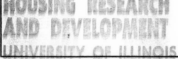

New Households New Housing

New Households
New Housing

Edited by

Karen A. Franck
New Jersey Institute of Technology

Sherry Ahrentzen
University of Wisconsin–Milwaukee

VNR Van Nostrand Reinhold
——————— New York

To Dorothea Seelye Franck and Lois Boland

Library of Congress Catalog Card Number 89-5351
ISBN 0-442-22486-9

Printed in the United States of America

Designed by East End Graphics

Van Nostrand Reinhold
115 Fifth Avenue
New York, New York 10003

Van Nostrand Reinhold International Company Limited
11 New Fetter Lane
London EC4P 4EE, England

Van Nostrand Reinhold
480 La Trobe Street
Melbourne, Victoria 3000, Australia

Nelson Canada
1120 Birchmount Road
Scarborough, Ontario M1K 5G4, Canada

16 15 14 13 12 11 10 9 8 7 6 5 4 3 2 1

Library of Congress Cataloging-in-Publication Data

New households, new housing.

   Includes index.
   1. Shared housing.   2. Single parents—Housing.
3. Single people—Housing.   I. Franck, Karen A.
II. Ahrentzen, Sherry.
HD7287.85.N48   1990   363.5′9   89-5351
ISBN 0-442-22486-9

Contents

Foreword by C. Richard Hatch — ix

Introduction — xi
Sherry Ahrentzen
   New Households — xi
   New Housing — xii
   New Households, New Housing — xiii

PART I   COLLECTIVE HOUSING

1   Overview of Collective and Shared Housing — 3
   Karen A. Franck
      History of Housing with Shared Spaces in the United States — 3
      Advantages of Shared and Collective Housing — 5
      Mingle Units — 7
      Quads — 8
      GoHomes — 9
      Sponsored Group Residences — 11
      Collective Housing — 13
      Overview of Chapters — 17
      Additional Information — 19

2   Apartments and Collective Life in Nineteenth-Century New York — 20
   Elizabeth Cromley
      Dwelling Practices of Pre–Civil War New York — 21
      Developing a Building for Collective Purposes — 22
      Collective Activities: Housekeeping, Cooking, and Dining — 32
      Collective Dwellings for Specific Tenant Groups — 35
      Lessons for Today — 43

3   Early European Collective Habitation: From Utopian Ideal to Reality — 47
   Norbert Schoenauer
      The Genesis of European Collective Habitation — 47
      Two English Prototypes: Catering Flats and Cooperative Quadrangles — 48
      A Danish Prototype: The *Kollektivhus* — 53
      A German, Swiss, and Austrian Prototype: The *Einküchenhaus* — 55
      A Russian Experiment: The *Dom-Kommuna* — 59
      A Swedish Prototype: The *Kollektivhus* — 62
      A Survey of Pre-War Collective Housing in Sweden — 67
      Conclusions — 69

4 **Communal Housing in Sweden: A Remedy for the Stress of Everyday Life?**　71
　　Alison Woodward
　　　Recent History of Swedish Communal Housing　72
　　　Tenure, Management Models, and Design　74
　　　Comparison of Four Communal Projects　79
　　　Who Wants to Live in Communal Housing and Why?　84
　　　Design Issues in Communal Projects　89
　　　Conclusions　92

5　**Cohousing in Denmark**　95
　　Kathryn M. McCamant
　　Charles R. Durrett
　　　Four Characteristics of Cohousing　100
　　　Evolution of the Concept of Cohousing　101
　　　The Participatory Development Process　109
　　　Design Guidelines　111
　　　Cohousing in the United States　121

6　**The Party Wall as the Architecture of Sharing**　127
　　Jill Stoner
　　　Qualitative Characteristics of the Party Wall　127
　　　The Transformation of the Party Wall　130
　　　Two Housing Competitions　135
　　　Conclusion　140

PART II HOUSING FOR SINGLE-PARENT HOUSEHOLDS

7　**Overview of Housing for Single-Parent Households**　143
　　Sherry Ahrentzen
　　　Housing Issues for Single Parents　144
　　　Early Developments in Europe　146
　　　Developments in the United States　149
　　　Overview of Chapters　158
　　　Additional Information　159

8　**Two Prototypical Designs for Single Parents: The Congregate House and the New American House**　161
　　Jacqueline Leavitt
　　　Dominant Images of Nuclear Families, the Elderly, and Single Parents　161
　　　Designing for Mobility　162
　　　Single-Parent or Intergenerational Congregate Housing　164
　　　The New American House Competition　170
　　　Conclusions　184

9　**Two Cases of Transitional Housing Development in Boston**　187
　　Joan Forrester Sprague
　　　Abigail West Shelter　188
　　　Tree of Life　195
　　　Comparisons and Lessons　204

10 Passage Community: Second-Stage Housing for Single Parents   208
    Christine C. Cook
        Planning and Developing   210
        Neighborhood Characteristics and Housing Design   212
        Support Services and Management   217
        Evaluation of the First Year of Occupancy   218
        Recommendations for Future Developments   219

11 Developing Two Women's Housing Cooperatives   223
    Gerda R. Wekerle
    Sylvia Novac
        Developing Women's Communities   223
        The Canadian Non-Profit Housing Program   224
        Two Women's Housing Cooperatives   225
        Creating Affordable Housing   234
        Who Lives in Women's Housing Co-ops?   235
        Women Exercise Control   236
        Creating a Supportive Community   237
        Security of Tenure   238
        Conclusions   239

PART III   SINGLE ROOM OCCUPANCY HOUSING

12 Overview of Single Room Occupancy Housing   245
    Karen A. Franck
        Rise and Decline of Single Room Occupancy Housing   246
        Homelessness   250
        Advantages of Renovating or Developing SRO Housing   252
        Policies and Programs for Preserving and Renovating SRO Hotels   252
        Three Cases of SRO Housing   254
        Overview of Chapters   261
        Additional Information   261

13 The Design of a Single Room with Furniture for a Residential Hotel   263
    Michael Mostoller
        Historical Research   263
        Contemporary Research   268
        Design Philosophy   271
        Room Studies   272
        Furniture Design   279

14 A Look at SRO Hotel Residents with Recommendations for Management and Design   285
    Mary Burki
        SRO Neighborhoods   286
        SRO Hotel Residents   286
        The SRO Resident's Life   289
        Managing SRO Hotels   292
        Designing SRO Hotels   296

15   The Single Room Occupancy Hotel: A Rediscovered Housing Type for Single People   308
   Karen A. Franck
      Social Advantages   309
      Hotels with Heterogeneous Populations   310
      Hotels Targeted for the Elderly   316
      Hotels for Younger People   317
      Design Issues   322
      Management Issues   326
      Policy Issues   328

Contributors   331
Index   335

Foreword

In 1949 the U.S. Congress passed the Urban Renewal Act. As readers of this book will know, that landmark legislation promised a decent, safe, and sanitary dwelling for every American. Although many of us do live in better housing now than when the Act was passed, the number of Americans who experience problems with housing quality or cost or both has changed very little. Moreover a grave new problem has arisen in recent years: widespread homelessness. This most serious form of housing deprivation—the negative side of urban revitalization—continues to show steady growth.

Not only has the number of households needing decent homes increased, but also the composition of these households has changed and their incomes relative to housing costs have declined. As we will learn in this volume, single parents with dependent children now represent nearly 20 percent of all U.S. family households. Most of these single parents are women, and most have low incomes. Another fast-growing group is single individuals, who now constitute nearly a quarter of those seeking housing. In fact only one household in ten today consists of an employed father, a homemaker mother, and children. While no demographic projections suggest significant changes, this minority remains the focus of public and private housing efforts.

This timely book describes the growing number of American households that do not fit the conventional family mold. Despite their numbers —which now approach half of all those seeking shelter—they are still commonly referred to as nontraditional households. This book elevates them to the central place they deserve in the housing debate and brings together in a single place the most successful experiments and thoughtful proposals regarding dwellings appropriate to their varied needs.

At the same time this book is concerned with new forms of dwelling for those households that, while still of conventional structure, seek closer social contact or increased amenity through sharing and cooperation. It describes a continuum of housing types, differentiated in terms of size, cost, and degree of self-containment—ranging from SRO units in reconditioned hotels in New York to residential clusters in Scandinavia designed to lighten the burden on working parents.

Karen Franck and Sherry Ahrentzen have addressed their book to that disparate group we call *housers*—the public officials, architects, planners, and developers who shape the nation's housing policies and production. Although this group has been a powerful collective force for more than a generation, in recent years dissension over building types (high-rises versus low-rises), locational strategies (revitalizing the slums versus integrating the suburbs), and financing (subsidies to buildings versus subsidies to households) has reduced its influence, permitting conservatives to dismantle the structure of public support for housing. This book, by providing a clear framework for rethinking American housing needs, will help reforge the consensus that effective housing action requires. By challenging housers' traditional assumptions, it will shift the agenda toward increased pluralism and user control.

Housing as a responsibility of government and a specific concern of architects and planners is a matter not much more than a century old: a frequently cited point of origin is the London County Council's decision to build its first low-income flats around 1890. Although there were isolated, private experiments in the United States in the latter half of the nineteenth century, it took the Great Depression of the 1930s to force government housing action here. In that time of national crisis, leading housers formulated a now-familiar program: lowered densities, increased light and air, and affordable apartments for nuclear families temporarily deprived of their birthright—a house with a yard of its own. These goals for individuals and dwellings were never seriously questioned: those as yet unmarried were destined to marry and have children; single parenthood was surely a temporary condition; and apartments (or any other form of collective living) were merely stepping stones on the way to family houses.

We now see that this conception of the housing task contains a number of dangerous myths. First, it accepts only one choice of marital status. Except for the young, failure to establish a conventional family is seen as a form of deviance justifying housing deprivation. But as we have seen, half of all households today are "nontraditional." Most remain so for long periods; many remain so for life.

Second, this conception assumes a perpetually rising economic tide that will float all ships into the desired port: a private home. In fact, the real incomes of young couples with children—the backbone of the single-family house market—have declined by nearly a quarter since 1980. Is it ambition or lack of housing choices that accounts for the fact that more than half of the women with children today go to work? What more affordable housing alternatives are there for them or for the still less-affluent single parents and young people leaving school?

Third, this conception is built on the belief that ours is and must remain a heartless world and that housing privacy is the appropriate response. The purpose of housing, it is implicitly argued, is to generate protective islands, each complete in regard to human complement and equipment. In his first book Lewis Mumford dubbed this the "Myth of the Country House." Tracing its origins and impact to the Renaissance villa surrounded by pleasure gardens and private hunting grounds, Mumford saw clearly that the proliferation of this myth diminished concern for the public realm. He wrote:

It does not matter very much whether [it] is an estate on Long Island or a cottage in Montclair . . . the Country House today tries to make up by an abundance of physical goods for all that has been lost through its divorce from the underlying community; more than ever it attempts to be self-sufficient within the limits of suburbia.

As the common possessions of the community dwindle, the private possessions of individuals are multiplied; and at last, there remains no other community than a multitude of anarchic individuals, each of whom is doing his best to create for himself a Country House.

This passage appears in *The Story of Utopias.* It was Mumford's point that the modern, private anti-utopia of the country house, even if it were feasible for an entire society and not just for its richest members, is destructive of human potential. In proper utopian fashion he makes no bones about his preference for active participation over passive enjoyment, creation over consumption, and a good measure of community over the extremes of privacy we Americans have learned to require.

In the Introduction Sherry Ahrentzen assures us that this book is not concerned with utopia, but rather with the practical and economic advantages of new housing for new households. Like good utopians, however, the editors see things whole—balancing the political, financial, administrative, and architectural aspects of housing. Like serious utopians they celebrate those who have persevered to find solutions to problems others ignored or wished away. Like generous utopians they argue the primacy of participation, creativity, and community. Their book— itself a collective effort—describes the kinds of housing that can satisfy these needs. It deserves close attention.

C. Richard Hatch
School of Architecture
New Jersey Institute of Technology

Introduction

Sherry Ahrentzen

This book is for architects, planners, developers, and others who are concerned with designing and developing housing for nontraditional households. The contributors to this book describe the physical design, development process, social characteristics, and management approaches of over 50 cases of contemporary and historical housing in the United States, Canada, and Europe. These buildings were designed specifically for those individuals and families whose needs have not been well accommodated by conventional single-family houses and apartments. Their housing needs are numerous and diverse: affordability and security, accessible social and support services, minimal housekeeping and maintenance responsibilities, convenient child-care services, ample opportunity to be with other residents, and other housing amenities that enhance daily life. This text provides information on the needs of particular households and how those needs have been addressed in specific housing cases.

While we use the word *new* in the title of this book, the diverse household compositions of today continue demographic trends that began in the past century and even earlier. Many of the household types described here are not new but rather have been unrecognized in recent years or are transformations of earlier types. Thus the term *new* is used with the understanding that what is now seen as new may have existed previously but now merits "renewed" attention and consideration from architects, planners, and developers, as well as from students, faculty, and residents themselves.

NEW HOUSEHOLDS

The image in the United States of the traditional family—a married couple with young children, with an employed husband and a homemaker wife—that characterized the 1950s and 1960s does not match today's demographic realities. Other types account for nearly 79 percent of the households created since 1980, whereas the traditional married-couple family accounts for only 21 percent (United States Bureau of Census 1985). The fastest-growing household type is the single person living alone; persons living alone comprise 24 percent of all households. Single-parent families account for 12 percent. America's 86.8 million households are still dominated by the 50.3 million families maintained by married couples. Yet even within the conjugal family, lifestyle changes have occurred. Over 60 percent of married women with dependent children are in the paid labor force, compared to 18 percent in 1950. Nearly 53 percent of married women with children under 6 years of age are employed (Oxford Analytica 1986). Only 10 percent of households consist of an employed father, a homemaker mother, and children younger than 18.

In addition to these changes, the financial prosperity of the 1950s and 1960s has dissipated for many American households. Only one-quarter of Americans age 15 and older have a personal income of $20,000 or more per year, while one-half earn less than $10,000 a year (Russell 1987). During the past decade the income distribution of American households has reflected less a normal, or bell-shaped, distribution and more a skewed distribution with the peak at the low-income end (Rose 1986).

NEW HOUSING

As the traditional economic "middle class" begins to shrink and household composition becomes more diverse, housing providers must develop new housing forms to accommodate these changes. The majority of housing built today consists of two standard types: the single-family house and the medium-density, multiunit building or housing complex. But at other times in history, societies provided a number of different types of housing to accommodate their varied populations. For example, in medieval times, although many peasant houses were designed for conjugal families, some were designed for single women and others for extended families with a large number of children and relatives. Since it was common for transient single men to roam from town to town, roofed shelters were provided for these vagabonds as well as for expelled university students, elderly men and women, and servants not lodged in their masters' homes. Castles, palaces, large urban hotels, university dormitories, and monasteries were among those residences that provided communal living models. Variety of population as well as housing was certainly a character of the medieval urban fabric (Barthelemy and Contamin 1988).

But we do not have to go as far back as the Middle Ages to witness a variety of housing types being provided for a diverse population. Developed during World War II, Vanport City in Oregon, which Hayden (1984) describes, had affordable housing for single persons, single-parent families, conjugal families with children, and nonfamily households. Several day-care centers were scattered throughout the development. Even before the war there were alternative housing types, as well as proposals for more. Ford (1936), for instance, after an assessment of the 1930 Census of New York City, proposed a comprehensive policy that would promote new housing types—such as special housing for working mothers with young children, residences for older women, and lodging houses with a mix of social facilities for the poor—and would increase the existing stock of housekeeping apartments for single women and nonfamily groups.

Nevertheless, the residential landscape we inhabit today is largely the product of post–World War II prosperity and values. In the 1950s the single-family house was built and marketed in cities, suburbs, and towns across the country. While the single-famly house effectively answers a number of needs for many Americans—space, sanitation, security, status, and privacy—today's demographics and household economics call into question the relevance of these cultural values, and in particular the means of achieving them, for *all* households. There is a new recognition and acceptance of the pluralistic character of American society. Television, the great portrayer of American normative, and idealized, family life, reveals an eclectic array of households: for several years two single-parent families shared a residence in "Kate & Allie"; four older women share a home in "The Golden Girls"; a widower and his two male friends raise three children in "Full House"; and "thirtysomething" has only one traditional family featured among a number of separated parents and singles.

This book presents a number of examples of alternative forms of housing that were developed to address the needs of those households whose daily lives are not sufficiently accommodated by conventional housing. It is true that no marketing survey has yet revealed a high demand for housing with features such as on-site day care or shared dining areas. However, such housing innovations are so rare in the United States that people would be unable to express a positive opinion of them since they have never seen or experienced such housing. We want to present these innovations to designers, developers, housing officials, and households who have never considered alternative forms of housing and to those who have thought of them in the abstract but have not been aware that such housing now exists.

We certainly are not the first to expound and promote this perspective. A number of architectural and social critics have recently challenged the ubiquity of the single-family house: Dolores Hayden (1984), for example, maintains that today the detached suburban house is generally too expensive for many households. In addition, the diverse character and needs of today's household population cannot be met by a single standard form that lacks flexibility and variety. She calls for redesigning the American dream.

NEW HOUSEHOLDS, NEW HOUSING

Actions to provide more housing options are already being taken by a number of architects and legislators. And many residents are directing their own efforts toward establishing new forms of housing. Across the country, homeowners are building accessory apartments and echo houses, many times illegally. These small attached (accessory) and detached (echo) units typically are occupied by relatives of the people who live in the main, larger home. Between 1970 and 1980, the Census Bureau estimates that 2.5 million conversions of single-family houses were made to create accessory apartments (Hare 1981). Shared housing is another grassroots movement reflecting a desire for new housing options. Sharing a home is no longer seen as suitable for only those in unstable living situations. Today there are over 400 shared housing programs nationwide that match nonrelated persons who wish to share one residence.

The New American House competition held in 1984 reflects the architecture community's acknowledgment of and concern for developing new housing forms for new household types. In universities studio design projects have included housing for single parents and for collective living arrangements. In 1987 the American Institute of Architects sponsored a student design competition for housing for the homeless.

State and federal legislation is starting to pave the way for new types of housing to be built (Leavitt 1988). California's proposed Family Housing Demonstration Program will offer incentives to private developers to build multiunit rental or cooperative housing with job-training and child-care services. Joseph Kennedy II has introduced into the House of Representatives the Community Housing Partnership Act, which provides, in part, $500 million in grants to subsidize the development of affordable rental hous-

ing and homeownership. Another proposed federal legislation package would provide $10 billion for building affordable housing with child-care and job-training services and for strengthening existing public housing.

But the most encouraging signs of change are the subject of this text—the numerous efforts in the United States and elsewhere to build housing to accommodate nontraditional households. This book focuses on housing designed for shared and collective living, for single-parent families, and for low-income single people. Accordingly the book is divided into three sections: the first on collective housing, the second on housing for single-parent households, and the third on single room occupancy housing. Each section begins with an overview of the types of households and housing discussed in that section, includes descriptions of a few historical and contemporary cases of such housing, and provides a short summary of the content of the chapters in that section.

Most of the cases described in these chapters have been built or are presently under construction. The few proposed but unbuilt projects were nonetheless designed to be built. Funding sources for construction and operation are diverse and include government agencies, nonprofit organizations, private developers, financial institutions, private donors, and residents themselves. Often a complex mixture of private financing and public subsidy made a project possible.

There are several themes that recur throughout the book. One is the integration of different types of households. Despite the book's division into three sections, many of the contributors describe and advocate housing that integrates different types of households, including single-parent families with single persons and couples, the elderly with younger people, and individuals with physical or mental handicaps or other vulnerabilities with more able-bodied residents. Housing designed to meet the needs of particular kinds of households, while also accommodating diversity, allows for a level of exchange and support between residents that is a benefit to all.

Another theme is the integration of housing with other uses, one being social services. On-site child care is strongly advocated in housing for single parents and in some collective housing communities. Spaces for counseling, job training, or other support services are provided in some single-parent housing and in some single room occupancy housing. Locating housing in proximity to social services is another solution, as is locating it close to public transit stations or bus stops. In a few cases, living space is integrated with work space; in other cases, workshops or photography studios are incorporated into the housing. And the integration of commercial spaces occurs in some single room occupancy housing as well as in housing for single parents. In many projects described in this book, housing is designed with a recognition of the interrelationship of the many activities of daily life and with a desire to see those interconnections enhanced by housing design.

Another common theme is the participation of residents in the planning, design, and management of their homes. This may mean managing the entry desk in a single room occupancy hotel or fully participating in all aspects of housing management and maintenance. Participation also may mean that residents initiate a housing project and direct its design and financing, or residents may participate in the construction. As demonstrated in many chapters, residents are empowered by their participation in the creation and ongoing management of their homes.

A particularly pervasive theme is the accommodation and balance of privacy and sharing. The dialectics between privacy and community, or sharing, is a particularly salient topic for housing in general (e.g., Chermayeff and Alexander 1963; Altman and Gauvain 1981). But for the households and housing described here, sharing is a much more central and prevalent concern than in standard housing. And sharing takes many forms. The type of shared relationship varies considerably among the housing developments described. Sharing can be simply co-presence: occupying the same room or space without any spoken acknowledgment of the other's presence. The necessity of this more passive form of sharing among residents must be recognized and accepted by architects and housing sponsors. As is frequently seen in the cases of shared housing, simply knowing that others are around and can

be found in times of emergency can enhance residents' feelings of security.

Sharing also can display an affiliative nature. Residents in Danish cohousing, for instance, use the communal dining room to sit and chat with neighbors as well as to hold occasional celebrations. And sharing also can have an instrumental aspect: the maintenance and nurturance of one's home and household can benefit from sharing resources, activities, and space with other residents. Such sharing can save money, time, and effort for individual residents while enhancing their quality of life. On-site child care in housing for single parents or a wood-working shop in a Danish cohousing community contributes to the ease and enjoyment of everyday life.

Achieving the delicate balance between privacy and sharing demands that housing sponsors and architects understand the type of sharing that is to occur and the reasons for it. A "shared" space can take on different forms depending on the type of sharing and the desired balance with privacy. Many residents may cook their own separate meals in a shared kitchen without coordinating their efforts with one another, as occurs among some single room occupancy residents; or a small group of residents may talk and socialize as they work as a team, preparing a dinner in a community kitchen for a large group of families, as happens in the cohousing communities in Denmark. In both cases residents later seek privacy: eating in their own rooms, as in SRO housing, or preparing tomorrow's breakfast in one's private kitchen, as in Danish cohousing. Providing options for the appropriate level and type of sharing and balancing these with sufficient options for household privacy has been the task of the many architects and sponsors of the housing described in this book.

Although we recognize and document the empirical fact of demographic diversity and financial distress among many households today, we realize that demographics and financial need alone do not dictate housing design and practice. Urban form ultimately rests on the visions, values, choices, and interests of powerful groups. We hope to show those persons and organizations responsible for providing and building housing that alternative types of housing can, and do, exist in concert with more conventional housing. We also hope that the cases presented here encourage individuals and families to place demands on the building professions and financial institutions to provide a more diverse and flexible housing stock. With a greater variety of housing options available, residents will no longer have to resign themselves to accepting a single standard type of house but will be able to choose and even create for themselves more suitable, and meaningful, places to live.

References

Altman, I., and M. A. Gauvain. 1981. A cross-cultural and dialectic analysis of homes. In *Spatial Representation and Behavior Across the Life Span: Theory and Application*, ed. L. Liben, A. Patterson, and N. Newcombe, 283–320. New York: Academic Press.

Barthelemy, D., and P. Contamin. 1988. The use of private space. In *A History of Private Life. II. Revelations of the Medieval World*, ed. G. Duby, 395–505. Cambridge, MA: Belknap Press of Harvard University Press.

Chermayeff, S., and C. Alexander. 1963. *Community and Privacy*. Garden City, NY: Doubleday.

Ford, J. 1936. *Slums and Housing*. Cambridge: Harvard University Press.

Hare, P. H. 1981. *Accessory Apartments: Using Surplus Space in Single Family Houses*. Chicago: American Planning Association.

Hayden, D. 1984. *Redesigning the American Dream: The Future of Housing, Work and Family Life*. New York: Norton.

Leavitt, J. 1988. Refuse, refuge, community. Paper presented at conference on Assisting the Homeless, Advisory Commission on Intergovernmental Relations (March 10–11), Washington, D.C.

Oxford Analytica. 1986. *America in Perspective: Major Trends in the United States Through the 1990s*. Boston: Houghton Mifflin.

Rose, S. J. 1986. *The American Profile Poster*. New York: Pantheon.

Russell, C. 1987. 25 things you should know. *American Demographics* 9(8):7.

United States Bureau of the Census. 1985. Household, families, marital status and living arrangements: March 1985 (advance report). *Current Population Reports: Population Characteristics*, Series P-20, No. 402. Washington, D.C.: Government Printing Office.

PART I

Collective Housing

Chapter 1

Overview of Collective and Shared Housing

Karen A. Franck

Collective housing, as defined in this book, is housing that features spaces and facilities for joint use by all residents who also maintain their own individual households. These spaces and facilities form a central characteristic of the housing and not simply an added amenity. Today in collective housing, the shared facilities supplement complete, self-sufficient dwelling units so that each household has its own kitchen even though there also is a larger, shared kitchen. In the past, shared facilities in collective housing often replaced facilities conventionally placed in individual dwelling units; thus individual units often lacked private kitchens, but the individuality and separateness of the households was acknowledged, both socially and spatially, in other ways.

Today's collective housing can be distinguished from shared housing, in which unrelated individuals share single dwelling units, forming joint or group households.[1] In shared housing, spaces or facilities that usually are part of the private domain of individual households, such as kitchens, bathrooms, and living rooms, are placed in the shared domain of the joint household. Shared housing differs from collective housing in the degree of autonomy and privacy of the occupants. In this overview both collective and shared housing are discussed, while the subsequent chapters in this section focus primarily on collective housing.[2]

While shared and collective housing differ in the degree of autonomy of the households and in the types of spaces that are shared, they are similar in other respects. In both types of housing, sharing means at the very least the joint use of common facilities and spaces by unrelated persons or households. Sharing may also mean social interaction between residents, group activities, and coordination and cooperation in pursuit of common tasks. Both are intended for long-term occupancy; they are not intended exclusively for special user groups; and they are not intentional communities where residents hold a common set of philosophical or religious beliefs that guide their everyday lives. In these different ways shared and collective housing can be distinguished from other types of housing with shared spaces and facilities—such as military barracks, dormitories, congregate housing for the elderly, community group homes for people with mental or other disabilities, convents, monasteries, and utopian communities. Several of these other types, however, are precursors of contemporary shared and collective housing.

HISTORY OF HOUSING WITH SHARED SPACES IN THE UNITED STATES

In the nineteenth and early twentieth centuries there was a great variety of housing with shared facilities and spaces. Utopian communities, both

3

religious and nonsectarian, located in rural areas, were particularly numerous between 1820 and 1850 (Hayden 1976) and some still exist, such as the Hutterite communities in New York State and elsewhere. Other forms of cooperative living, including cooperative living clubs and early cooperative apartment buildings, were not intentional communities but were based on the premise that joint use of spaces and facilities by unrelated individuals or households had economic, practical, and social advantages.

One cooperative living club was the Jane Club, organized by Mary Kenney in Chicago for young, single female workers and managed by the residents. The building for the Jane Club that opened in 1898 included 30 private bedrooms, a social room, a dining room, a kitchen, a laundry room, and a bicycle and trunk storage room (Hayden 1981). From 1885 to 1920, women in other cities organized cooperative boarding clubs. In an exhibition in the Woman's Building at the Columbian Exposition, Mary Coleman Stuckert displayed her drawings and model of a proposed new community with cooperative housekeeping facilities. Facilities in her plan included a meeting hall, library, kindergarten, kitchen, dining room, and laundry. In 1916 Alice Constance Austin planned an entire cooperative colony to be built in Llan del Rio, California. Hot meals were to arrive at each house from a central kitchen and dirty dishes were to be returned to the kitchen via an underground tunnel. The dwellings themselves had no kitchens at all (Hayden 1981). While the Jane Club depended on cooperation and exchange among residents and Stuckert's plan expected residents to eat together, in Austin's plan the individual households would eat in their own houses. The advantage of the central kitchen was practical rather than social: to save the time and energy that individual households spend preparing their own meals.

The first speculative cooperative apartment buildings in New York also contained extensive common facilities. Hudson View Gardens—built in 1924—contained a restaurant, a staff of maids, a commissary, a supervised playground, a beauty shop, and a barber shop (Hayden 1981). In 1925 the United Workers Cooperative Association built in the Bronx the Workers' Cooperative Colony, consisting of 750 units, an auditorium, a library, a kindergarten and nursery, and, nearby, other commercial facilities and a cafeteria. In addition to family apartments, private rooms were clustered around a shared kitchen; these were intended for single people and the elderly, whose relatives also sometimes lived in the project. A cooperative restaurant and then, in 1937, a cooperative dining club did develop. Early rental apartment houses and apartment hotels for the well-to-do in New York and Boston also were frequently equipped with extensive common facilities, as were residences for single men and single women (see chapter 2).

Experiments with collective living in the United States declined significantly following the 1930s, particularly after World War II, when the single-family detached house, long an American ideal, became affordable to many more families. Prime among its characteristics are spatial and social privacy and self-sufficiency: ideally it is to be occupied only by members of a single household who are related to each other by blood or marriage; no spaces or facilities are to be shared with other households; and all household tasks are to be performed by each household, separately (Franck 1987). With growing economic prosperity and increases in retirement benefits after World War II, both young single adults and elderly people were able to afford to live as independent households (Glick 1984). And they were expected to live in dwelling units, often apartments, that approximated the ideal of the social and spatial privacy of the single-family house even when these dwellings were occupied by single adults. Alternatives that entailed the sharing of a single-family house by several unrelated adults often were forbidden by local zoning ordinances, as they still are. Both the dwelling unit (house or apartment) and the household occupying it became increasingly privatized and isolated (Slater 1970).

At present the types of housing in the United States that do have shared facilities as a central defining feature tend to be exclusively for students, the elderly, or other particular types of residents. Moreover, the housing segregates these different types of residents from each other and from other kinds of households. In congregate housing for the elderly, residents' complete private apartments are supplemented by communal dining rooms and other common spaces and by recreational and health services. In retirement communities the elderly have individual houses that are supplemented by club houses or community centers and other facilities that provide a great variety of recreational activities. Security, assistance in case of emergency, and lack of maintenance responsibilities are additional benefits. Life-care communities also provide private apartments and shared spaces, offering residents increasing levels of health-care and housekeeping services as they become increasingly frail. Dormitories and other forms of housing exclusively for students are examples of housing with shared facilities for short-term residence. Students may have single rooms and share bathrooms or they may share apartments; in either case these units are supplemented by additional shared spaces for studying or relaxing. Community group homes are supportive housing for people with mental disabilities or other handicaps; they provide bedrooms, shared bathrooms, shared kitchens, and additional common social spaces. Residence in these may be short or long term.

The predominance in the United States of housing with shared spaces and facilities for particular groups indicates how much contemporary American society tends to view such housing as appropriate for people with specialized needs. This assumes that those who are not in school, not elderly, and not handicapped do not desire, and would not benefit from, more sharing of spaces and facilities than is currently available in conventional housing, in which a high degree of social and spatial separation is the norm.

It is hard to tell whether other types of households in the United States would in fact appreciate more opportunities to share spaces and facilities in the residential setting since there are so few cases for them to see or experience. One survey, conducted by Leavitt and Saegert, of readers of *Ms.* magazine indicated a strong willingness among women to share living spaces (Van Gelder 1986). Twenty-six percent were willing to share a kitchen or a living room (18 and 17 percent already did so); 19 percent were willing to share a bathroom (15 percent already did so). One reason for sharing living space is to share

housing costs. Of those with annual household incomes under $10,000, 53 percent would like to share housing costs. But even among those with incomes over $75,000, 21 percent said they would like to share housing costs. Respondents also drew their own plans of ideal homes and mentioned other advantages of sharing. When describing her plan one woman mentioned "the opportunity for group work and play." Another, who saw an advantage in service professionals living together, referred to a "place where life and living blur into an unsegmented whole" (Van Gelder 1986, 40). While the questions in the survey referred to being "willing" to share spaces, respondents also seemed to express a desire to do so.

ADVANTAGES OF SHARED AND COLLECTIVE HOUSING

Shared housing—housing in which a single dwelling is occupied by independent and unrelated adults who use the same kitchen within the unit—has economic, practical, and social advantages. Cost savings from sharing facilities can significantly lower the rent or the mortgage payments for each individual. The sharing of costs also allows for amenities that no resident could afford alone, such as a large living room, a garden, or an excellent location (Raimy 1979). Practical advantages can result from sharing household responsibilities, such as grocery shopping, preparing meals, and cleaning, which can give residents more time for other activities. Taking advantage of this potential, however, requires coordination and cooperation.

The social benefits of shared housing include the increased security and support provided by the simple presence of others; possibilities for social interaction, companionship, and friendship between residents; and organized group activities. One form of shared housing that has developed in the United States is the purchase or rental of large houses by nonprofit organizations for occupancy by unrelated individuals who are often, but not exclusively, elderly. In her research on eight cases of such housing, occupied primarily by elderly people, West (1981) makes a clear distinction between the support and security of co-presence and other more active forms of sharing. West found that a primary reason for moving to these group residences is "not to be alone." Sometimes a move followed a frightening event such as fainting or a criminal attack. These residents may be seeking the security of shared presence rather than more frequent social interaction. And, indeed, the degree of actual sharing of activities was relatively low. Most residents, 60 percent, reported that they spent most of their time in their own rooms. Almost half of the residents interviewed reported that they had imagined that group living would generate a lot of enjoyable group activities, but it had not. Except for group meals that were served to residents, the kinds of sharing that occurred most frequently were between a few residents and were part of a brief, unplanned encounter.

Significantly those residents in West's research who were most satisfied with group living were living in groups of 6 to 10 members; those least satisfied were in groups of 16 to 20. Building form contributed significantly to the amount of active social sharing among residents. The greatest amount of social interaction occurred in buildings of several stories, such as townhouses, and the least amount occurred in sites with detached, horizontal layouts. Residents in the former also were more satisfied with the amount of privacy they had. Since these were older houses, West speculates that the townhouses may have had more transition spaces and niches (stair landings and breakfast nooks) that allowed casual exchanges between residents when they were on their way somewhere.

Contemporary collective housing, in which shared spaces and facilities supplement complete dwelling units, is very rare in the United States (when collective housing is distinguished from housing for special groups). The advantages of such housing, as demonstrated by research on collective housing in Denmark and Sweden, are somewhat different from the advantages of shared housing (see chapters 4 and 5). The economic advantage of collective housing is primarily the opportunity to have amenities that might be difficult for single households to afford, such as darkrooms, workshops, one or more guest rooms, or very large living rooms. The actual cost of a dwelling unit is not likely to be reduced in

collective housing; in many cases it is the same as or higher than the cost of conventional apartments or houses. The practical and social advantages are considerable, but many of them, as in shared housing, depend on coordination and cooperation among residents to perform tasks. The regular sharing of meals saves individual households the time and effort of preparing every evening meal on their own (and of the related efforts of grocery shopping and cleaning up). This can be particularly desirable for working parents. The shared spaces also provide greater opportunity for sharing child-care responsibilities. Beyond the security and support extended by the presence of others, there is the social interaction and companionship generated by joint activities, particularly the sharing of meals and their preparation, which make for a richer domestic life for adults and for children. In this way collective housing offers advantages over the separation of conventional single-family houses.

Interaction and independence, community and privacy are significant issues in the design and use of shared and collective housing. In shared housing the single common kitchen reduces the independence and the privacy of each resident; however, the provision of private baths and private entrances in shared housing can enhance independence. Social interaction and the development of community can be enhanced by having a social space large enough to accommodate all residents for a meal. Day-Lower, West, and Zimmers (1985) recommend that seating areas, such as window seats or breakfast nooks, be placed near circulation paths or adjacent to transition spaces such as doorways and stair landings. Similarly, a variety of spaces for sitting, both indoors and outdoors, that have a sense of intimacy can invite private conversations between residents.

In collective housing the presence of complete dwelling units *and* common spaces allows for a greater balance of community and privacy, but whether social interaction and the development of community actually occur depends on the residents, just as it does in shared housing. Thus many of the same design features suggested for shared housing are useful in collective housing. These include a space to accommodate the entire community for a meal, additional shared spaces and facilities, and spaces indoors and outdoors that offer residents an opportunity to linger and chat. (For more suggestions see chapters 4 and 5.)

In both types of housing the shared spaces can only accommodate and encourage interaction between residents; they cannot ensure that it occurs. When the common spaces are truly used, especially when they are used for regular common meals, the potential social benefit of such housing for generating active social sharing is realized. Simply having the spaces for such activities is not enough to realize this potential; a high proportion of the residents must be committed to organizing and performing the tasks that regular group activities require. A lack of regular group activities does not, however, diminish the other advantages— enjoying shared amenities and the support and security provided by the simple presence of other residents.

The range of economic, practical, and social advantages of shared and collective housing is apparent in the following contemporary American cases and in the historic and contemporary American and European cases described in subsequent chapters in this section. The American cases of shared housing include mingle units, quads, GoHomes, and sponsored group residences. Two cases of American collective housing also are presented.

MINGLE UNITS

Mingle units are apartments or single-family houses that are purposely designed for occupancy by two people who wish to share housing costs without sacrificing too much privacy or independence. The motivation for sharing is thus largely economic rather than social or practical, although the simple presence of another person offers the kind of comfort and security offered by other types of shared housing. The distinguishing design characteristic of mingle units is the floor plan: it contains two "master," or principal, bedroom suites of comparable size and amenities, each with its own bathroom. Only two people share the dwelling; they often are co-purchasers and therefore share a mortgage and the financial and legal responsibilites it entails.

One of the hallmarks of the post–World War II American single-family house has been the social and spatial hierarchy of the bedrooms; a single master bedroom that is relatively large and private and often has its own bathroom with one or more subsidiary bedrooms that are smaller and less private and may share a bath. The underlying assumption is that the master bedroom will be shared by mother and father and the subsidiary bedrooms will be occupied by children, preferably one for each child. The desirability of this arrangement may be questionable even for the traditional nuclear family. It is, however, not at all suitable for a household that is not hierarchically organized, such as one consisting of two independent single persons, a single parent and a grown child, or two couples. The mingles plan, by virtue of the equal size and amenities of the two bedroom suites and their privacy, can better meet the needs of these other household types.

The term *mingles* was most likely coined by developers who began using the plan in the late 1970s as a way of attracting buyers who could not afford to buy a house or an apartment without sharing the costs. In 1981 about 20 percent of the homes built by Berkus Group Associates were designed for this "tandem living style," as were one third of the units built by Fisher Friedman (Gottschalk 1981). Visits to new developments in southern California in 1984 indicated that the mingles plan was routinely included in new tract housing of single-family detached and attached homes, comprising from 10 to 30 percent of all units.

One type of mingles plan, illustrated in the plan from Tierra Vista in Serrano Highlands, California, shows bedrooms of equal size with comparable bath and storage space (Fig. 1-1). Moreover, the suites are separated by the shared living/dining spaces, giving each bedroom some privacy. While the dining space is somewhat separated from the living space, it is not separated enough to constitute a second, distinct social space. While all the two-bedroom plans at Tierra Vista feature two complete and separate bedroom suites, only this plan was described in the sales brochure as "the perfect plan for sharing singles." Of the 12 two-bedroom units sold as of June 1984, three had been sold to tandem buyers, in all cases to women who work together.

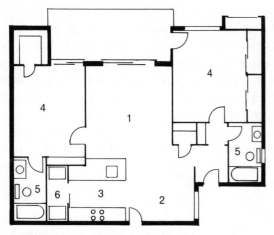

1. Living room   4. Master bedroom
2. Dining area   5. Bathroom
3. Kitchen   6. Washer / dryer

Figure 1.1. Mingles unit at Tierra Vista in Serrano Highlands, California: floor plan.

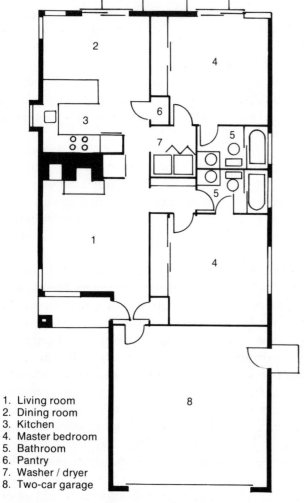

1. Living room
2. Dining room
3. Kitchen
4. Master bedroom
5. Bathroom
6. Pantry
7. Washer / dryer
8. Two-car garage

Figure 1-2. Mingles unit at Las Flores in Upland, California: floor plan.

Another mingles plan, from a development built by Lewis Homes in Upland, California, provides two social spaces—the living room and the kitchen (Fig. 1-2). These are separate and more distinct than the comparable spaces at Tierra Vista. This plan allows each resident to use a space outside of his or her own suite without intruding on the other resident.

In many essential features the mingles house is no different from the traditional single-family house. What is different is the expectation of who will live there, the nature of their relationship, and their need for two social areas and for equal and complete bedroom suites that are as private as possible. Privacy and equality of members within the unit have thus become more important than in the traditional single-family house, where hierarchy of members is the rule. Indeed, privacy, independence, and equality seem to be more significant design issues than sharing in the mingles plan.

QUADS

Quads are a type of rental housing built by private owners, for profit, to house students, single working people, or elderly people who are willing to share a kitchen and a bathtub/shower with other residents. Each room has its own toilet and sink. Each kitchen is shared by four persons, hence the term *quad*, which seems to be a local term in Eugene, Oregon, where 10 or 15 quad complexes were built in the early 1970s. Some cater to students and others to single working people and the elderly.

The site I visited, Campus Court, has 26 quad units, or a total of 104 bedrooms. The bedrooms range from 130 to 190 square feet; rents range from $215 to $235 a month with a lease that extends from September to June. The striking characteristic of the quad is a floor plan that allows each bedroom to have its own door to an exterior corridor, creating a private entry and exit for each resident (Fig. 1-3). A bed, a dresser, and a refrigerator are provided in each room. Four bedrooms are grouped around a kitchen to which each room has access. The kitchen, narrow and rather uninviting in layout, serves a purely utilitarian function (Fig. 1-4). There are no other

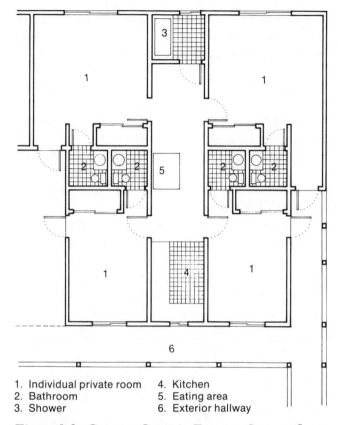

1. Individual private room 4. Kitchen
2. Bathroom 5. Eating area
3. Shower 6. Exterior hallway

Figure 1-3. Campus Court in Eugene, Oregon: floor plan of a quad.

Figure 1-4. Campus Court: kitchen.

gathering spaces except the roof, which is used for sunbathing.

The physical appearance of Campus Court is more like a motel than a college dormitory. The intention is to provide affordable housing at a profit to the owner. At the same time aspects of dormitory life are present. A live-in manager interviews new residents and tries to place them with people they will get along with. Housekeeping services, including weekly vacuuming, are provided; residents provide their own linen. The manager has found it preferable to restrict residency to students because of their common lifestyle; the habits of working people tend to conflict with those of students.

The intentions behind quads are economic and practical: to give students and other single persons housing that has a high degree of privacy and security and is affordable by virtue of the single-room accommodations, the shared kitchens, and the shared shower and tub. The social benefits of sharing—such as social interaction, group activities, and performance of common tasks—may develop among residents, but these are not explicit objectives. Nor does the design of the kitchen appear to encourage such activities.

GOHOMES

GoHomes are the invention of architect Ted Smith. The first one was built in 1983 in Del Mar, outside San Diego (Fig. 1-5). It was built as a four-unit cooperative house that combines work space with living space in each unit and provides private bathrooms, private entrances from the outdoors, and a shared kitchen.[3] Smith's intentions were to provide affordable housing, with work spaces, within walking distance of the beach and to meet the local zoning requirements for a single-family house (by having only one kitchen). The building is cooperatively owned by shareholders, who each paid $10,000 per share and then paid for or did most of the interior and facade work for his or her unit. Each shareholder pays $350 a month in carrying costs. Of the four original residents, one is a professional musician who gives music lessons; another uses his work space for drafting; a third does stained-glass work; and a fourth is a computer buff.

Figure 1-5. First GoHome in Del Mar, California: front facade. *(Ted Smith, Architect; Photo: Tim Street-Porter)*

Each unit has two levels—the second a loft space—and each has its own very small bathroom (one is only 3 feet by 8 feet). Most of the units have a little less than 500 square feet of floor space on the two levels. Each unit has two entrances from the outdoors, one for professional use and one for residential use, and one entrance to the shared kitchen (Fig. 1-6).

In this GoHome Smith wanted to maximize the individuality and the independence of the units and to limit the connectedness between them. In his observations of housesharing among his friends, he noticed how much they prized their privacy: to be able to come and go without passing through common areas and to eat in their own spaces. Therefore the kitchen is primarily utilitarian. Smith reported in 1984 that this GoHome "was not meant to be a beautiful communal living space. . . . It is missing the thing that makes a place feel like a home—the kitchen. Most of the GoHome is workspace." Privacy and independence more than shared use were the guiding concerns in the design of the first GoHome.

Two subsequent GoHomes, also built in Del Mar, follow the same principles of providing affordable living and working spaces near the beach, with a shared kitchen, private baths, private entrances from the outdoors, and private entrances from the units to the kitchen. Like the first GoHome these are designed to allow for possible future conversion to a single-family house in order to increase their flexibility. The number of units, or what Smith calls "suites," has been increased to six and the shared kitchens are larger. Rents or carrying charges for suites in the latest GoHomes are $450 to $500, while rents for newly built efficiency apartments in Del Mar are about $650.

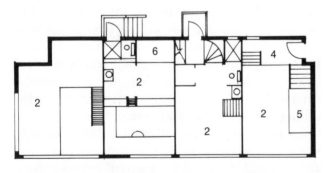

1. Lower level of private unit
2. Upper level of private unit
3. Shared kitchen
4. Landing
5. Loft bed
6. Built-in bed

Figure 1-6. First GoHome: plans of first and second floors.

In the second GoHome one of the six suites is used as an office/workshop by three of the residents—two architects and a furniture maker. This work space is contiguous with the shared kitchen/dining area. Smith reports that there is much more active sharing between residents here than in the first GoHome, with sharing of meals and assignment of tasks. "There is less independence," he says. "It's more like a big family and less like independent houses." In the third GoHome a domed ceiling graces the 20-by-14-foot kitchen, which opens onto a deck. A pair of units joined together provides a place for a couple to live. Smith is keen to encourage a mixture of households—both singles and couples.

Smith adopted the term *GoHome* from the lyrics of a song written by a friend. According to Smith, the word refers to getting back to basics and returning to an earlier, "sweeter time." The concept reflects his desire to see a more integrated city, based on combinations of uses instead of separations. As a model the GoHome is a way "to put the city back together" (Katkov 1984, 51). The basic model remains constant: affordable living and working spaces that support privacy as well as community and that have various sizes and shapes, where ceiling height is as important as amount of floor space. Possible variations are numerous, including the incorporation of varying amounts of shared space and the integration of GoHomes with other dwelling units. A combination of GoHomes and row houses is to be built on a site in downtown San Diego.

SPONSORED GROUP RESIDENCES

Sponsored group residences are houses purchased (or leased) and managed by nonprofit organizations for occupancy by unrelated individuals or small households such as couples or single-parent families. These and other organizations also operate services to match renters with homeowners. The National Shared Housing Resource Center in Philadelphia, which provides technical assistance, resource development, and training for shared housing and matching programs, estimates that there are 400 such programs nationwide (Damiani 1988).

One such program is the Boston Aging Concerns (BAC), which owns and manages one of the earliest intergenerational group residences in the country, the Shared Living House in Boston's Back Bay. It was established in 1979 in what had originally been a private home and then a lodging house. Currently the Victorian building contains 14 bedrooms and one complete apartment in addition to a common kitchen, living room, and dining room. The bedrooms vary in size; some are as small as 80 square feet. In 1985 rents ranged from $165 to $312 a month. In August 1985, 12 of the 13 tenants in residence were women and 9 of them were age 50 or over.

Residents are expected to share household maintenance chores and to contribute to the purchase of food staples for the kitchen. Once a week residents have dinner together and hold a meeting that is attended by a facilitator from BAC. Although the intention of BAC is for additional meals to be shared, residents tend to cook individually, with two or three sometimes cooking jointly. The original goal was to create a strong sense of community where there would be frequent group activity, but residents' strongest reason for living there is economic rather than social; people choose to live there for its desirable location in the Back Bay, its pleasant atmosphere, and its low rent rather than for the opportunity to interact with others. As in the group residences studied by West (1985), sharing primarily takes the form of common use of facilities and informal, unplanned contacts rather than frequent group activities or coordination and exchange among residents. Several residents are frustrated by the lack of social interaction and the infrequency of group activities.

Innovative Housing, a shared housing program in Mill Valley, California, sponsors and manages 100 shared houses. Their activities include leasing or purchasing houses for sharing and aiding the operation of these houses through workshops and other support activities, facilitating shared homeownership, developing living and working spaces for sharing, and designing and developing small cooperative communities of shared houses. One example of the last activity is a vest pocket community of seven group residences, designed by Dan Solomon, to be built on two adjacent sites in Fairfax, California (Fig. 1-7). Each of the

Figure 1-7. Innovative Housing Vest Pocket Community in Fairfax, California: site model. *(Daniel Solomon and Associates, Architects. Photo: Peter Xiques)*

seven houses will have a study, a shared kitchen, and a spacious living/dining area with a fireplace (Figs. 1-8 and 1-9). Two of the houses also will have community rooms that residents from all the houses will be able to use. The functions of the community rooms will be decided by the residents, with funding for furniture or equipment from Innovative Housing. Possibilities include a library, an exercise room, and a computer room. To enhance privacy, the bedrooms, with the exception of the bedrooms for handicapped residents, will be placed on the second floor. Two rooms will share a bathroom but each will have its own sink. House Three also will have sleeping porches on the second floor, which can be furnished with a desk, a window seat, or an addi-

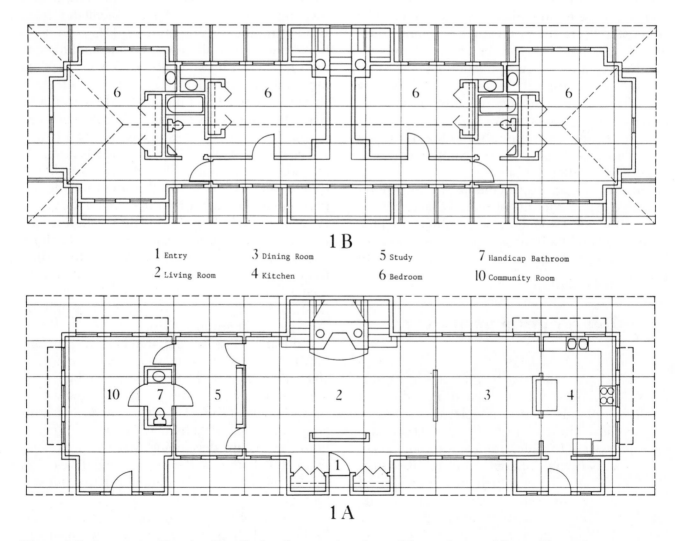

1 B

| 1 Entry | 3 Dining Room | 5 Study | 7 Handicap Bathroom |
| 2 Living Room | 4 Kitchen | 6 Bedroom | 10 Community Room |

1 A

Figure 1-8. Innovative Housing Vest Pocket Community: plans of first and second floors, House 1.

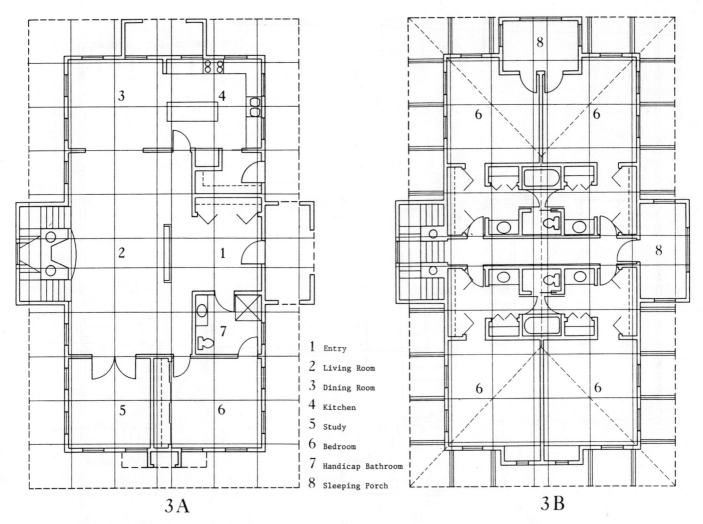

1 Entry
2 Living Room
3 Dining Room
4 Kitchen
5 Study
6 Bedroom
7 Handicap Bathroom
8 Sleeping Porch

3 A   3 B

Figure 1-9. Innovative Housing Vest Pocket Community: plans of first and second floors, House 3.

tional bed, depending on residents' wishes (Fig. 1-9). Each cluster of houses will have its own outdoor space, and there also will be a trellis and a barbecue pit for use by the entire community.

All together the houses can accommodate 30 people, with single parents having the option of renting one of the rooms with an adjoining sleeping porch to give them more space. Innovative Housing encourges residents to share meals, but the decision to do so is left up to each household. Initially, core groups of two to three residents for each house will participate in a series of workshops conducted by Innovative Housing. These core groups will then set up the houses, make decisions on sharing arrangements and the final interior design and furnishings, and interview additional residents for the house. Rents are projected to be $350 to $400 a month.

COLLECTIVE HOUSING

338 Harvard Street in Cambridge, Massachusetts, and Sunlight in Portland, Oregon, are cases of collective housing where a common kitchen and living space are provided in addition to private dwelling units that have their own kitchens, baths, and living spaces. 338 Harvard Street is a former Lutheran rectory that has been renovated by developer/architect Gwen Rono (Fig. 1-10). The house, with a new addition, now contains ten complete one- and two-bedroom apartments and several shared spaces: a large living/dining room served by an adjacent kitchen (with laundry), a study, a garden, a sun deck, and a guest room and bath (Fig. 1-11). The condominium apartments cost between $130,000 and $220,000 and range in size from 556 to 935 square feet.

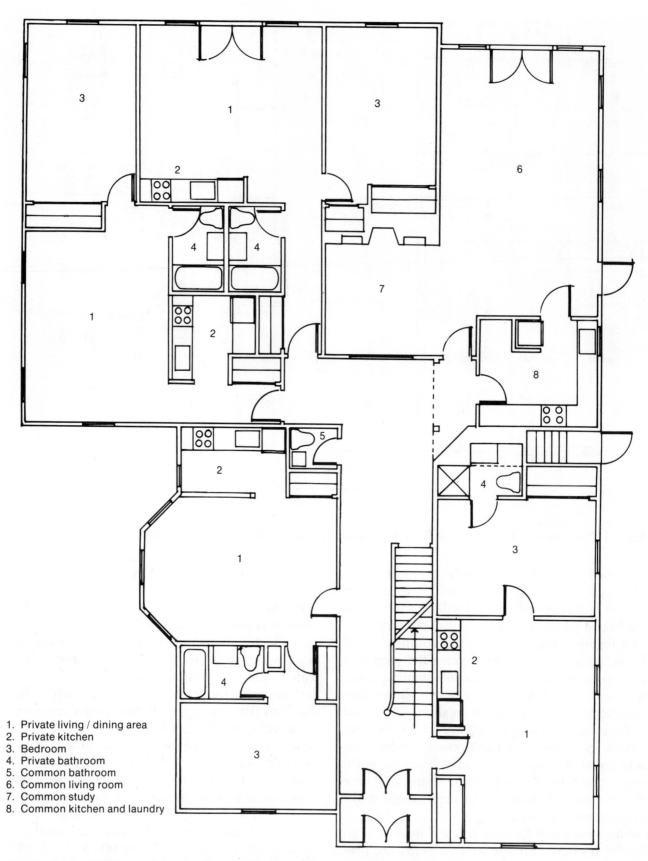

1. Private living / dining area
2. Private kitchen
3. Bedroom
4. Private bathroom
5. Common bathroom
6. Common living room
7. Common study
8. Common kitchen and laundry

Figure 1-11. 338 Harvard Street: plan of first floor. *(Gwen Rono, Architect)*

Figure 1-10. 338 Harvard Street in Cambridge, Massachusetts.

Figure 1-12. 338 Harvard Street: common study.

The shared living/dining room is 700 square feet, with an adjacent study (Fig. 1-12). The design details are planned to create a "sense of gracious living." These include hardwood floors, a fireplace in the shared living room, a large and elegant entry hall, and terraces for five of the apartments.

Rono's goal was to provide housing for empty-nesters that would encourage social interaction between residents and a strong sense of community while removing the cost and burden of maintaining a private home. She aimed to achieve an age mix, with 80 percent age 60 or over. The original sales brochure emphasized "an ongoing opportunity for residents to participate in the evolution and development of their own supportive community; ten attractive apartments designed to preserve privacy and independence; gracious common spaces to encourage the community life of the house."

As it turned out, the age range of residents is wider than expected; 60 percent are over 50, and three owners do not live in their units but lease them to students or young professionals. People's reasons for living in the house are thus more diverse than originally expected, with less of a central focus on the creation of a supportive community. Nonetheless, monthly potluck dinners and house meetings are held in the common living room and several residents gather there for coffee on Saturday mornings. Residents also use the living room for their own parties. The guestroom was so heavily used that another room, intended to be an office, was converted to a second guestroom. Although the common living room and study are not heavily used, the residents appreciate these rooms very much: they provide a sense of space and present additional options. Since the condominium association was established, residents have taken on more responsibility for common household tasks, such as sorting the mail, and as more of the owners begin to live in their apartments, the use of common areas and the sense of community are likely to increase.

While 338 Harvard Street was created by an

Figure 1-13. Sunlight in Portland, Oregon: common house.

outside sponsor, Sunlight in Portland is a community created by the residents themselves. Beginning in the early 1970s, a group of six families, including Bill Church, a local architect and planner, held regular potluck suppers in their neighborhood in northwest Portland, sometimes two or three times a week. They also shared a sailboat. In 1976 they decided to buy and share an apartment building but later decided against it because of the lack of privacy between apartments. The group grew to eight families who met regularly; all decisions were made by consensus. Eventually the group decided to build on land that was suitable for solar design, on a bus line, and 20 minutes from downtown Portland. A site was found and purchased, and construction of 15 single-family detached houses and one community building began in 1977 on 6½-acre sloped, wooded site.

The group also agreed on a number of design restrictions by which all would abide: parking in one location separated from all the houses; houses built above the shadow line, using passive solar heating; and houses made of weathered cedar only one story in height and unobtrusive in the landscape. Each family contributed an equal amount to the purchase price of the land and to the cost of the community building, but the cost of the construction of the individual houses varied. Each family owns its own house and the ground beneath it; all other land is owned in common.

Church and another architect in the group served as planners and advisors. Each family designed its own house within the restrictions. The houses range from 800 to 2,400 square feet; there are no garages or basements. The result is, indeed, unobtrusive houses of different sizes nes-

Table 1-1. Characteristics of Contemporary Shared and Collective Housing in the United States[1]

	No. of People or Households Sharing	Bathrooms	Kitchens	Entrances from Outdoors
Shared housing				
Mingle units	2 people	1 per person	1	1 for 2 people
Quads	4 people	1 sink/toilet per person 1 tub/shower for 4 people	1	1 per person
GoHomes	4–6 people	1 per person	1	1 per person
Group homes	4–20 people	Sometimes 1 per person	1	1 for whole house
Collective housing[2]	10–15 households	1 or more per household	1 per household and 1 for all households	Sometimes 1 for each household

[1] In shared housing unrelated individuals share a single dwelling unit and thus constitute a single household. In collective housing each household has its own complete dwelling unit and then all the households share additional spaces and facilities.

[2] This is based on only two examples, which are described in the text.

tled into the slope, surrounded by trees and reached by winding lanes. The community building contains a large gathering/dining space that can seat 75 people for a meal, a kitchen, a guest room/study with bath, and a workshop with tools donated by residents (Fig. 1-13). A potluck dinner is held every Wednesday evening and usually is attended by about 20 people. Outside groups can rent the community space for gatherings. An athletic field was added in 1984. Decisions are still made by consensus.

In collective housing, unlike in shared housing, the comfort and security of co-residence are offered without sacrificing the privacy and independence created by complete individual dwelling units (Table 1-1). The luxury of having community *and* privacy with spaces designed for both extremes should a be more frequent design consideration in all kinds of housing. Even households happy with the privacy and independence of traditional dwellings may desire, in addition, common spaces that support shared activities between households and between households of different ages and lifestyles. The chapters in this section present additional cases of communities that offer these opportunities.

OVERVIEW OF CHAPTERS

Nineteenth- and early-twentieth-century collective housing is the topic of chapters 2 and 3. In "Apartments and Collective Life in Nineteenth-Century New York," Elizabeth Cromley describes the development of a variety of accommodations that offered various combinations of individual rooms, suites, or apartments with shared spaces and facilities. The apartment hotel or family hotel offered permanent residence in private suites of living rooms and bedrooms, supplemented by shared dining rooms and parlors. Middle-class families with children and young couples often lived in such buildings. Buildings also were designed for other groups, including single working women and bachelors. Cromley reviews the kinds of design and occupancy issues architects, developers, and residents faced during this time. What should be private and what might be shared was not a foregone conclusion but rather a question to be debated and explored.

In "Early European Collective Habitation: From Utopian Ideal to Reality," Norbert Schoenauer describes the rich array of early collective housing that was built or proposed in England, Denmark, Germany, Austria, Switzerland, Sweden, and the Soviet Union. In these examples, as in those described by Cromley, meal preparation and other housekeeping tasks were performed by building staff, and the buildings were designed for various types of households, including families with children. Collective housing in Europe, however, was more often part of a larger political or social agenda than it was in the United States.

Chapters 4 and 5 chronicle contemporary efforts in Sweden and Denmark to develop collective housing and describe the results of these efforts. In "Communal Housing in Sweden: A Remedy for the Stress of Everyday Life?" Alison Woodward focuses primarily on rental housing built by public authorities. A variety of shared spaces and facilities supplement complete apartments. The buildings house a mixture of residents, including many families with children. In some of her examples meal preparation and other tasks are done by the residents themselves; in others this service is provided by a staff hired by the management. Woodward gives a detailed history of the recent development of collective housing in Sweden and presents findings from a survey of residents in four projects.

In "Cohousing in Denmark," Kathryn Mc-Camant and Charles Durrett outline the development and the essential social, design, and management characteristics of Danish collective housing. These communities supplement complete individual dwellings with a community house that contains a common kitchen, a dining/living area, and various other shared spaces and facilities. Significantly, these communities are planned, designed, and managed by the residents themselves. Community life centers most directly on regular, shared evening meals prepared by the residents. The authors suggest how the Danish collective housing model can be adapted in the United States.

In "The Party Wall as the Architecture of Sharing," Jill Stoner proposes a cultural and architectural transformation of the party wall into a membrane that connects as much as it separates households. This transformation would require changes in the structure, program, and regulations for multifamily housing in the United

States. The changes in program center on the idea of larger, more inclusive households, each composed of several smaller subgroups. Examples include two-generation households, households of single-parent families, and households of single adults. The households would occupy "suites" consisting of private and shared spaces. The design and function of the shared spaces, which are generated by the redefined party wall, would vary according to the particular composition of the household.

ADDITIONAL INFORMATION

For additional information on nineteenth- and early twentieth-century collective housing in the United States, see Hayden's *The Grand Domestic Revolution* (1981). For a more complete description of collective aspects of early apartment buildings and apartment hotels in New York, see Cromley's *Alone Together: A History of New York's Early Apartments* (1989). Suggestions for designing group residences are given in Day-Lower, West, and Zimmers' *Designing Shared Residences for the Elderly* (1985). Additional detail and analysis of Danish collective housing are given in McCamant and Durrett's *Cohousing: A Contemporary Approach to Housing Ourselves* (1988).

NOTES

1. This definition of shared housing seems to have been widely accepted in the United States following the development of shared housing programs in the 1970s (Streib 1984; Day-Lower 1983; Raimy 1979), but this particular distinction between collective and shared housing has not been made before, as far as I know. Collective housing as defined here also has been called *communal housing* (see chapter 4) or *congregate housing* (see chapter 8). The latter term, however, tends to refer primarily to housing for the elderly.
2. This overview is based in large part on research conducted by the author on social and spatial innovations in American housing with funds from the National Science Foundation (Grant CE-839721-13). I am grateful to Jerry Finrow for draw-

ing the quad floor plan, to Stephanie Kidd for drawing the mingles units and the GoHome, and to Daniel Solomon and Associates for providing drawings of the Fairfax Vest Pocket Community project.
3. Two units have since been added to the first Go-Home.

References

Cromley, E. 1989. *Alone Together: A History of New York's Early Apartments.* Ithaca, NY: Cornell University Press.

Damiani, D. M. 1988. Shared lives—Shared experiences—Shared resources. *Shared Housing Quarterly: Special Issue* 5 (1):1–3.

Day-Lower, D. 1984. *Shared Housing for Older People: A Planning Manual for Group Residences.* Philadelphia: Shared Housing Resource Center.

———, Sheree L. West, and H. Zimmers. 1985. *Designing Shared Housing for the Elderly.* Philadelphia: National Shared Housing Resource Center.

Franck, K. A. 1986. Together or apart: Sharing and the American household. In *Discipline of Architecture,* 79–89. Washington D.C.: Association of Collegiate Schools of Architecture.

———. 1987. Shared spaces, small spaces, and spaces that change. In *Housing and Neighborhoods,* ed. W.

Van Vliet, H. Choldin, W. Michelson, and D. Popenoe, 157–172. Westport, CT: Greenwood Press.

Glick, P. 1984. American household structure in transition. *Family Planning Perspectives* 16: 305–211.

Gottschalk, E. C. 1981. Doubling up. *The Wall Street Journal* (Apr. 17):18.

Hayden, D. 1976. *Seven American Utopias.* Cambridge, MA: MIT Press.

———. 1981. *The Grand Domestic Revolution: A History of Feminist Designs for American Homes, Neighborhoods and Cities.* Cambridge, MA: MIT Press.

Katkov, R. 1984. The GoHome. *Arts & Architecture* 3:48–51.

McCamant, K. and C. Durrett. 1988. *Cohousing: A Contemporary Approach to Housing Ourselves.* Berkeley, CA: Habitat Press.

Raimy, E. 1979. *Shared Houses, Shared Lives.* Los Angeles: J. D. Tarcher.

Slater, P. 1976. *The Pursuit of Loneliness.* Boston: Beacon Press.

Streib. G., F. Foltz, and E. and M.A. Hilher. 1984. *Old Homes—New Families.* New York: Columbia University Press.

Van Gelder, L. 1986. Special *Ms.* Poll: Dream houses. *Ms.* (April):34–36, 40, 88.

West, S. 1981. *Sharing and privacy in shared housing for older people.* Ph.D. dissertation. New York: City University of New York.

Chapter 2

Apartments and Collective Life in Nineteenth-Century New York

Elizabeth Cromley

Dwellings with collective features, those that emphasize group settings and activities, offer an alternative to the single-family house that is the norm for dwellings in the United States today. Creating collective settings in housing seems a promising way to diminish the isolation of the elderly, to share child-care burdens among parents, and to increase the social networks available to both families and single people. Designing for these concerns has occupied many socially conscious architects and planners over the last few years, and it appears to be a fresh direction in housing (Hayden 1984; Birch 1986). Given the rising prices of houses and the high demand for land near metropolitan areas, most new housing, socially conscious or not, is going to have to incorporate shared elements of one kind or another.

Some historic precedents for collective housing in America come from communities with strong religious or political aims (Hayden 1976). Fourierists, Perfectionists, and other groups created dwellings to support utopian programs where collectivity was a valued political tenet. Similarly many European examples of collective housing emerged out of politically progressive or radical programs, as recounted in chapter 3. One might forget that housing types with spaces and facilities designed for the domestic life of groups,

as distinct from individuals, also have a substantial history in nonutopian, nonradical American urban architecture. In apartment houses of the 1870s, 1880s, and 1890s, many city dwellers found themselves living in collective or cooperative settings as they pursued conventional domestic lives.[1]

Apartment design issues of that period reveal the many tensions between collectivity and privacy that arose for people not motivated by a utopian vision. The idea of sharing a roof, and perhaps many other spaces and facilities, with other families was problematic for middle-class city dwellers of the later nineteenth century. According to contemporary commentators, the sharing of living quarters rightly belonged to bachelors, salesmen on the road, and working girls living away from their families—that is, people in what they saw as unstable situations. With their strong orientation to the nuclear family,[2] middle-class New York husbands and wives worried that their privacy and independence would be compromised by a group dwelling. They understood that there were many advantages to living collectively, *collective* implying only living in a setting that made sharing of resources and facilities easy. Many of the appealing aspects of an apartment house—such as central heating, the services of a doorman, or stylish and imposing architecture—were directly linked to its group nature. But at the same time tenants worried about living too close to strangers and about losing the integrity and individuality of the family. The idea of living collectively or "cooperatively"[3] held both promise and threat.

Designers and developers created nineteenth-century apartment buildings not to support or encourage social change but to protect familiar life patterns. But of course change occurred. By the first decade of the twentieth century, many varieties of apartment buildings had been constructed and definitions of *home* had shifted from an insistence on privacy to include the benefits of collective living in apartment buildings. Tenants learned to interpret group settings and behavior in ways that did not violate the prevailing understandings of family privacy. As we consider housing alternatives for emerging new household forms in the present, we should not naïvely take "collectivity" as an unmitigated benefit. Seeing how family-oriented Americans of this earlier time dealt with the challenges of group life can make us aware of the complex relations between dwellings and the people who live in them.

DWELLING PRACTICES OF
PRE–CIVIL WAR NEW YORK

From 1850 to 1860 New York City's population expanded by over 56 percent. The supply of dwellings was inadequate to meet this demand, and real-estate prices rose to the point that moderate-income families could no longer afford houses of their own. When looking for alternatives to a private house, New Yorkers tried several kinds of ad hoc, collective dwelling practices. Common in the mid-century city were nonprivate living arrangements such as living in a boarding house or a hotel or subdividing a private house among two or three families. *Putnam's Monthly* magazine recommended hotel life in 1854 ("New York Daguerreotyped"). Their writer pointed out that private houses were really only "what Fourierists call the 'isolated household.'" In eschewing isolation families could obtain a share in resources and even luxuries otherwise denied them. But residents of the mid-nineteenth century often expressed dismay at the loss

of privacy they felt in this ad hoc housing (Vaux 1857; Richardson 1874, 65).

Privacy appears to be the very keystone of successful Victorian family life. Sentimental descriptions of "home" pointed to the "beneficent influence of its delightful seclusion," where the family members could thrive because they lived separate from others (Ware 1866; *Women's Own Book* 1873). This prized privacy, it should be noted, was sought for the family unit; it was not a question of assuring individuals within the family privacy from each other. The home, because it had to be an appropriate representation of a family's social status, needed to be separate and individualized. "A house to be a true home must be strictly adapted to the owner's position in society," asserted John Ware in his 1866 book on the home. Above all, home was a moral place where true values could be maintained, usually through the dedication of women, in the face of the world's darker aspects. Home, wrote Ware, is "an anchor by which he [the male houseowner] holds amid the tossing temptations of life,—a place of refuge and of love, whose charms, whose solid, pure delights, prevail against all that pleasure offers or appetite suggests." To truly represent social status and to guarantee a moral life, a home had to belong to an individual family and should not be shared with others.

In contrast to the secluded and private home, housing alternatives that New Yorkers could actually afford placed home-seekers in situations of what was then called "publicity," or being under public observation. Subdivided houses put two or three families into a house constructed for one. Savings on the rent through sharing appealed to many, but physical remodeling often did not accompany these changes in use. This meant that families used baths and kitchens in common, losing some of the privacy they treasured. Boardinghouse owners rented separate rooms out to individuals but served meals to all the tenants together, and sociability took place in the boarding house's collective parlor. Critics focused on those two collective spaces, dining room and parlor, for their harshest condemnations of boarding, citing the food as loathsome, the company at table as unacceptable, and the parlor flirtations as verging on the immoral (McCabe 1872; Furniss 1871).

Many families chose hotels as permanent residences where they would live in suites of furnished private living rooms and bedrooms. The remainder of the parents' and children's hotel activities took place in public dining rooms and group parlors. Sometimes hotels offered private bathrooms, but it was more common to have shared facilities. The Windsor Hotel, which opened on Fifth Avenue in 1873, provided shared parlors and dining rooms for its permanent family residents, including two dining rooms for children and one each for white and "colored" servants (*New York Times* 1873). In this hotel sharing space could work only if class and race divisions were respected.

Hotel staff also could serve centrally cooked meals in tenants' private rooms. The staff did the laundry, cleaned the rooms, and sometimes helped with child care. But the high level of household work taken care of by the hotel left wives without their usual household duties. The *New York Times* reported in 1873 that women enjoyed hotel life because it gave them relief from hiring, training, and paying servants and, provided the benefits of a lavish house in only a few rooms. But, they reported, men prefer privacy. Both male and female critics found hotel life especially threatening to women's role as wife and mother, the moral guide and emotional center of family life (Browne 1869, 398).

Such a history of living in group settings that were not designed especially for family use left tenants with apprehensive feelings about sharing spaces. Yet New York's crowded conditions and costly real estate prevented most middle-class residents from obtaining their own private houses. The basic building type created to answer city dwellers' housing needs was what we now call an apartment house. It contained separate, independent dwelling units for at least three households under a single roof. Usually a kitchen was understood to be part of the independent dwelling unit but, as we will see, this characteristic and many others were questioned by the variety of designs for apartments produced by the end of the century.

Writers of the period did not agree on terminology; what was an *apartment house* to one was a *family hotel* to another. In the 1860s and 1870s, writers often called apartment buildings *French flats* or sometimes *Parisian dwellings* because Parisians were known to live in apartments, even though French multiple dwellings differed from New York apartments. By the end of the century, *flats* named the inferior version of multiple dwellings, just a step up from *tenements*, while *apartments* designated the better form in popular nomenclature. Another variant was called an *apartment hotel*. This name pointed to a hybrid of two ideas, the privacy of a self-contained family dwelling unit plus the elaborate housekeeping and food-preparation services offered in hotels. In addition to these many kinds of family-oriented buildings, there also were multiple dwellings especially designed for single people.

The ways that nineteenth-century designers rethought the activities associated with home are provocative and suggest a willingness to try new ways of balancing collective facilities and experiences against private ones. There were apartment houses where all cooking and eating went on in restaurants outside the building, while in others, a family's personal cook prepared family meals in a private kitchen. Another type of apartment house had one central kitchen, a staff cook, and a collective dining room, while another alternative proposed private dining rooms in which families ate centrally prepared meals. The multiplicity of ways to think about the meal carries through to many other aspects of home life, all raising possibilities for using the collective potential of a multiple dwelling and for questioning privacy as the only way to live.

DEVELOPING A BUILDING FOR COLLECTIVE PURPOSES

Apartment houses raised issues of collective life in different ways for architects, tenants, and developers: For architects physical design decisions related to group use were most prominent; tenants focused on issues of meaning and shared use; while developers looked to assure a good return on investment by securing an appropriate tenancy. The requirements of these three groups overlapped, but, for the sake of this analysis, I will consider as separate issues some aspects of physical design, collective activities, and specially defined tenant groups.

Physical Design Issues in a Collective Building

Architects developed specific spaces for group use that included lobbies, reception rooms, dining rooms, elevators, stairs and corridors, and the outdoor spaces of courtyard and roof garden. Facade designs took on a special importance because they conveyed to the public eye meanings about the building. Architects had to discover ways of expressing subtle relations between the individual and the collective as they developed appropriate space relationships and suitable styles for apartment exteriors.

The entrance, the lobby, the stairs, the elevators, and the corridors had to serve collective needs. These were routes for all the tenants, all their guests, and sometimes for their servants, too. Designers made a range of choices in public circulation either to emphasize or to play down the group use of the building. In these spaces tenants' encounters with each other could be friendly and pleasant or socially threatening, depending on both the designers' decisions and the tenants' interpretations.

The path of movement starts in the street: how should one enter a collective dwelling? One kind of small apartment house that was common in the 1870s and 1880s was a French flat that occupied a house-sized lot. Bruce Price's design for 21 East 21st Street looks almost like a private house when approached from the street (Fig. 2-1). Its front door is raised above the sidewalk, reached by a flight of steps just like the stoops of contemporary private row houses. A building four times as long, Richard Morris Hunt's Stuyvesant Apartments on East 18th Street also makes use of a few steps up to its small front doors, a pair of them centered on the facade (Fig. 2-2). These designers suppressed the group nature of their apartment houses by emphasizing the single-family house qualities of small doorways and raised stoops.

Larger buildings, such as Central Park Apartments on Seventh Avenue at 59th Street, made more imposing architectural statements out of their front doors, handling them more like those of a public building, hotel, or club (Fig. 2-3). Elaborate two-story-high door frames received additional architectural attention in the form of

columns, entablatures, or other embellishments, and owners attempted to appeal to tenants by mentioning a glamorous group entrance in newspaper ads. At the entrance a marquee or porte-cochère extending out over the sidewalk was one way of asserting collective control over the unpredictable traffic of the sidewalk. This manner of handling the entrances of large apartment buildings continued into the twentieth century, offering one point at which collective use created an opportunity for architectural enrichment.

On the interior, the problems that arose over the meaning and use of group space concerned unclear boundaries between public and private behavior. Would shared regions within apartment houses be read as encouraging sociability and exchange among tenants, and what level of exchange would tenants find comfortable? Would dress and codes of deportment suitable to "public" places or "private" places prevail? Front door, lobby, and public stairs or elevators had to be used by the whole group of tenants and by their guests. Such "publicity," however, made some critics very uncomfortable. Corridors received condemnation for their "liability to espionage, noise, difficulty of policing . . ." (Potter 1879). All the halls, elevators, and lobbies, lamented an 1890 writer, were open territory where other tenants and their visitors may wander ("Apartment Houses" 1890, 194). Privacy-loving tenants feared harrassment from strangers under such circumstances.

The city street was a neutral territory where one did not speak to strangers (Young 1872, 474). Some architects believed apartment house lobbies ought to be mere extensions of the street (Hubert 1892). A simple, austere architectural expression suited the interpretation of extended street space. If the lobby were not public space, but instead private space, then it should be treated architecturally as a kind of collective drawing room, with decoration appropriate for conviviality. In drawing rooms certain codes of manners were in force: one dressed suitably and addressed others as social equals. A lobby on the drawing-room model assumed that people wanted intimacy.

An ornamented lobby also might be an affront to economy. At the Central Park Apartments, the architects argued for simple, good-quality mate-

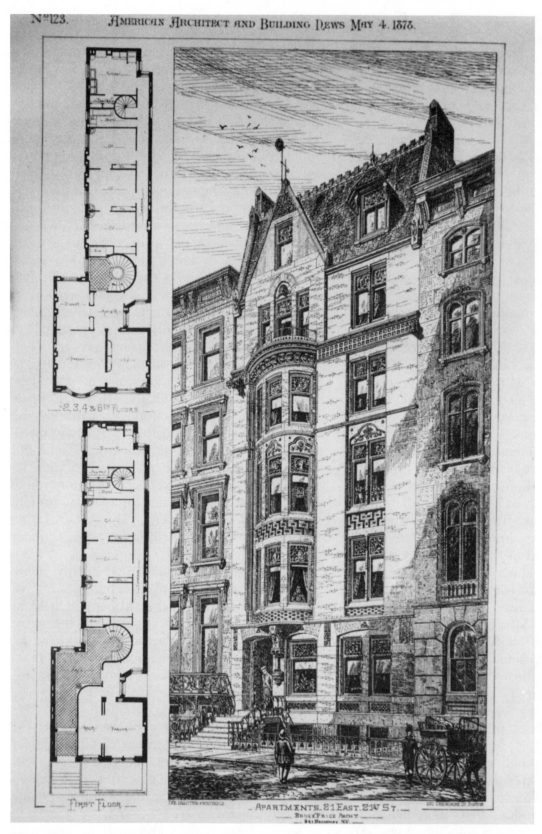

Figure 2-1. Apartment house by Bruce Price, 1878, 21 East 21st Street, New York. (*Source: Apartment House on East 21 Street*, American Architect and Building News 3, *May 1878, Pl. follows 156*)

Figure 2-2. Stuyvesant Apartments by Richard Morris Hunt, 1869, on East 18th Street, New York. *(Source:* Architectural Record *11, July 1901, p. 479)*

rials instead of wasting money on lavish draperies and upholstery. By the turn of the century, however, many advertisements based their promotion of apartment buildings on the richly ornamented character of the lobbies.

Architect John Pickering Putnam (1890) contrasted the apartment's "privacy line" to that of a single-family house, where private terrain begins at the edge of the public street and sidewalk. The sidewalk, Putnam wrote, belonged to public life, and it extended into the apartment house's public lobby, elevator, and upper-floor public corridors; an apartment's private terrain started at the individual unit's front door. Putnam took advantage of the opportunities that lobbies and circulation spaces provided for group sociability because enhancing social exchange was in keeping with his Nationalist theories, derived from Bellamy's utopian novel *Looking Backwards*. In his apartment house designs for Boston, Putnam defined his lobby and parlor spaces as congregating spaces

Figure 2-3. Central Park Apartments by Hubert, Pirsson and Hoddick, 1883, at Central Park South (59th St.) and Seventh Avenue. *(Photo: Courtesy of Henry Francis du Pont Winterthur Museum Library, Collection of Printed Books)*

for tenants; but by doing so he set clear limits on the "public," encouraging tenants' interactions with each other but excluding outsiders.

Like the lobby the public stairs of an apartment house must be "nothing but a street," asserted architects Hubert, Pirsson, and Hoddick when describing their Central Park Apartments in 1882. They relied on a French apartment tradition, in which the halls and stairs were considered extensions of the street. In this view, public behavior, the kind employed when walking down the sidewalk, was appropriate for stairs or public halls. But not all tenants agreed that the line separating group life from private life fell at their individual front doors. Some tenants understood that the stairs and landings of the building were theirs for individual activities and would hold intimate conversations there. In summer these unrestrained tenants conducted a busy social life on the front stoop of their apartment house, dressed as if in private (Hubert 1892, 57). This embarrassed tenants with a stricter sense of decorum. Contemporary critics believed that unresolved conflicts over the "privacy line" could force the more particular residents to move out, resulting in the social decline of an apartment house.

For its principal vertical circulation paths, Bruce Price's design (Fig. 2-4) included a main stair and a service stair, both circular. The main stair toward the front of the building rose around a circular, open well in the center, a gracious, Paris-inspired approach to the one-per-floor apartments inside; the service stair in the rear was a tight spiral. Price clearly separated the paths of movement for tenants and for servants, recognizing that unclear class boundaries might limit people's willingness to use group circulation spaces.

An additional circulation element, apparently private, was the dumbwaiter provided for housekeepers' or servants' use in the kitchen. In a lively description of 1890's apartment life in a flat building with two units per floor, novelist Theodore Dreiser uses the dumbwaiter as a space for social contact in *Sister Carrie*. His heroine, Carrie, meets her next-door neighbor when both women

Figure 2-4. 21 East 21st Street: floor plan. *(Source: Apartment House on East 21 Street, AA&BN 3, May 1878, Pl. follows 156)*

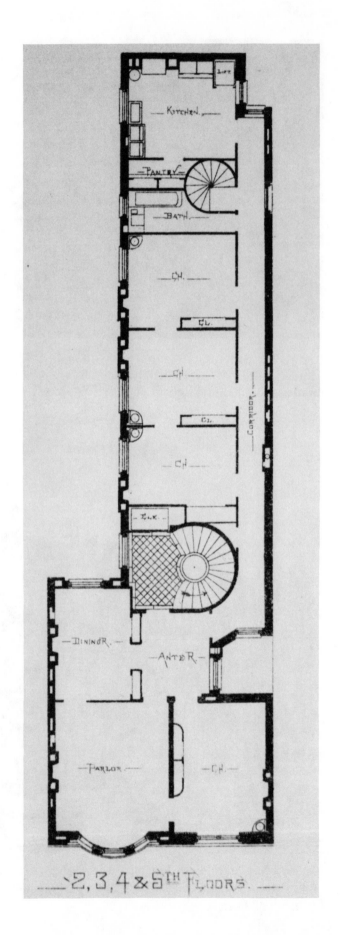

open their dumbwaiter doors at the same moment to retrieve the cream and the morning paper and see each other across the open shaft. This begins a welcome friendship for the two women that expands to include jaunts together out into the city.

Apartment houses in the 1870s rarely included additional collective social spaces; these spaces seemed unsuited to good domestic life because of their association with full-blown hotels. The ground-floor parlors, ballrooms, and other social spaces for group use typically found in hotels challenged nineteenth-century commitments to privacy. However, by the turn of the century, a revived interest in family hotels or apartment hotel forms led to increased use of these semiprivate social spaces. Architects advertising the services of their firm in 1902 (Associated Architects) listed the types of collective rooms that they would include in an apartment house: a library, rooms for social entertainment, a gymnasium, a lounge, a billiard room, and a café ("if the house contains bachelor or boarding apartments"). Architect Walter Kilham noted in 1904 that while the amount of ground-floor space given over to collective use varied, it was generally on the increase and included at least a "palm room" with tropical plants and another small reception room where tenants could meet their friends.

Collective Outdoor Spaces: Roof and Courtyard

The roof was a part of apartment house space that had a mobile identity. In many cases roofs were collectively used, but by servants. Typically they provided space for clothes drying in every scale of building from a tenement to a luxury house. In the flat building described by journalist Christine Herrick (1890), each household was assigned a day to use the clothesline on the roof, so if it rained on their day, their apartment had to be draped with wet clothes. Here strict ideas of privacy and individuality prescribed limits on the collective use of the roof, sometimes causing problems for tenants. Another way of assigning roof space was to build drying rooms of wood slats, stretched with clotheslines, such as were provided at the Stuyvesant or recommended for

the garret of an ideal apartment building proposed in *Appleton's* (Carroll 1878).

Yet roofs also had properties of the belvedere where a lovely view could be enjoyed by a select company. In 1872 journalist O. B. Bunce recommended that apartment houses develop their roofs as recreational spaces from which to take in stunning views of the city (Fig. 2-5). In his article on bachelor flats, E. T. Littell (1876) suggested that part of the roof be fenced off, roofed with wood slats, and provided with benches for the tenants' recreation. In this case, since the tenants were all single men, Littell's idea would prevent these young men from having raucous parties on their individual balconies, which would disturb other tenants and give the building a bad name. For the 1884 Dakota apartment building's roof, Henry Hardenbergh designed gazebos, pergolas, and sunshades (Birmingham 1979, 35). Roof gardens associated with theaters took their places in New York night life beginning in 1882 with the roof gardens on top of the Casino Theater and at Madison Square Garden. In theater roof gardens patrons could enjoy informal entertainment, such as vaudeville and cabaret, after the more formal plays in the theater proper. In both theaters and apartment houses, roof gardens provided spaces for people who arrived singly, in couples, or small parties, but did not feel obliged to be sociable with others using the space (Editor's Table 1881).

In apartment houses roof terraces offered an exceptional experience since the grandest 1880's apartment blocks had the most splendid views, being higher than neighboring buildings. Roof gardens continued to be featured in high-quality apartment houses at the turn of the century and became almost a standard feature. This shift in use from laundry to pleasure was facilitated by elevator rides to the roof and by new kinds of drying equipment introduced into apartment basements.

Apartment house courtyards might have provided a space for collective activity, but most architects did not interpret them in that way. Planned activities associated with courtyards were popular in the later nineteenth century for working-class tenement houses, such as A. T. White's 1890 Riverside Apartments in Brooklyn, where the large court served as a children's play-

Figure 2-5. Roof Gardens of the Future. *(Source: Illustration from O. B. Bunce, The City of the Future, Appleton's Journal 7, 1872, p. 156)*

ground and had a bandstand for concerts. However, this level of collective activity out of doors seemed unappealing to middle-class tenants. Large central courtyards, such as those at Henry Hardenbergh's Dakota and Van Corlear apartments, were relatively rare in nineteenth century middle-class apartment houses. Their principal purpose was to bring light and air into the building; sometimes courtyards also facilitated deliveries, as at the Central Park Apartments (Fig. 2-6). Although these courtyards had a clear function, they also added a landscaping opportunity to big buildings. Fountains, paths, and plantings became pleasing visual features of the larger courtyards.

Facades as Messages about the Group and the Individual

The problem of designing a suitable facade for apartment blocks focused architects' attention on the conflict between issues of collectivity and images of the private home. One way to use collectivity to create architectural expression is illustrated by Calvert Vaux's proposed Parisian Buildings of 1857 (Fig. 2-7). Vaux claimed that a well-lit, spacious, and attractive staircase was essential to convince Americans that apartment houses were acceptable. If the stair were given less than full architectural treatment, Vaux believed, people would turn against living in flats. Thus the shared stair becomes the principal motive for facade design and declares the group nature of the house on the exterior.

An energetic display of style also could proclaim an apartment's group use. Private houses of mid-nineteenth-century New York had rather plain facades with tall, ornamented stoops and front doors; their details and small scale set them apart as individual homes. Toward the end of the century, owners renovated facades to give stylistic individuality to each house front. Unable to use these private house features, apartment designers developed an individualism of style to mark out a large apartment block from other nearby buildings. Henry Hardenbergh's Dakota (Fig. 2-8) on 72nd Street at Central Park West, loosely based on northern Renaissance sources, has contrasting colors and varied brick, stone,

Figure 2-7. Parisian Buildings project by Calvert Vaux. (*Source: Harper's Weekly 34, Jan. 11, 1857, p. 30*)

terra-cotta, and iron materials, many different window forms, tall roofs, and a multitude of dormers. The assertive style of such a building made it stand out from the city context, allowing tenants to point it out as their collective home.

But what of the individual family home that privacy-loving people might prefer? In a vast building eclectic styles also could supply clues for single-family identification. To passersby and to residents viewing the Dakota up close, the variety of color and ornament created a perception of differences rather than of unity. The Central Park Apartments' facade design (see fig. 2-3) had this same disjunctiveness, with its separate towers, changes in color and texture, projecting bays, and corner turrets. Because of the differences from one detail of the facade to the next, residents could point out their own particular set

Figure 2-6. Central Park Apartments: courtyard. (*Source: Blanke, Cliff Dwellers, Cosmopolitan 15, July 1893, p. 357*)

Figure 2-8. Dakota Apartments by Henry Hardenbergh, 1884, New York. (*Source:* Architectural Record 6, *Oct.–Dec. 1896, p. 337*)

of windows, towered corner, projecting bay, or bit of ornament on the exterior and say "That's my part." In this way the style preferences of the 1870s and 1880s allowed tenants to locate their own individual parts of a perhaps uncomfortably large building, enhancing their personal attachment to it.

By 1910 the characteristic style of architecturally ambitious apartment houses had shifted toward the classical, which historians have always credited to a change in taste inspired by the 1893 Chicago World's Fair. Critics, such as architect Charles Israels (1901), praised this shift and argued for the virtues of classicism to give apartment houses more dignity. An example of this new taste is Israels's 1901 design for an apartment

building at 78 Irving Place (Fig. 2-9), organized like a classical column with a strong two-story base, shaft, and cornice.

This new classical architectural style presented the apartment house as a unified compositional whole rather than as a set of fragments. In a reversal of the 1880s experience, passersby would register its unity first, then perhaps recall that apartment houses contained many separate families. Charles Israels praised apartment buildings for their modern convenience that "eliminates the individual for the common good." The classical architectural expression of circa 1910 declares the value of subsuming multiple architectural parts within a clear whole, paralleling tenants' ability to appreciate collective living.

Figure 2-9. 78 Irving Place by Israels and Harder, 1900. *(Source: New York Apartment Houses,* Architectural Record *11, 1901, p. 494)*

COLLECTIVE ACTIVITIES: HOUSEKEEPING, COOKING, AND DINING

The collective activities that interested designers, critics, and tenants were the interrelated ones of cooking, dining, and housekeeping. To support these successfully, designers had to analyze and understand where the particular activity fit along a continuum from all group to all individual and had to design spaces to suit. When tenants moved into apartment houses, they often expected cooking, dining, and housekeeping activities to be purely private and internal to the single-family household. In order to take advantage of the collective potential of apartment houses, both architects and tenants had to question these expectations.

In the early period of apartment design, the 1860s and 1870s, critics recognized that living in a flat made housekeeping much simpler than it had been in a house. At first, however, this simplicity seemed to be a feature only of the small size of a flat and of its being on one floor. A housekeeper had fewer rooms and pieces of furniture to keep in order and no stairs to climb within the home. At the 20-unit Stuyvesant Apartments, individual households still had to manage all the housework on their own. There was no elevator, although a rope-and-pulley dumbwaiter aided in bringing goods up, trash down, and laundry to the basement for washing and to the roof for drying. Coal or wood had to be carried up for each individual cooking stove. Private fireplaces had to be lit for heat; individual deliveries of ice kept foods cold in personal iceboxes. Each family was expected to employ its own live-in servant. Each apartment unit in the Stuyvesant worked like a miniature private house of the period, where housekeeping was a labor-intensive problem that was internal to the private household (Littell 1876).

But it was difficult to maintain a conception of all household labor and equipment belonging to separate household units in an apartment house that contained 5 or 10 or 50 households, all engaging in the same sort of housework. While apartment units were workplaces for both servants and housekeepers, the apartment house as a whole enabled collective meal preparation and other kinds of housework to be performed by a central staff. The group building facilitated the installation of central heating, elevators, hot and cold running water, and other centralized technological features that saved housekeepers and their maids substantial effort. As early as 1876 architectural writer E. T. Littell recommended that apartment designers stop creating apartments as a collection of fully independent households and start thinking of cooking and other housekeeping services as properly collective.

Cooking and Dining

Centralized cooking and group meals often have served as a focal point of utopian communities. It is interesting to see how this aspect of collectivity developed in apartment houses and how it enhanced the daily lives of households not engaged in radical social movements. That centralized cooking provided advantages seemed to be a widely held opinion. Writing on the new dwelling places emerging in New York of the mid-1870s, James Richardson (1874) argued that the abandonment of private kitchens would be a money-saving choice and that centralizing laundry work also would provide benefits to household budgets. Writing to the *New York Times* in 1876, a reader suggested that all laundry and cooking work be done in apartment house basements rather than within private family units. There, centrally hired cooks and laundresses would perform the work required by individual households, while a family's own servant would perform just the duties of waitress and chambermaid, would always be neat and tidy, and would be ready to serve a meal or answer the door.

The experiences of dining in a fairly expensive apartment house of the later 1870s was described by a writer for *Appleton's Journal*, a general interest magazine (Carroll 1878). An apartment-dwelling family invites their visitors to stay for dinner, happy that they can spontaneously extend the hospitality that their collective dining arrangements allow. They take the elevator down to the house dining room, encountering en route well-dressed tenants from other floors in the building. The ground-floor dining room is "handsomely furnished and frescoed" and has separate, rather than group-sized, tables with fine napery, china, and silver. The menu and wine list are just like those in a good hotel, and the meals are served by attentive waiters. While the food is well prepared, it retains a hint of the monotony associated with any food produced "in the mass." The writer praises the way such an apartment house lessens so many of the housekeeping burdens of middle-class families. He also notes that there is an unavoidably high level of socializing with one's neighbors because of collective dining, yet the small size of individual apartment units makes large-scale entertaining impossible to accomplish privately.

Many apartment houses provided such a restaurantlike dining room, usually off the lobby, raising questions about the relation between collective and private values. Should family meals be private events? Then centrally located and staffed kitchens could cook meals for tenants to eat in private. At the 35-unit Haight House, for tenants who wanted such privacy, a house steward received marketing orders for the family's favorite foods. House cooks then centrally prepared the meals, which were served in private.

In 1890 the *New York Times* advertised a nine-room "kitchenless" apartment in The Florence at 18th Street and Fourth Avenue. One of its features was a large pantry "with refrigerators, gas heaters, sinks, etc.," which complemented the full array of centralized kitchen equipment at the Florence. In this apartment, house meals cooked in the building's kitchen by cooks employed by building management could be served in one's own dining room by a family-employed servant. This fully equipped pantry took up far less room than the standard kitchen, yet it probably also allowed servants to create smaller meals as well as to serve larger ones.

Should meals instead be collectively eaten in sociable surroundings with fellow tenants? This tradition derived from hotels and continued into the twentieth century with apartment hotels. Public dining rooms might be restricted to the tenants or might include nonresidents who would pay for meals as if in any restaurant. Individual tenants welcomed kitchenless apartments because they believed that kitchens gave off smells and attracted bugs.

The Sherwood House on Fifth Avenue at 44th Street advertised its apartments in 1875: "Suites of 3 to 8 rooms . . . with every comfort and luxury, without the cares of housekeeping; meals supplied at table d'hote or by private table. . . ." Architect Ernest Flagg's 1883 prospectus for a 52-unit cooperative apartment, the (never-built) Fifth Avenue Plaza, included on an upper floor of the building a dining room–restaurant where tenants could take their meals and enjoy a view over Central Park at the same time. Not only did a house dining room and centralized kitchen save the tenants work and money, he claimed, but also the profits from this restaurant could pay many of the general expenses of running the building. In addition, when wives and children went away for the summer months, the husbands who remained behind still could get a decent meal. Collective dining in these houses was welcomed mostly for reasons of economy and efficiency; sociability was a by-product rather than the goal.

Parallel to these developments in ordinary apartment houses were more politically charged proposals for communal services, as seen in the writings of feminist reformers such as Helen Campbell and Charlotte Perkins Gilman (Hayden 1981). In a program to free women from "domestic slavery," they wanted to introduce professionalism into housework. Gilman claimed that the modern family was no longer a self-contained production unit as it had been in the earlier nineteenth century. The modern family ate in restaurants, used the labor of commercial laundries, and would not hesitate to hire professional child-care workers (Gilman 1904). Campbell wanted to professionalize household work along the lines of efficient industrial production, introducing the concept of "domestic science," a rational and skilled pursuit (Campbell 1897). Like so many writers who dealt with apartment design in the 1870s and 1880s, these feminists believed that improved household design could lead to more freedom for women. Campbell put forward a proposal for suburban houses that, like apartment houses, would have a common kitchen and laundry, and envisioned a domestic environment of "great clustering palaces; whe[re] the private houses ray out in wings and ells of lawn-ringed separateness, all its industries subservient and reduced to order, and the whole great building expressing the thought of human living at its best" (1897, 59). Her suggestion fuses the apartment house idea of collective services with the suburban ideal of a house with its own lawn. Some kitchenless houses were patented in the 1890s, but no examples of this landscape-oriented type were built in New York (Hayden 1976; Handlin 1979).

Collective Aspects of Housework

The Haight House on Fifth Avenue at 15th Street opened as an apartment house in 1871. Each apartment had "hot and cold water day and night." A fireplace in each room was supplemented by steam heat in halls. Traditional housekeeping labor, such as lighting a fire in each room, co-existed with modern conveniences within each unit, such as hot and cold running water. The question facing designers and tenants was how much and what kind of centralized effort and equipment would make for the best living conditions while violating privacy the least. This careful balance was achievable when "different households touch only at such points . . . where cooperation is proper, convenient, and economical" (Carroll 1878, 534).

Housekeepers and other servants had many kinds of work to perform, and apartment houses helped ease these burdens in two ways. First, apartment houses had at least a janitor, if not a full staff, who took care of some cleaning and repair work of the building and the family unit. Second, apartment houses had some kinds of centralized equipment, such as central heating and other utilities, that all tenants shared. While these are not collective activities in the sense that tenants do them together, nonetheless they are possible only in a collective dwelling where the group's resources support centralized labor and equipment (Herrick 1904).

At the Central Park Apartments, collective dwelling enabled tenants to pool their resources to pay the wages of a janitor, hall boys, and an engineer (needed to run early elevators). The equipment and the supplies needed to run it, paid for out of the group's combined rents, included coal-powered central steam heat and hot water (water supplied by the building's own artesian well); gas for lighting and a back-up installation of incandescent electric light, should anyone prefer it to gas; and one service elevator and one passenger elevator for each of the eight towers of this large apartment house. These were items that did not impinge on any family's privacy or required only a small stretch of tolerance for strangers, as when people who did not know each other had to share a ride in the elevator.

An individual family might add to the ease of housekeeping by having private family work done by apartment building staff rather than within the individual household. Linked to Haight House apartments by dumbwaiters and private service stairs was a serviced laundry in the basement so the formerly private labors of clothes washing and ironing could be displaced to building-wide staff and facilities.

Child care was another feature of the housewife's work that apartment buildings could have taken on. A *Harper's Monthly* contributor writing about housing problems in New York ("Problem of Living" 1882) asserted that apartments were not intended for children. Landlords sometimes refused to allow children in their buildings or charged extra rent to families with progeny. However, other observers noted that the doorman or concierge kept an eye on children, who then could play safely in an apartment house courtyard. By 1907 a writer for *American Architect and Building News* suggested that apartment house developers would increase potential markets for their rental units by offering a central child-care service, akin to central laundry and food preparation, which had long been staples of the large apartment house ("Editorial" 1907). However, centralized child care did not find a ready market in the early twentieth century. Contemporary commitments to private child rearing, the tradition of privately hired nurses for middle-class children, and fixed ideas of women's responsibilities and mothering roles prevented this service from being implemented.

Although many tenants and critics welcomed the centralized management of household work, it also led to centralized rules, as recognized by architect P. B. Wight in an 1870 article. He observed that the maintenance of good order in an apartment house is extremely important and is not the result of merely controlling who is allowed to rent an apartment. It also depends on the efforts of a janitor or a porter who enforces proper conduct and must perform "no inconsiderable amount of police duty" (Wight 1870). Herrick (1890) noted that in her family's flat building, the hall door was locked and the public corridor lights turned off at 9:45 each evening, a practice that she found in conflict with her social life.

Along with the centralized labor of apartment house staff, multiple dwellings provided the perfect site for collectively used technological additions to household convenience. By the late 1890s electricity was finally supplied beneath the streets throughout all the developed areas of Manhattan, and electric lights became a feature of most moderate-rent apartment buildings. Advertisements for apartments of the 1890s began to include specifics about electricity and additional plumbing, both centrally installed enhancements to individual convenience.

By the first decade of the twentieth century, a balanced array of both centralized and individual technologically aided conveniences were expected in average buildings, such as those beginning to fill the avenues of New York's Upper West Side. Improved plumbing allowed apartments to have multiple toilets and shower baths within each unit. The Berkeley Arms at Riverside Drive and 95th Street advertised in 1904 that its tenants not only enjoyed the benefits of all-night elevators and electric lights, through centrally supplied electric power, but also were offered an individual telephone in each apartment. A bachelor apartment building on East 48th Street provided a centralized refrigeration plant that chilled individually installed refrigerators to enhance the single life in modest kitchenless apartments of two rooms and a bath.

This led some contemporaries to stress the advantages of collective dwelling for achieving the most modern efficiency and convenience. Apartment households of this era were the beneficiaries of advanced housekeeping conveniences available only to tenants in large buildings. Single families dwelling in private houses did not have access to this array of conveniences unless they were very wealthy. Moderate-income apartment dwellers could make use of central refrigeration

and vacuum-cleaning systems, electric lights, speaking tubes, laundry washing and drying equipment, and telephones. The "cooperative" character of apartment living "follows a distinct tendency of this age of concentrated effort," wrote architect Charles Israels in 1901. For him "cooperative" life did not imply unwelcome intimacy but simply the level of cooperation necessary to make a large building run smoothly for each tenant. He welcomed the aggregate nature of the large apartment houses on the grounds that "it eliminates the individual for the common good."

COLLECTIVE DWELLINGS FOR SPECIFIC TENANT GROUPS

The people who shared an apartment house could be seen not merely as an accidental gathering of tenants but as a group that shared a common social status or lifestyle. This was a choice made by developers, who established the income level of prospective tenants when they determined rents, building location, and elaboration of design. It also was a choice made by tenants, who selected buildings to live in on the basis of congenial neighborhoods and culturally familiar fellow tenants. As the design of physical settings for "home" expanded beyond the single-family house, attention was directed beyond the nuclear family to the variety of persons who constituted "households" needing a home. Apartment buildings were specifically designed to take into account the needs of working women, bachelor men, single parents, childless couples, or employees whose work kept them traveling, as well as of the complete nuclear family.

Single Women and the Working Women's Home

The kinds of middle-class people in need of housing extended beyond the middle-class nuclear family, leading designers to produce alternatives to the full family apartment. The Working Women's Home of the 1850s was created out of rehabilitated tenement buildings at 45 Elizabeth

Figure 2-10. Working Women's Home by John Kellum, begun 1869, New York: view and floor plan. (*Source: Mr. Stewart's Hotel*, Appleton's Journal 1, 1869, *pp. 417–419*)

Street (Browne 1869, 548). There some 500 women were provided with a bed in a dormitory setting, with curtains rather than walls for privacy. On the main floor were parlors, a reading room, a laundry, and a common dining room that served meals paid for by the week along with the rent. In the basement were a common kitchen and the bathrooms. The age range of the tenants was 18 to 35, and they made around $6 to $7 a week. For $1.25 women could get a bed and have their laundry done; for another $1.75 to $3.25 they could get meals. For an extra 25 cents, tenants could be let in after 11 P.M.

Sales clerks were the intended residents at department-store owner A. T. Stewart's "hotel for women of modest means," begun in 1869 (Fig. 2-10). The planned "hotel" included 16-by-18-foot bedrooms for two women to share and 8-by-9-foot rooms for single women ("Mr. Stewart's

Hotel" 1869). Shared facilities such as parlors and reading rooms made this house similar to a hotel, as did a central dining room and kitchen. Since it was just for women, however, it escaped the moral criticism leveled at hotels occupied by both sexes. Stewart had planned a duplicate building for young men that was never built.

A grand entrance portico with columns, a marble floor, and elevators added elegance and convenience to Stewart's hotel; interiors were to be enhanced with good-quality furniture and even fine paintings. However, construction lagged, and the hotel did not actually open until 1877. By then the set rents were too high for working women and the intended tenants also were beleaguered by too many rules and regulations (Williamson 1930). The experimental was then converted to the conventional: the women's home became the Park Avenue Hotel. A greater

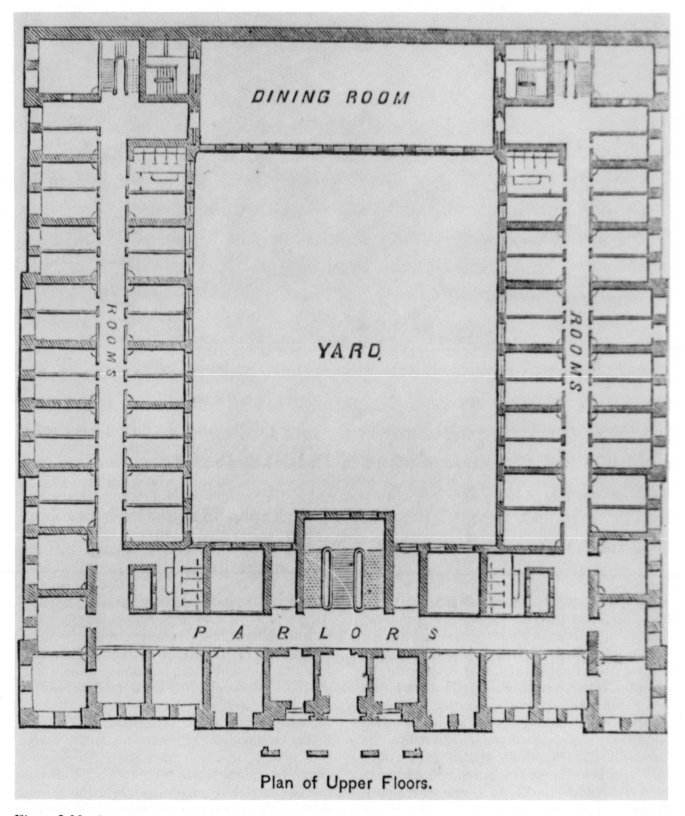

Figure 2-10. *(cont.)*

Figure 2-11. Bachelors lounging in their hotel home. (*Source:* Harper's Weekly, *Dec. 1857, p. 825*)

impediment to producing a good apartment building for single women was the fact that, in the 1870s and 1880s, younger respectable women did not have society's blessing to make independent homes of their own.

Single Men and the Bachelor Flat

Bachelors, some 125,000 strong in the New York of 1871, constituted a group acknowledged to be less committed to privacy than the traditional family. Single men in New York seemed to have serious difficulty in finding suitable housing, according to several articles that dealt with the question. Hotels were available to bachelors (Fig. 2-11), but critics complained that only the wealthy could afford them, while boarding houses were an unacceptable alternative for those who valued privacy (Littell 1876; Potter 1879). Bachelors' needs suggested relocating services and entertainment spaces outside the family unit and redefining somewhat the spaces and functions that a residence should contain.

Solving the bachelor's housing problem required a suite of rooms scaled to the needs of a single person, perhaps consisting of only a parlor, a bedroom, a bath, and closets. Architect E. T. Littell proposed in 1876 that developers create a bachelor dwelling unit with a parlor, 14 by 16 feet; a bedroom, 8 by 10 feet; and a bathroom, 5½ by 8 feet (with perhaps a bigger parlor for those who wish to "chum together"). His proposal was much like later-executed bachelor apartments, such as The Century of 1900 (Fig. 2-12). Some suites could be connected so two friends could share quarters if desired. Bachelors usually took their meals in clubs and restaurants or with friends. Some suggested that a bachelor flat building be run like a club, with membership fees and dues and a common dining room where the bachelor could find good food as well as privacy.

Bachelor flats, then, suggested a modification to the assumed set of rooms for family needs; with that modification came some redefinitions of the boundary between collective and private spaces. Bachelors' apartments kept the private definition of a parlor, a bedroom, and a bathroom as other middle-class apartments of the 1870s had done. Entertainment and dining activities were shifted to public spaces (clubs, restau-

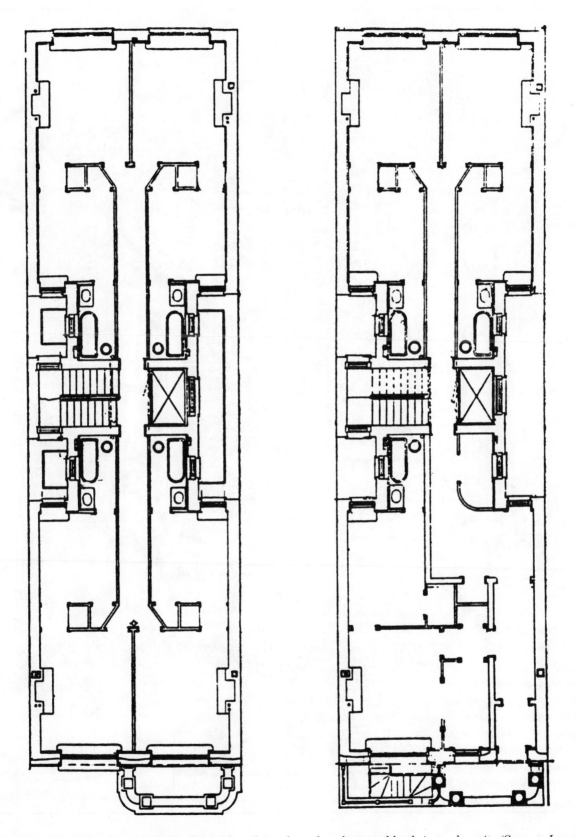

Figure 2-12. The Century: a bachelor flat with only parlor, chamber, and bath in each unit. *(Source: Israels, New York Apartment Houses, Architectural Record 11, 1901, p. 507)*

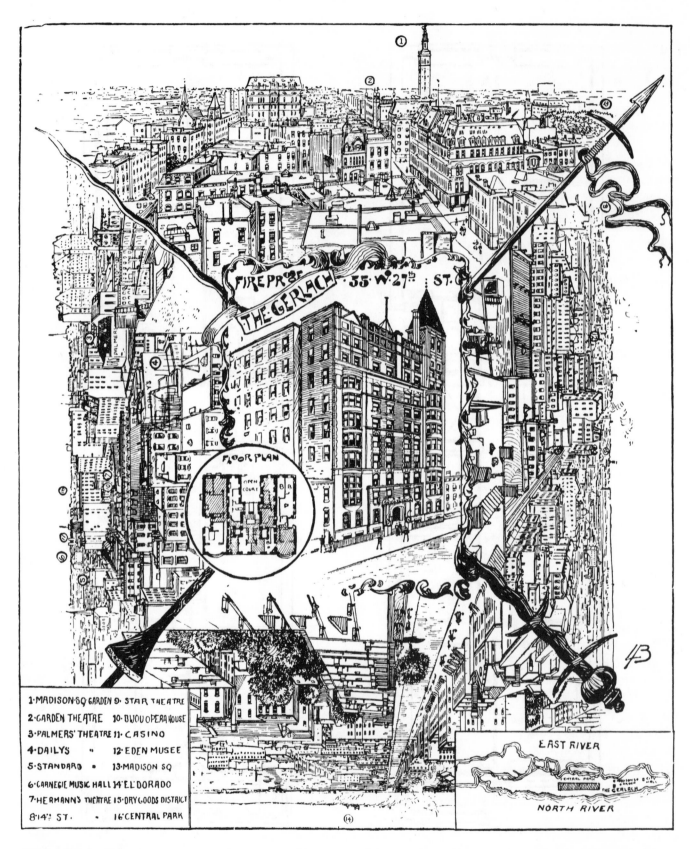

Figure 2-13. The Gerlach, circa 1890, on West 27th Street, New York: an apartment hotel. (*Source:* King's Views of New York, *1895, p. 598*)

rants, and roof terraces) and, since cooking was not considered a likely skill for bachelors to possess, kitchens were omitted.

Bohemians

At the turn of the century, after four decades of experience with apartment life, some urbane New Yorkers welcomed further variations on the apartment building. One of these was called an apartment hotel, the combination of apartment-unit privacy and hotel services that had been explored in the 1870s (Fig. 2-13). Disapproving critics felt that such apartment hotels were "unhomelike" and that people who enjoyed being near the bright lights of Broadway might be irresponsible, perhaps immoral ("Over the Draughting Board" 1903, 89). However, for people whose employment kept them traveling, for young couples without the resources to buy furniture or pay servants, and for the adventuresome, apartment hotels could be a reasonable solution to housing needs.

The Ansonia (Fig. 2-14) was an apartment hotel on Broadway at 74th Street that opened in 1904 (Bolton 1903). This building offered services such as food preparation or house cleaning through its own staff but also provided apartments equipped to support the same work internally in the private household. The Ansonia's developer and architects assumed that tenants were not all alike in their needs and gave them a range of apartment sizes, from bachelor unit to full family apartment.

The Ansonia's designers interpreted certain conveniences as appropriately collective, building-wide services. These included a fully staffed laundry with steam clothes dryers in the basement, a Turkish bath, a staff of cooks, and a conservatory dining room on the 17th floor (whose cooks would also prepare private meals for service in individual homes). Lobby shops on the ground floor made it convenient to purchase middle-class comforts such as flowers and cigars. The management even provided an automobile garage that could both service and store tenants' cars, although it believed that automobiling was just a passing fad.

Figure 2-14. The Ansonia by Stokes and Duboy, 1902, on Broadway New York: an apartment hotel. (*Source:* American Architect and Building News 91, Jan. 1907, p. 7)

Technologically advanced Ansonia housekeeping apartments included a gas or an electric kitchen range, porcelain washtubs, and pantries within the private unit (Fig. 2-15). Built-in refrigerating compartments "with appliances for freezing artificial ice upon the spot" added an innovative touch. Nonhousekeeping units for those who had no interest in food preparation or private dining had only a parlor, a bedroom, and a bathroom. These apartments assumed the least amount of housekeeping effort on the part of tenants, whose cleaning would be done by hotel staff while they dined in restaurants or in the Ansonia's dining room. Like adjoining bedrooms in hotels, some suites at the Ansonia had doors both into the public corridor and into adjacent rooms. Enhanced flexibility was available by renting a suite comprised of a parlor, a bath, and two bedrooms, then renting an additional adjoining bedroom/bath unit to create a larger apartment. Should a household member depart, the enlarged apartment could be scaled down again at the lease's end.

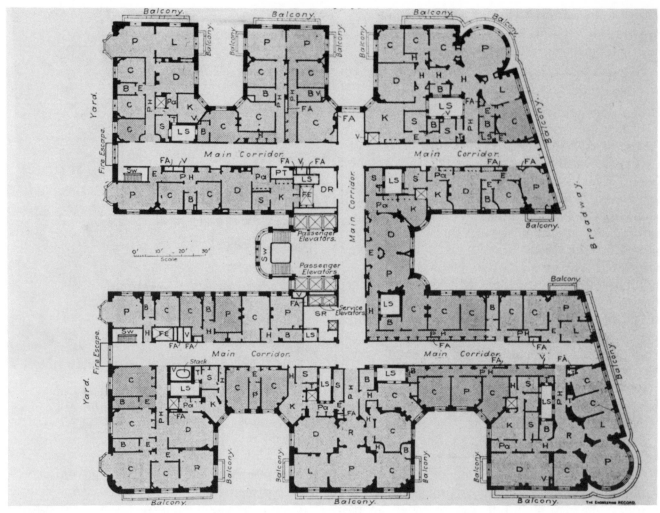

P: Parlor   S: Servants' room   LS: Light shaft   FE: Freight elevator
C: Chamber   L: Library   FA and V: Fresh air and ventilation flues in halls   Pa: Pantry
D: Dining room   R: Reception room   E: Entry   H: Hall
K: Kitchen   PH: Private hall   B: Bath

Figure 2-15. The Ansonia: floor plan *(Source: American Architect and Building News 91, Jan. 1907, p. 7)*

Redefining the Residential Group

If residents were not self-selected by common beliefs, as they would have been in a utopian community, what would enable them to live harmoniously together? "An apartment house must be built to accommodate a class of tenants who are in a nearly uniform social scale," asserted architect P. B. Wight (1870, 312). Nineteenth-century writers theorized that, to be successful, an apartment house must have more or less the same level of accommodations throughout so that the tenants would feel comfortable with each other. The quality of homogeneity had been recognized by contemporary writers as a po-

tentially positive feature of apartments in the earliest years of apartment development. For example, the Haight House, a fashionable apartment conversion at 15th Street and Fifth Avenue, was described as an example of a New York trend toward "the clustering of particular social sets about particular centers" (Richardson 1874). The writer felt that apartment houses had the capacity to encourage such groupings of like-minded people. In the case of Haight House, these were "artistic and literary people who are able to find home, society, recreation —almost everything which goes to distinguish civilized life —without passing from under their own roof."

In the pamphlet "The Central Park Apartments," the authors assert that Americans insist on preserving the boundaries of social classes and that this often is done by applying high rents to ensure the exclusivity of a building (1882, 18–19). They intend their apartment house for people "socially suited to each other and intending to make the house not a temporary stopping place but a permanent home."

A sense of social comfort in apartment houses became ever more widespread as elevator apartment buildings replaced earlier walk-ups in new construction at the turn of the century. Higher floors in walk-ups commanded lower rents, but elevators equalized rents for all floors. This allowed tenants to count on an apartment house occupied by people of a similar class (or at least of similar income). Thus the apartment house became its own neighborhood and helped alleviate the worries of middle-class families in the face of the city's disturbing growth. Although some homogeneity of income was likely among a building's tenants, other social barriers could be, and were, erected. In a 1911 article in the *Architectural Record*, the author cautions against allowing a "peroxide Juno" or a "hook-nosed tenant" into an apartment building, destroying privacy and impairing the value of one's investment ("The Duplex" 1911, 327).

As the idealization of a secluded private house as home gave way to the realities of urban life, so, too, did some fantasies about women as securers of home values. Apartment houses brought women together in the daily flux of housekeeping, food shopping, child care, and visiting. The collective home may have acted to facilitate women's enjoyment of the city because apartment houses tended to be located on streets convenient to public transportation. Street cars, elevated trains in the 1870s, and subways by the early twentieth century accompanied apartment houses as essential features of New York's real-estate development. Thus women tenants without private carriages could easily travel to shop in Ladies Mile or to attend operas or lectures. Men complained that the women of 1900's New York wanted to be anywhere but waiting patiently by the fireside (Boyer 1985; "Over the Draughting Board" 1903). Insofar as apartment houses allowed women to meet each other and to have

access to the city, they helped break down the notion of a private home as women's only proper sphere.

In 1901 apartments were extolled as enabling New Yorkers to obtain through "cooperation . . . the ultimate amount of comfort and convenience with the minimum effort" (Israels, 1901, 508). Yet in 1902 ("Editorial") *American Architect and Building News* expressed doubts about that cooperation. The editorial noted that the early apartment buildings of New York had been built "on the supposition that they would be occupied by congenial people, who would like to meet in the common reception room or restaurant." However, this writer continued, tenants moved so often that intimacy among them turned out to be impossible and so apartment house developers had shifted toward providing no common rooms at all. The first article stresses the success of "cooperation" achieved in apartment houses while the second reports on the decrease in common social spaces, which would seem to have provided the site for cooperation among tenants.

This apparent contradiction points up the way that apartment dwellers made collectivity work for them at the turn of the century. When trying out new shared housing forms, they selected the nonsociable points of sharing as least problematic. Lobbies, elevators, corridors, common laundry facilities, or landscaped courtyards made few demands on tenants' sense of family independence. The more personal and difficult occasions for collectivity, such as dining together or engaging in the greater intimacy that common parlors and reception rooms implied, challenged their concern for maintaining privacy. These they avoided. The cooperative nature of apartment houses that Charles Israels had praised was grounded in utilitarian and economic sharing, not in the sociable sharing that knits a group of people together into a community.

LESSONS FOR TODAY

The high costs of land development and the high prices of houses guarantee that American housing will have to become more and more "cooperative," sharing land, infrastructure, party walls, and even more. People who already are dedicated to collective living for political reasons are willing to give up some degree of separation and privacy, but for most Americans privacy has great symbolic power. It seems important to examine precedents in history to see where privacy can be successfully diluted and where it should be upheld if we wish to add more collective qualities and more diversity to the housing choices of the 1990s.

Comparisons with nineteenth-century experiences of home may help us clarify the meanings and the performance of private homes that residents have required. For nineteenth-century commentators *home* as a private house had a strong symbolic function. It spoke of family, of women's nurturant role, of men's money earning capabilities; it portrayed a family's individuality to society. In contrast with the idealized home, homes in nineteenth-century apartment houses caused people to confront some of those ideals and perhaps to discard or at least to modify them. Apartment houses demonstrated that groups of households could, while living together, preserve what they felt was important about individual family values. In order to arrive at that point, many alternatives to a secluded family unit were tested and some were rejected. As we review these early experiments, we may find them suggestive for rethinking the boundaries of privacy that have become habitual today.

What is the best combination of labor and equipment needed to do a household's work? Since the 1920s most household machinery has been sold in individually scaled pieces to be operated by unpaid housekeepers: the washing machine, the dryer, the freezer, the refrigerator, the vacuum cleaner, the range, and now the microwave oven are taken for granted as single-family possessions (Cowan 1983). For the nineteenth-century apartment house, this equipment was collectively supported and of a size suitable for building-wide use. Furthermore many items entered the apartment house accompanied by someone hired to operate them. Washing machines came with laundresses who would not only wash and iron but also mend, inspect, and otherwise keep wardrobes at their peak. Likewise, cooking was done on large-scale ranges, and meals were prepared for all the tenants by cooks hired through collective resources. These shifts

in the location, size, and operation of housekeeping equipment reveal the privatizing choices that have been made over the last few decades. Thinking about these choices can allow us a new perspective on what should happen inside a household unit and what can happen elsewhere in support of it.

What is the best architectural expression for the public facade of collective life? Nineteenth-century apartment buildings show architects struggling over whether to stress images recalling private houses and individuality or to create group imagery. Hybrids of architectural form recalling hotels and other public building precedents implied collective uses but perhaps shortchanged tenants' needs for domestic scale and meaning in residential architecture. A current example of housing for single parents by architect Lars Lerup (Beers 1987) hovers between these two poles, choosing images from each. Single-family housing has a long history as a site for personal expression within community norms (Cromley 1982). Housing for multiple households will have to continue the search for appropriate imagery to convey the same balance between the individual and the group.

Attention to specialized tenant groups meant that designers worked out a type of building for underpaid shop-girls' budgets, for bachelors' lifestyles, or for the preferences of couples on the road. Single parents who wanted to devote their time to child care rather than to housework had numerous apartment hotels to choose from. The diversity of multiple dwelling types tried during the nineteenth century suggests the potential in American housing for much more support for the needs of different life stages. Post-war America's tendency to isolate and privilege the nuclear family has had the effect of effacing these many alternative models of household and homelife.

If we are to learn from the explorations of our predecessors, then in addition to reviewing the pragmatic potential of collective buildings, we also must focus on their ideological grounding. The boundaries of class and race were assumed to be appropriate divisions in the social body that nineteenth-century collective facilities always respected. For families and single people at the turn of the century, gender differences and gender-assigned roles were important cornerstones of culture that they had to protect. Thus it was not easy to introduce child care into the collective services of an apartment house because it interfered with women's assigned roles in the family. Maturity and stability were defined by family independence and individuality; to be mature meant to establish an independent household. Sharing, in contrast, was regarded as a sign of instability. Thus, single people or Bohemians could live collectively, but married couples with families risked being labeled as immature or "flighty" if they wanted to try collective life. It is clear that our Victorian predecessors organized their housing around such ideological commitments.

Unfortunately many of these same ideas are current in the United States today. Proposed changes in house form imply changes in these long-standing ideas about family form and gender relations and threaten assumptions about the inherited social order. To raise these ideological assumptions to the conscious level can help us identify where the impediments lie in creating new dwelling forms for the future. Until we can examine publicly the nature of these assumptions, however, the lessons we could learn from the history of collective housing will remain inaccessible.

NOTES

1. The history of apartment buildings in New York has been dealt with in a few recent books. Andrew Alpern's *Apartments for the Affluent* (New York: McGraw-Hill, 1975), has recently been reissued by Dover under the title *New York's Fabulous Luxury Apartments* (1987). It has mainly period photographs and plans, with a short introductory text. *Living it Up, a guide to named apartment houses of New York* is by Thomas Norton and Jerry Patterson (New York: Atheneum, 1984). This lists hundreds of apartment buildings that have names (such as the Dakota); it has a useful introductory essay on their development. M. Christine Boyer's *Manhattan Manners* (New York: Rizzoli, 1985) recounts a history of real-estate development in New York with a chapter on the apartment building. See also Elizabeth Cromley's *Alone Together: A History of New York's Early Apartments* (Cornell University Press, 1989), which considers the cul-

tural ramifications of these buildings for middle-class tenants.

2. The word *family* is problematic here. When nineteenth-century sources worry about family values or family privacy, they usually mean the nuclear family comprised of a married couple with children plus their servants. When we speak of a single-family home, we mean a house that contains a single household. But when the census defines *household*, it means the person or persons living under one roof who are not necessarily related. An idea such as "family privacy" may certainly have been an ideal for single-person households or for households comprised of several unrelated people, as well as for nuclear families.

3. In nineteenth-century sources the word *cooperative* is more common than *collective* and usually implies shared responsibilities and shared expenses, but it does not imply a high level of social interaction. Blanke (1893, 355) uses "cooperation" to describe the sharing of building-wide costs; Appleton's editor ("Editor's Table," 1876, 182–183) calls apartment buildings that have central heating and plumbing systems and centrally hired building staff "cooperative structures."

References

Apartment houses. 1890. *American Architecture and Building News*, Part 1, v. 29 (Sept.):194–195; Part 2, v. 30 (Nov.):97–100; Part 3, v. 31 (Jan.):20–23.

Apartment house on East 21st Street by Bruce Price. 1878. *American Architect and Building News* 3 (May):plate follows 156.

Associated Architects. 1902. *Artistic Modern Homes*. New York: [Associated Architects].

Beers, D. 1987. Redesigning the suburbs. *Image*, Sunday magazine of the *San Francisco Examiner* (July 12):12–21.

Birch, E. 1986. *Unsheltered Woman: Women and Housing in the '80s*. New Brunswick, NJ: Rutgers University Press.

Birmingham, S. 1979. *Life at the Dakota*. New York: Random House.

Blanke, E. N. 1893. The cliff dwellers of New York. *Cosmopolitan* 15 (July):354–362.

Bolton, R. 1903. The apartment hotel in New York City. *Cassiers Magazine* 24 (Nov.): 27–32.

Boyer, M. C. 1985. *Manhattan Manners*. New York: Rizzoli.

Browne, J. H. 1869. *The Great Metropolis: A Mirror of New York*. Hartford, CT: American Publishing Co.

Bunce, O. B. 1872. The city of the future. *Appleton's Journal* 7:156–158.

Busbey, K. 1910. *Home Life in America*. London: Methuen.

Campbell, H. 1897. *Household Economics*. New York: Putnam's.

Carroll, C. 1878. Apartment houses. *Appleton's Journal* n.s. 5:529–535.

The Central Park Apartments. 1882. New York: American Banknote Company.

Cowan. R. 1983. *More Work for Mother*. New York: Basic Books.

Cromley, E. 1982. Modernizing, or "You never see a screen door on affluent homes'. *Journal of American Culture* 5 (Summer):71–79.

Dreiser, T. 1981. *Sister Carrie*. New York and London: Penguin.

The duplex apartment house. 1911. *Architectural Record* 29 (Jan.–June):326–334, 327.

Editorial. 1902. *American Architecture and Building News* 75 (Jan. 11):9.

———. 1907. *American Architecture and Building News* 91 (Jan. 5):1–2.

Editor's Table. 1876. *Appleton's Journal* 15 (Feb.): 182–183.

———. 1881. *Appleton's Journal* n.s.11 (Dec.):568–569.

Flagg, E., et al. 1883. *Prospectus for the Fifth Avenue Plaza Apartments*. New York.

Furniss, L. E. 1871. New York boarding houses. *Appleton's Journal* 5 (Mar. 4):259–261.

Gilman, C. P. 1904. The passing of the home in great American cities. *Cosmopolitan* 38 (Dec.):137–147.

Handlin, D. 1979. *American Home*. Boston and Toronto: Little, Brown and Co.

Hayden, D. 1975. Two utopian feminists and their campaigns for kitchenless houses. *Signs* 4 (Winter):275–290.

———. 1976. *Seven American Utopias*. Cambridge, MA: MIT Press.

———. 1981. *Grand Domestic Revolution*. Cambridge, MA: MIT Press.

———. 1984. *Redesigning the American Dream*. New York: W. W. Norton.

Herrick, C. 1890. Their experience in a flat. *Harpers Weekly* 34 (Jan. 11):30–31.

———. 1904. Cooperative housekeeping. *Munsey's Magazine* 31 (May):185–188.

Hubert, P. et al. 1892. New York flats and French flats. *Architectural Record* 2 (July):55–64.

Israels, C. 1901. New York apartment houses. *Architectural Record* 11 (July):477–508.

Kilham, W. 1904. Planning of apartment houses—Part IV. *Brickbuilder* 13:2–8.

Lerup, L. 1987. *Planned Assaults*. Montreal: Canadian Centre for Architecture; Cambridge, MA: Distributed by MIT Press.

Littell, E. T. 1876. Club chambers. *American Architect and Building News* 1 (Jan.):59–60.

McCabe, J. 1872. *Lights and Shadows of New York Life*. Philadelphia: National Publishing Co.

Mr. Stewart's hotel for working people. 1869. *Appleton's Journal* 1 (July 3):417–419.

New York daguerreotyped—Private residences. 1854. *Putnam's Monthly* 3 (Mar.):233–248.

New York Times. 1873. (Aug. 13):2–6.

———. 1876. (Sept. 3):5–4.

Over the draughting board. 1903. *Architectural Record* 13 (Jan.):89–91.

Potter, E. T.. 1879. Urban housing—V. *American Architect and Building News* (Sept. 27):99.

The problem of living in New York. 1882. *Harpers Monthly* 65 (Nov.):918–924.

Putnam, J. P. 1890. Architecture under nationalism—I. *American Architect and Building News* 29 (July):21–25.

Richardson, J. 1874. New homes of New York. *The Century* 8:63–76.

Schuyler, M. Henry Janeway Hardenbergh. *Architectural Record* 6:335–375.

Vaux, C. 1857. Parisian buildings. *Harpers Weekly* 1 (Dec. 19):809–810.

Ware, J. 1866. *Home Life: What it Is and What it Needs*. Boston: Wm. V. Spencer.

Wight, P. B. 1870. Apartment houses practically considered. *Putnam's Magazine* (Sept.):306–313.

Woman's Own Book. 1873. Jewett City, CT: Reade Publishing Co.

Williamson, [E.] J. 1930. *The American Hotel*. New York and London: Knopf.

Young, S. G. 1872. Foreign modes of living. *The Galaxy* 14:474–482.

Chapter 3

Early European Collective Habitation

From Utopian Ideal to Reality

Norbert Schoenauer

In one of the Grimm brothers' fairy tales, an apprentice to a joiner received from his master a magic table as a reward for his cheerfulness and industry. When instructed "Table, cover thyself," this magic table would at once be set with a fine tablecloth, plates, cutlery, and sumptuous dishes accompanied by wine (Grimm and Grimm, 116). The magic table of this fairy tale represents an inspiration that parallels the utopian ideals of nineteenth-century social and housing reformers; they attempted to provide meal service to inhabitants of multiunit housing, thus making obsolete the need for food preparation in every household.

In the age of industrialization, when small-scale handicrafts were gradually replaced by large-scale industries, it was not surprising that domestic activities also came under close scrutiny. The application of two particular forces—centralization and mechanization—that fostered industrial development was thought to offer the greatest promise of utopian domestic life, first by easing and thereafter by reducing the burden of housekeeping. Since these two forces were complementary, one would have expected equal emphasis to be placed on both their applications in order to improve housekeeping. However, in the evolution of housekeeping reform this was not the case, and the unequal emphasis manifests itself in two different developments. The Euro-

pean emphasis on centralization led to the establishment of collective habitations where resources for household services were pooled in order to free tenants from doing repetitive domestic work, whereas an American reliance primarily on mechanization encouraged the development of servantless households where mechanical appliances did away with most of the manual chores of housekeeping. The mechanization of household work processes, which eventually led to the American servantless home, has been well described by Siegfried Giedion (1969) and Dolores Hayden (1981).

THE GENESIS OF EUROPEAN COLLECTIVE HABITATION

The roots of collective habitation are found in early nineteenth-century France, where a major social upheaval gave rise to efforts to bring about social harmony. An important proposal for social reform was developed by Charles François Marie Fourier during the first decade of the nineteenth century. Believing that individualism and competition led to imperfect and immoral social organizations, he proposed the formation of a cooperative society based on social units called *phalanges*, consisting ideally of 1,620 members (the minimum being about 300 and the maximum about 2,000 persons) inhabiting a common building with a new domestic arrangement—centralized kitchen service. Fourier advocated the abolishment of individual food preparation mainly to emancipate women and to avoid the wasteful practice of simultaneous cooking inherent in private housekeeping. Conceived as a large palatial building complex, the so-called phalanstery was to consist of individual apartments complemented by a series of common rooms for conversation, reading, and dining. The common "dining rooms on the second floor were to be served by raising the tables (decked with food) through trap doors from the kitchen below" (Hayden 1976, 151). This was not a completely new idea. Louis XV's hunting lodge at Choisy, where the king went for privacy with Madame de Pompadour and friends, was equipped with a similar mechanism that enabled a set table with the food already on it to be elevated into the dining room from the kitchen below so that there need be no servants present (Mitford 1968, 45).

Two attempts to establish an experimental *phalanstère* during Fourier's lifetime were initiated in 1832, but, being insufficiently funded, both Fourierist communities failed shortly after their establishment (Fourier 1971, 145). Patiently, Fourier waited many years for a philanthropist who would be willing to underwrite the initial cost of a new *phalanstère*, but no one ever came. He died disillusioned and in poverty in 1837.

Five years after Fourier's death, Jean-Baptiste André Godin, an industrialist, adapted some of Fourier's ideas for his workers' housing and established in 1859 a collective habitation called *familistère* in Guise, France. Instead of installing individual kitchens in every dwelling, he built a central kitchen with a common dining room for the occupants of the *familistère*.

Godin's *familistère* was visited in 1885 by Johan August Strindberg, a Swedish author and journalist, who wrote enthusiastically about the social relationships of its inhabitants. Strindberg was particularly impressed by the relationships between men and women in this collective habitation. Because husbands and wives had their own separate rooms and all housekeeping functions were collectivized, including child care, he observed that the wife ceased to be the "beast of burden" of her husband. Moreover, if the couple proved to be incompatible, divorce without bitterness was greatly facilitated. And, since the community took care of the children, their lot remained unchanged despite their parents' divorce (Vestbro 1979, 4).

Strindberg's enthusiasm for collective habitation was not widely shared by his compatriots, and collective habitation remained but a utopian ideal in Sweden until 1907.

Toward the end of the nineteenth century, however, the concept of centralized household services gained ever wider acceptance, at least in theory, and many social reformers extolled its virtues of efficiency, especially for women in the labor force. The social philosopher Prince Petre Alekseevich Kropotkin, for example, advocated the adoption of centralized kitchen service for apartment dwellers. He, too, bemoaned the inefficiency of innumerable housewives concurrently cooking meals for their families and estimated that every day in England and the United States alone "eight million women spend their time to prepare this meal, that perhaps consists at the most of ten different dishes" (1906, 145).

Similar sentiments also were expressed by H. G. Wells, who asserted that an "ordinary Utopian would no more think of a special private kitchen for his dinners than he would think of a private flour mill or dairy farm" (Purdom 1913, 98). Wells visualized the prosperous utopian living in "residential clubs" that offered to their occupants not only furnished bedrooms but also elaborate suites of apartments that could be furnished to suit individual tastes. Among such luxuries as pleasant boudoirs, private libraries, studies, and private garden plots, Wells allocated merely "little cooking corners" for these suites because a central kitchen was to cater to the utopian.

TWO ENGLISH PROTOTYPES: CATERING FLATS AND COOPERATIVE QUADRANGLES

By the end of the nineteenth century, a new residential building type came into existence in London: the serviced apartment building, which was designed mainly for affluent people. Called *catering flats* these buildings were developed to fulfill the demands of a certain segment of society, namely well-to-do singles and elderly couples who sought the "homelike" quality of a luxurious apartment building combined with the services offered by a hotel (Perks 1905, 54).

The development of this new building type was attributed to the increasing difficulty of obtaining good servants, but another reason was the demand for an agreeable form of dwelling for non-traditional households of affluent people who were willing to pay for the conveniences they obtained.

Catering flats (the British counterparts of American apartment hotels) consisted of a number of self-contained suites of various sizes, usually with a pantry but without kitchens and servants' rooms. Household services and meals in the common dining room were paid for at a fixed charge, whereas the use of all other common rooms, such as the drawing rooms and billiard rooms, was included in the rent.

One of the largest blocks of catering flats in England was Queen Anne's Mansions in West-

minster, designed by E. R. Robson. In addition to their private luxury suites, the occupants of this building also had access to a number of well-appointed common rooms, including several dining and drawing rooms.

Marlborough Chambers on Jermyn Street in West London was another example. This corner building, designed by Reginald Morphew, contained at sidewalk level a number of shops in addition to two entrance lobbies. Above the shops were four floors of apartments that were considered to be "some of the best and most expensive suites in London" (Perks 1905, 155). And on the top floor, in the garret, were a central kitchen and various living accommodations for the staff. Provision was made in this building to serve all meals for the tenants in their respective suites.

Another block of catering flats was designed by E. J. A. Balfour and Thackeray Turner. Named Campden House Chambers, this building consisted of suites ranging from two to four rooms (Figs. 3-1, 3-2, and 3-3). In contrast to the previous example, here the common dining room

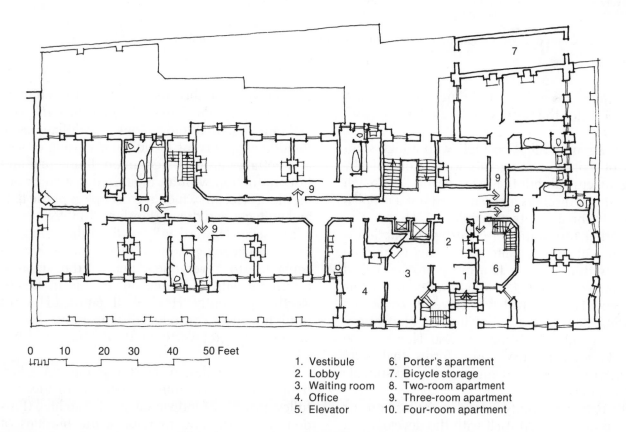

| 0 | 10 | 20 | 30 | 40 | 50 Feet |

1. Vestibule
2. Lobby
3. Waiting room
4. Office
5. Elevator
6. Porter's apartment
7. Bicycle storage
8. Two-room apartment
9. Three-room apartment
10. Four-room apartment

Figure 3-1. Campden House Chambers, London: ground-floor plan of catering flats. *(Balfour and Turner, Architects)*

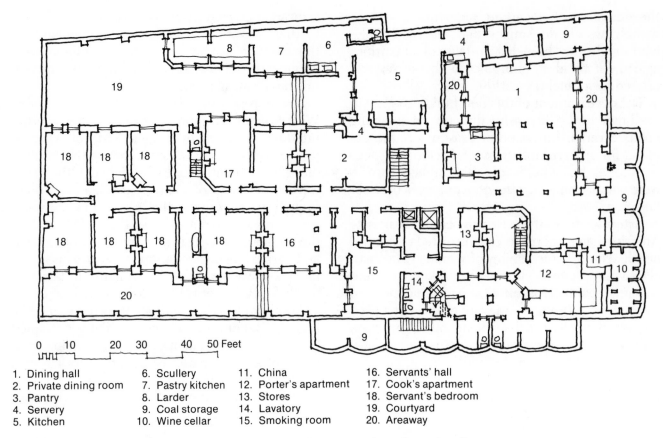

1. Dining hall	6. Scullery	11. China	16. Servants' hall
2. Private dining room	7. Pastry kitchen	12. Porter's apartment	17. Cook's apartment
3. Pantry	8. Larder	13. Stores	18. Servant's bedroom
4. Servery	9. Coal storage	14. Lavatory	19. Courtyard
5. Kitchen	10. Wine cellar	15. Smoking room	20. Areaway

Figure 3-2. Campden House Chambers, London: basement plan of catering flats.

and kitchen, as well as all the necessary accommodations for the staff, were located in the basement.

Serving an affluent clientele with a high standard of living, catering flats were economically quite successful, but they were beyond the reach of most city dwellers and remained but a utopian dream to the majority of people.

Another forerunner of collective habitation—but this time in a satellite town rather than in an urban setting—was a housing prototype called *cooperative quadrangles*, which was conceived by Ebenezer Howard. Just as he fervently advocated building new garden cities instead of continuously expanding existing ones, so Howard also tried to develop new house forms that were "modern in design and equipment" and suitable for the times.

The first opportunity to implement his housing reform ideas offered itself with the development of Homesgarth (1909–1913) in Letchworth. Later renamed Sollershott Hall this garden apartment

project was described four years after its completion in C. B. Purdom's *The Garden City* as a "scheme designed to overcome the difficulties of the domestic servant by building a group of flats and cottages around a common dining hall and in conjunction with an organized system of domestic service on which the occupiers of the flats and cottages can draw" (Purdom 1913, 99).

Ebenezer Howard fully realized that cooperative housekeeping did not offer a way of life acceptable to everyone, hence the modest beginning with only one quadrangle in Letchworth. Apparently "H. G. Wells taunted Howard until he finally introduced cooperative housekeeping at Letchworth in 1909" (Hayden 1981, 231).

Homesgarth, designed by the architect A. Clapham Lander, was arranged both to provide "the fullest privacy of individual and home life" (Purdom 1913, 99) and to remove the burdens of housekeeping through the application of the principles of cooperation and a new kind of domestic organization. This domestic organization was based on a new relationship between "master" and "servant" that ensured greater freedom to both. The "master" could now obtain a variety of domestic services without the responsibility, anxiety, and expense that usually were implied in the engagement of private servants. But an even more important aspect of this new relationship was the relative freedom that service personnel could enjoy. This freedom emanated from two basic facts, namely, that the nature of service tasks was now clearly defined and that service personnel were no longer directly responsible to the person serviced but to a third and more neutral party, the management of the organization offering the service. Moreover, since the charges were paid to the management and not directly to the service personnel, the outdated and degrading social status of "servant" no longer applied to service employees of collective habitations.

Figure 3-3. Campden House Chambers, London: perspective.

Thirty-two dwelling units with their complementary collective facilities were built around a central court to form three sides of a quadrangle and part of a fourth side (Fig. 3-4). The common facilities located in the central wing comprised a dining hall, a tea room, a reading room, a smoking room, and ancilliary facilities including a kitchen, a laundry, and accommodations for the domestic staff. Meals were served in the common dining hall or, on request, in the tenants' flats or townhouses. Dwellings were centrally heated and connected by a house phone to the central administrative office. On demand, domestic help for housekeeping services, including the cleaning of boots, was available at fixed rates of payment to all tenants.

This cooperative housekeeping project at Letchworth offered a variety of living accommodations, ranging from one- to three-bedroom units. In addition to bedrooms each unit had a sitting room, a bathroom, and a "pantry" equipped with a small gas stove.

Dwelling units were built either as flats or as houses (Fig. 3-5). The former were entered from common stair halls and the latter, like townhouses, through private vestibules. The one-bedroom unit was available only as a flat and the three-bedroom unit only as a house; the two-bedroom unit could be rented either as a flat or as a house, according to preference. The rent for a house was slightly higher, but housekeeping service charges were the same for all the dwelling units. Efficiency apartments consisting of only a bed-sitting room also were planned for this development, but none of these smaller flats was ever built. Each ground-level dwelling, whether a flat or a townhouse, had its own private garden space.

Two years after the completion of Homesgarth, another cooperative quadrangle called Meadow Way Green (1915–1924) was built in Letchworth. For a short while Howard himself lived in Homesgarth, and when Welwyn Garden City was established he saw that it, too, was to receive a cooperative quadrangle, called Guessens Court.

Howard was convinced that only a small segment of this new town's population, primarily childless couples, the elderly, and singles, was ready to accept a collective life style. Thus it was

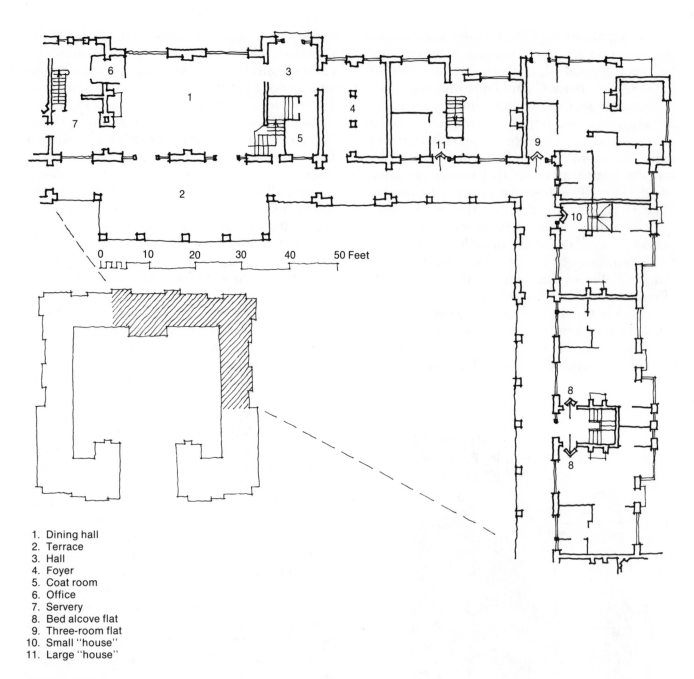

1. Dining hall
2. Terrace
3. Hall
4. Foyer
5. Coat room
6. Office
7. Servery
8. Bed alcove flat
9. Three-room flat
10. Small "house"
11. Large "house"

Figure 3-4. Homesgarth, Letchworth: ground-floor plan of part of the cooperative quadrangle. *(A. Clapham Lander, Architect)*

caution rather than lack of conviction that prompted him to a slow start. He predicted that his cooperative housekeeping units would eventually make people "green with envy" rather than "red with laughing" (Hayden 1981, 231). In Purdom's opinion the success of Howard's novel housing development would be assured by the desire of many people "to lighten for themselves the burden of housework" and "to bring back comfort into the home" (Purdom 1913, 99). After all the concept of cooperative housekeeping was not different in principle from that of the innumerable social clubs of Great Britain, where the sharing of common kitchen facilities was an accepted custom.

In spite of such reasoning and the convincing

economics of cooperative housekeeping derived from sharing the wages of domestic help and purchasing food at wholesale prices, Howard's housing reform ideas did not meet with the anticipated widespread success. Families with children were reluctant to embrace collective habitation. But cooperative quadrangles continued to be popular housing in garden cities for single people, the elderly, and childless couples.

A DANISH PROTOTYPE: THE *KOLLEKTIVHUS*

At the beginning of this century, Otto Fick, an energetic Dane with a lively imagination and a sincere commitment to the betterment of living conditions, formulated a new concept for apartment living that was to complement imminent changes in society. His efforts eventually led to

Figure 3-5. Homesgarth, Letchworth: perspective.

the development of a *kollektivhus* (collective house), a new prototype of multiple dwellings that was to be emulated later not only in the Scandinavian countries but also in several other countries in Europe.

It is not clear whether Otto Fick knew about the catering flats of London or the apartment hotels of North America, but there is an uncanny similarity between these and his proposed *kollektivhus*. Fick, too, envisaged his building to be administered so that all housework and food preparation would be carried out by service staff, relieving tenants of the worry and the labor of house cleaning and cooking after they came home from work.

Fick's plan for an ideal housing development was realized in 1903, when a *kollektivhus* was built in accordance with his design principles. The plans for this apartment building were prepared by the architect L. Christian Kofoed, and the building was located at the corner of Forchhammersvej and Sankt Markus Plads in Copenhagen. The building site was owned by the municipality, which also held the first mortgage on the property. Because Fick could not raise sufficient capital for the construction of his building, it had to be financed as a cooperative.

Fick's collective apartment house was composed of 26 kitchenless but otherwise self-contained dwelling units ranging in size from three to five rooms. Apartments were centrally heated and had a hot water supply, garbage disposals, and a central vacuum pipe outlet to which vacuum cleaners could be attached.

Twenty-seven common rooms for collective services were included to serve the inhabitants of the building, including a central kitchen, a laundry, a drying room, an ironing room, and maids' rooms. All the dwelling units were served by dumbwaiters for the delivery of meals from the central kitchen. Fick argued that it was senseless to have 26 housewives cooking individually when it would be much easier and much more efficient to have meals prepared centrally for every household. Other housekeeping services also were available to tenants, such as house cleaning, window washing, shoe polishing, and even mending clothes, all on request at fixed charges (Waagensen and Rubin 1949, 13–15).

Fick was concerned, however, that contact between neighbors could become too "liberal" if collective services were extended to include all family activities. For this reason neither a common dining room nor a nursery for children was planned for the building. Food was simply sent to each apartment unit via the dumbwaiter and, in order to preserve the element of surprise or the illusion of having home-cooked meals for which there had never been any choice, there was no provision made for menu selection. If, however, certain members of a family did not like a particular dish, the central kitchen was notified and something else was delivered.

In 1907 a detailed account of Fick's collective house services was published in a periodical (Schwimmer 1907, 1024–1029), and the amenities enjoyed by the tenants of this new establishment were described in great detail. Breakfast was delivered as requested at a specific time and announced by an electric bell in the apartment. At lunch or dinner, if guests were to be entertained, notice had to be given only one hour before meal time so that food could be delivered on more attractive and festive dinnerware. Laundry service and special errands were arranged by management on request for a charge that was reasonable because of the efficiencies inherent in centrally organized housekeeping.

As a social reformer Fick was primarily concerned with the working class and would have liked to have his collective house built for them. However, before World War I, very few workers were able to afford the luxury of any housekeeping services. Consequently, although originally designed for lower-income groups, his *kollektivhus* attracted only middle-income dwellers. To remedy this situation Fick later attempted to create collective services on a wider basis by establishing central kitchens, laundries, and other services for an entire city district, but this concept was too advanced and found no supporters.

Fick's *kollektivhus* was predominantly composed of large dwelling units for large families rather than smaller units for childless couples or single tenants. Thus 26 large families with relatively few wage earners had to bear the costs of collective services, whereas a larger number of smaller households with correspondingly more wage earners would have made these services more affordable. In spite of this the collective house continued to function well during World War I, until food rationing was imposed and the central kitchen service had to be suspended. After the war, when things returned to normal, tenants once again requested meal service; the central kitchen functioned satisfactorily until 1942, when the building was sold and when, incidentally, food rationing again was enforced.

A GERMAN, SWISS, AND AUSTRIAN PROTOTYPE: THE *EINKÜCHENHAUS*

In 1901 the German social democrat and women's activist Lily Braun published in Berlin a book entitled *Frauenarbeit und Hauswirtschaft (Women's Work and Home Economics)*. In it she proposed the formation of housekeeping cooperatives as a means of accelerating the supply of homes for lower-income groups suffering from an acute housing shortage. She envisaged these cooperative societies providing apartment buildings of 50 to 60 kitchenless dwelling units in landscaped garden settings with a centralized kitchen (Uhlig 1979, 159).

Lily Braun believed that these housing cooperatives, in addition to reducing costs by providing kitchenless apartments, would bring about (1) the end of "dilettante" food preparation, (2) the improvement of child rearing, (3) the emancipation of women, and (4) the phasing out of servants or maids through their replacement by workers hired by the management.

Apart from a few socialist colleagues, Braun's housing reform proposals were rejected by her contemporaries and the kitchenless apartment buildings ridiculed as comparable to "rabbit warrens" where home life was limited to "bedroom activities" only. But, a few years later, news of Otto Fick's collective house in Copenhagen reached Germany, and many former antagonists of kitchenless apartment buildings changed their attitudes. After Rosika Schwimmer's 1907 account of the *kollektivhus* in the periodical *Die Umschau*, the virtues of this new Danish dwelling form were discussed in the Berlin press. Some hailed the collective house as the "urban apartment house of the future," while others still feared that this dwelling type would spell the be-

ginning of the end of the sanctified status of marriage and the family.

Undeterred, however, a group of housing reformers formed a "one-kitchen house" society in 1908 and published an informative pamphlet extolling the virtues of collective habitation. Plans and model photographs of proposed collective apartment buildings in Lichterfelde and Friedenau, both garden suburbs of Berlin, were published, and Hermann Muthesius and Albert Gessner were identified as their architects (Uhlig 1979, 167).

To forestall any negative reaction and to reassure potential clients, a promise was included in the cooperative's prospectus asserting that by living in these new types of apartment buildings, closeness and intimacy between family members would not be endangered; on the contrary they would be strengthened because centralized kitchen and housekeeping services would free the mother from housework and enable her to devote greater attention to the healthy development of her children. Four types of collective services were proposed: centralized food service, centralized housekeeping service, child care in a "house-kindergarten," and recreational facilities for free-time activities.

Five one-kitchen houses were opened on April 1, 1909. The initial success was tremendous since all apartments were rented before the completion date, but only one month later the owners went bankrupt. Thus the much publicized collective habitation movement that had promised extensive gastronomic and housekeeping reform to apartment dwellers experienced a major setback. A new owner attempted to continue operation by increasing the charge for services, but eventually individual kitchens had to be retrofitted into every apartment unit and centralized food service was discontinued.

Two noted architects, W. C. Behrendt and Henry van der Velde, sought to rescue the collective habitation movement. But because they were unable to raise enough funds, both architects had to be satisfied with giving only moral support to the cause.

Of course not all German architects shared the views of Behrendt and van der Velde, especially conservative architects such as Paul Schultze-Naumburg. The latter saw in collective service buildings "the atrophy of the soulful (family) life" and a manifestation of "the oddity of an ignominious large city" (Uhlig 1979, 154–155). It did not help the cause of collective habitation that centralized kitchen services were viewed by Schultze-Naumburg and others as leading to other collective organizations which were associated with communism.

Nevertheless an apartment building with a centralized kitchen was built in 1910 at Wilhelm Zürichstrasse of Wilmersdorf, Berlin (Waagensen and Rubin 1949, 18). Modeled on Fick's *kollektivhus* but featuring larger dwelling units then its Copenhagen counterpart, this apartment house met with reasonable success. With the outbreak of World War I four years later, however, most building construction stopped, and further experimentation with collective house forms ceased in Germany.

In neutral Switzerland a collective habitation project was started in 1915 with the founding of a cooperative society called Wohn-und-Speisehausgenossenschaft (dwelling-and-boarding cooperative society). The initiator of this venture was Oskar Schwank (Troesch 1976, 6–11 and 30).

A building-construction foreman by training, Schwank worked for some years in architects' offices and thereafter declared himself to be an architect. He gave the impression of being a conservative burgher, but his appearance was misleading since he was anything but conventional. Most likely Schwank read about one-kitchen-house experiments in architectural journals and may even have heard of the success of apartment hotels in North American cities before he formulated and "patented" his design for collective habitation.

With conviction and persuasiveness approximating those of a preacher, Schwank had little difficulty in convincing eleven building tradesmen and building material suppliers, all burghers of Zürich, to form a cooperative society. Not one of the founding members of this society had any intention of living in the projected one-kitchen apartment house, however. Schwank prepared the necessary plans for the project, and a building permit was issued by the municipal authorities in the summer of 1915. By January 1916 a mortgage for two-thirds of the anticipated building cost was

secured and the suburban building site on the corner of Ida and Gertrude streets of Zürich-Wiedikon was acquired. Construction commenced shortly thereafter, and in the spring of the following year about 50 dwelling units were ready to receive the first tenants. During the construction period, though, Schwank made several major errors and lost control of the development. As a consequence he was forced to withdraw from both the job and the cooperative.

The Amerikanerhaus (American House) apartment building offered to its residents several collective services, of which the central heating system was the most admired. Bathing facilities for the occupants of the 45 dwellings were communal and were located in the basement. Individual bathtubs were not installed in the apartments. The small private washrooms near the entrance door of each apartment contained merely a sink and water closet; they were ventilated through an airshaft.

The building was designed around a central courtyard with gallery access to the various dwelling units (Figs. 3-6, 3-7, and 3-8). These galleries were unusually wide and were expected to function as social spaces for informal get-togethers. In fact they were used as such during the 1920s and 1930s, a period identified by the long-time tenants as "the golden age" of the development. Originally Schwank planned for the courtyard to be covered with a glass roof, not dissimilar to Godin's *familistère* at Guise, but this plan was abandoned during construction in favor of glazing the galleries only.

Subsequently several changes were made to Schwank's original plans. First, a large commercial space at sidewalk level, originally conceived as a food market (anticipating today's supermarket), was subdivided into smaller shops. Second, office and atelier spaces planned for the top floor of the four-story building were converted into dwelling units. Third, a library located adjacent to the entrance lobby was abandoned. Finally, the common dining room projected for the exclusive use of the tenants was replaced by a public restaurant. Nevertheless, the central kitchen service was retained to serve both the tenants and the patrons of the new restaurant.

The majority of the tenants were artisans and

clerical workers, but an industrialist also was listed as a resident. In 1946 the cooperative society that had built the Amerikanerhaus was dissolved, and the building was subsequently taken over by a real estate company. In 1976 the long-time residents of the Amerikanerhaus were interviewed by a journalist. Their anecdotes of partying and celebrating birthdays clearly reflected great satisfaction with the social life of this collective habitation (Troesch 1976).

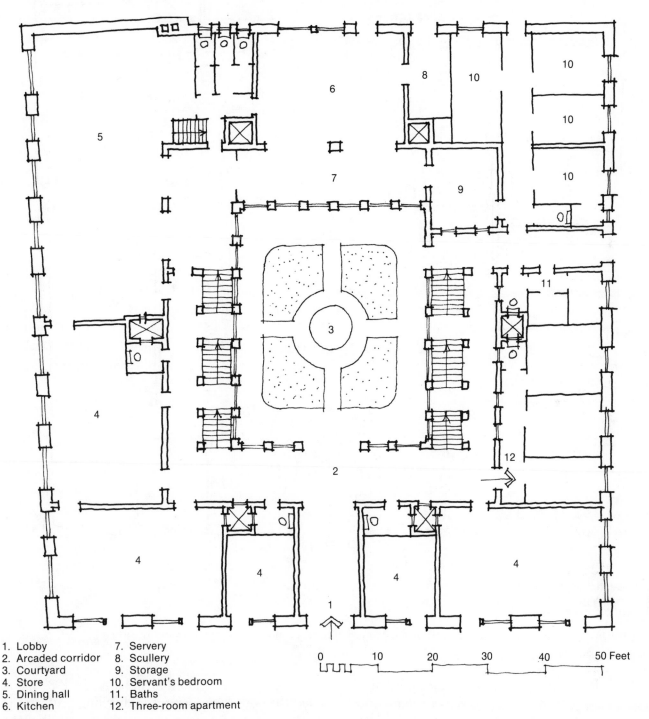

1. Lobby
2. Arcaded corridor
3. Courtyard
4. Store
5. Dining hall
6. Kitchen
7. Servery
8. Scullery
9. Storage
10. Servant's bedroom
11. Baths
12. Three-room apartment

0   10   20   30   40   50 Feet

Figure 3-6. Amerikanerhaus, Zurich-Wiedikon: ground-floor plan of collective apartment house. *(Oskar Schwank, Architect)*

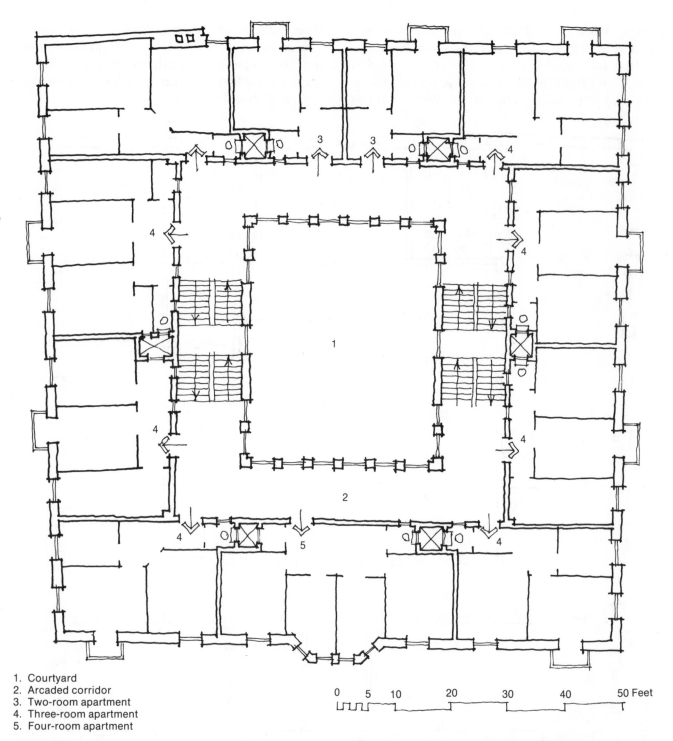

1. Courtyard
2. Arcaded corridor
3. Two-room apartment
4. Three-room apartment
5. Four-room apartment

0   5   10   20   30   40   50 Feet

Figure 3-7. Amerikanerhaus, Zurich-Wiedikon: typical floor plan of collective apartment house.

The idea of collective habitation also reached Vienna, and plans for an *Einküchenhaus* (one-kitchen house) were drawn up by the architect Otto Hellwig (Troesch 1976, 9), but its realization was postponed until after World War I and its aftermath of economic instability. In 1922 a collective house comprising 25 dwelling units (ranging from one to five rooms each) was built as the first phase of a large project. With an additional 246 apartments, this project, called Heimhof

Figure 3-8. Amerikanerhaus, Zurich-Wiedikon: principal elevation.

(Home Court), was completed four years later. Although the new dwellings were rather small (mostly one and two rooms each), they nevertheless became very popular. Collective services made housekeeping easy and common facilities —such as dining halls, bath houses, a kindergarten, and social rooms stocked with daily newspapers—were luxuries greatly appreciated.

Each floor of the apartment block was cleaned by a maid who also served meals in one's own apartment, if requested to do so. Laundry services as well as other housekeeping services were offered at cost since this housing development was run by the occupants themselves as a non-profit cooperative. Each year members elected new executives whose responsibility was to manage the building.

After the German occupation of Austria in the 1930s, the cooperative administration of Heimhof ceased and its central kitchen service, together with all other housekeeping services, was discontinued and the social common rooms were closed.

A RUSSIAN EXPERIMENT: THE *DOM-KOMMUNA*

As might be expected after the Revolution of 1917, the notion of collective habitation also was embraced in Russia. Between 1926 and 1930 nearly 30 percent of all newly erected dwelling accommodations were housing communes, or *dom-kommunas*, which in their organization were very similar to the *kollektivhus* concept.

In his book *Town and Revolution*, Anatole Kopp attributes the development of *dom-kommunas* to the creative forces of the Russian revolutionary society. From the outset of the Soviet rule, it was an accepted notion that life was to change and that corresponding changes would have to follow in the home. Social changes coupled with a great housing shortage made it necessary to look beyond the traditional bourgeois apartment building for a new form that would act as a "social condenser" and would require a reduced volume of building construction per household.

According to Anatole Kopp the responsible people among the proletariat were "inspired by a legitimate desire to free women from domestic slavery, which in the conditions that existed in the U.S.S.R. of the twenties meant back-breaking labor" (1970, 145). Additional considerations were, first, "the need to release as many of the non-active population as possible [again mainly women] to play their part in industrialization of the country," and, second, "the economic impossibility of giving each one individually the comfort and conveniences that it was rightly believed could be more easily provided for groups" (Kopp 1970, 145). El Lissitzky recounts that "the Soviet architect was given the task of establishing a new standard of housing by devising a new type of housing unit, not intended for single individuals in conflict with each other as in the West, but for the masses" (Lissitzky 1970, 35). Finally, in a desire to transform in a few brief years a traditional society based on capitalism to a new communalistic one, architects were asked to devise housing communes that would assist this process.

As early as 1919 the management of a large Soviet state industrial plant prepared specifications for the construction of apartments of the hotel type. This project contained the germ of an idea that later led to the development of the *dom-kommuna*, or housing commune concept, described in 1925 in the program of a housing design competition organized by the Moscow Soviet. Two years later an inquiry into the *dom-kommuna* concept was followed by a series of fraternal competitions, all of which led to the creation in 1928 of a research and design group headed by the architect and editor of the architectural magazine S.A., Moses Ginsburg. Other members of this group were M. Barshit, A. Pasternak, G. Sum-Shchik, and V. Vladimirov.

Only a few months after the formation of this research group, the drawings of five prototype dwellings, which became known as *stroikom* units, were published by the group. Four out of the five prototypes were conventional designs, but the fifth, namely the F-type unit, represented a real innovation and a genuine response to the needs of the day. This innovative design featured two superimposed one-bedroom units serviced by a single-loaded corridor at mid-level between the two units. Each dwelling was a floor-through unit, allowing cross-ventilation and exposure to two orientations. The favorable exposure toward the south featured living rooms that were one-and-a-half stories high, thereby allowing deep penetration of sunlight into the dwelling during the long winter months.

In a slightly modified form, this F-type dwelling unit was employed in the design of Narkomfin, a collective apartment building on Novinsky Boulevard in Moscow (Figs. 3-9 and 3-10). Built between 1928 and 1929 for the People's Commis-

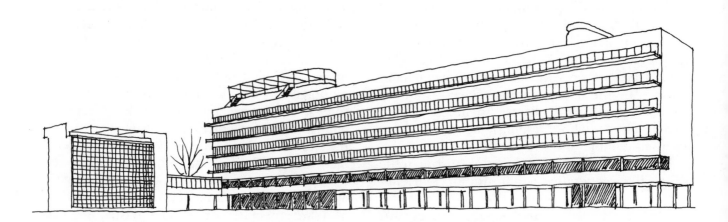

Figure 3-10. Narkomfin *dom-kommuna*, Moscow: perspective.

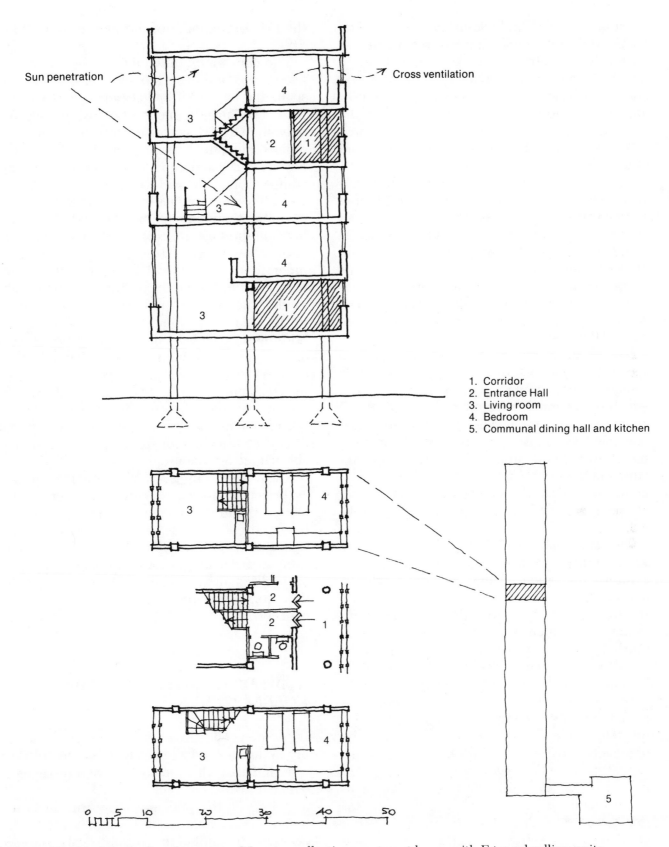

1. Corridor
2. Entrance Hall
3. Living room
4. Bedroom
5. Communal dining hall and kitchen

Figure 3-9. Narkomfin *dom-kommuna,* Moscow: collective apartment house with F-type dwelling units. *(Moses Ginsburg, I. Milinis and S. Prokhorov, Architects)*

sariat of Finance, this building contained several collective facilities and common rooms, such as a canteen, a central kitchen and dining room, a laundry, a gymnasium, a library, a day nursery, and a roof garden. Moses Ginsburg, I. Milinis, and S. Prokhorov were the architects of the building, which in many respects anticipated subsequent developments by Le Corbusier and others in the West.

After the completion of the Narkomfin building, many other collective apartment houses were constructed in Russia. In the northern part of the country, an enclosed corridor gave access to the various dwelling units, while in the south an open gallery–type access corridor linked the entrances of individual apartments with the stairways and the building's collective facilities. The number of residents of a *dom-kommuna* ranged from 400 to 800.

The idealism of Russian housing reformers of the 1920s is summed up by Lissitzky, who wrote: "The important thing is that the housing block, which up to now has merely represented the algebraic sum of self-contained private apartments, has now been transformed into a synthetic complex for total communal living." And only after "the functions of the individual elements become better defined" will it be possible "to give more consideration to individual desires" (1970, 41–42).

The *dom-kommuna* with its collective facilities was to release women from domestic labor for gainful employment in the labor-short industry and was to make them responsible members of a socialist society. Moreover, through living communally, with their everyday housekeeping needs satisfied by collective services, all inhabitants of the *dom-kommuna* would have the opportunity to improve and educate themselves in order to make a maximum contribution to society. It was hoped that this new way of life would discourage the self-centeredness of the individual and the materialism manifested by the bourgeois class in capitalistic societies, whose members are perpetually engaged in a race to acquire more consumer goods. Lenin himself suggested in his manuscript *The Great Initiative* that, like true communism, the true emancipation of women would come about only when the microeconomics of the individual household were replaced by the macroeconomics of the socialist state (1961, 419).

The *dom-kommuna* building program did not live up to these expectations. It had a short life span, and by 1932 it had already been discontinued. The abandonment of Russia's collective habitation experiment is attributable to four conditions. First, the housing shortage in Russia during the 1920s and early 1930s was so acute that compact one-bedroom dwellings often were occupied by large families or, in extreme situations, by more than one family. Second, the acute housing shortage necessitated the postponement of the construction of some collective facilities in order to free labor and building materials for more essential building construction. The promise that the omitted "nonessential" services were to be installed at some future date, when the housing shortage was alleviated, did not prevent daily aggravation and discontent. Third, in Russia there was no previous experience with the management of collective apartment houses. Mismanagement often resulted in large-scale dissatisfaction among tenants. Fourth, the concept of collective habitation presupposes a considerable degree of urban sophistication and affluence on the part of its users, which was hardly the case at the time in Russia. In summary, overcrowded living conditions; incomplete facilities; poorly managed collective services; and, perhaps most significant of all, the difficult and rapid transition from an agrarian and rural folk society to an industrialized urban society are not ideal conditions for testing the validity of a new housing concept.

A SWEDISH PROTOTYPE: THE *KOLLEKTIVHUS*

In Sweden collective habitation experiments also began during the first decade of this century and were initiated with the construction of Hemgården, an apartment building built between 1907 and 1909 in the middle-class district of Ostermalm in Stockholm. This building was not conceived in the spirit of the socialist ideals expressed by Johan August Strindberg, but rather it was designed to cater to middle-class families who wanted to take advantage of centralized household services at a time when servants were increasingly more difficult to find. The apartment sizes varied from two to five rooms each, and a total of 60 dwellings were provided. Each apartment was provided with a kitchenette and closely resembled the dwelling units of American apartment hotels as well as those of Fick's *kollektivhus* in Copenhagen, the latter built only a few years earlier.

Located in the basement the central kitchen supplied three meals a day to Hemgård's inhabitants. An internal telephone was used to order the food, and 12 dumbwaiters linked the various apartments with the kitchen. The inhabitants of this building also had access to cleaning, laundry, and ironing services in addition to nursing help in case of illness. The service employees were housed in small, dark flats in a separate building at the rear of the property.

During World War I the investment company that owned the building went bankrupt, and the building was purchased by a housing association formed by the tenants. The central kitchen service had to be abandoned soon after. Gradually all other collective services were discontinued, but in the 1960s, when young families of professional people moved into the building, some basement rooms were reconverted into communal rooms (Vestbro 1979, 4).

The Hemgård experiment was not emulated by other developers, although the difficulty of obtaining hired help was aggravated after the war and a request for more collective habitation was expressed not only by the middle class but also by the leaders of the labor movement.

In the 1930s a lively debate was conducted on the merits and demerits of collective habitation. Most people agreed that working-class women had to be helped because their housework chores were particularly burdensome; they could afford to buy neither semimanufactured food products nor modern household appliances. Therefore collective habitation would be especially advantageous to them. Moreover, single women and men who were gainfully employed requested collective habitation not only for easing their household chores but also for the social interaction these buildings offered to their residents. Although members of the Social Democratic

Union of Swedish Women and of the Communist Party supported these requests for collective habitation, the majority of the labor movement leaders favored a conservative housing policy of providing detached, privately owned homes to nuclear families.

In the general discourse about new house forms with collective installations, Alva and Gunnar Myrdal, both sociologists, emerged as protagonists in the Swedish collective habitation movement. Also engaged in the women's emancipation movement, Alva Myrdal saw in collective habitation the liberation of women from housekeeping chores, which would lead to opportunities in the work force equal to those of men. Sven Markelius, an architect and town planner, was sympathetic to Alva Myrdal's ideals, and together they set about to translate these ideals into buildable substance (Mühlestein 1975, 5).

Two large collective housing projects were designed by Markelius in Stockholm, but neither of these was built. One project—designed in 1931–1932—entailed three apartment buildings in Bromma, and the other—designed one year later—entailed five apartment blocks on Kungsklippan. Finally, in 1935 a true albeit small collective house for family living was built by Markelius at 6 John Ericssonsgatan, in the center of Stockholm.

Markelius's collective house was designed for family accommodation. Since there was little previous experience with similar buildings in Sweden, this new endeavor received no support from investors and had to be financed as a cooperative venture, with each tenant advancing as a downpayment the equivalent of 9.3 percent of the building's value, an amount slightly in excess of one year's rent.

All 57 apartment units of this collective house commanded magnificent views of the waters of Malaren. Most of the dwellings were one-bedroom or bed-alcove units and all had balconies. Markelius himself occupied one of the flats for many years and acted as a resident handyman. Four dumbwaiters, each serving a set of two apartments on each floor, linked the pantries of the kitchenless dwellings to a service corridor adjacent to the communal kitchen. The ground-floor level accommodated, in addition to an

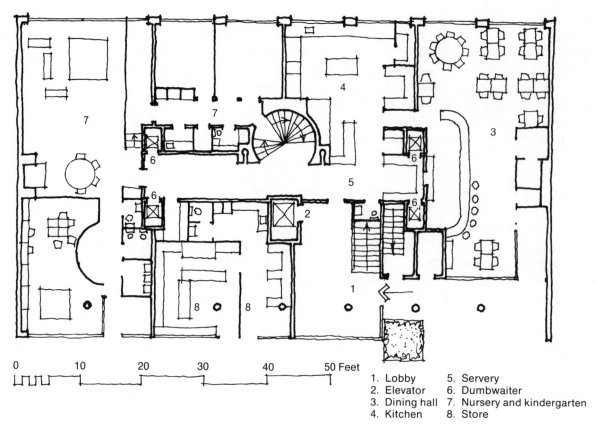

1. Lobby   5. Servery
2. Elevator   6. Dumbwaiter
3. Dining hall   7. Nursery and kindergarten
4. Kitchen   8. Store

Figure 3-11. 6 John Ericssonsgaten, Stockholm: ground-floor plan of collective apartment house. *(Sven Markelius, Architect)*

entrance vestibule and a lobby, a small self-service restaurant in lieu of a common dining room, a small convenience store, and a combined nursery and kindergarten for 20 preschool children (Figs. 3-11, 3-12, and 3-13). These facilities were accessible from the elevator lobby and directly from the street. Behind the elevator core was a central kitchen with a connection to the corridor containing the dumbwaiters.

The utopian ideal of collective habitation for people from all walks of life did not materialize in this building. To Markelius's disappointment only academics and self-employed people took advantage of this new house form, in spite of the fact that the dwellings were designed to be small in order to be affordable to low-income groups. A further disappointment derived from the fact that some tenants, having become accustomed to the amenities offered by the *kollektivhus*, were reluctant to move from the building when their children grew up. Others, who had more than

two children, found the apartments too small and left, so that the kindergarten eventually lost its viability and had to be closed. Because the population of the building had decreased, the economic viability of the centralized food and laundry services diminished and the kitchen, the restaurant, and the laundry had to rely increasingly on revenue received from the public. The decollectivization of this building's services was further advanced by rising salaries for employees and by the small size of its service facilities. For example, the laundry facility was too small to be commercially viable and so was the restaurant, although the latter continued to function under private ownership after its collective management by the tenants ceased.

Before these economic problems were encountered by the management of Markelius's collective house, and following some favorable newspaper reportage, public opinion accepted the concept of collective habitation, particularly

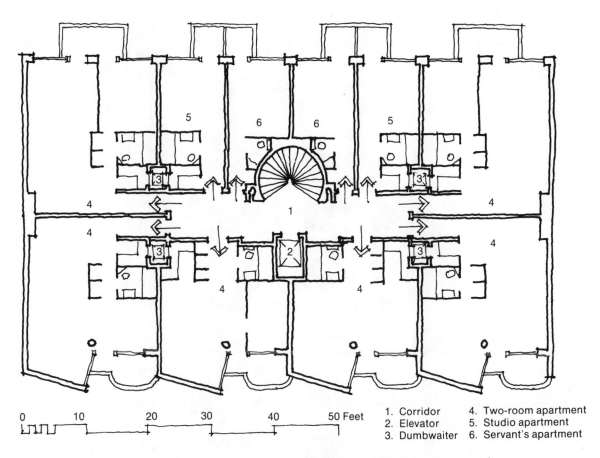

1. Corridor   4. Two-room apartment
2. Elevator   5. Studio apartment
3. Dumbwaiter   6. Servant's apartment

Figure 3-12. 6 John Ericssonsgaten, Stockholm: typical floor plan of collective apartment house.

for single persons. In fact a few years before Markelius's project was built, a collective house with housecleaning services—Rålambhus at 76 Norr Malarstrand in Stockholm—was established exclusively for bachelors. Designed by the architect Ragnar Ostberg—famous for his design of the Stockholm City Hall—this building featured a ground-floor restaurant that catered to tenants and the public alike. This building served as a model for subsequent collective houses for single people.

In 1938 Olle Engkvist, a private builder, initiated the construction of an apartment house, Smaragden, with collective services for single women only. Designed by the architects Backström and Reinius, this building was constructed on Kungsholmen in Stockholm on a site leased from the city for 99 years. It contained 200 one-room flats, each with a kitchenette and access to collective housekeeping services. The common dining hall, with a seating capacity of 130, and

the club room, with daily newspapers, were located at roof level and offered beautiful views of the city. A roof terrace and a gymnasium also were available to the residents (Waagensen and Rubin 1949, 39).

A similar building, Yrkeskvinnornas Hus (Working Women's House), was built by a women's organization with a membership of mainly professional and business women. Located in the Gårded district of Stockholm and designed by the architects Albin Stark and Hillevi Svedberg, this building contained 62 self-contained dwelling units ranging in size from one to four rooms each, all with standard kitchens despite the fact that a central kitchen service was designed to supply meals to its tenants. Between 1939 and 1944 two more collective houses were built in Stockholm. Elfvinggården in Alvik served single women, and Gårdesgården in the Gårded district served childless couples. Both these buildings were very successful and still function as collec-

Figure 3-13. 6 John Ericssonsgaten, Stockholm: perspective.

tive houses, while Smaragden and Yrkeskvinnornas Hus lost some of their collective services (Vestbro 1979, 7).

Olle Engkvist revived the concept of family collective habitation with the building of Lundagården (1941) and Marieberg (1944). Engkvist realized that many married women also were choosing professions that gave them not only a good income but also positions of social importance. He recognized that "the housewife will always have to shoulder great responsibility" and

therefore would benefit from the services provided by a collective house. Living in collective habitation also would ensure "that she does not break down under the burden, and that the comfort and happiness of her home is not jeopardized" (Berkeley 1973, 56). It must be noted that in the early 1940s, "joint" responsibility of the couple for their home and children was not yet accepted by Swedish society. Only much later was a government policy introduced "designed to loosen up the roles of the sexes and to equalize the burdens of parenthood" (Berkeley 1973, 56).

Designed by Albin Stark, Lundagården had 67 dwelling units and was built in the Soder district of Stockholm. Initially its collective facilities consisted of a central kitchen, a kindergarten, a nursery, a laundry, and three small commercial outlets.

Marieberg, the other collective house built by Engkvist, was designed by the architect Svend Ivar Lind. This building complex consisted of two parallel blocks connected at ground level by a corridor and contained about 200 one- to four-room dwelling units, each with a kitchenette and bath. An additional 12 smaller flats were provided for the service staff. Most collective facilities were on the ground floor of the Wennerbergsgatan wing, including a central kitchen with a dining room, a kindergarten, a nursery, and health-care office.

Marieberg represents a new trend in Swedish collective habitation. Realizing that the financial feasibilty of collective services is a function of the number of its users, Engkvist considerably increased the size of his development and introduced the compulsory consumption of a minimum of 24 main meals per month by each tenant for 10 months of every year. Direct food service to apartment units was discouraged by an extra charge levied to its users, resulting in a greater popularity of the in-house restaurant.

A SURVEY OF PRE-WAR COLLECTIVE HOUSING IN SWEDEN

During World War II an extensive survey of collective habitation was undertaken in Sweden by Bent Waagensen, a civil engineer, and Jenny Rubin, a social worker, both refugees from German-occupied Denmark. The survey was sponsored by Stockholm's Home Research Institute with the aim of gathering relevant information on this new housing form. The findings of the study were published after the war in Denmark in a book entitled *Kollektivhuset og dets Forudsaetninger (The Collective House and Its Pre-Conditions).*

The demographic and socioeconomic background of the inhabitants of Swedish collective houses was described in the survey as follows.

Tenant Age Group

About 75 percent of the inhabitants (out of a total of 552 surveyed) were adults, the balance being predominantly preschool-age children. Less than 4 percent of the inhabitants were school children. Approximately 50 percent of the *kollektivhus* households were headed by persons in the 30–50 age group, 33 percent by persons over 50, and 16 percent by persons under 30.

Tenant Family Composition

The majority of households were small. For example, 38 percent had only one person per dwelling unit, 32 percent had two, and 15 percent had three. Single-parent households represented 40 percent, and by far the majority of these were headed by women, outnumbering men four to one. Households with one or two children accounted for 25 percent.

Tenant Income

The survey revealed that practically all tenants belonged to either the middle- or the upper-income group. Only 1.5 percent of the households represented the lower-income group, and some of the heads of these households actually were employed in one of the service facilities attached to the apartment building. At the time the survey was taken, the national classification of Sweden's population consisted of 5 percent upper-, 37 percent middle-, and 58 percent lower-income families. Hence the inhabitants of collective houses did not represent a cross section of the Swedish population.

The researchers calculated that in order to take maximum advantage of the services offered in a *kollektivhus*, a family with one child had to have a minimum yearly income of 12 thousand Swedish Kroner, a figure closer to the average of the upper-income group than to the average of the middle-income one. As could be expected some tenants could not always afford to make full use of the services offered in these apartment buildings; consequently the economic viability of the service facilities suffered.

An interesting fact uncovered by the survey was that about 66 percent of all married women without children, as well as almost 50 percent of the mothers with one or two children, had a permanent job outside the home. There is little doubt that for these families the extensive housekeeping services that were available on short notice were a great inducement to live in a *kollektivhus*. Nevertheless, the expense of this type of accommodation must have obliged many of the women either to assume greater responsibilities outside the home in order to increase income or to reduce expenditures in areas other than lodging.

Tenant Status

It was found that the majority of the tenants were professional people, artists, or self-employed business people; 75 percent of the heads of household in the upper-income group had higher education.

The researchers reasoned that professional persons and artists were less inclined to be conventional and the public at large accepted their nonconformity. Hence these nonconformists were more apt to experiment with new forms of habitation and were not restricted by preconceived notions of what forms of dwellings were conventionally acceptable.

As a new dwelling form, the *kollektivhus* was the object of much criticism, particularly by those who had never seen one before, who had never lived in one, and who did not understand even its elementary principles. The survey produced many absurd comments from the public at large, such as "It sounds so Russian and uniform," "No doubt there must be a great deal of interference with one's private life," "It sounds like living in a glass house," "They must be strange people to live in one of those," and "Isn't it like living in an institution?"

In reality, however, the survey found that people could live quite privately in a collective house if they so wished because the degree to which people came in contact with their neighbors varied from household to household. Some tenants knew many of their neighbors and had social ties with them, while others did not even greet their neighbors in spite of having lived next door to them for many years. Social contact was found to be dependent primarily on the individual. Using the same elevator, stairs, and corridors was not enough to spur conversation between tenants of the same building. While the *kollektivhus* did permit frequent social contacts, it also allowed people to avoid them because collective services provided by paid staff rendered interdependence between neighbors unnecessary. The survey found that tenants' backgrounds or working conditions determined their social behavior to a great extent. People who met the public often during the course of their daily work, preferred privacy and quietness in the evening. Of course, greater social interaction was inevitable between tenants who partipated in the administration of a cooperative building.

Waagensen and Rubin's survey also attempted to establish why people moved into collective houses and investigated what type of buildings the tenants had occupied previously. About 66 percent of the inhabitants moved to these serviced apartment buildings because of the desire to reduce the chores of housework. This desire to ease the burden of running a home was primarily motivated by the wish to work outside the home or to spend more time with the children. The remaining 33 percent of the inhabitants had not intended to live in these serviced apartments but were induced to do so because of the acute housing shortage.

Most of the families interviewed in the survey moved to a *kollektivhus* from conventional apartment buildings; only newlywed couples had not previously had dwellings of their own. A considerable number of families moved to these serviced apartment buildings from single-family homes. The reason for giving up private homes was that they could not find adequate household help. In many of these latter cases, it was the husband as much as the wife who desired the conveniences of a *kollektivhus*.

Finally, the Waagensen and Rubin survey revealed that most inhabitants of collective houses were satisfied with their accommodations and only a small minority desired to move elsewhere (Waagensen and Rubin 1949, 42–51).

CONCLUSIONS

The evolution of collective habitation in Europe demonstrates the long and elusive pursuit of the "magic table" ideal of collective habitation. To change housing traditions is always an arduous task, but change is nevertheless inevitable in the wake of emerging trends towards smaller families, new nonfamily households, and new domestic demands.

The concept of collective habitation evolved from a utopian ideal to reality most closely in Sweden and Denmark. Nonetheless, in the Scandinavian countries collective housing issues continue to be debated. With the traditional nuclear family—consisting of mother, father, and children—clearly in the minority, advocates of collective houses (more recently called service houses) feel that the need for such buildings will increase rather than diminish, in the future. Collective habitation is particularly well-suited for singles, both young and old; for single-parent households; for young childless couples; and for empty-nesters because of its easy access to services and, equally important, its integration of age groups. All Swedish women's organizations endorse the concept of service-house dwelling; they rank central kitchen service and child care as mandatory services while they consider house cleaning and laundry service dispensable, at least for healthy adults. The most compelling proof of the desirability of collective habitation is the fact that in the late 1970s, 13,000 Stockholm residents signed a waiting list for service house accommodation (Vestbro 1979, 12).

To meet an increased demand and to ensure economic viability, recent collective housing projects have tended to be too large, in both Denmark and Sweden. This resulted in collective houses acquiring an undesirable institutional atmosphere instead of a homelike ambience. For example, the Danish collective housing development Vaerebro Park (1968) in Rodovre, a suburb of Copenhagen, has 1,327 dwelling units distributed in three high-rise and five four-story blocks, while Sollentuna, a Swedish high-rise *servicehus* built in 1972 in Stockholm, has 1,246 dwelling units (the population of children under 15 years of age numbers about 1,000). Shortly after Sollentuna's completion, Jutta Zilliakus, a Finnish columnist and an advocate of collective habitation, admitted that it was a "terrible grey monster" but consoled herself that it worked and people liked it (Berkeley 1973, 59). Subsequently, however, its excessive size did create some problems because self-policing was inoperative and drug- and alcohol-addicted people made it a habit to gather in the corridors. After guards were hired to patrol the public areas and evict the squatters, the operation of Sollentuna returned to normal.

The moderate-size collective house, with between 60 and 100 dwelling units and collective services limited exclusively to its tenants, may be very desirable from a social point of view, but unfortunately it has proven not to be financially viable. Coupling the concept of collective habitation with mixed-use housing, where collective services are provided by commercial outlets with a clientele that extends beyond the residents of the building to include inhabitants of the neighborhood, may broaden the base of users enough to ensure economic viability. Such a development would be consistent with the existing trend of urbanity with housing constituting a part, albeit an important part, of a mixed-land-use pattern. Failing such developments, moderate-size collective habitation with services will continue to be a utopian dream for many and a reality for only a few.

References

Berkeley, E. P. 1973. The Swedish 'servicehus.' *Architecture Plus* 5:56–59.

Fourier, C. 1971. *Design for Utopia: Selected Writings of Charles Fourier.* New York: Schoken Books.

Giedion, S. 1969. *Mechanization Takes Command.* New York: W. W. Norton.

Grimm, J. and W. *Fairy Tales and Stories.* New York: George Routledge.

Hayden, D. 1976. *Seven American Utopias: The Architecture of Communitarian Socialism, 1790–1975.* Cambridge, MA: MIT Press.

———. 1981. *The Grand Domestic Revolution.* Cambridge, MA: MIT Press.

Kopp, A. 1970. *Town and Revolution: Soviet Architecture and City Planning 1917–1935,* trans. T. E. Burton. New York: George Brazilier.

Kropotkin, P. 1906. *The Conquest of Bread.* London: Chapman and Hall.

Lenin, V. I. 1961. *Die Grosse Initiative*. Berlin: Dietz Verlag.

Lissitzky, E. 1970. *Russia: An Architecture for World Revolution*, trans. E. Dluhosh. London: Lund Humphries.

Mitford, N. 1968. *Madame de Pompadour*. New York: Harper and Row.

Mühlestein, E. 1975. Kollektives Wohnen gestern und heute. *Archithese* 14:3–23.

Perks, Sydney. 1905. *Residential Flats of All Classes*. London: Batsford.

Purdom, C. B. 1913. *The Garden City*. London: J. M. Dent and Sons.

Schwimmer, R. 1907. Zentral haushaltung. *Die Umschau* 52:1024–1029.

Troesch, P. 1976. Idastrasse 28, Zurich-Wiedikon. *Tages Anzeiger Magazin* 3:6–11 and 30.

Uhlig, G. 1979. Zur geschichte des einküchenhaüser. *Wohnen in Wandel*, ed. L. Niethammer, 151–170. Wuppertal, West Germany: Peter Hammer.

Vestbro, D.U. 1979. *Collective Housing Units in Sweden*. Stockholm: Svenska Institute.

Waagensen, B. and J. Rubin. 1949. *Kollektivhuset og dets Forudsaetninger*. Copenhagen: Nyt Nordisk Forlag. Arnold Busck.

Chapter 4

Communal Housing in Sweden

A Remedy for the Stress of Everyday Life?

Alison Woodward

All those different moments of stress when the kids were small and you ran at seven in the morning to the day-care center, ripped their clothes off and left, then off to the city, then back, stuff them back in the clothes, tear them away from their friends, off to the store, throw some boxes in the cart, and then home and shriek and yell at them and up the stairs and food on the stove and off with their clothes again. . . . It was stress, stress, stress, you just didn't have time to have fun . . . and then came the weekend . . . you'd built up a kind of castle in the air, and instead came the Big Fight. . . . Well I think living here is fantastic. . . . At last, I'm living in harmony!
—*Mother of two in Prästgårdshagen*

While Sweden exhibits far-ranging equality between the sexes in many areas (Ruggie 1984), equality within the private sphere of the home has been difficult to achieve. With almost all women now in the labor force, the issue of juggling everyday chores with work has led women to challenge existing housing arrangements. This chapter presents one answer to that challenge: communal multifamily housing. Sweden is one of the few Western societies to experiment extensively with introducing communal living into *all* sectors of the housing scene, including public housing.

In the 1960s and 1970s, Sweden saw wide experimentation with communal living, primarily through private initiatives. Variants where small groups of friends or movement members share housing around *one* central kitchen are to be found both in cities and in rural areas. These are called *storfamilj*, or big family groups such as those studied by Palm-Lindén (1982). Many of the examples presented by Gromark in his 1983 European survey also are of this more traditional commune form.

In contrast to such traditional communal living, the newer Swedish projects treated in this chapter provide each household with its own private living space, including a kitchen. Communal facilities supplement the basic apartment. The communal housing solution unites two or more households around a number of shared services, the most important of which is an alternative for daily meals. These services can be purchased or provided by tenants themselves.

This chapter focuses on the new communal forms recently produced by traditional housing providers, such as the cooperative movement and the public housing firms. These buildings are called *kollektivhus* in Swedish, as they are collective or communal dwellings. After a brief history of these specific alternatives, this chapter surveys several projects constructed in the last 10 years. It then considers some of the architectural and social issues raised by the introduction of this alternative living form into the established Swedish multifamily-housing sector.

RECENT HISTORY OF SWEDISH COMMUNAL HOUSING

Sweden has had a relatively continuous history of attempts to introduce shared domestic labor into family dwellings (Vestbro 1982). The Social Democratic Women's movement envisioned many alternative housing solutions for lessening housework for women. These visions found concrete expression in a number of privately financed projects in the 1920s and 1930s similar in spirit to projects in the Soviet Union (Caldenby and Walldén 1979) and elsewhere in Europe (Pearson 1987; Hayden 1981, 1984). (This housing was described in chapter 3.)

In the 1960s a new variation on this theme appeared in publicly financed projects, coupling support services with multifamily housing. For the first time the vision of common services for private households was adopted by the public sector. The best known of these projects—the Service House in Sollentuna, completed in 1972 —housed 1,246 households in apartment units within a single complex and included day care, a reception service, and a restaurant. In contrast to much multifamily housing, it attempted to house various types of households by mixing apartment sizes and including some social-welfare clients.

Demand for Communal Housing in the 1970s

By the mid-1970s many criticized the large-scale service house model and pleaded for smaller projects that might encourage an informal exchange of services between neighbors. Demands for housing better suited to the creation of community and the easing of everyday life came from at least two groups—the rejuvenated women's movement and the more amorphous alternative-living movement.

The Swedish women's movement has always combined demands for equality with dreams of a better everyday life. In the 1970s new groups joined the more traditional women's groups. Women became more vocal in their demands and more concrete in their vision. The Social Democratic Women's movement published studies for ideal future neighborhoods, including *Service and Community Where We Live* (Åkerman et al. 1975), while radical women's groups such as Group 8 and the Women's Building Forum worked out new housing forms (Cronberg et al. 1979). With arguments echoing those of Dolores Hayden's "material feminists" (Hayden 1984, 72) women looked for ways in which people could share everyday tasks in order to increase the joy of free time.

The second, related branch of the movement for communal solutions was the commune movement. The 1970s brought extensive questioning of the traditional nuclear family and its way of life. Experimentation with communal living was widespread (Jonsson 1983; Palm-Lindén 1982). Many communes and "big families" (*storfamilj*) had difficulty finding housing for their needs. The problems ranged from insufficient kitchen space to bedrooms with widely differing sizes and amenities. Although many communes dreamed of an alternative social order, they had to fit their solutions into traditional spaces.

The combined thrust of the women's movement and the alternative living activists found its most effective architectural expression in the work of the BIG (Bo i Gemenskap/Live Together in Community) group. These female architects, interior designers, and journalists developed an influential model for better living, the "little collective," or communal home. The characteristics of the model included the following:

Small scale: between 20 and 50 households

Shared work: sharing the everyday tasks associated with housing

Speculation free: publicly financed rental housing with democratic participation for tenants in management

Varied population of tenants: to increase contacts between different generations and social groups (BIG-gruppen 1982, 32).

The plan circulated informally in 1977, stimulating debate about future Swedish housing. Later the group published their plans (BIG-gruppen 1982) and the book became a major source of inspiration for planners and tenants.

Politically the various demands for new forms of housing found a focus in the conflict over the closing of one of Sweden's first communal projects, the Hässelby Family Hotel (opened in 1956), by its private owner in 1976. After serious dispute, including police intervention when tenants tried to keep the restaurant kitchen open, the tenants regrouped. They undertook the preparation of weekday suppers in a pantry and have since run a food service (Blomberg et al. 1986). The struggle inspired those believing in communal housing and demonstrated the need for a public statute to guard against the whims of private owners. The drive for communal housing became a political movement; in many cities political pressure groups began carrying the banner "Communal Housing Now!"

However, information about the size of the demand for housing with more communal facilities was very limited. As one Stockholm housing official lamented, it is difficult to ask people whether they want something that does not yet exist. A Stockholm housing survey in 1975 found that 13 percent of those seeking new housing were interested in some form of communal housing (Stockholms Kommuns 1983). A 1982 survey in suburban Stockholm demonstrated that almost one-third of the respondents would be interested in exchanging one-tenth of their private housing space for common space for food preparation, hobbies, and other community activities (Stockholms Kommuns 1983, 7). In 1986 nearly 5,000 people were registered in the Stockholm County Housing Authority office as seeking housing in a communal alternative (Stockholms Stads 1986,9).

Material and Social Advantages of Communal Housing

The definition of a communal project remained somewhat vague at the end of the 1970s. Most projects retained private space for the household combined with communal facilities. Two distinctive emphases emerged, focusing on either the material or the social advantages of communal living. The communal dwelling form could remedy financial and time problems for families through the convenient, economic provision of services that otherwise would have to be purchased privately. Furthermore, families could save money by common purchasing and efficien-

cies of scale. Such advantages can be called "material" improvements. Earlier projects had included purchased services, but now visionaries suggested cooperative production of services by the tenants themselves to increase the material advantages. Another, newer emphasis accented the advantages of sharing experiences, including the tasks of everyday life. Living communally and sharing facilities could improve the social quality of life.

As discussion evolved, it became increasingly difficult to separate the material and social advantages. Proponents argued that through the cooperative production of such services as meals, which also provides material advantages, a better sense of social community would develop.

The material problems of everyday life are pressing, especially for families with children. The evening meal—a major source of stress that involves last-minute shopping, preparation, and dish washing—takes from one to three hours of labor a day, depending on family size and the use of prepared foods (Boalt 1983). A central element in most solutions is the sharing of meal preparation on a large scale, saving both time and money. Rushing to day care located in another part of the city is another unwelcome chore for many families. In the communal solution day care can be provided within the same building, again saving time.

Less easy to categorize are the social advantages of communal-living alternatives. Through the sharing of tasks and management, people meet each other in ways that are not usual in Swedish multifamily housing, and these contacts can be the source of informal babysitting arrangements, helping and borrowing networks. Communal living also offers opportunities for casual encounters between adults and sources for new friendships.

The most vigorous arguments in the drive for communal solutions have been those stressing improvement of the quality of everyday life both materially and socially. Play contacts for children and children's contact with a variety of adults are difficult to find in most traditional Swedish housing. Within communal housing both parents and nonparents hope to find both the security of knowing one's neighbors and a better social environment for all.

TENURE, MANAGEMENT MODELS, AND DESIGN

By the 1980s the communal model in Sweden came to mean multigenerational, multifamily housing that included communal facilities and the potential for common meals. Communal living appeared in a variety of tenure and management forms as multiple alternatives flowered. Table 4-1 presents an overview of completed communal projects in the 1980s.

Legal responsibility, turnover, and tenant influence all become more problematic in the communal situation. In the 1970s many small communes foundered on the crux of capital and ownership. Individual, rather than cooperative, ownership of separate units in a single building is difficult because Swedish law prohibits dividing real estate properties horizontally, for example, into condominiums. Swedish cooperative apartments give residents "use" rights, but not ownership rights, to their apartments. Problems of continuity and transfer of owned shares in a building also create difficulties for communes. The existing, privately owned projects are all rather small and are usually organized in the *storfamilj* model.

A better alternative may be cooperative ownership. Sweden has a well-established cooperative movement that has been responsible for many of the new ideas in housing in this century. Communal housing is particularly well suited to the cooperative ownership form (Sollbe 1982; Ågren 1981). Many of the problems arising from joint ownership or relations to a private landlord are resolved within the cooperative form. Indeed, in Denmark, many communal housing projects have been built with some form of cooperative ownership (Vestbro 1982). (McCamant and Durrett describe one type of Danish communal housing in chapter 5.)

By the mid-1970s the major Swedish firms in the cooperative housing sector, HSB and Riksbyggen, had communal projects on their drawing boards, but neither seemed to support the undertaking wholeheartedly. The management of these firms in the 1970s was rather conservative, and while architects and social philosophers within the cooperative movement were enthusiastic, the management was cool to what it felt

was an untried idea with an uncertain market. However, since 1980, six cooperatively owned projects have been completed.

The possibilities for introducing communal housing forms into public rental housing did not look promising. [Public housing constitutes the majority of multifamily housing in Sweden and therefore is not stigmatized as it is, for instance, in the United States (Kemeny 1981; Byggforskningsrådet 1985)]. However, changes in tenant influence in management (Cronberg 1986) and in the management of municipally based public housing firms opened the door to creative new initiatives for communal dwelling.

Generally, recent communal projects in the rental sector can be divided into those with a *service* approach—where tenants pay for services that management provides, such as meals and communal facilities for recreation—and those with a *tenant-management* approach—where tenants themselves decide on the level and type of services and may undertake the provision of services themselves. The two models differ not only in focus but also in scale because the service model usually is much larger. The service and the tenant-management models exist in cooperatively owned and rental projects in about the same proportions.

The Service Model in Public Housing and Goals of Integration

In the 1970s not only tenant groups but also social-service agencies were looking for alternative housing solutions. Institutional solutions for the handicapped and the elderly fell increasingly into disrepute. A new philosophy of social welfare suggested that social and health services be integrated into the community (Lagergren et al. 1982; Lidmar 1981).

Linköping was one of the first communities to attempt to translate this social philosophy into a physical solution, using communal housing as a tool to achieve more integrated care of individuals across the life cycle. Social-welfare services for the aged, preschoolers, and the disabled were combined in Linköping into one project called Stolplyckan (Vestbro 1982, 273–275; Pedersen 1981; Arkitektur 1985). The intention was to fol-

Table 4-1. Recent Swedish Communal Projects by City

Project	Year	Total Units	Management Model	Tenure	Building Type
Eskilstuna					
Nålmakaren	1983	102	Service	Rental	3 connected blocks
Gothenburg					
Stacken	1980	33	Tenant mgmt.	Rental	Renovated high-rise
Trädet	1985	38	Tenant mgmt.	Rental	Renovated high-rise
Gävle					
Blomstret	1985	37	Tenant mgmt.	Co-op	2 connected tower blocks
Karlskoga					
Solbringa	1984	86	Service	Rental	Block
Landskrona					
Yxan	1983	21	Tenant mgmt.	Rental	Renovation
Linköping					
Stolplyckan	1982	186	Service	Rental	12 connected blocks
Malmö					
Södervärn	1984	9	Tenant mgmt.	Rental	Renovation
Orebro					
Sörbyängen	1984	84	Service	Co-op	4 connected towers
Stockholm					
Rio	1983	111	Service	Rental	2 connected high-rises
Fristad	1984	133	Service	Rental	3 connected blocks
Taljan	1985	9	Tenant mgmt.	Co-op rental[1]	Tower
Prästgårdshagen	1984	31	Tenant mgmt.	Rental	Tower
Orion	1985	157	Mixed models[2]	Rental	7 towers
Kupan	1986	50	Tenant mgmt.	Co-op	2 connected towers
Katthuvudet	1986	18	Tenant mgmt.	Co-op	Tower
Trekanten	1986	78	Tenant mgmt.	Rental	Lamel bldg.[3]
Svärdet	1987	118	Tenant mgmt.	Rental	Tower
S. Station	1987	63	Tenant mgmt.	Rental	High-rise
Flygtrafiken	1987	52	Tenant mgmt.	Rental	Block complex
Vildkornet	1988	82	Tenant mgmt.	Rental	2 connected blocks
Upplands Väsby					
Prästgårdsmarken	1984	56	Mixed models	Co-op	9 small multiplex units
Uppsala					
Blenda	1983	24	Tenant mgmt.	Rental	2 connected gallery buildings[4]
Arken	1985	29	Tenant mgmt.	Rental	Renovated high-rise

[1] Tenure is a combination of cooperative and rental forms with low deposit.
[2] Each building has chosen its own form of management and maintenance, usually some form of tenant management scheme.
[3] Building type developed by Swedish Functionalists, thin and slicelike to allow light and air into apartments.
[4] The corridors connecting the apartments are outdoors.

low the new directions in social policy with a high degree of economic efficiency. Facilities provided by the various welfare agencies for the elderly could also be used by other tenants. For example, Swedish housing for the elderly is provided with a wide range of facilities, including hobby rooms, physical-therapy facilities, and food service (Lidmar 1981). Likewise, most day-care facilities have a kitchen. In Stolplyckan the community hoped to engage all tenant groups around a central set of services and thereby to improve not only the level of social care but also social life for all.

The 186-apartment project includes 35 units for the elderly (equipped with alarm buttons) and nine units adapted to the needs of the physically handicapped. The project consists of point-block towers connected by common corridors to facilitate indoor circulation and opportunities for impromptu meetings. The apartments were reduced in size from the legally regulated Swedish standard in order to provide the common facilities, which include hobby rooms, a large meeting room, a library, and gymnastic and sauna facilities (Fig. 4-1). Kitchens and dining rooms were provided by the welfare agencies mentioned above. In total some 2,000 square meters of floor space are devoted to common facilities.

Stolplyckan opened in 1979–1980 and proved inspirational for a number of subsequent large-scale projects, primarily in the Stockholm area. In Stockholm the pressure for communal housing was especially intense and coincided with a severe housing shortage for all age groups. In response, politicians in 1978 directed housing firms to convert three proposed projects for the elderly into communal projects following the Linköping model. Again the idea was to minimize the extra expense of communal services by common financing and common utilization of facilities by several target groups. Housing authorities felt that there was a financial risk involved in providing large-scale kitchen facilities in a residential project and that some of the risk could be reduced by the cooperative use of the dining area with the elderly. Politicians believed that cooperative use with younger households would prove stimulating for the elderly. However, planners did not consider the fact that most employed residents would take their meals at other times than the elderly.

Each project was to contain the full range of social services, including day care, apartments for the handicapped and elderly, and a library. Service and social integration were hallmark words in the plans for the buildings. Since the end of the 1970s, six projects in the large-scale service-integration tradition have been constructed. They range from 86 to 135 communal apartments, including some specially adapted to the needs of the handicapped and the elderly. The projects vary in degree of social integration and services, ranging from sporadic evening cafeteria service exclusively for the communal tenants to highly organized daily restaurant service for all tenants. They also display a wide range of voluntary associations, such as choirs, exercise groups, and management groups. The projects are very popular among the elderly to the extent that two have become dominated by the elderly and no longer refer to themselves as communal projects.

The Tenant-Management Model

The initiatives based on self-help and tenant management have been called "little communal houses" by Swedes. They usually are much smaller than the service-oriented projects and are the closest descendants of the work done by the women's BIG group discussed previously. The first was a renovation project in Gothenburg initiated by a professor of architecture and a Communal Housing Now group in that city. The municipal housing authorities faced difficulties when renting apartments in unpopular buildings constructed in the 1960s in outer suburbs. The Communal Housing Now group rented an entire tower block from the housing authority and renovated it as a communal project with self-management. Thus the tenants have a contract agreement with the Communal Housing Now group rather than individually with the housing authority. The project, known as Stacken (which means "ant hill" in Swedish and refers to the work capacity of the tenants), went from proposal to occupancy in less than two years, despite a radically different tenure arrangement and

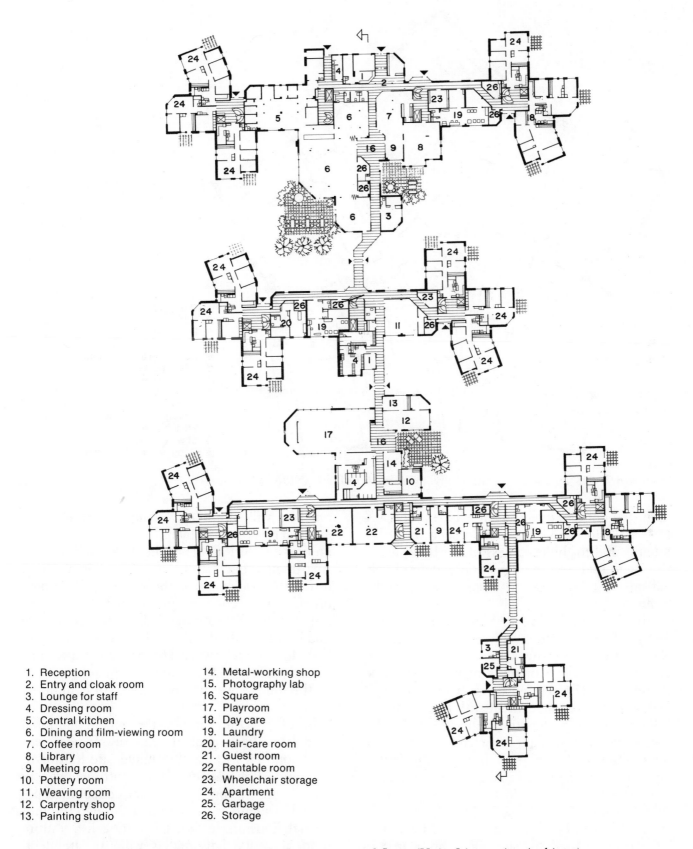

1. Reception
2. Entry and cloak room
3. Lounge for staff
4. Dressing room
5. Central kitchen
6. Dining and film-viewing room
7. Coffee room
8. Library
9. Meeting room
10. Pottery room
11. Weaving room
12. Carpentry shop
13. Painting studio
14. Metal-working shop
15. Photography lab
16. Square
17. Playroom
18. Day care
19. Laundry
20. Hair-care room
21. Guest room
22. Rentable room
23. Wheelchair storage
24. Apartment
25. Garbage
26. Storage

Figure 4-1. Stolplyckan: plan of common facilities on ground floor. *(Höjer-Ljungqvist, Architect)*

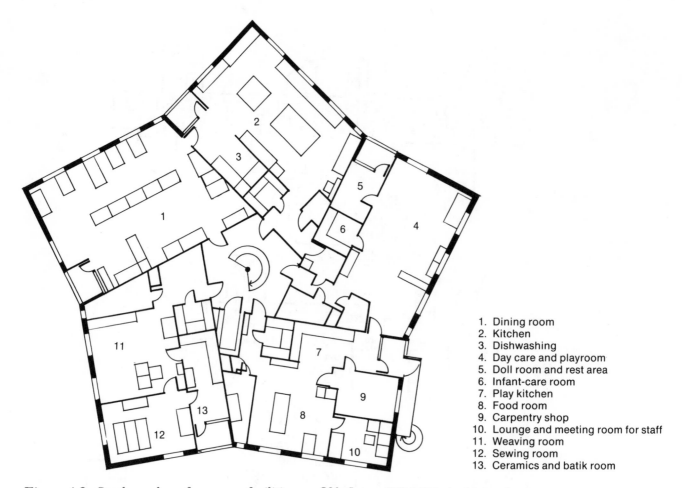

1. Dining room
2. Kitchen
3. Dishwashing
4. Day care and playroom
5. Doll room and rest area
6. Infant-care room
7. Play kitchen
8. Food room
9. Carpentry shop
10. Lounge and meeting room for staff
11. Weaving room
12. Sewing room
13. Ceramics and batik room

Figure 4-2. Stacken: plan of common facilities on fifth floor. *(NOARK, Architects.)*

management agreement (Ågren 1984). This testifies both to the organizational capacity of the tenants and to the eagerness of the housing authority to find new solutions to problems of vandalism and vacancy in their less attractive buildings.

About 50 adults live in Stacken in 34 apartments. They prepare evening meals five days a week, run a parent-owned cooperative day-care center, and carry out most maintenance tasks themselves. The residents negotiated their special management agreement with the municipal housing authority in part to achieve a higher degree of decision-making power and self-management than was then possible under the rental laws. Typical of the self-management projects is tenants' express desire to exercise control over their housing, much as owners do.

The Stacken building is a star-form tower in a suburb considered to have social problems. In part authorities hope that projects similar to

Stacken will stimulate change in other such areas. The common facilities are located on the ground and fifth floors of the building (Fig. 4-2). Apartments open onto a large staircase that forms the backbone of the building. This plan provides an open artery for circulation and communication. The dining hall is located in the middle of the building so that no one is more than four floors away. The Stacken experience was so successful that three years later a second Gothenburg tower was renovated for communal living.

In other communities the little communal model has been applied primarily in new construction. Two unusual examples are Katthuvudet and Prästgårdsmarken. Katthuvudet, in Stockholm, was built as a private cooperative; potential residents were recruited through the municipal housing authority's waiting list. Future residents worked intimately with the architect, also a cooperative member, on the design of the building. Households had far-ranging influence over the design and cost of their individual apartments. What was to be shared and how work would be accomplished were decided by the group long before moving day. In Katthuvudet there are 18 apartments. Households eat together two nights a week.

Prästgårdsmarken, outside of Stockholm, consists of nine free-standing buildings. Each building is a small commune, housing from four to six households, with varying degrees of communality from simply sharing the stairwell and laundry room to sharing all the facilities and rooms of the entire house, except bedrooms. Residents from all the buildings form one cooperative council.

By the beginning of the 1980s, it was clear that the little communal house was by far the more popular model. In Stockholm the city government instituted a special committee to investigate and coordinate the communal housing situation. This committee and politicians considered the service model an interim solution. Although the city government had originally planned three projects of the combined service model, only two were built. The third, Orion, underwent substantial modifications. Orion now consists of seven free-standing, smaller apartment buildings, each rented out to its own communal group (Larsson and Reikko 1985).

Presently there are 12 communal projects organized as little communal houses and managed by public housing firms, ranging in size from 9 to 78 apartments. In all projects of this form, tenant organizations assume some of or virtually all the management tasks, such as cleaning the stairs and halls, maintaining the grounds, and changing the light bulbs. The core of the little communal model is the food service: meals are prepared by the tenants at cost.

COMPARISON OF FOUR COMMUNAL PROJECTS

The following discussion compares residents' experiences in communal projects managed in the two dominant models—the service approach and the tenant-management approach.[1] This comparison is based on information gathered during a three-year study of public sector communal housing in middle Sweden conducted by the author in collaboration with Dick Urban Vestbro (architect) and Maj-Britt Grossman.[2] The core of the research was an in-depth evaluation of four projects. Residents completed lengthy questionnaires (90 percent of all households responded) and participated in group discussions. Central research concerns were the success of the projects in reaching goals of social integration across the generations and between handicapped and non-handicapped tenants and in promoting tenant participation in management. Additionally the research paints a portrait of the new communards, their social background and their wishes and experiences after several years of communal living. Finally, the research aimed to increase understanding of the role of the physical environment and of housing managers in promoting or deterring the communal aims of the projects.

Two Service-Integration Projects

The two projects that represent the service-integration model are Rio and Fristad. Both are located in Stockholm and were the first public housing communal projects in the region. Tenants moved in between 1983 and 1984.

Rio, with 111 communal apartments and 143 service apartments for the elderly, is located in an extremely attractive inner-city neighborhood. The service apartments are allocated through the social-welfare agencies to elderly in need of around-the-clock alarm service. Elderly without special care needs can apply for the standard apartments in the communal project. In some projects service and standard apartments are physically integrated, as in Stolplyckan. In Fristad and Rio, however, the two types of apartments are physically separated.

Fristad is larger, with 133 communal apartments and 175 service apartments for the elderly (Fig. 4-3). It is located in a suburban area with inconvenient public transportation. Rio consists of four eight- to nine-story towers; two are communal housing and two are service-supported, noncommunal housing for the elderly. Fristad contains eight buildings from four to five stories in height. Here also, one-half the project houses

Figure 4-3. Fristad: perspective. *(Svenska Bostäder, Architects)* Buildings on the left are the service housing for the elderly. Communal housing is on the right. A corridor and a central stairwell connect the communal building to the dining room placed midway between the two groups of residents.

the elderly and the other half contains the communal housing. In both Rio and Fristad, there are facilities for extended nursing care for the elderly. In both, the communal buildings and the apartments for the elderly are connected by an interior corridor, but the large size of the projects effectively separates the two ends of the project. Common facilities are located on the ground floor in both projects, with the dining room midway between the elderly and the communal apartments (Fig. 4-4).

Each project also includes a number of apartments specifically designed for the physically handicapped and allocated by the Social Welfare Board to handicapped applicants. In both, a number of facilities have been built specifically for the communards and are located on "their" side of the project. The designers' intention was that all residents would have access to these facilities, such as the library, as well as to hobby areas located adjacent to the elderly housing, which are used for therapy during the day.[3]

Both communal projects contain a wide range of apartment sizes (one to six rooms each). Rents are comparable to other recently built rental housing in Stockholm, but households are required to purchase a set number of meal coupons per month as part of their rental agreement. A restaurateur prepares meals for staff and residents. Elderly citizens in the surrounding neighborhood are entitled to eat in the restaurant at reduced prices. The restaurant also is open as a commercial facility for lunch and dinner seven days a week. In practice the different user groups patronize the restaurant at different times of the day. Elderly residents eat during the day while communal residents eat in the evening.

All communal tenants are full members of the communal project's general assembly, and all adults in the communal apartments have voting rights. Questions of management, organization, and relations with the restaurant are dealt with by the tenant governing board elected by the assembly. The service apartments are managed separately. Both projects hold monthly meetings to resolve conflicts and organizational difficulties.

Two Tenant-Managed Projects: Combining Work and Community

The second pair of projects share the philosophy of the little communal house. Blenda, located centrally in Uppsala, a university town to the north of Stockholm, opened in 1983. The project has 24 apartments in a four-story building with exterior connecting balconies. The building is located in an area of similar but noncommunal apartment buildings. The building originally was intended to contain standard apartments, but, in response to pressure for communal solutions, the public authority decided during construction to convert one building to a communal design. Prästgårdshagen, occupied in 1984, is located in an inlying Stockholm suburb. It has 32 apart-

ments and was specifically designed as communal housing with tenant-prepared meals. The building is at one corner of a quadrangle of low tower buildings. The other three buildings are service housing for the elderly, but the communal building is run independently of the rest of the quadrangle, even though the four buildings are connected by an interior corridor on the ground floor (Fig. 4-5).

Both projects include a range of apartment sizes from one to five rooms each, and in both, apartments have been reduced in size to provide common facilities. Blenda includes the most drastic reductions: Tenants in one-and two-room apartments have only a "cabinet," or pullmanlike kitchen, and showers rather than bathtubs. Larger units have a combined living/kitchen space. In Prästgårdshagen only the eating space in the kitchen was eliminated. Both have day-care facilities and a wide variety of hobby and social rooms on the ground floor (Figs. 4-6 and 4-7). On each floor in Prästgårdshagen there is a

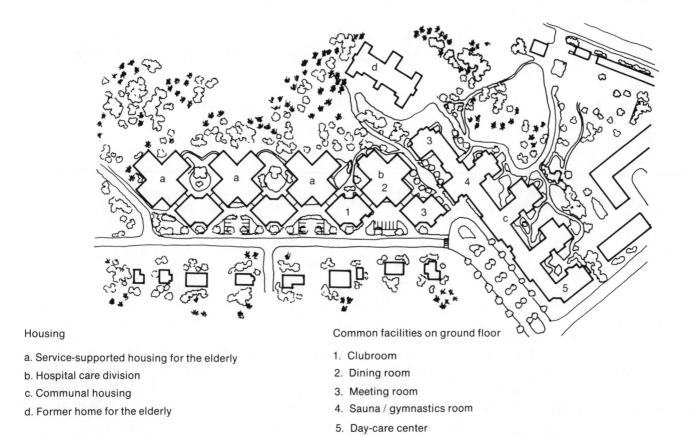

Housing	Common facilities on ground floor
a. Service-supported housing for the elderly	1. Clubroom
b. Hospital care division	2. Dining room
c. Communal housing	3. Meeting room
d. Former home for the elderly	4. Sauna / gymnastics room
	5. Day-care center

Figure 4-4. Fristad: site plan and location of common facilities on ground floor.

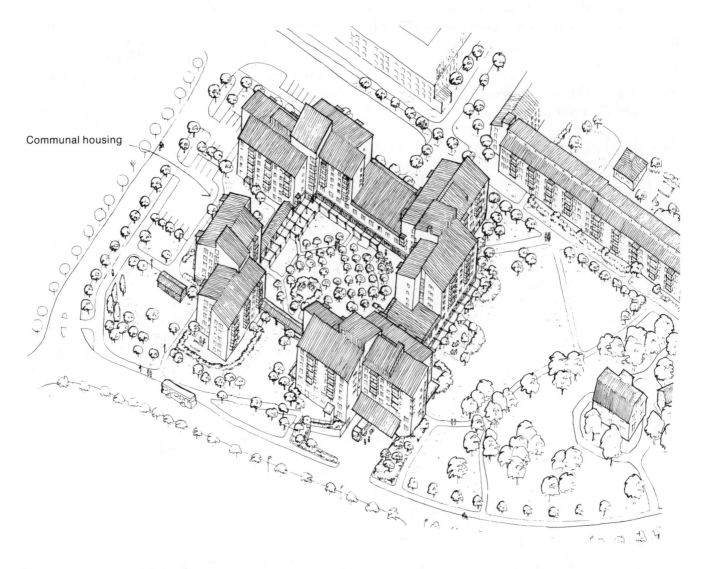

Communal housing

Figure 4-5. Prästgårdshagen: perspective. *(Courtesy of Coordinator Architects)* One building is communal housing, which is managed independently of the three buildings for the elderly.

common room furnished according to the desires of the tenants, which acts as an extension of tenant living rooms.

A major difference between the service integration projects and these two projects is the extent of tenant involvement. Here, tenants prepare meals five days a week, purchasing their own food. Tenants eat at cost, for about half the cost of the meals in the service buildings. Tenants were selected long before moving day and began planning all aspects of the communal ex-

periment two years in advance. Both groups worked with architects to design the projects. In the case of Blenda, many of the significant design decisions had already been made because the building originally was intended to house standard apartments, but an advisory group did help design some aspects of the kitchen and the common spaces.

The group in Prästgårdshagen was able to profit from the experiences of Blenda and Stacken. They obtained a better communal

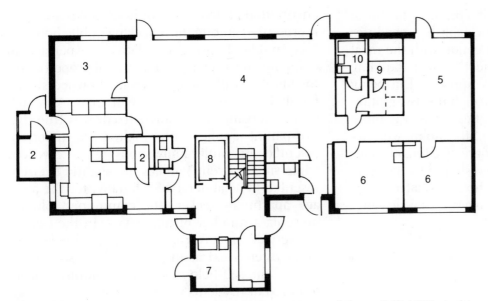

Figure 4-6. Blenda: plan of common facilities on ground floor. *(NOARK, Architects)*

1. Kitchen
2. Storage
3. Meeting room
4. Dining room
5. Day-care and TV room
6. Hobbies and day-care room
7. Garbage
8. Elevator
9. Sauna
10. Bathroom

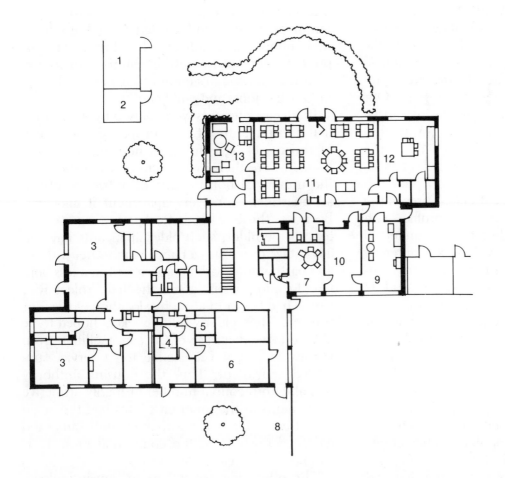

Figure 4-7. Prästgårdshagen: plan of common facilities on ground floor. *(Coordinator Architects)*

1. Bicycle storage
2. Garden shed
3. Day-care room
4. Sauna
5. Photography lab
6. Ceramics room
7. Carpentry shop
8. Covered outdoor walkway
9. Laundry
10. Playroom
11. Dining room
12. Kitchen
13. TV and coffee room

kitchen and layout of their common facilities. Both groups attempted to establish procedures for work delegation in connection with the meal service as well as in connection with building maintenance. Tenants were interested in being able to reduce their rent through the assumption of maintenance responsibilities. This was more successful for the tenants in Stockholm, who negotiated one of the most progressive tenant-management contracts in Swedish public housing today. Blenda tenants, who negotiated their agreement earlier, do not have such a wide-ranging maintenance agreement.

WHO WANTS TO LIVE IN COMMUNAL HOUSING AND WHY?

Few studies have been conducted on the social characteristics of the residents of Swedish communal housing. Caldenby and Walldén note that Stacken residents are well educated, work in the public sector, and tend to be between 25 and 45 years old. Single female parents are overrepresented (Caldenby and Walldén 1984, 94–99). Our research shows similar demographics, as can be seen in Tables 4-2 and 4-3. Households with children make up slightly more than half of the households and slightly more than half of these are one-parent households.

Table 4-3 indicates the age profile. Three of the projects have a markedly younger profile, with over 70 percent of the adult tenants under 40 years of age. Project Rio, however, has a different age profile brought about through housing allocation. In Rio 37 percent are under 40 and 22 percent are over 65 years of age. This project, given its connection with the service buildings for the elderly, is in danger of becoming an old people's enclave. (Because of its demography it shows a different profile than the other buildings; among the older respondents to our survey, the service aspect of communal housing is much more important than the social components.)

When considering the population characteristics, several factors should be kept in mind. All these projects are in rental public housing and many factors in the Swedish housing situation

ensure that certain types of households are overrepresented among those seeking public housing. New public housing is relatively expensive in comparison with either older rental properties or, for families with capital, privately owned single-family homes in outer suburban areas. Although public housing is not stigmatized, it is true that two-parent families with children are underrepresented in multifamily housing in Sweden, while single-parent families are slightly overrepresented (Thelander 1985). Finally, for the average apartment seeker, the communal solution presents a number of unknowns. In the case of the service models, the required meal ticket formula offered extra, unpredictable costs; in the case of the self-help model, the amount of work required of residents was uncertain.

Those who finally came to these four projects, therefore, cannot be expected to be a cross section of the apartment-seeking public in either Stockholm or Uppsala. Rather, they are pioneers. That there seems to be an overrepresentation of women and single-parent households may nonetheless indicate that the communal project offers an interesting solution for groups with the greatest difficulties in balancing household work, jobs, and child care.

In all cases tenants were chosen by the municipal housing authorities from special waiting lists of those seeking communal housing. In Stockholm, where there is a severe housing shortage, the municipal housing authority tries to obtain an apartment for every apartment it allocates. Because those with better-quality apartments tend to be older, such older applicants have an advantage over younger applicants either without an apartment or with an apartment in a less popular location. This factor affected Project Rio, which had the most attractive location of the four projects. Here elderly home-seekers hoped to be able to take advantage of the care facilities, even if they were not yet eligible for a service-supported apartment. Thus the housing authority was able to recoup a number of highly attractive apartments in the inner city. This had the negative effect of filling Rio with many individuals too old to contribute to the communal project, as can be seen in Table 4-3.

The other decisive factors in housing allocation were, first, the applicant's degree of interest

Table 4-2. Household Types in Four Communal Projects (%)

	Fristad	Rio	Blenda	P-hagen	All Projects
One Person	20	29	45	21	25
Couple	18	21	5	14	18
Single Parent/Child	32	24	15	34	28
Two Parents/Child	28	27	25	31	28
Other Household Type	2	0	10	0	1
Number of Households	110	97	20	29	256

Table 4-3. Age of Residents Interviewed in Four Swedish Projects (%)

	Fristad	Rio	Blenda	P-hagen	All Projects
19–35 Years	55	20	56	56	43
36–64 Years	39	58	38	44	46
Over 65	6	22	6	0	11
Number of Respondents	(161)	(135)	(32)	(41)	(369)

and commitment to communal living and, second, the applicant's ability to contribute to the demographic diversity of the project. The housing authority hoped to lessen the chance that one household type (for example, single mothers with very young children) would dominate the project.

In terms of social class the tenants in the communal projects differ significantly from other tenants in Swedish public housing. While Lindberg (1985) estimates that 67 percent of public housing tenants are situated in the working class, our figures indicate that only 28 percent of the employed tenants in these projects have working-class jobs and virtually none of them works in the more traditional blue-collar jobs, such as factory work. A striking 41 percent are employed in what Erik O. Wright (1979) calls the "semiautonomous" positions of teachers, journalists, consultants, and architects, and another 24 percent are in middle-level management or supervisory positions. In all, 69 percent are employed in the public sector. Thus the tenants in these pioneer projects are similar to what Inglehart (1977) calls the "post-materialists," those liable to vote for an alternative political party, such as the Greens, or to have been active in an alternative movement,

such as the women's movement: that is, those who prioritize social values above material ones (Woodward 1987).

Although many factors contribute to a decision to move to a new home, the most important reason given for choosing to move to these projects was their communal nature. Sixty-seven percent of the respondents gave this as their reason for moving, while other considerations—such as the proximity to work, the location, and the quality of the apartment—followed.

Respondents were asked to evaluate various aspects of their experience in the projects (after one or two years of residence). What is most striking about the results is the clear emphasis on the social aspects of the housing form. In open-ended interviews with groups of residents, the same emphasis on the social aspects of communal living was evident. Meals, which might be considered to be a material aspect of communal living, were also important, especially in the smaller projects. However, these residents stressed the social aspects of eating and preparing meals together over the material aspects of saving money or time. Community and security for children and adults received the highest ratings in all buildings.

Meals: The Heart of Communal Life

As we can see in Table 4-4, meals are very important to those living in the smaller projects; those in the larger projects seem to have mixed feelings about the role of meal service. Although the provision of meals is perhaps the biggest difference between communal and conventional housing, our observations indicate that it is not only the meals themselves but also the way they are organized and served that is important in whether communal living is successful in relieving some of the stress of everyday life.

In the service models meals have been provided by a contracted restaurateur for a fixed price. Both Fristad and Rio have experienced their most significant conflicts around the meal service.[4] In both buildings tenants have formed alternative food groups to prepare meals themselves in other locations in the building. Both organizationally and physically the service model has problems. Organizationally most meals are prepared for elderly tenants and elderly citizens in the surrounding neighborhoods. These people eat early in the day and the restaurateur has been loath to prepare fresh meals for the communards who eat later. Physically the dining rooms are planned to seat nearly 200 people. With the self-service cafeteria-style setup, the dining areas have a cool, modern restaurant atmosphere rather than the warm, bistrolike ambience that many communards desire. Specifically, tenants complained about the lack of influence over decisions; the quality of the food; the injustice of the coupon system; and the physical problems with the dining room (for example, no specific area for the communal dwellers and inappropriate furniture for larger groups wishing to eat together) (Fig. 4-8).

Tenants are not integrated into the decision-making process concerning food service and have had to fight to be included on the committee of social workers and elderly tenants that meets regularly with the contractor to discuss food quality. Problems, such as offering alternative meals for vegetarians, have been difficult to resolve. Combining the meal service for the elderly and for the communal housing residents has led to irritation. The major client is the social-welfare office and the food service plans meals primarily for older people in terms of spicing, portions, and preparation. The communal residents have different food preferences. In effect the older people dominate, and this shows in the menu. The problem spills over into the atmosphere in the dining rooms. Only one-third of the residents in both projects find the atmosphere in the dining rooms even relatively pleasant. Communal residents complain that because the restaurant is open to outsiders, they never really feel that the dining room is their own. Some feel it is like eating in a nursing home. This feeling is intensified by the design of the dining rooms which, while containing well-designed furniture, nonetheless have an institutional atmosphere because of their scale.

Instead of promoting integration across the generations, the predominance of the elderly seems to have created conflict. In Rio the communal residents have succeeded in reserving a place in the dining room for the communards for specific hours in the week. In Fristad the tenants have renegotiated the coupon arrangement, acquired different furniture, and worked out a better communication system with the restaurant owner. However, the protracted conflicts have led a number of tenants to avoid the dining room and to use their meal tickets to purchase food portions for their freezer. This still eases every-

Table 4-4. Aspects of Housing Rated as Important or Very Important (% of respondents)

	Blenda	Prästgårds hagen	Fristad	Rio
Social Aspects				
Community	86	83	85	77
Community for children	80	93	83	80
Security	80	76	86	79
Meals	81	90	48	53
Physical Facilities				
Social rooms	93	85	74	65
Hobby rooms	78	80	70	63
Sauna	40	56	52	47
Material Aspects				
Potential to lower rent	15	88	80	78
Potential to lower food costs	28	61	66	68

Figure 4-9. Blenda: dining room. *(Photo: Dick Urban Vestbro)* Tenants participated in the design of the dining area and furnished it themselves. The wall textile depicts the helping hands of all Blenda residents.

day tasks, but for many families eating meals together has become an unpleasant duty rather than a pleasure. Nonetheless the majority of tenants in both projects do not wish to convert to a self-help food system. They are still interested in a service model and see its value as an alternative. What they want is a system that is more responsive to their needs and more sensitive to their eating habits.

The atmosphere in the dining rooms of Blenda (Fig. 4-9) and Prästgårdshagen contrasts dramatically with the more formal restaurant atmosphere of Rio and Fristad. Children and adults press around large refectory tables and, especially at the beginning of the dinner hour, the atmosphere is noisy and intense as people talk about the experiences of the day and try to persuade their children to settle down and eat. Later the children troop off to the nearby playrooms while the adults settle down for coffee and dessert. Some drift over to the TV room to watch the evening news while one or two from the evening cleanup crew begin to collect plates. Residents in the smaller projects prepare meals five days a

Figure 4-8. Fristad: restaurant. *(Photo: Dick Urban Vestbro)* Tables separate families from each other. Tenants agitated for larger tables so they could eat together.

week throughout the school year for 20 to 70 diners, depending on the number of advance reservations. Meals are simple and economical, with a focus on recipes that can be prepared by inexperienced cooks in less than two hours. Purchasing and meal planning are done by an elected crew who thereby are excused from meal preparation.

All adults are required to help with meals regularly. Setting up a system with amateur cooks has not been problem-free, but the pride residents feel in their achievement neutralizes the various economic and organizational problems they have faced. The most serious issue, which has begun to surface after a few years of experience, is project size. Because the project is small it has the advantage of limiting the number of meals that have to be prepared, but it also limits the number of hands available to prepare meals. With a high percentage of one-parent households, both projects have occasionally experienced a shortage of people to prepare dinner, and both have discussed the frequency of shared meals. Although our survey showed that over 66 percent of Blenda respondents and 87 percent of Prästgårdshagen respondents reported eating from three to five times a week in the dining hall, this frequency has often dropped lower. Residents in these projects experience meals as the heart of the collective experience, but in group interviews and in observations some problems did surface. Some parents feel that the children need a chance to calm down at home and that life in the dining room is just an extension of the public life at the day-care center or school. They prefer to eat at home occasionally, just to enjoy each other's company, or to be sure the children get enough to eat without distractions.

In discussions, in observations, and in response to our questionnaire, it seems that the social advantages of eating together and the material advantages in terms of simplified everyday life are equally valued among residents in all four projects. A large number of residents in both models (from 48 percent in Fristad to 90 percent in Prästgårdshagen) emphasize the social importance of the common dining room. Residents have realized their vision of both easing and enriching the everyday with a reliable source of prepared meals. As one female teacher in Blenda expressed it:

> The dining room is the heart of the house and therefore enormously important. Even though I am not able to eat there regularly, I do my turn at work willingly. . . .

Social Integration and Sense of Community

Communal living aims not only to ease the stress of everyday life materially but also to improve its social quality. Above all, those coming to live in these four projects hoped that the quality of their own and their children's social lives would improve. Eighty to 93 percent of the respondents described social opportunities for children (including new playmates and increased contact with nonrelated adults) as one of the most important aspects of their life in communal buildings while 77 to 86 percent rated community and companionship for themselves as vital in their new life as communards (see Table 4-4). In one of the smaller projects, a single mother related the following:

> My expectations were that it would be different than living in a normal apartment building, with more companionship, but I think you need something to gather around to get this community, something you are doing together.

In Fristad many agreed with this woman:

> I wanted to try another way of living and come to live closer to other people even during the working week. I was looking for community and companionship. I don't think people should live alone.

In all the projects except Rio, more than half of the respondents feel they have met people who are different from their earlier acquaintances and that their social life has changed significantly since moving to the project. People mentioned having more contact with others from different ethnic backgrounds, different age groups, and different social classes. Socially some found they had more time for informal socializing or that they were seeing more of their new acquaintances than of those people whom they knew before moving in.

Women were more aware of the change than men perhaps because, as our observations showed, they feel freer to leave their children unattended in the corridors of the building than they did in their previous living arrangements and they have more opportunity for spontaneous contacts with their neighbors. Many commented on the atmosphere in the corridors, where everyone greets everyone else, something that seldom occurs in conventional Swedish multifamily housing. For women this is important; they feel more secure in the knowledge that they know their neighbors. A single woman noted,

> You're never afraid here. If you meet someone, it's someone you know . . . but even if you don't know them, you say hello here. It gives you a feeling of security.

The chores in the smaller buildings give residents repeated opportunities for getting to know each other. Fristad also has some common maintenance tasks. This resident engagement in the project may help explain the similarity between the social atmosphere in Fristad and the smaller projects. Rio, however, where residents share no common tasks except house meetings, has experienced extreme conflicts about the direction and nature of the project. Residents complain about anonymity or animosity. At this stage the planners' and politicians' belief that shared work tasks build social community and trust seems justified. Through sharing of some of the tasks of daily life, a more diverse social life develops than in standard multifamily living.

In describing the best aspects of living in communal housing, the largest proportion of answers referred to aspects of community, neighboring, and the nice people in the buildings. This kind of answer ranged from one-third of the answers in the larger projects to one-half in the smaller. Concerning the worst aspects of communal living, there was less agreement. Residents in the larger buildings criticized aspects of the meal service; residents in the smaller buildings focused on specific details, such as the organization of the parent-run day-care center in Blenda or the recruiting of new communal members. The only aspect perceived as a problem at all four projects was the rent—92 percent found it too high. The expense of living in communal housing was one of the main reasons given for those who were considering moving, even though communal living is not more expensive than any other newly produced multifamily housing. Overall these pioneers feel quite positively about the experiments. Despite criticism of the rents, there is

lower residential mobility in buildings with communal structures than in other new housing (Stockholms Stads 1986, 3).

DESIGN ISSUES IN COMMUNAL PROJECTS

Recent Swedish communal projects, whether of the service or the tenant-management model and regardless of tenure form, pose a number of architectural problems. The projects have specific social aims that demand a different physical setting from that of traditional multifamily living. As the Stockholm Municipal Council expresses it, communal residences should "increase social contacts between people and stimulate community at the same time as the private household is eased from some of the practical tasks in the home" (Stockholms Kommuns 1983, 1). Yet these social aims must be met within financial constraints.

One of the first bargains struck is to trade a certain amount of private floor space for space in common facilities. The architectural discussion in Sweden has primarily been about where this subtraction can best be accomplished. Some argue that kitchens can be smaller because main meals will be eaten in the common facilities. This was the typical solution in the very first communal projects in Sweden in the 1920s, which were intended to end the drudgery of kitchen work for women. In these projects meals were prepared in common kitchens and could be transported to the private apartment or consumed in the common dining room. A number of new projects also reduce the size of private kitchens. The argument against a substantial reduction of private food-preparation space is that in the majority of projects thus far, group meals are provided only in the evenings during the work week. For families with young children, the reduced kitchen space can sometimes cause problems as many mothers prefer to keep the mess of children's snacks and meals in the kitchen and often combine child-minding with the preparation of meals.

Other solutions have been to reduce the size of the living rooms or bedrooms. The argument for reduction in private space is that in communal living, recreation and free-time activities usually pursued in the private domain can be shared. The communal projects have TV rooms, hobby rooms, game rooms, library space, and other facilities for activities usually carried out in the private home. Those arguing for more communal projects often claim that one of the reasons that public life and community life have stagnated in modern multifamily housing is the relative lack of gathering places outside the home.

In the Stockholm area, where public authorities have been following communal projects closely, between 4 and 14 square meters of floor space per apartment are set aside for communal facilities. Not all projects have compensated for the extra facilities by reducing private apartments. Some of the builders prefer to maintain a certain flexibility by producing standard-size apartments and communal space that can be converted to apartments in the event that the communal experiment fails. Generally, however, a rule of thumb has been the reduction of between 5 and 10 percent in private floor space (Stockholms Kommuns 1983, 25).

Closely related questions are what the functions of these common facilities should be and who should decide their function. Architects involved in the design of the projects have sometimes been able to work with prospective tenant groups in the predesign phase. Tenants enter the design process at different stages. In Katthuvudet tenants determined with the architect virtually every design decision. In the two large service-integration models in Stockholm, tenants influenced only minor decorative features and furniture for common rooms. Generally the smaller the project, the greater the degree of tenant participation in design. Architects interviewed in this research were almost universally enthusiastic about the tenant collaboration, even though—as is often the case in user participation on multifamily projects—those who eventually were able to move into the project were not always those who had been involved in design decisions.

Importantly, when tenants have been preselected for projects, the opportunity to participate in the design process also has stimulated their thinking about the nature and goals of the communal arrangements. To provide information for

the architect, they need to decide how many meals a week they will be preparing, for what size groups, and in what kind of atmosphere. Do they want to spend money on the installation of a photography studio, or do they prefer to keep their hobby space flexible? What facilities should there be for teenagers? How will the maintenance and cleaning of the building be handled? These and other questions are addressed by tenant groups in preoccupancy collaboration with the housing firm and the architect. Interestingly, in the projects we reviewed, the more extensive the preoccupancy collaborations, the more management tasks residents have been willing to assume. Preoccupancy participation seems to stimulate tenants to assume management tasks and strengthens their feelings of self-confidence in dealing with housing management. However, this also may result from the smaller size of these projects.

Once tenants or management have decided on the goals of communal living, design decisions can be made to further these aims. Unfortunately, experience with design of alternative housing forms is very limited and there is little documentation. It is only now that architects can begin to study the record on such concerns as kitchens and circulation space.

Kitchen and Dining areas

Designing a kitchen to be used by amateur cooks preparing meals for 20 to 80 people is a very different design problem than designing an institutional kitchen. In the communal kitchen children and other tenants can be expected to come in and out during meal preparation, meaning that extra space is needed for social interaction and for extra helping hands. Another difference is in storage requirements. Some projects hope to achieve food economy through wholesale purchasing or use of biodynamic or home-grown produce and need storage areas to suit these goals. The issue of cleanliness also presents difficulties. How does one best provide an easy-to-clean meal center and still retain a homey atmosphere?

For all the communal projects an important, if not the major, design concern has been the creation of a functional yet warm heart for the project, centering on the dining and food-preparation areas (Fig. 4-10). Even in the projects using employed restaurant personnel, the tenants hoped to find a welcoming atmosphere in the dining areas. However, experience in creating a noninstitutional atmosphere for this sort of living form is difficult. All architects involved in these projects faced problems.[5] Those designing a kitchen to be shared between a social-care facility and tenants were constrained by legal regulations for institutional kitchens, for example. Stainless steel, because of its superiority in terms of hygiene, is the dominant material in sinks and surfaces but creates a cool and sterile impression. Architects and residents have attempted to compensate for an institutional atmosphere through choice of colors and use of wood in tables and kitchen furniture. Smaller projects, such as Orion and Katthuvudet, have installed kitchens closely mirroring private domestic kitchens in material and form, yet this too is not an ideal solution when one hopes to encourage group preparation of meals.

Figure 4-10. Prästgårdshagen: kitchen. *(Photo: Dick Urban Vestbro)* Two residents clean up after an evening meal.

Circulation Spaces

A second, perhaps less explicitly expressed need in these projects is the furthering of social contact in circulation spaces, such as halls. Earlier experience with communal projects in Sweden underlined the importance of interesting and well-designed corridors to encourage spontaneous interaction among tenants on their way in and out of the buildings (Blomberg et al. 1986; Vestbro 1982). Varied corridor widths and materials and the positioning of furniture groupings near circulation nodes seem to create socially successful semiprivate spaces (Fig. 4-11).

As the facilities were meant to serve all tenants, an important concern was accessibility for the handicapped to the various common areas and provision of play and interaction space for children within the surveillance radius of adults. Again, these aspects of communal living have been respected in varying degrees in the diverse attempts. Some plans, such as those with broad central stairs and welcoming spacious entrances, seem definitely more encouraging of sponta-

Figure 4-11. Fristad: entry hall. *(Photo: Dick Urban Vestbro)* The hall offers a buffer zone between the cold outdoors and the communal spaces. Tenants meet incoming residents when they pass by here on their way to dinner or to hobby rooms.

neous, unplanned interaction than others. But like most architectural-social equations, a number of different factors, including tenant organization and project size, interact to produce these circumstances.

Evaluation of Design and Space

With the many different types of residents in these buildings, there are various opinions about design. The elderly and those residents involved in maintenance are much less enthusiastic than parents or children about long, unbroken connecting corridors between buildings, which are used actively by children on scooters and roller skates. Where common facilities, such as the day-care center or hobby rooms, are used by two or more user groups at different times of the day, organizational problems have arisen concerning access and security for hobby materials. Day-care personnel have complained that residents do not clean up; residents worry that their equipment may be damaged by children. More storage space that can be secured against theft seems to be an unanticipated need. Highly flexible common facilities are most appropriate; as tenant groups change, new hobbies may replace old. Rooms that can be divided easily to separate smokers from nonsmokers or to provide small gathering places are heavily used where they exist and desired where they do not. Reaction to the reduced size of the private kitchen depends on household composition and the extent the family is integrated into the communal project. A family that chooses to eat most of the evening meals at home may feel more frustrated by the reduced kitchen.

In the projects presented here, the design scorecard is not yet in. A preliminary conclusion is that in the projects where tenants have partici-

pated in design decisions, satisfaction with the results is higher as tenants have been able to inform architects about their anticipated needs and about a lifestyle very different from traditional multifamily living.

CONCLUSIONS

Sweden probably now has the most varied experiences in providing alternative forms of multifamily housing in the public sector. The experience has not been free of conflict. Both among residents and between residents and the various bureaucracies involved in managing the projects, there have been lively and at times di-

Figure 4-12. Prästgårdshagen: entry to communal housing. *(Photo: Dick Urban Vestbro)* The day-care center is adjacent to the main entrance and other common rooms. Children are integrated into the daily activities of the building.

visive discussions about everything from tenant democracy to vegetarian meals (Woodward et al. 1988). There are still a number of problems to be resolved if communal living is to become an alternative not only for the informed minority but also for a wider public.

Important lessons have been learned about the design of facilities for common use—such as kitchens, corridors, and dining rooms—and about the potential for rehabilitating older buildings for new housing forms. In trying different types of housing, the Swedes have had the chance to test questions of scale and management and to offer alternatives for different kinds of communal living. But questions remain. The issue of size is still unsettled. The service-integration model has had a number of problems that are perhaps as much a matter of organizational form and demographic imbalance as of scale. The large-scale projects do have the advantage of resources in the form of people. Rio has a choir and Fristad has a football team, and the two projects have greater potential to organize courses and trips. The smaller projects enjoy the advantages of intimacy but are hard pressed at times to find three people to prepare a meal. Small scale provides an opportunity for everyone to know everyone else, but the familiarity that lends security can also lead to conflict.

The Swedish communal housing experiments combining sufficient private space for independent living and substantial common facilities, including an affordable dining alternative, seem to provide a very attractive answer to the problems of many modern households. The one-person household, which is the most predominant household type in Sweden, obtains an expanded social network without a lot of effort. Families with children get help with daily problems such as day care (Fig. 4-12), babysitting, and meal preparation, and they find easy opportunities for meeting other adults in unconstrained circumstances. The elderly and the handicapped become members of a wider community that includes people from all generations. The projects presented here have come a long way toward realizing an old dream of the Swedish women's movement and a new dream for an increasing number of families: a better social life combined with simpler, easier living every day.

NOTES

1. Other authors have evaluated residents' experiences in one of the oldest communal projects in Sweden after tenant takeover of the food service in 1977 (Blomberg et al. 1986) and in the first self-management commune, Stacken (Caldenby and Walldén 1984).
2. The research was supported by the Royal Institute of Technology, Department of Building Function Analysis, and the Swedish Building Research Council. It is presented in full in Woodward, Vestbro, and Grossman (1988).
3. The different agencies involved in planning these projects were not always in agreement about usage of common facilities. Thus, for instance, the Social Welfare authority that manages the facilities for the elderly had not planned on sharing certain hobby facilities with the wider group of tenants from the communal apartments. Similarly, the Social Welfare authorities argued that most facilities should be placed closest to the housing for the elderly because of their lower physical capacity. The organizational difficulties in designing for common use are treated more fully in Woodward, Vestbro, and Grossman (1988).
4. In an internal survey in Rio (with a response rate of over 90 percent), 89 percent of the respondents found that the dining room was not working as the heart of the building and 80 percent felt that the food was not sufficiently good and nourishing for its price (house newspaper *Karnevalen*, Oct. 1984:1).
5. Interior designer Gunilla Lauters has collected architectural examples of communal kitchens in her research and provides suggestions in a guidebook to communal living and design (Lauters 1982).

References

Ågren, L. 1984. *Kollektivhuset Stacken*. Gothenburg: CTH-Architecture Department/Korpen.
———(ed.). 1981. *Bogemenskap. En seminarserie om kollektivt boende.* (R35). Stockholm: Swedish Council for Building Research.
Åkerman, B., et al. (ed.). 1983. *Den okända vardagen —om arbetet i hemmen*. Stockholm: Akademilitteratur.
———, et al. 1975. *Service och gemenskap där vi bor i Stockholm*. Stockholm: Tiden.
Arkitektur. 1985. Theme issue on collective/communal housing. *Arkitektur* 85:3–30.
BIG-gruppen. 1982. *Det lilla kollektivhuset: En modell för praktisk tillämpning* (T14). Stockholm:

Swedish Council for Building Research.

Blomberg, I., I. Goodridge, B. Olsson, G. Wiklund, and P. Wistén. 1986. *Levande kollektivhus: Att leva, bo och arbeta i Hässelby familjehotell* (R19). Stockholm: Swedish Council for Building Research.

Boalt, C. 1983. Tid för hemarbete. Hur lång tid då? In *Den okända vardagen—om arbetet i hemmen*, ed. B. Åkerman et al., 39–69. Stockholm: Akademilitteratur.

Byggforskningsrådet. 1985. *Forskare om förvaltning och förnyelse* (T7). Stockholm: Swedish Council for Building Research.

Caldenby, C., and Å. Walldén. 1979. *Kollektivhus: Soviet och Sverige omkring 1930*. Stockholm: Swedish Council for Building Research.

———. 1984. *Kollektivhus Stacken*. Gothenburg: Korpen.

Cronberg, T. 1986. Tenants' involvement in the management of social housing in the nordic countries. *Scandinavian Housing and Planning Research* 3:65–87.

———, et al. (ed.). 1979. *Bygge och bo på kvinners vilkår. Rapport fra en konferanse i Kungälv 4–6 mai 1979*. Copenhagen: Nordiske kvinners bygge—og planforum [Nordic Women's Building and Planning Forum].

Gromark, S. 1983. *Boendegemenskap: En kritisk granskning av boendegemenskap som samhällsangelägenhet, av dess värden, villkor och forutsättningar*. Gothenburg: CTH Architecture Department, Institute for Building Planning.

Grossman, M. B., and D. U. Vestbro. 1982. *Aktuella kollektiva bostadsprojekt*. Stockholm: Royal College of Technology, Building Function Analysis.

Hayden, D. 1981. *The Grand Domestic Revolution: A History of Feminist Designs for American Homes, Neighborhoods and Cities*. Cambridge: MIT Press.

———. 1984. *Redesigning the American Dream: The Future of Housing, Work and Family Life*. New York: Norton.

Inglehart, R. 1977. *The Silent Revolution: Changing Values and Political Styles among Western Publics*. Princeton: Princeton University Press.

Jonsson, B. 1983. *Alternative rörelse och samhällsutveckling i Sverige*. Academic dissertation. Uppsala, Sweden: Uppsala University, Department of Sociology.

Kemeny, J. 1981. *The Myth of Home Ownership*. London: Routledge and Kegan Paul.

Kollektivhuset Rio. *Karnevalen* 1984–1986.

Lagergren, M., L. Lundh, M. Orkan, and C. Sanne. 1982. *Tid för omsorg*. Stockholm: Liber.

Larsson, M., and L. Reikko. 1985. Orion: En uppsats om kollektivhus. [Essay in community planning, May.] Stockholm: University of Stockholm, College of Social Welfare.

Lauters, G., 1982. *Kollektivets Bostad*. Stockholm: Litteratur and Föreningstjänst.

Lidmar, K. 1981. *Från ålderdomshem tillservicehus—ett historiskt perspektiv*. Stockholm: Social Welfare Board Care for the Elderly Program.

Lindberg, G. 1985. Ekonomi, organisation och kooperation i kooperative bostadsförvaltning in Byggforskningsrådet. *Forskare om förvaltning och förnyelse* (T7). Stockholm: Swedish Council for Building Research, 63–84.

Palm-Lindén, K. 1982. *Att Bo i Storfamilj* (Rapport R2). Lund: University of Lund, Architecture, Building Function Analysis.

Pearson, L. 1988. *The Architectural and Social History of Cooperative Living*. London: Macmillan.

Pedersen, B. 1981. *Stolplyckan: Kommunalt kollektivhus i Linköping*. (Unpublished working paper.) Lund: University of Lund, Architecture, Building Function Analysis.

Ruggie, M. 1984. *The State and Working Women: A Comparative Study of Britain and Sweden*. Princeton: Princeton University Press.

Sollbe, B. (ed.). 1982. *Bo Kollektiv—erfarenheter och visioner* (M82:20). Gävle: Swedish Institute for Building Research.

Stockholms Kommuns Kollektivhuskommitté. 1983. Kollektivboende i Stockholm—Slutrapport från kollektivhuskommittén. (Feb.) Stockholm: City of Stockholm.

Stockholms Stads uppföljningsgrupp för kollektivhus. 1986. *Om kollektivhusen i Stockholm*. Lägesrapport nr 2 maj. Stockholm: City of Stockholm.

Thelander. A. L. 1985. Den svenska bostadssituationen. Förändringar och utvecklingsmönster. In *Forskare om förvaltning och förnyelse*, Byggforskningsrådet, 15–36. Stockholm: Swedish Council for Building Research.

Vestbro, D. U. 1982. *Kollektivhus fran enkökshus till bogemenskap*. Stockholm: Swedish Council for Building Research.

Woodward, A. 1987. Public housing communes: Swedish response to post-material demands. In *Housing and Neighborhoods*, ed. W. van Vliet et al., 215–238. Westport, CT: Greenwood Press.

———, Dick Urban Vestbro, and Maj. Britt Grossman. 1988. *Det nya kollektivhuset*. (Working papers from the Department of Building Function Analysis.) Stockholm: Royal College of Technology.

Wright, E. O. 1978. *Class, Crisis and the State*. London: New Left Books.

Chapter **5**

Cohousing in Denmark

Kathryn M. McCamant
Charles R. Durrett

In Denmark people have developed a new housing type that redefines the concept of neighborhood to fit contemporary lifestyles. Tired of the isolation and impracticality of conventional single-family houses and apartment units, they have built housing that combines the autonomy of private dwellings with the advantages of community living. This concept is called *bofællesskab* in Danish, and we have termed it *cohousing*. The developments vary in size, financing method, and ownership structure but share a consistent idea about how people can cooperate in a residential environment to create a stronger sense of community and to share common facilities.

Each household has a private residence and shares extensive common facilities with the larger community (Fig. 5-1). The common facilities typically include a kitchen and a dining room where dinners are served two to seven nights a week; children's playrooms, which also may house organized child-care and after-school programs; workshops; a meeting/living room; and laundry facilities. Although individual dwelling units are designed to function self-sufficiently and include their own kitchens, the common facilities, and particularly common dinners, are an important aspect of community life.

In this chapter we examine what has made cohousing successful, present design guidelines, and suggest how to apply the concept in the United States. Our research is primarily based on information gathered in 1984 and 1985, when we spent more than a year studying cohousing in Denmark, Sweden, and the Netherlands.[1] During that time we visited or lived in 46 projects and interviewed residents, architects, bankers, attorneys, and government officials. We also worked directly with the Danish Building Research Institute and Royal Academy of Art and Architecture in Copenhagen. By far the most valuable part of all our work was living in cohousing and personally experiencing day-to-day life in these communities.

This chapter focuses on Danish examples because we believe that they are the most applicable to the American context. In addition the concept was first pioneered in Denmark and the largest number of cohousing developments are located there. The Dutch *centraal wonen* are similar in concept.[2] The Swedish *kollektivhus*, or "housing with services," differs in that it is usually developed by housing professionals or local authorities, resulting in a more institutional solution (Andersen 1985). The Danes also have built *kollektivhuser* but have done little with this model since the 1950s. (For more information about the Swedish examples, see chapter 4.)

Figure 5-1. Trudeslund. This cohousing community is comprised of 33 privately owned row houses and a large common house (*upper center*). Although the houses were built at the same density as single-family houses in the area (*upper right*), residents chose to cluster the dwellings along two pedestrian streets, to localize parking, and to preserve the wooded portion of the site.

Cohousing is a grassroots movement that began in the early 1970s and grew directly out of people's dissatisfaction with existing housing choices. Although the concept has gained the support of the government, it was first initiated by the residents themselves. Based on democratic principles the communities espouse no ideology other than the desire for a more convenient and more sociable home environment. Unlike other housing innovations that target specific populations, cohousing integrates different types of households and age groups. In Denmark today cohousing is an accepted, mainstream housing alternative.

By the spring of 1988, 67 cohousing communities had been built in Denmark (Table 5-1) and another 38 were being planned. Almost 70 percent of these were built between 1982 and 1987.[3] Existing communities range in size from 6 to 80 households, with the majority being between 15 and 33 units.[4] Most are clustered housing developments, although five are detached single-family houses. The majority are located just outside metropolitan areas where sites are affordable and still within half-an-hour's drive to workplaces, schools, and the other attractions of urban centers. Generally cohousing is new construction because of the difficulties inherent in creating

Table 5-1. Danish Cohousing and Common Facilities[1]

COMMUNITY	YEAR BUILT	# OF UNITS	TENURE[2]	SIZE OF COMMON HOUSE (s.f.)	COMMON AREA PER UNIT (s.f.)	MEALS/WEEK[3]	LIVING ROOM	LAUNDRY	CHILDREN'S RMS[4]	CHILD CARE	TEEN/MUSIC RMS	WORKSHOP(S)[5]	STORE OR FOOD CLUB	GUEST/RENTAL ROOM	SITE PLAN (E)=Existing CH=Common House
1 Sættedammen	1972	27	Private (P)	3,010	112	6d	X	X	X	X		2	X	2	2 Courtyards
2 Skråplanet	1973	33	P	3,770	114	5d	X	X	X	X	1				Semi-detached terraced houses
3 Nonbo Hede	1974-76	15	P	3,530	235	3	X	X	X		2		4	2	2 Clusters
4 Gyldenmuld	1976	12	P	3,900	325	5	X	X		X	1	1	2		Cluster
5 Gyndbjerg	"	14	P	2,150	154	4	X	X	X	X	1	1			Street/CH in (E) farm house
6 Drejerbanken	1978	20	P & Rental	5,110	226	7	X	X	X	X	2	2		2	2 Courtyards
7 Tinggården	"	79	Rental	9,680	122	0-2	X	X	X	X	4		16		6 clusters w/seperate CH's
8 Tørnevangsgård	"	6	P	2,040	340	2	X	X		X	1		1		Courtyard /CH in (E) bldg.
9 Jerngården	"	8	P	2,010	251	7	X	X	X		2				Renovated rowhouses
10 Æblevangen	1979	36	P	6,460	179	6	X	X	X	X	3			4	4 courtyards
11 Mejdal I	"	12	P	2,150	179	3	X	X	X		1				Clustered detached single family houses
12 Stavnsbåndet	"	26	P	5,170	199	4+	X	X	X	X	1	1	1	1	2 courtyards
13 Bakken	1980	25	P	5,800	232	5	X	X	X	X	2		3		Street / 3 rentals in (E) bldg.
14 Bofælleden	"	8	Private Coop.	?	?	7	X	X			1				Reused school bldg.
15 Faldengrund	"	12	P	3,860	322	5	X	X	X		2	X	3		Detached single family houses
16 Frugthaven	"	12	P	2,480	207	4	X	X	X		1		1		4 clusters
17 Gug	"	22	P	4,520	205	7	X	X	X		2		6		Rowhouses
18 Overdrevet	"	25	P	6,840	274	7	X	X	X		2	X	1	2	2 courtyards
19 Sol & Vind	"	27	P	5,920	219	7	X	X	X		2	X	1	1	Streets & courts/50% detached houses
20 Vildrosen	"	12	P	4,306	359	5	X	X	X	X	3	X	1	1	3 courtyards /detached houses
21 Jernstøberiet	1981	21	P	3,230	154	5	X	X		X	1	X			Reuse of factory bldg. /interior court
22 Kolbøtten	"	6	P	1,185	197	1	X	X	X		1				Units & CH attached
23 Trudeslund	"	33	P	8,610	261	7	X	X	X	X	2	X	1		Street
24 Bondebjerget	1982-83	80	Rental	15,500	194	3-7	X	X	X		8	X	4		4 clusters w/seperate CH's
25 Drivhuset	1983	18	Cooperative	2,530	140	5	X	X	X	X	2	X	2	4	Glass covered street
26 Grønmosegård	"	7	P	3,230	461	4	X	X			1			1	Rowhouses w/ CH in (E) farm house
27 Ibsgården	"	21	Cooperative	3,730	178	7	X	X	X		1	X			Courtyard w/ CH in (E) farm house
28 Norgårds Plantage	"	24	Cooperative	1,185	49	7	X	X	X		1				Streets w/carport next to each home
29 Uldalen	"	18	Cooperative	2,700	150	5	X	X	X		1			3	Rowhouses
30 Vejgård Bymidte	"	40	P	1,350	34	5	X	X							Reuse of factory bldgs. + new rowhouses
31 Abakken	1984	15	Cooperative	4,430	295	3	X	X	X		1		5		Courtyard
32 Andedammen	"	18	Cooperative	3,000	167	7	X	X	X	X	1	X	1		Rowhouses w/ CH in (E) bldg.
33 Askebakken	"	17	Cooperative	2,820	166	5	X	X	X		2		2		Rowhouses
34 Savværket	"	21	Cooperative	4,310	205	7	X	X	X		3	X	4		Glass covered street
35 Blåhøjen	1985	25	Cooperative	5,920	237	7	X	X	X		2	X	2	3	3 Courtyards
36 Håndværkerparken	"	32	Rental	5,670	177	5	X	X	X		1		2		Glass covered street
37 Mejdal II	"	14	P	1,600	114	?	X	X	X		1		1		Clustered detached single family houses
38 Thorshammar I	1986	20	Cooperative	3,230	162	7	X	X	X	X	3		4		Courtyard w/glass covered walkway

X Includes at least one such facility.

1 Subset of total of 46 cohousing communities studied by the authors in 1984/85. All have common kitchens and dining rooms, and many have additional facilities not shown here. Covered street space and out buildings are not included in size.

2 Private refers to forms of ownership similar to condominums. Cooperatives use government-sponsored financing which limits members' equity. Rentals are owned by private, non-profit housing developers.

3 "d" represents weekly dinner clubs in which residents typically participate once or twice a week, although dinners are available five to six times a week.

4 Child care is readily available in Denmark and therefore not a high priority in cohousing. Danish communities often organize programs when they have a group of similar age kids and switch to other facilities when there is less need. Both past and current programs have been included.

5 Includes wood working, bicycle repair, auto repair, photographic dark rooms, sewing, and craft work spaces.

Figure 5-2. Bondebjerget. *(Faellestegnestuen, Architects)* Children play in front of one of the four common houses, each of which has a kitchen/dining room, a living room, a children's playroom, a workshop, and a craft room. The 80 units are rentals owned by a local nonprofit housing developer, but the complex was initiated and planned and is now managed by the residents.

the desired relationships between spaces in existing buildings. Nevertheless two communities—Jernstøberiet, built in 1981, and Vejgård Bymidte, built in 1983—adapted old factory buildings (see figs. 5-18 and 5-19) and another—Bofælleden—adapted a school building. Jerngården residents renovated nine deteriorated row houses in 1978 to create a charming community in the inner city of Aarhus. Residents of another ten communities sought a rural setting and sometimes used old farm houses for the common house.[5]

Cohousing developments employ a variety of financing mechanisms and ownership structures: privately owned condominiums, limited-equity cooperatives, rentals owned by nonprofit organizations, and a combination of private ownership and nonprofit rental units. In almost all cases residents initiate, plan, and manage the community regardless of whether the units are owner occupied or rented. Eighteen of the 20 developments built before 1982 are completely privately owned, similar to American condominiums. Since then most projects have taken advantage of new government-sponsored, index-linked loans that structure the development as a limited-equity cooperative. Four projects, including Bondebjerget, resulted from collaborations between nonprofit organizations and resident groups (Figs. 5-2 and 5-3). Other than determining who can afford to live in the development, financing makes little difference in the actual functioning of cohousing.

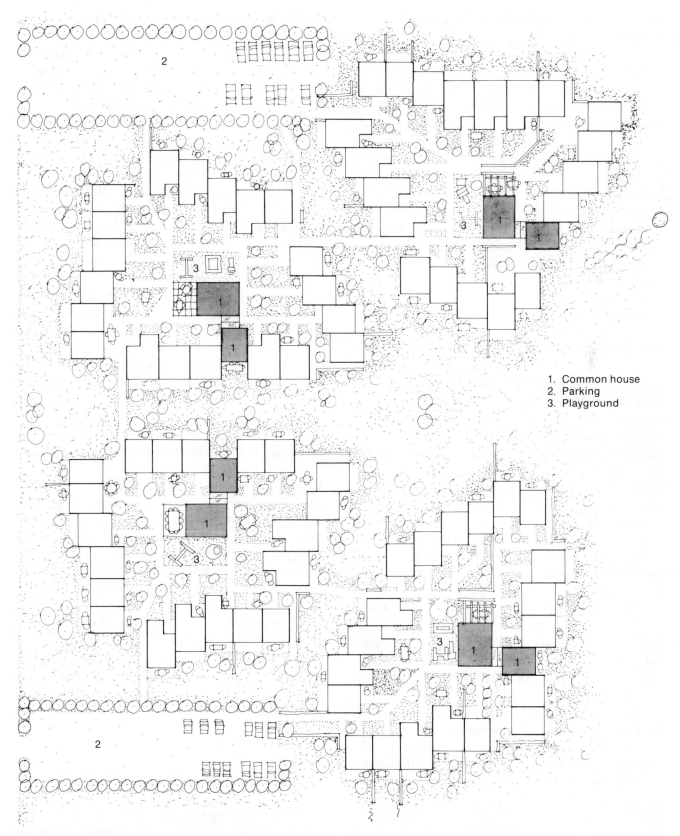

1. Common house
2. Parking
3. Playground

Figure 5-3. Bondebjerget: site plan. In order to maintain the intimate scale residents desired, the community is divided into four clusters of 20 residences with their own common houses.

FOUR CHARACTERISTICS OF COHOUSING

Despite their diversity all cohousing developments consistently incorporate four characteristics: extensive common facilities, an intentional neighborhood design, a participatory development process, and complete resident management. Each of these attributes is briefly described in this section. This is followed by a history of cohousing in Denmark with two case studies, a description of the design and development process, and a closer look at the most important design criteria. The chapter concludes with a discussion of American applications.

Common Facilities

The common house is the place for common dinners, afternoon tea, a Friday night bar, children's games on rainy days, child care, crafts workshops, laundry facilities, and other organized or informal activities. Through cooperation and pooling resources, residents enjoy facilities they could not afford alone, such as a photography darkroom or a well-equipped wood-working shop. The functions incorporated depend on the needs and desires of the residents and are likely to change with time.

Common facilities have both practical and social benefits. Not having to worry about shopping for, cooking, and cleaning up after dinner every night allows residents to relax after work, to spend time with their children, or to attend classes. Common dinners are the ongoing social link that allows people to discover mutual interests, to share experiences, and to keep in touch. Thus a social network grows from the practical functions.

Common space in clustered housing is not in itself so unusual; condominium developments in the United States often have a clubhouse or a community room. A common house differs from a clubhouse, however, in the way the space is used and in its extensiveness. In cohousing the common house is perceived as an extension of the private residences. Ranging in size from 1,185 to 8,610 square feet (110 to 800 square meters), the common house is used by residents on a daily basis and considered an essential part of community life.

As cohousing has evolved the common house has increased in size and importance. Today the size of private dwellings often is reduced in order to afford more extensive common facilities. Initially many residents hesitated to commit to common dinners, imagining them to be inconvenient or imposing on a frequent basis. Yet no community has decreased the frequency of shared dining, and several have increased the number of dinners available each week. Now most groups plan for nightly meals in the common house, with more than half the residents participating on any given evening.

Common houses also are used by the surrounding neighborhoods for meetings, classes, union organizing, and a refugee day-care program. Savværket residents organized a film club that attracts participants from the whole town. The common house provides the community meeting place that most of today's neighborhoods lack.

Intentional Neighborhood Design

Cohousing residents set out to create an environment that directly responds to their desire for a sense of community. Beginning with the initial programming, residents consistently emphasize design aspects that "increase the possibilities for social contact" rather than those that protect individual privacy. The neighborhood atmosphere is enhanced by placing parking at the edge of the site, allowing the majority of the development to be pedestrian oriented and safe for children's play. Meeting places are created with benches and tables, and play areas for small children are placed in central locations where they can be seen from the houses or by other people in the vicinity.

A Participatory Development Process

Residents not only participate in the development process of cohousing but also initiate and control it. This is distinguished from the more common form of user participation, in which residents have input in the planning and design but do not control decision making. Even in cases where a resident group collaborates with a non-profit developer to build rental cohousing, the residents maintain control of the project. Residents organize the group, write the program, hire the architect, choose the financing, participate in the design process, and often do some of the construction and landscaping. The consistency with which resident participation is found in cohousing leads us to believe that this component plays an essential role in its success.

Complete Resident Management

Once a development is built, residents (renters and owners alike) remain responsible for the ongoing management of the project. Major decisions are made at common meetings, usually held once a month. These meetings provide a forum for residents to discuss issues, to solve problems, and to work out differences of opinion. Unlike earlier Scandinavian cooperative housing that employed people to provide services, cohousing residents do most of the work themselves. Responsibilities are divided among work groups in which all adults participate. Duties such as cooking common dinners and cleaning the common house are rotated. In most cases management and community duties become less formally structured as residents get to know each other better.

Although the participatory process and resident management are important aspects of cohousing, they also are the primary source of frustration, particularly the long discussions and debates involved in making decisions cooperatively. Residents told us that over time they become more effective at working together and take the lessons learned at home to work and school. The frustrations arising from group decision making are apparently balanced by the rewards of a community based on democratic principles.

Each of the four characteristics builds on the others and contributes to the success of the whole. None is unique alone, but the consistent combination found in cohousing is.

EVOLUTION OF THE CONCEPT OF COHOUSING

The first attempt to build cohousing began in 1964 when Danish architect Jan Gudmand-Høyer and a group of friends gathered to discuss their dissatisfaction with available housing options, namely the single-family house or the multistory apartment building. They sought a neighborhood that gave higher priority to children and lower priority to cars and that allowed for more cooperation around daily household activities such as laundry, meals, and child care.

The group bought a site in a Copenhagen suburb and proceeded with plans to build 12 terraced houses around a common house. Although the local officials were supportive of the project, the neighbors were not. They opposed it because of the number of children and the subsequent noise they feared would intrude on their quiet neighborhood. They organized against the project and bought the land Gudmand-Høyer's group needed for access to the site. Eventually the group was forced to sell the site and most of the families gave up. In the contemplative period that followed, Gudmand-Høyer wrote an article entitled "The Missing Link between Utopia and the Dated Single-Family House." Published in 1968 the article attracted enormous response. A new group was formed that eventually split into two over the issue of location. In 1972, 27 families moved into the first cohousing community, Sættedammen, designed by Teo Bjerg and Palle Dyreborg. A year later 33 families moved into Jan Gudmand-Høyer's Skråplanet (Figs. 5-4 and 5-5).

In the following years other groups organized to build cohousing. By 1980, 12 communities had been built in Denmark and many more were in the planning stages. Ten of those built were privately owned with the cost of a unit close to that of nearby single-family houses, although the cost of a unit also included a share of the common facilities.

The majority of residents in these early developments were young, two-income families who chose cohousing as an alternative to the conventional single-family-house developments in which 65 percent of the Danish population live. Emphasizing the benefits for children, residents are consistently attracted by the social aspects of

Figure 5-4. Skråplanet. *(Jan Gudmand-Høyer, Architect)* The 33 privately-owned residences are situated on the sloped site so that every living room has a view to the south. The front entrances are on the north side.

cohousing. One resident explained that "our primary motive for wanting to live in a [cohousing] community was the desire for a more social environment for both children and adults. The many practical advantages we later discovered the community gave us we hadn't even thought of initially" (Byggeriets Udviklingsråd 1983). The initiators of cohousing were people who could afford large, modern houses. Yet instead they chose smaller houses, assumed the financial risks, and spent the personal time to develop a cohousing community.

Acknowledging the benefits of cohousing, nonprofit housing developers and the Danish Building Research Institute took an interest in making it affordable for people of lower income. The 79-unit development, Tinggården, built in 1976 as a result of a design competition sponsored by the Institute, was the first cohousing rental project. Built by a nonprofit housing developer, the complex is divided into six clusters of 12 to 15 units around common houses with one large meeting house for the whole development. Drejerbanken, completed in 1979, successfully combines ten rental and ten owner-occupied units.

In 1981 new legislation made it easier and less expensive to finance cohousing projects in Denmark. This law allows any group establishing a housing cooperative of at least eight units to apply for a government-sponsored loan, thereby decreasing the initial investment and the monthly mortgage on new construction. In addition rental developments owned by nonprofit housing associations have opened cohousing to lower-income households who qualify for rent subsidies.

The availability of cooperative financing and the growing interest of nonprofit developers in building rental cohousing have greatly diversified the population of cohousing. Whereas earlier communities were almost exclusively two-income families with children, a sampling of six cooperatively financed communities built between 1983 and 1985 shows the households to be 16 percent single people, 29 percent single parents, 1 percent couples without children, and 54 percent couples with children. The diversity increases even more in three nonprofit-owned rentals built between 1978 and 1982: averaging 28 percent single people, 36 percent single parents, 14 percent couples without children, and 22 percent couples with children. Adult residents range in age from their early 20s to mid-70s. The majority still move into the community between the ages of 30 and 45, but the number of elderly participants is increasing continually; several com-

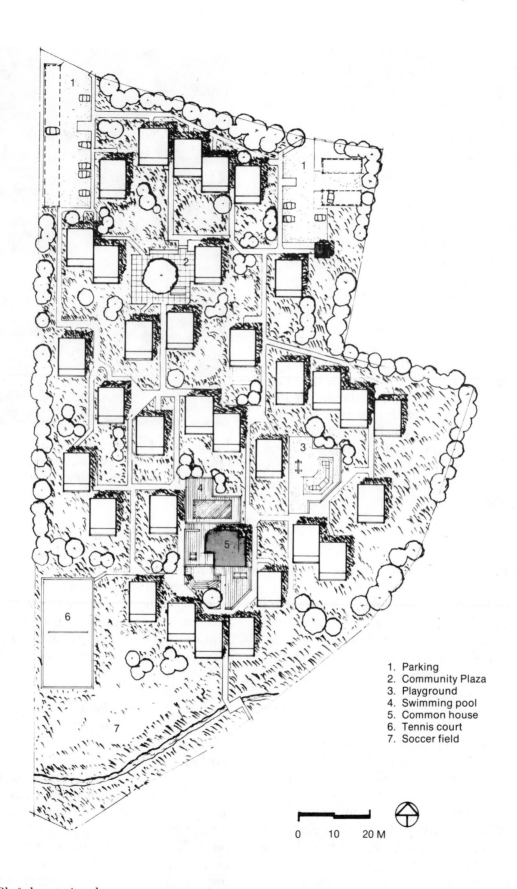

1. Parking
2. Community Plaza
3. Playground
4. Swimming pool
5. Common house
6. Tennis court
7. Soccer field

0   10   20 M

Figure 5-5. Skråplanet: site plan.

munities have been initiated by seniors as an alternative to elderly housing. Today cohousing is cross-generational, attracting singles, single-parent families, couples without children, two-parent families, and elderly.

The most important factor in determining who lives in cohousing is not income but rather the desire and ability to get a project built. Low turnover rates, averaging 3.3 percent a year, and long waiting lists for available units often require that people interested in living in cohousing start their own development. In fact many new communities are initiated by people on the waiting lists for other projects.

The growth and acceptance of cohousing in Denmark attest to its success as as a viable housing option. Recently some of the basic ideas have been adopted in speculative developments and subsidized housing as professionals begin to realize that these ideas successfully address the needs of a growing segment of the population. In 1982 residents converted a section of a modern 1,500-unit nonprofit housing project to cohousing in order to reduce the anonymity of this large, impersonal environment, which was creating problems of vandalism and a high turnover of residents. Similar conversions have improved problematic projects in Sweden.[6]

A Closer Look: The Trudeslund Community

Situated in the town of Birkerød just north of Copenhagen, Trudeslund's 33 residences and common house were completed in 1981. The development, designed by Vandkunsten Architects, uses the natural features of the sloping site: the buildings line two pedestrian streets and the common house occupies the highest corner where the streets meet. By keeping parking at the site's edge and clustering the houses, much of the lower portion is left as wooded open space, becoming a favorite place for children to play (Figs. 5-6 and 5-7).

Like other cohousing communities Trudeslund was initiated by its residents, who purchased the site, formulated a program, and then held a limited competition to choose the architect. The development process, from the first meeting to occupancy, took 2½ years.

Figure 5-6. Trudeslund: pedestrian street. *(Tegnestuen Vandkunsten, Architects)* Row houses with small front gardens line the pedestrian street, where much of the community socializing takes place.

The split-level and two-story residences range in size from 970 to 1,500 square feet (90 to 140 square meters) each and are privately owned, so that each household owns its home and a portion of the common areas. The cost of a Trudeslund residence is comparable to that of single-family houses in the area and resale values have steadily increased since the complex was completed.

The 8,610-square-foot (800-square-meter) common house is one of the largest in Danish cohousing. Facilities include a kitchen and a dining room, two children's playrooms, a music/guest room, a teenagers' room, a library, a TV room, a workshop, a common store supplied with most daily household goods, laundry facilities, a photography darkroom, a walk-in freezer, and storage space (see fig. 5-15). A more recent addition is the computer. A government study of different possibilities for working at home has provided every household with a personal computer connected to a central computer in the common house and outside computer lines. Twenty-nine

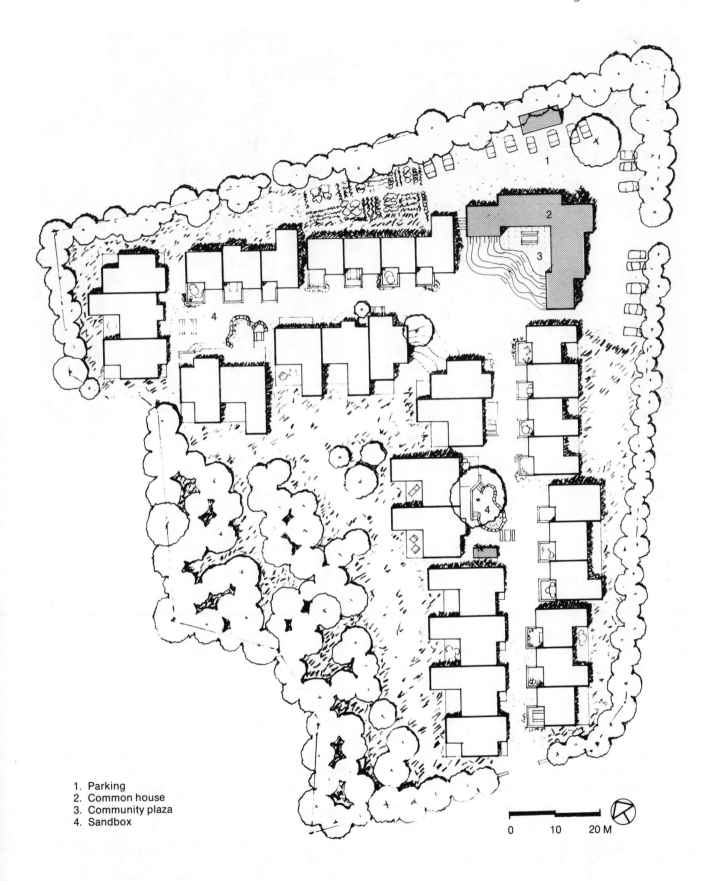

1. Parking
2. Common house
3. Community plaza
4. Sandbox

Figure 5-7. Trudeslund: site plan.

Figure 5-8. Jystrup Savværket: Glass-covered street. *(Tegnestuen Vandkunsten, Architect)* The covered street provides a protected area outside the dwelling, which can be used all year round.

of the households also have pooled their resources to buy a 17-room vacation house in Sweden.

Dinner is available in the common house seven nights a week (except for two Saturdays a month when the room is used for private parties). Two different adults are responsible for the menu, shopping, preparation, and cleanup each night. With an average turn out of 45 to 70 people, it is a big job, but in return the two cooks can enjoy common dinners for the next month. Residents sign up for dinners two days in advance and pay for the meal after dinner when the cooks have divided the cost by the number eating— typically $1 to $1.50 for adults, half price for children less than 13, and free for toddlers under 3.

Other duties are divided among the nine work groups who take responsibility for the cooperative store, the outdoor areas, the special children's activities, the monthly newsletter and minutes of meetings, the heating system, the laundry room, the general maintenance, the social events, and the overall coordination of community activities.

Jystrup Savværket

Like all of Denmark, Danish cohousing has two personalities: summer life and winter life. Residents complain that in the long, cold winters the amount of socializing decreases significantly— people do not sit outside or drop by the common house as often. Architects have responded with glass-covered pedestrian streets. Also designed by Vandkunsten Architects, Jystrup Savværket has a site plan similar to Trudeslund but the buildings are connected by a giant skylight (Fig. 5-8).

"But the street! Nobody can imagine how we could function without it—here there is life all year round. Here we sit, talk, and drink coffee 'til one in the morning, here the kids play when it rains or snows—the glass-covered street is simply one of the best parts of our house." As this resident describes, Savværket's narrow, blue-walled, glassed-covered street is a success. Completed in 1984, the community orients 21 residences along two streets that meet at the 4,350-square-foot (404-square-meter) common house (Fig. 5-9). Not only the common house but also the whole

Figure 5-9. Jystrup Savværket. The common house sits at the junction of the two covered streets with a library in the highest tower. Private decks that extend over the street and ground-level patios provide every household with sunny private space overlooking the shared outdoor area.

street becomes an extension of one's living space, functioning as a vestibule to leave coats and boots, as a play area, and as a gathering place.

The one-, two-, and three-bedroom residences range in size from 680 to 1,050 square feet (63 to 98 square meters) each. Residents reduced the average unit size to 10 percent below that required to qualify for government-assisted cooperative financing in order to afford more common facilities. As a cooperative resale values are limited by the government to reflect the rate of inflation and building improvements.

At the junction of the two pedestrian streets, the common house is separated from the unheated covered area by a glass wall so that one can see directly in (Fig. 5-10). There is a professionally equipped kitchen and a comfortable dining area where residents can eat every night of the week, a fireplace and a sitting area, two children's rooms, a youth lounge, a billiard room, and a music room. A child-care program uses the facilities during the otherwise quiet daytime

hours when most adults are away at work. In addition there are two workshops (one for textiles, the other for wood working), a laundry room, and two supplementary rooms on each of the two streets. The supplementary rooms, each with its own bathroom, are used as guest rooms, office space, or teenagers' bedrooms. The flexibility of these rooms allows maximum use of the extra space that every household occasionally needs. A previously existing building is used for auto repair and storage.

After the first year of occupancy, not one resident felt that the interior street and the resulting close proximity between private and community areas was uncomfortable, despite the fact that many households moved from larger single-family homes. The number of new communities with private residences and the common house under one roof—five built by 1986 and several more planned—points to a continuing trend in northern countries where the long winters drastically reduce the use of outdoor areas.

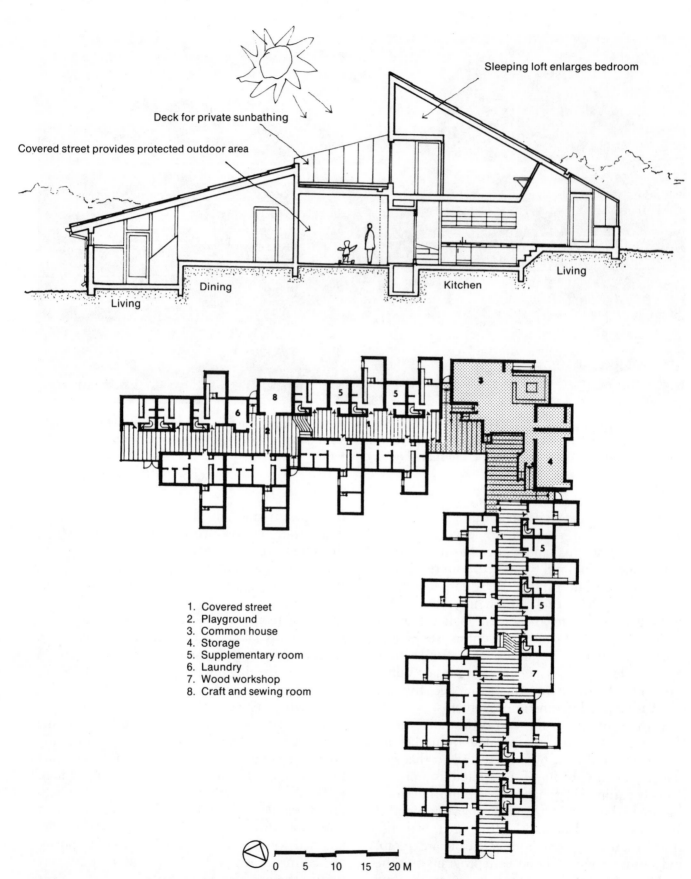

Sleeping loft enlarges bedroom

Deck for private sunbathing

Covered street provides protected outdoor area

Living

Dining

Kitchen

Living

1. Covered street
2. Playground
3. Common house
4. Storage
5. Supplementary room
6. Laundry
7. Wood workshop
8. Craft and sewing room

0   5   10   15   20 M

Figure 5-10. Savværket: first-floor plan and section through covered street.

THE PARTICIPATORY DEVELOPMENT PROCESS

Although resident participation often complicates the development process, in the case of cohousing it is the driving force in getting projects built and contributes significantly to the community atmosphere. When financial institutions questioned the feasibility of cohousing projects, it was the residents who risked their own assets, convincing banks to give them construction loans. When a city council denied approval of a cohousing project, it was the residents who built models, went to meetings, and eventually convinced the council that they were respectable citizens with sound intentions. When cuts had to be made to build within construction budgets, it was the residents who insisted that the architects cut the size and amenities of the individual units in order to preserve the common facilities. Resident involvement in the planning process provides a rare opportunity for architects to incorporate nontraditional design ideas that few developers will risk, let alone fight for.

Cohousing is as much about a development process as it is about shared facilities. While the latter provides ongoing community ties, the active participation of residents in the development process is critical in building the community atmosphere initially. Bonds between residents are spawned during the planning and design process as the group works together on issues closely tied to their personal values. Participants say that during this process they gain new perspectives and become more willing to try ideas they would not have considered before.

As cohousing evolves, becoming better known and more clearly defined, the participatory process itself evolves. When a new *bofællesskab* is advertised in Denmark today, people know what it is. Groups begin the planning process by visiting existing developments. Aspects now taken for granted, such as common dining and smaller individual residences, required months of discussion and many compromises in the first projects. The first cohousing projects took between five and eight years to develop; today it can take as little as two years from the first meeting to occupancy.

Nevertheless, the participatory development process has its difficulties. Residents usually have little knowledge of financing, design, and construction. Participants need to maintain an efficient time line, to avoid the domination of strong personalities, and to integrate new members without backtracking. Without a conscious supportive effort from group members, individuals who lack self-confidence and organizational skills (often the very people most in need of community) are intimidated by the process. In dealing with these issues today, we can learn from two decades of cohousing experience.

The participatory process often begins with a notice about a proposed project being placed in a local newspaper. Several groups, however, have experienced the frustration of attracting too many people before setting the basic parameters of the project. To facilitate a project in a more timely manner, groups have found it is easier to start with five to fifteen households who develop the initial program, find a site, identify financing possibilities, and choose an architect. When these decisions have been made, other people can decide if they are interested in the project. Indeed, as a project becomes more clearly defined, more people are attracted to it. Most cohousing developments are filled and have a waiting list well before construction is completed.

Enlisting the assistance of facilitators, architects, lawyers, and financial consultants who are supportive of the group's goals expedites the process considerably. An architect or a planner can facilitate the initial planning and programming stages by giving an overview of the process, recommending time lines, and identifying when certain decisions need to be made. At the same time professionals must be careful not to dictate decisions for the group because this can create a power struggle and, in at least one case, caused the firing of an architect.

A cohesive development program defines the group's social goals, priorities, financing capability, and design requirements. It must establish a strong foundation so that new members can be easily integrated, the design and construction phases be made less time consuming, and the costs be kept down. Cohousing groups have found that clarifying the desired outcomes is more important than laying out specific architectural requirements (as is commonly done in conventional housing programs). For instance, clarifying the functions to be accommodated and the cost limitations of the common house is more valuable than just listing its square footage requirements. The preparation of the program should be considered a learning period for all participants, including the architect (Cronberg and Jantzen 1982). If the program is rushed or incomplete, the project will be built on a weak base that may disintegrate before it is completed.

A participatory process should not, however, be taken to mean endless meetings and discussions. Like any other effective business venture, it requires that efficient organizational structures and work methods be established early. One commonly used method is to divide participants into work groups covering different areas, such as investigating financing and energy options; developing public relations; recruiting new members; researching the common facilities and outdoor areas; contacting the building department, public officials, architects, and engineers; publishing a community newsletter; and coordinating the efforts to keep track of what everyone is doing. Work groups then present options and recommendations at common meetings, where most of the decisions are made.

Meeting formats vary, but it is most important to devise a system where everyone has an opportunity for input without allowing a few people to dominate. Small group discussions work well in this respect, as do roundtable discussions where each person has an opportunity to comment on a topic. Decision-making procedures also need to be carefully considered and agreed on early in the planning process. Although many groups move toward making decisions by consensus after moving in, the time pressures of the development period cause most to make decisions by majority or two-thirds vote.

Numerous participatory methods are used in the design process—models, field trips, questionnaires, discussions, and paper furniture cut-outs to develop floor plans are a few. Models with movable pieces, whether of house plans or of site plans, and field trips to experience different architectural solutions and building densities are considered the most useful by both architects and residents. More important than specific methods are the relationship between the archi-

tect and the residents, the cohesiveness of the group, and the architect's ability to translate social goals into the design of a physical environment. Architects must be able to educate participants about the social consequences of various design decisions and must be honest about their own biases. Residents and designers must respect each other and yet be willing to fight for the solutions they believe are best. The architect must learn when to challenge residents and when to compromise.

One of the difficulties in a participatory process is the inevitable turnover of participants. Some families are pressured to find other housing before the project is completed, some move for job opportunities, and still others become discouraged or decide they are not ready for co-housing. Although new members are easily attracted, this turnover means that in some projects with long planning periods, as few as three or four households have participated from the beginning to the completion. The number of residents who participate in the entire process, however, does not seem to affect the success of a project once it is completed. The backbone of the project is people committed to it because they intend to live there.

It can be a difficult process for all participants, but it also is an exciting one with unique results. One resident commented "those meetings created an openness between us as we learned each other's strong and weak sides . . . without that phase I would not have the same relationship to the common house or outdoor areas" (Byggeriets Udviklingsråd 1983). The early involvement of residents motivates them to take responsibility for the project's success and allows them to understand the restrictions and choices that must be made.

Most cohousing developments rely on residents to do some of the construction themselves. In some cases residents complete only the landscaping. In others, such as Sol & Vind, residents do a good portion of the interior construction—laying floors, installing cabinets, and finishing walls. In Denmark exterior and structural walls usually are built of concrete or brick, making it difficult for unskilled residents to build the whole structure. Nevertheless, residents of Jerngården and Bofælleden did extensive renovations of existing buildings. In both cases the project consisted of only eight units and members of. the group had considerable construction experience among them. In two other communities, Mejdal I and II, residents built the common house after moving in.

The main reason communities adopt the owner-build option is to reduce the required cash investment by doing some of the work themselves. In addition the owner-build approach allows for customizing interiors to fit the aesthetic choices and financial limitations of different households.

Owner building has its limitations as well. In order to have an incentive to contribute a substantial amount of labor, residents must have equity in the project. Although residents' installation of landscaping has been successful in rental housing, renters cannot be expected to contribute substantially more than that. Cohousing demands a lot from residents both before and after construction. For some, particularly for single parents, elderly, and those with time-demanding jobs, the added burden of putting in construction time may be too much. In addition, construction efforts can take energy from other community activities. At Sol & Vind, finishing the building interiors and landscaping so exhausted residents that other community activities did not fully develop until two years after occupancy. The key to incorporating the owner-build option successfully is being realistic about the trade-offs and the amount of work the group is ready to take on. Careful consideration needs to be given to financial limitations, the amount of construction experience within the group, and the time residents can contribute.

DESIGN GUIDELINES

Design guidelines for cohousing build on those already established for clustered housing (Alexander et al. 1977; Davis 1977; Gehl 1987; Cooper, Marcus, and Sarkissian 1986). Cohousing, however, requires special considerations because residents have chosen this type of development for its strong sense of community and consequently come to know each other much better than neighbors usually do. In addition, the social im-

plications of the relationships between buildings are not something people generally think about, but in programming cohousing they are very important. This makes it more critical for architects to understand and communicate these implications to residents involved in the planning and designing of cohousing. With this in mind we have devised the following guidelines based on our observations and the experiences of residents in Danish cohousing.

Transitions from Private Areas to Common Areas

The attention and sensitivity paid to the transitions between the private, common, and public realms affect the ease with which residents move from one to the other and define the relationship between the community and surrounding neighborhood.

Many architects give priority to protecting individual privacy rather than to creating opportunities for meeting other residents. Yet of the hundreds of cohousing residents we interviewed, not one complained of lack of privacy. Many, however, could point out design features that discouraged sociability. In cohousing there is less need for territorial definitions, and the relationships between private and community areas can be more relaxed than in other housing types.

The importance of casual interaction in cohousing should not be underestimated. Common facilities provide practical advantages and a place for residents to become acquainted, but it is the general social atmosphere that residents most value—chatting with neighbors, feeling comfortable asking them for a cup of sugar or to watch the children, and allowing children to wander freely around the development.

The transition spaces between the private home and the common areas can greatly support this community life. Generally the kitchen/dining area is the room where residents spend most of their time. A door with a window between the private kitchen and the common area allows a parent to watch children playing outside or to call out to a passing neighbor. Visual access to the common areas, whether these areas are indoors or outdoors, also allows people to see activities they may want to join. As one resident said: "I can't decide to join the neighbors sharing a pot of tea in the common area if I can't even see that they're there." Studies have shown that direct access between the dwelling and a semiprivate garden patio increases the use of the outdoor space in other housing types (Bundgaard, Gehl, and Skoven 1982; Gehl 1987; Marcus and Sarkissian 1986). As the threshold to the common areas, this relationship is particularly important in cohousing.

A "soft edge," that is, a semiprivate area between the private dwelling and the common area, further increases the opportunities for casual socializing. This transitional zone provides a place for residents to set out tables and chairs or to plant a small garden. Distinguished from circulation paths by plantings, low fences, or merely a change in paving, this edge need only be 8 feet deep to provide a place to sit. A study comparing outdoor activities in two Danish clustered housing developments showed that when a soft edge was provided, residents spent 68 percent of their time outdoors in front of the houses and only 32 percent of their time in the more private backyards. When there was only a hard edge and no semiprivate area, residents spent only 12 percent of their outdoor time in front. Even more important, the total number of hours people spent outdoors increased fourfold when there was a soft edge (Bundgaard et al. 1982; Gehl 1987). Our findings show that people's preference for sitting or playing in front of their houses is even more pronounced in cohousing. As the "front porch," both literally and figuratively speaking, this area immediately in front of the home allows people to observe and take part in community life as they choose.

The activities that occur between houses on a warm day at Trudeslund illustrate how sensitive design encourages social interaction. Along the walkways between houses, children play, people relax with a beer after work, and families enjoy leisurely Saturday morning breakfasts. All the residences have private patios in the back, but people prefer sitting along the community streets where the action is, where they can visit with neighbors or just watch the activity.

In Trudeslund the kitchen/dining areas have big windows looking onto the walkway, and most have a door directly to the front patio (Fig. 5-11). Next to the door are sitting areas, sometimes defined by a small fence and sometimes by an open patio. Those few households who have neither a door for direct access (having to go through the vestibule instead) nor a sitting area simply do not use the front area as often as other residents (Fig. 5-12).

With interior streets and courts, the transition area between the dwelling and common space is reduced and becomes less clearly defined, but it still plays an important role. Not having to worry about putting on shoes or warmer clothing to go outside their residences, people can move even more casually from private to common areas. At Savværket private entrances that are set back from the street provide vestibules for storing shoes, children's toys, and outdoor clothing. Casual sitting areas along the street are well used all day long.

The two mistakes most commonly made with regard to transition areas are providing only a hard edge, so that one steps directly from the individual residence into the community realm, and placing storage buildings in front of the dwellings. Without a soft transition between private and common areas, residents cannot move informally from one to the other. Storage buildings located in front of the house impair communication by preventing residents from observing passersby, watching children play, or seeing what is happening in the common areas.

Transitions within Common Areas

The common areas themselves should be designed to provide different types of gathering spaces—from those that are just outside the private dwellings to the "community plaza." Again sensitive transitions from the most intimate gathering spaces to the most public encourage an active community life. For example, along the pedestrian streets at Trudeslund five to eight houses share a picnic table. Here neighbors often share a pot of tea. Within sight of most kitchen windows, each street also has a sandbox where toddlers can play for hours while their parents work or visit with neighbors. The play areas become meeting places for both children and adults.

Figure 5-11. Trudeslund: entrances to private house. The formal entrance, on the right, leads to a vestibule for winter use. The entrance on the left provides informal access directly to the kitchen/dining room.

Some residents express concern that these local gathering places promote cliques. Our observations indicate, however, that gathering places benefit the whole community by bringing residents into the common areas. It is natural for people to become better acquainted with those who live in closest proximity because of their frequent encounters.

Equally important is a community plaza for larger gatherings. When located outside the common house, as at Trudeslund, this area functions as the community's "front porch." It is here that residents gather before and after dinner, have summer barbecues, and hold other community celebrations. Ideally residents should be able to pass by the community plaza on their way home to see if others are there.

Transitions between Community and Public Areas

One other transition that should be carefully considered is that between the development and the surrounding neighborhood. As members of a tightly knit community, cohousing residents are already set apart from their neighbors in the surrounding area. One way to reduce the insularity of cohousing developments is through the design of their physical boundaries. Possibilities include sharing recreation areas, integrating neighborhood pathways, or sharing a public plaza. At Sol & Vind a neighborhood path passes through the site. Trudeslund shares a basketball court with the neighbors. Jerngården residents painted their houses different colors to blend with the rest of

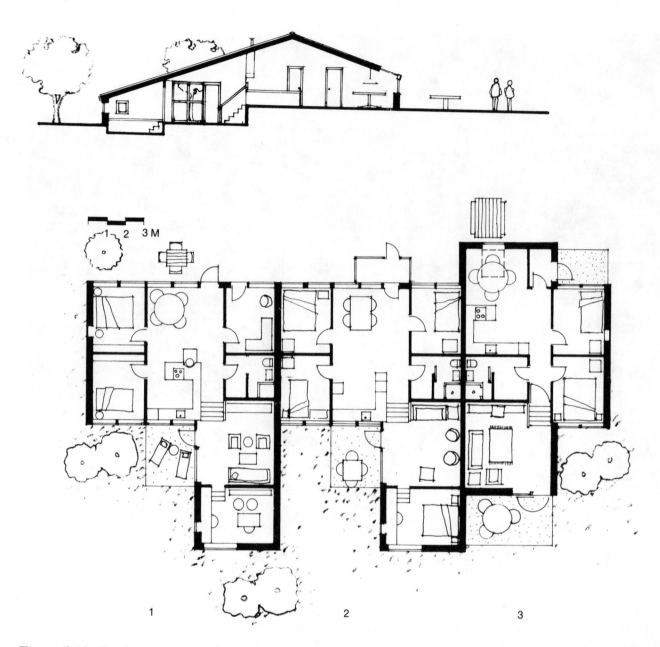

Figure 5-12. Trudeslund: private house floor plans and section. (1) A 1,184-square-foot unit with formal entrance to vestibule or office space and informal entrance directly to kitchen/dining area; (2) a 1,184-square-foot unit with greenhouse entrance; (3) a 969-square-foot unit with entrance through vestibule.

the street. Håndværkerparken shares a plaza with the surrounding housing development.

Unfortunately, in spite of the well-meaning intentions of cohousing residents, neighbors are not always interested in socializing. When the Trudeslund architects and residents presented their design to the local planning commission, neighbors insisted that they plant a hedge around

the site to hide the development. As people learn more about cohousing, their fears that it will attract strange people and be detrimental to the neighborhood decrease so that the links between communities and surrounding neighborhoods can develop more fully. Nevertheless, neighborhood integration has been one of the most difficult design ideas to realize.

A Child-Friendly Environment

One of the main objectives of cohousing has been to design "child-friendly environments" that give children many different opportunities for playing and interacting. Close proximity of peers and familiarity with other residents allow children in cohousing more freedom than in conventional single-family-house developments. This freedom is further enhanced by keeping most of the site free of cars. Because children are undoubtedly the primary users of outdoor areas, these areas should be designed to accommodate a variety of types of play and to avoid conditions that deter children's full use of the site.

In addition to keeping cars at the site's edge, a responsive site plan provides centrally located play areas for the youngest children within sight of home and, whenever possible, undeveloped areas for the older ones to explore. An area where children can build forts, make up secret games, and create their own world is always well used. The wooded area behind the houses at Trudeslund offers an example: the seven- and eight-year-old boys spend hours there with their forts and campfires.

Surfaces conducive to a variety of types of play also are important. This includes hard surfaces for bicycle riding and ball games and grass for rolling and sitting on. Studies show children play more often on hard surfaces than on grassy areas when both are provided (Cooper Marcus 1974; Cooper Marcus and Sarkissian 1987), so particular attention should be paid to providing adequate hard-surfaced areas where playing will not be a problem. Wide pathways and courtyards offer this possibility. Many Danish communities use a thin layer of gravel on walkways, courtyards, and parking areas to provide an inexpensive hard surface conducive to many types of play.

Children are attracted to places where there is activity and thus spend a great deal of time along major circulation paths. When designing these areas, architects should provide sitting places where the banter of children will not intrude on nearby residences. Conflicts between children's normal activities and the needs of adults often can be avoided by considering, during the design phase, how children will use the site.[7]

Parking

All the cohousing developments we studied—with the one exception of Nørgårds Plantage—are pedestrian oriented, with parking relegated to the periphery of the site. Architect Jan Gudmand-Høyer, who has been designing cohousing since 1964, notes that in every case where residents have participated in the design (cohousing or otherwise), cars have been restricted to the site's edge. People may want to drive to individual houses to deliver groceries, drop off a disabled or elderly person, or move furniture, but residents do not want cars parked next to the houses. Given the harsh Danish winters, this is no easy choice. People have clearly stated that they would rather walk in snow and rain than compromise their immediate living environment.

In addition to the increased safety of children, the community benefits from the resultant meetings between residents as they walk to and from the parking area. The importance of such possibilities cannot be overstated; people meet in the parking lot going to and from work, arrange car pools, and start friendships through casual chats on the way home.

The choice of scattered parking or centrally located parking depends on the site, size, and preferences of the community. Most communities have one or two centrally located lots. This works because of the relatively small scale of cohousing and the informal treatment of most parking lots, which often are surfaced with gravel. Parking lots, usually empty during the day, make fine play areas for bicycle riding and ball games after school.

The primary factors affecting the number of cars owned by residents are site location and availability of mass transit. Nevertheless, living in cohousing improves the potential for sharing cars; a family who needs a second car can easily arrange to share one with another household. Although Danish planning codes typically require a minimum of 1.5 parking spaces per unit, cohousing developments average considerably fewer cars, often fewer than the total number of units.

Figure 5-13. Jernstøberiet: central hall leading to common house. Residents enter through the central hall, which provides a covered court for playing and socializing. Private residences line either side, with kitchens facing the hall.

The Common House

The location of the common house greatly affects the frequency of its use. Specific activities —attending common dinner, using the laundry facilities, or picking something up from the cooperative store—bring residents there. Three often-conflicting requirements for the location of the common house are (1) that residents pass it on their way home from locations outside the community, (2) that it be visible from the dwellings, and (3) that it be more or less equidistant from all the dwellings. Of these, our observation is that the first is most important. When residents pass the common house on their way home, they can see if something of interest is going on. At Trudeslund residents often pass through the common house—to see if their children are there, to see what is for dinner, or to check the bulletin board. Because it is along their path home, it becomes part of their daily routine. At Jernstøberiet residents pass through the central hall to get to their dwellings, making it the community's primary socializing space (Fig. 5-13). Residents will rarely make an extra effort to go by the common house if it is out of their way. Similarly, when residents can see the common house from their homes, they can see if there is some

Figure 5-14. Trudeslund: common house. Residents relax after dinner while the evening's cooks clean up in the kitchen beyond.

activity or if the lights are on. One resident told us that he kept his binoculars by the window to see if there was anyone he wanted to talk with at the Friday night bar. As for the third consideration, no dwelling should be so far from the common house as to feel isolated, but we did find that some residents prefer to be further from the action than others.

Careful consideration of the relationships between functions inside the common house also can encourage its use. When practical errands bring people to the common house, the design should allow them to see if other people are there. In this regard the location and design of the kitchen can be a great asset because the cooks usually are working throughout the afternoon and evening (Fig. 5-14). Trudeslund's kitchen works well in this manner; from any of the common house entrances, one walks by but not through the kitchen so the cooks know who is coming and going. When the kitchen is closed off from the dining room and circulation (as in Sol & Vind), the cooks are isolated from other activities in the common house.

Another critical relationship is between the children's play area and the dining area. Although parents want to be able to hear young children, play areas must be separated from the

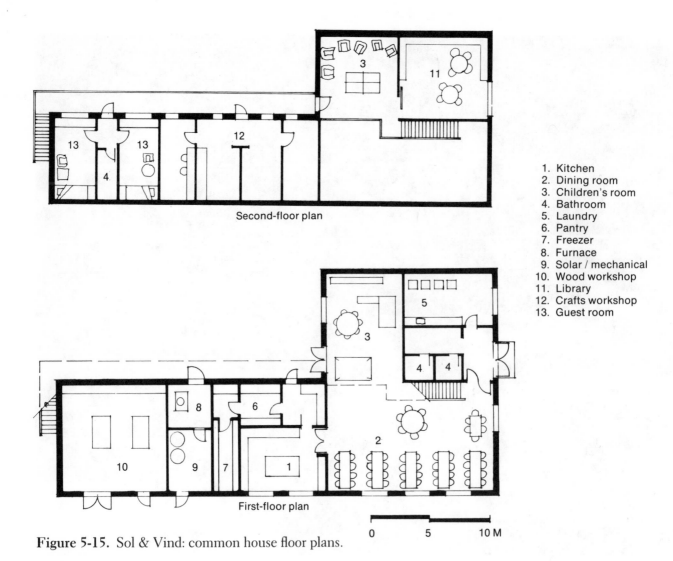

Second-floor plan

1. Kitchen
2. Dining room
3. Children's room
4. Bathroom
5. Laundry
6. Pantry
7. Freezer
8. Furnace
9. Solar / mechanical
10. Wood workshop
11. Library
12. Crafts workshop
13. Guest room

First-floor plan

0   5   10 M

Figure 5-15. Sol & Vind: common house floor plans.

dining area to enable adults to relax after dinner. At Sol & Vind we were surprised to find that residents rushed home after eating, claiming that their small children needed to get to bed. Yet in other communities with many small children, adults like to relax together after dinner, drinking coffee and talking while the children play. The difference is that in the Sol & Vind common house the play area is directly adjacent to the dining room (Fig. 5-15). At Trudeslund the play room is down the hall, still within hearing distance but separated from the dining room (Fig. 5-16). The children can play as noisily as they like while the adults sit and talk. In another community, Gyldenmuld, after many years of having the play area at the edge of the dining room, residents built a separate sitting room in one corner.

"It's a grand success, every night we talk and drink coffee there instead of rushing home like we used to," commented one resident.

Nearly every community contends that it needs yet a larger common house, regardless of whether the house is 1,000 or 8,000 square feet. Residents often cite the need for extra guest rooms that also can be rented out to teenage children, to couples having relationship difficulties, or for work space. Such rooms are now included in many of the new communities. More children's space also is a common request. Building costs, however, limit the space and amenities any community can afford, making it all the more important for the design to allow maximum use of what is available.

Designing for multiple use is one possible re-

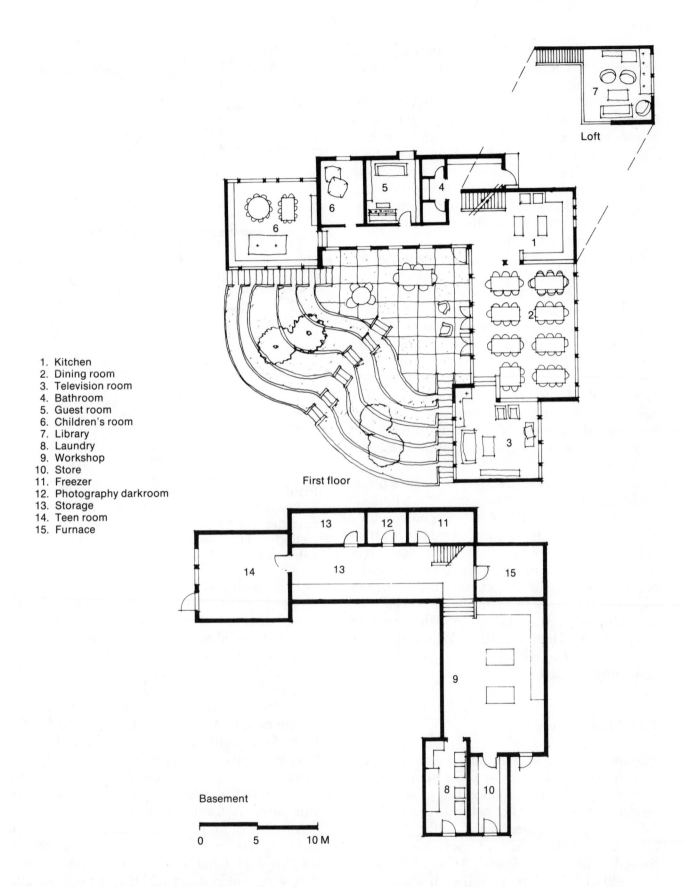

Loft

1. Kitchen
2. Dining room
3. Television room
4. Bathroom
5. Guest room
6. Children's room
7. Library
8. Laundry
9. Workshop
10. Store
11. Freezer
12. Photography darkroom
13. Storage
14. Teen room
15. Furnace

First floor

Basement

0   5   10 M

Figure 5-16. Trudeslund: common house floor plans.

sponse to this need. In its common house Savværket has four 200-square-foot rooms that can accommodate a wide variety of uses. Currently two are used for a child-care program, one is a music room, and the other is a youth lounge where the teenagers gather and listen to music. "In the future, maybe we'll rent out rooms for a teenager to live in or for someone who wants to work at home," speculates one of the residents. In addition along the covered street there are the four supplementary rooms that are used as guest rooms or extra bedrooms.

One difficult design problem is creating an intimate atmosphere while also providing for the needs of a large group. The dining room should be comfortable and not cafeterialike, and there must be places in the common house where a few people can gather informally and other places where the whole community can meet. The kitchen should be efficient and include professional facilities adequate for preparing large meals, but at the same time it should not be institutional. Visual access between the kitchen and the dining area assists in creating a residential feeling.

Good acoustics are necessary to create a pleasant atmosphere. If residents cannot talk comfortably in a conversational voice during dinner, they are likely to eat at home more often. At Skråplanet complaints about noise are the primary reason residents do not eat in the common house more often (few Skråplanet residents eat in the common house more than once a week). The flat, hard-surfaced ceiling is the main source of this problem. High, angled ceilings and absorbent surfaces should be incorporated to reduce noise amplification.

The Private House

The average size of individual cohousing units built in Denmark today is 895 square feet (83 square meters).[8] The average size of cohousing units decreased by almost half between 1975 and 1985, and perhaps more significantly, the range of unit sizes diversified. Private residences in Sættedammen varied from 1,500 to 1,940 square feet (140 to 180 square meters) each when it was built in 1972,[9] compared to Thorshammer (built

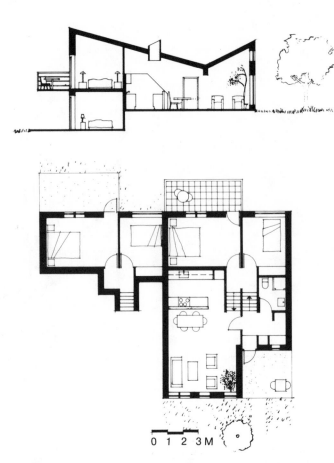

Figure 5-17. Bondebjerget: private house floor plan and section, a 1,205-square-foot unit. Direct access from the entrance to downstairs bedrooms allows teenage children and temporary boarders greater autonomy.

in 1985), with unit sizes ranging from 580 to 1,120 square feet (54 to 104 square meters) each. Although this reduction is due as much to the increase in building costs and requirements for cooperative financing as to the addition of a common house, community facilities certainly make it easier for residents to adjust to smaller units.[10] The common house supplements the private dwellings so that space is no longer needed in the home for laundry, guest rooms, or workshops. In Savværket private kitchens have only two-burner stoves because residents usually eat dinner in the common house, which can also be used for private parties or formal dinners.

A variety of unit sizes encourages a diversity of household types to live in the development: studios for singles and three-bedroom units for families with children. In addition a range of unit types allows residents to move within the community as their spatial requirements change. If people must move from the development to find larger or smaller units, the long-range benefits of a stable community are jeopardized.

Other ways to provide flexibility are designing for future additions and for the possibility of renting out a room within the house. Future additions should be anticipated in the initial design to ease the process at a later date. More important than specific physical characteristics are allocating area for private expansions and suggesting the style and form for additions. Specifying expansion requirements initially will prevent many conflicts between residents about this issue later. When designing larger units, architects should provide for the future possibility of renting out a room to a student or to another adult. Many households can use this rental to supplement their income during temporary financial difficulties. Renting out a room is facilitated by having direct access from the entrance to one bedroom so that one does not have to go through the living areas to get to it. Some of Bondebjerget's floor plans offer this possibility, which also can be an asset when living with teenage children in a small house (Fig. 5-17).

Smaller unit sizes require residents to be more careful in establishing priorities and designers to be more creative in the use of space—both when constructing new buildings and when adapting existing buildings (Fig. 5-18 and 5-19). Sleeping lofts and high ceilings help make small spaces feel larger. In this regard, design considerations are similar to those for all small housing units—how to make the most of little space—and are not specific to cohousing other than recognizing which amenities are provided in the common house and avoiding any overlap.

COHOUSING IN THE UNITED STATES

Today cohousing is a viable and accepted housing option in Denmark. Given the demographic, economic, and domestic changes affecting American society, cohousing appears to be both appropriate and applicable in the United States as well.

Although the ideals of individualism, private property, and the detached single-family house are embedded in our culture, changing circum-

Figure 5-18. Jernstøberiet. *(Jan Gudmand-Høyer, Jes Edvars, and Helge Christiansen, Architects)* Converting an iron foundry into 21 cohousing units led to the first design to incorporate private units under one roof. The living units are situated in the shed-roofed wings with the central foundry hall serving as the interior courtyard. The common house is located at one end of the central hall, with exterior decks facing the shared outdoor area.

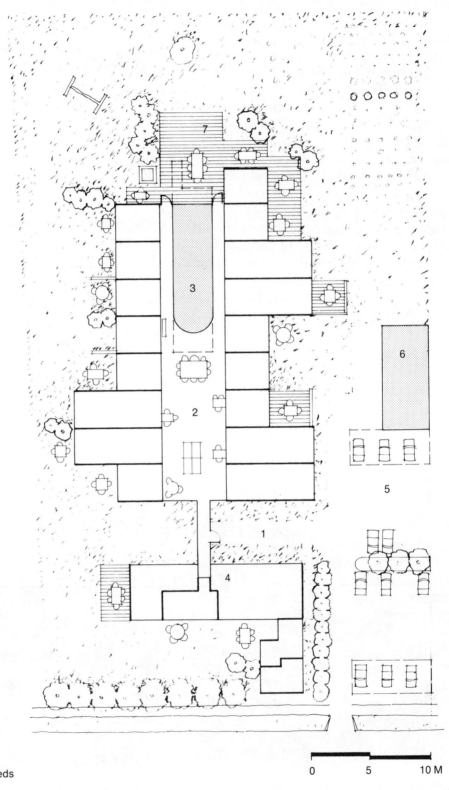

1. Entrance
2. Central hall
3. Common house
4. New annex
5. Parking
6. Workshop and storage sheds
7. Terrace

0   5   10 M

Figure 5-19. Jernstøberiet: site plan.

stances are leading people to question the usefulness of these ideals. In the United States families continue to decrease in size; women work outside the home in ever-increasing numbers; and a growing proportion of the population consists of single parents, elderly, and single people living alone. At the same time rising housing costs place greater demands on individual households. The transience of the population and the social isolation inherent in today's housing options (primarily single-family houses and apartment complexes) contribute to a lack of community support and cohesion. Traditionally support services such as child care and assistance for the elderly were provided informally within the extended family and the local community. By re-establishing a community-based structure, cohousing offers solutions to these various problems that are currently unavailable to individual households and are more effective than institutional programs.

In addition, technological advances make it increasingly common for people to work part-time or full-time at home. In most of today's housing situations, working at home only further isolates people. The daily social contacts of most adults revolve around the workplace rather than around the home environment. If the home is to be a viable workplace, it must be restructured to provide for a broader range of social and practical needs.

The mobility of the American population raises a question about our commitment to community and thereby about our ability to develop cohousing. Currently the lack of social ties within most neighborhoods offers people few incentives to stay. A home that is tied to a community and relationships that one values, on the other hand, provide good reasons for moving less frequently. One Danish cohousing resident remarked: "Before living here [in cohousing], I found the jobs I wanted and then moved. Now I look for the jobs near here."

The multicultural society of the United States presents unique challenges for the development of cohousing. As a relatively homogeneous culture, the Danish people share many traditions, values, and expectations that provide an immediate cohesion not readily available in the United States. Within the diversity of the American population, however, there are many people who share the basic values needed to live together successfully in cohousing: an appreciation of the benefits of community and a willingness to work together to achieve them. As in Denmark, different cohousing communities in the United States will reflect a range of different values and levels of commitment. Although it may require greater effort to establish shared values and expectations, the cultural diversity of the United States should provide the opportunity for anyone interested in cohousing to find a group he or she can live with.

The possibility of encouraging contemporary patterns of residential and social segregation presents an additional problem in the United States. While it is certainly possible for cohousing to be used as a variation of the walled-in, planned communities of the rich, this contradicts one of the reasons for people's interest in the concept, namely, the desire for an integrated residential environment. In Denmark cohousing groups consistently "seek a varied resident composition with diverse incomes, interest, and political perspectives . . . encouraging an attitude of openness and tolerance" (Trudeslund Program). They also make special efforts to integrate their community into the existing neighborhood. Cohousing groups now forming in the United States voice similar goals as they grapple with issues of affordability and diverse priorities. Cohousing offers people an opportunity to overcome the current pattern of segregation—by interest, age, income, and household composition—that they deem undesirable. In choosing cohousing, residents also choose to respect each other's differences while building on their commonalities.

Americans have a strong tradition of local organizing around issues of public concern, whether in the Pilgrim settlements and pioneer towns of the past or in the neighborhood organizations and grassroots political movements of today. The fact that cohousing is a small-scale model based on private initiative rather than on government policy makes it especially applicable to the American market.

A Growing Interest

Throughout the United States there is already a growing interest in housing that incorporates shared facilities and offers a stronger sense of community; several models are discussed in this book. Another is unrelated people sharing an existing house; this option is becoming increasingly popular among singles of all ages and among single parents. Innovative Housing, a San Francisco Bay Area nonprofit organization, is recognized as a national leader in the development of cross-generational shared housing. Responding to the demand for housing that is more affordable and less socially isolated, Innovative Housing has developed a pilot program for facilitating and managing shared houses. Their recent Vest Pocket Project in Fairfax, California, designed by Dan Solomon, further accommodates this lifestyle by clustering seven new houses, each to be shared by four or five unrelated people. Nevertheless, shared houses have limitations for families and individuals who need more autonomy than this option provides. Cohousing fills the gap between shared and single-family houses, offering the advantages of an intergenerational community with the autonomy of private units.

Shared facilities are being incorporated into other types of housing as well. Developers have discovered an attractive market for planned retirement communities that often include shared dining and other common spaces. Congregate housing for the elderly is another growing market. Housing for single parents, such as those described in this book, often include child-care facilities. In Santa Rosa, California, a Quaker group initiated a 27-unit cooperative called Santa Rosa Creek Commons, which includes a common meeting room and outdoor space. Participating in both the development and ongoing management, residents of different ages, incomes, and religions have created a strong community feeling. All across the country nonprofit organizations representing a wide variety of constituencies are advocating the development of intergenerational housing with shared facilities. These types of projects are becoming increasingly accepted by bankers, planners, and housing professionals. Cohousing builds on these precedents.

Getting Started

Our experience in introducing the cohousing model to American audiences has confirmed that there is indeed a market for this housing alternative. We have given presentations to a variety of audiences, including housing and planning professionals and the general public. The overwhelmingly positive response indicates that many Americans feel a void in available housing options. Two of our public presentations sponsored by Innovative Housing on the Palo Alto Peninsula attracted coverage from all the local newspapers and more than 200 people attended. We have spoken to similar audiences (a combination of young families, established homeowners, single people, and older couples) in Los Angeles, Denver, Seattle, and elsewhere. Inspired by the Danish examples, people interested in living in cohousing have begun meeting with each other to explore local possibilities.

In order to facilitate the development of cohousing, we are collaborating with Innovative Housing to provide consulting services. Because the public cannot demand what it has not yet conceived of, our first efforts have been a series of public "introductory presentations" on the cohousing concept. The presentations include slides of the Danish communities and related American examples, followed by discussions of local development possibilities.

The next step is finding others interested in developing cohousing in the same area. Groups have started through discussions with friends or advertisements in a local newspaper. Neighborhood organizations, churches, and worker's unions also are good places to start. To bring interested people together and to provide technical assistance for groups, we offer cohousing workshops, a newsletter, and a clearinghouse in conjunction with Innovative Housing.

The first "Getting Started" workshop, consisting of three sessions on organizing, financing, and design aspects, took place in June 1987 in Palo Alto, California. The 26 participants, all of whom paid to participate in the workshop, ranged in age from their mid-20s to their late 60s and included 13 singles, three couples, and three families with children, as well as both renters and homeowners. During the workshop we found that most of the group shared similar goals, with the only major difference being preference for an urban or a rural setting. (In Denmark, the issue of site location also was the major reason for groups splitting.) As a result participants have formed two groups, urban and rural, both of which are continuing to meet weekly to explore further the possibility of working together.

People's concerns focused primarily on two issues: financing and their ability to work together. Apprehensions about money are to be expected any time people are considering investing in property. As the people become more familiar with the financial possibilities and with each other, these concerns diminish. It appears that meeting others interested in the concept and working together are more important in overcoming people's concerns than is the technical information provided in the first workshop. Nevertheless, it also is clear that professional facilitation at this early stage assists the group in establishing momentum and direction. We are now offering a full range of workshops, programming assistance, and consulting and design services to assist people through the development process. This focus on providing services to support resident groups allows them to take and maintain control of the project, an important factor in developing successful cohousing.

In spite of these initial successes, barriers to developing cohousing remain: the conservative biases of financial institutions and planning departments, legal and liability issues, and people's skepticism. Although very real these problems are not insurmountable. Cohousing can utilize well-established financing and legal structures, such as condominiums and planned unit developments. We have adapted, for different stages of the process, legal agreements that outline shared and individual responsibilities. Those who believe that the benefits outweigh the difficulties will make cohousing possible. After all, similar barriers existed in Denmark.

A partnership between a resident group and either a for-profit or not-for-profit developer can take advantage of the strengths of each: the direct input and dedication of residents and the expertise and track record of a knowledgeable developer. The developer is guaranteed immediate occupancy, which decreases marketing expenses, while the residents get the community they want. Within such a project a nonprofit developer also can assist in financing affordable units, either as rentals or as lease/buy options.

Another development scenario is for a nonprofit housing developer to initiate a site-specific project. In this case a special marketing strategy to attract residents interested in this option should be started early in the planning process to incorporate residents in the design. The less residents are involved in the planning stages, the more important a move-in orientation is in establishing effective management participation by the residents.

It is, of course, also possible to design housing with extensive common facilities without resident participation. In this case tenant selection and management efforts are critical in encouraging use of the common facilities. Our research consistently shows that when residents are not involved in the planning process, they use the common facilities less frequently and usually require outside management assistance.

In the coming years much more will be learned about adapting the Danish cohousing model to an American context. We have already noted striking similarities. When workshop participants in Palo Alto described their interest in cohousing, it was almost a direct translation of what we had heard from the Danes. People mentioned seeking a balance betwen community and privacy, being frustrated with the isolation of current housing options, lacking a spontaneous social life that does not depend on making appointments with friends, wanting more contact with people older and younger than themselves, and concerns for a better place to raise children. These words echo others we have heard from Americans all across the country, not only from single parents and seniors but also from successful professionals and established homeowners. It is apparent that many people are searching for alternatives that the traditional housing industry is not providing and that some are ready to do something about it.

NOTES

1. This research is presented in full in a book by the same authors entitled *Cohousing: A Contemporary Approach to Housing Ourselves* (1988), published by Habitat Press, 48 Shattuck Square,

Suite 15, Berkeley, CA 94704. The research was partially funded by grants from Byggeriets Realkreditfond, Ib Henriksens Fond, Kreditforeningen Danmark, and the Fabruar 3 Fond. McCamant and Durrett are now working with resident groups, nonprofit organizations, and government agencies to develop and design cohousing in the United States.

2. Although they were developed with little knowledge of the Danish counterparts, the Dutch *centraal wonen* incorporate the same characteristics as Danish cohousing but differ in the placement of common facilities. In Denmark most common facilities are centrally located for use by the whole development; in the Netherlands clusters of four to eight households usually share a living/kitchen/dining area. As a result, common facilities for the entire development generally are smaller and do not include dining facilities. The first cohousing project built in the Netherlands was the 50-unit Hilversum community designed by Leo de Jonge and Pieter Weeda and completed in 1977. Ten years later 30 cohousing communities had been built in the Netherlands and approximately 40 were being planned.

3. The actual number of cohousing communities is difficult to verify (our accounting relies on many sources). Smaller developments, of less than eight households, are not as well known and some may have been overlooked in this accounting, as may have several that are in the planning stages.

4. There are many communities with fewer than six households that also could be called cohousing. We have, however, chosen to follow the Danish precedent of not including these because the relationships between residents in such a small group are closer to those in a "shared house" than in most cohousing communities.

5. *Rural* refers to having enough land to raise animals or possessing a rural atmosphere. Most residents still commute to nearby cities for work.

6. The Danish housing project mentioned is Farum Midtpunkt built in 1973 outside of Copenhagen. The best-known Swedish example is Stacken, a 33-unit, nine-story high-rise outside of Göteborg that was converted to a *kollektivhus* in 1980. The success of Stacken has led to similar conversions of other Swedish housing projects.

7. For more specific guidelines on designing child-friendly environments, we recommend the work of Cooper Marcus (1974) and Cooper Marcus and Sarkissian (1987).

8. The national average size of multifamily housing units is 840 square feet and 1,389 square feet for single-family houses. These national housing averages are from 1980; the cohousing unit size average is from developments built between 1984 and 1986. In addition there are fewer single-person households and more families in cohousing than in other multifamily housing, thereby further affecting the direct comparability of these figures. Despite the differences these figures help to place the size of cohousing units in the context of other Danish housing.

9. Units at Sættedammen are even larger today, up to 2,370 square feet each, because of private expansions.

10. The Danish Ministry of Housing limits the maximum average unit size to 1,023 square feet (95 square meters) each for any housing development to qualify for cooperative financing.

References

Alexander, C., S. Ishikawa, M. Silverstein, et al. 1977. *A Pattern Language*. New York: Oxford University Press.

Andersen, H. S. 1985. Danish low-rise housing cooperatives (bofællesskaber) as an example of a local community organization. *Scandinavian Housing and Planning Research* 2 (May):49–66.

Bundgaard, A., J. Gehl, and E. Skoven. 1982. Bløde Kanter (an English summary of Soft edges). *Arkitekten* 21:421–438.

Byggeriets Udviklingsråd. 1983. *Veje til Bofællesskab [Way to Cohousing]*. Copenhagen.

Cooper Marcus, C. 1974. Children in residential areas: Guidelines for designers. *Landscape Architecture* 65 (Oct.):372–377.

———, and W. Sarkissian. 1986. *Housing as if People Mattered*. Berkeley: University of California Press.

Cronberg, T., and E. Jantzen. 1982. *Building for People: The Theory in Practice*. Hørsholm: Statens Byggeforskningsinstitut [The Danish Building Research Institute]—Sætryk 299 [Report 299].

Davis, S. 1977. *The Form of Housing*. New York: Van Nostrand Reinhold.

Gehl, J. 1987. *Life between Buildings*. New York: Van Nostrand Reinhold.

Gudmand-Høyer, J. 1968. Det manglende led mellem utopi og det forældede en familiehus [The missing link between utopia and the dated single-family house]. *Information* (June 26): n.p.

Trudeslund Development Program, Birkerød: Bofællesskaber Trudeslund, 1979.

Chapter 6

The Party Wall as the Architecture of Sharing

Jill Stoner

This chapter is both analysis and provocation. The analysis breaks down the conventional aspects of the party wall into their constituent possibilities. The provocation directs those possibilities through analogy, metaphor, and invention toward the problem of urban housing. The chapter is organized as follows: (1) the qualitative aspects of the party wall are explored, (2) four strategies for transforming the party wall are presented, and (3) the author's design solutions to recent housing competitions are presented to illustrate these strategies.

The party wall, as a traditional element of urban housing, plays a dual role. In keeping with its name, it is shared, but, paradoxically, it also separates; that is, while the wall belongs to the configuration of both dwellings, it is the element that prevents the dwellings from belonging to each other. Architecture can bridge this dichotomy. Through the engagement of idea and built form, the party wall can be actively shared.

The party wall in this investigation illustrates the complex relationship between architecture and culture. Cultural aspects of urban life can be used to inform the architecture of the party wall. The wall itself, as a mediator between adjacent housing units, encourages us to focus on the potential for social relationships to act as generators of dwelling form. Finally, if the architecture of the party wall can be informed by cultural and physical conditions, perhaps it also can inform us about some of the more subtle agendas in contemporary housing design.

QUALITATIVE CHARACTERISTICS OF THE PARTY WALL

As part of the enclosure of a dwelling space, the party wall is distinguished from other walls by the fact that it participates in the enclosure on both sides. While other walls separate domains that can be defined as interior and exterior independently of one's position, the space on either side of the party wall is either "interior" or "exterior" relative to one's own position; that is, the side that one is on is "interior" and the other side is "exterior." The very premise of the party wall —the premise of sharing—implies this absence of an objective interior and exterior, or the presence of an equality between the two sides. The geometry of the party wall, and its immediate program on either side, is symmetrical.

The party wall may reflect a quality of hostility, of neutrality, or of friendship. Each of these has a corresponding physical nature that, when combined with the geometric principle of symmetry, gives us the diagrammatic conditions shown in Figure 6-1. The quality of hostility implies protection also, and thus the wall has a physical

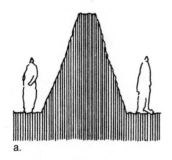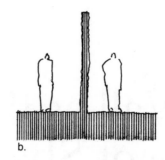

Figure 6-1. Physical manifestations of the party wall: (a) hostility; (b) neutrality; (c) friendship.

Figure 6-2. Found party walls in the landscape and designed party walls. In the landscape: (a) political border in open terrain—an invitation to hostility; (b) political border following mountain range—conducive to maintaining neutrality; (c) political border following river—catalyst to trade and thus friendly relations. Designed party walls: (d) the wall between the Yooks and the Zooks from Dr. Seuss's *Butter Battle Book* (1984) —manifesting hostility (illustration after Dr. Seuss); (e) the wall between telephone stalls—manifesting neutrality; (f) the hole in the wall between apartment bathrooms, from a mouthwash commercial where the medicine cabinet is a "window" into the neighbor's unit—manifesting friendship.

mass, or thickness. Neutrality implies a kind of indifference, and thus the wall is a planar, economical, opaque membrane. Friendship implies communication and engagement, and thus the wall is partially transparent and/or pierced.

The qualities of hostility, neutrality, and friendship, represented in the physical phenomena of mass, opacity, and transparency, also are at the very core of our personal and political relationships. These relationships may result from a wall's prior existence (usually, but not always, in the landscape), or may stimulate the creation of a wall. But whether the physical nature of the wall determines the politics or the other way around, the response is essentially passive. That is, although the wall is shared, it separates; it does not connect. These pre-existing "found" walls, which may stimulate a social response, and "designed" walls, which result from an existing politics, begin to illustrate the range of examples that can serve as metaphors for the design of the urban-dwelling party wall (Fig. 6-2).

The traditional party wall, usually of masonry (or wood studs in apartment house construction), is designed with neutrality in mind (see fig. 6-2e). An element of both structural and spatial convenience, it is in many ways an urban equivalent of the suburban side yard. The side yard, traditionally narrow and unused, in contrast to the more private back yard, is a space that emphasizes the neutrality between neighbors. In the urban context this space is metaphorically "squeezed" in the interest of economy. The side yard hedge and the space on either side is condensed into an 8-inch-thick mass.

This virtual substitution of the side yard with a wall effects the transformation from single-family detached house to row house (Fig. 6-3). Yet the illusion of separation is maintained. Separateness, autonomy, and privacy, the touchstones of the American dream house, become ever more precious as the need for housing density increases. Then the illusion is reinforced because the brick party wall, unlike the side yard hedge, is impermeable, inviolable, and mute.

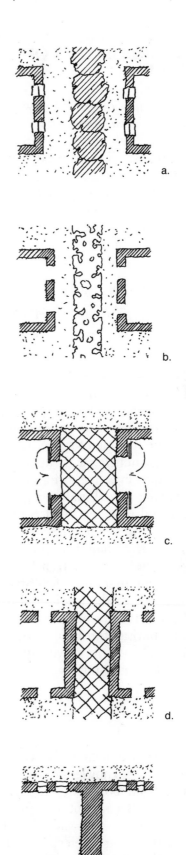

Figure 6-3. Transformation from single-family detached house to row house with party wall. **(a)** Side yards separated by dense wall of trees; **(b)** side yards separated by friendly waist-high hedge; **(c)** side yards merge in shared outdoor terrace; **(d)** side yards contract into alley for service between rear yard and street and windows disappear from side walls for privacy; **(e)** houses touch, separated by only party wall.

THE TRANSFORMATION OF THE PARTY WALL

The lens of contemporary culture, when focused on the party wall as a design element, reveals a set of conditions that can more directly inform our design process. These conditions can be grouped into physical and cultural aspects on the one hand and into subjective and objective aspects on the other. When organized into a matrix, the conditions can be identified as tactility, program, structure, and regulations.

	Physical	**Cultural**
Subjective	Tactility	Program
Objective	Structure	Regulations

Tactility, the condition that is both physical and subjective, is our personal experience of materiality. Program, which is cultural and subjective, involves the making of space in response to social factors. Structure, with its aspects being both physical and objective, brings technics into the design vocabulary. Finally, regulations are both cultural and objective, first conforming to changing needs and desires that affect qualities of urban life and then requiring conformance on the part of the designer. Each of these in turn, and some in combination, offers strategies for the transformation of the traditional party wall. The goal of such transformations is to create the potential for sharing through, within, and in place of the wall, as a positive aspect of such proximity in urban dwelling.

Tactility

The wall as a passive element between dwelling units implies an acknowledgment of surface only: the wall from both sides is planar rather than volumetric. Because it is perceived only from the inside, the party wall has little or no expression on the exterior elevation. Its opacity complements its thinness (usually only 8 inches) in the service of privacy. Thus the proximity of one's neighbor is mitigated, even denied, through the prevention of association. Because of this lack of visual contact, the next-door neighbor may seem farther away, say, than the person across the street, to whom one may call and wave through an open window.

The transformation of the wall with regard to tactility assumes recognition of its three-dimensional property. The wall exists not only in plan as an organizer of space and in elevation as a surface, but also in section, where it can become part of a spatial element in the dwelling.

When the wall is used as a spatial element, the space within it becomes less abstract and more tactile. In its transformation the wall becomes thicker and, at the same time, more permeable. The thickness, once the wall is pierced and light enters, is significant. Like a balloon as air is blown into it, the wall takes on identity, character, and shape. It becomes active rather than passive; it becomes a space to be experienced, a participant in the dialogue between two dwellings. The volume of the wall can be hollowed out in deliberate ways to create shared spaces in the service of program. As a shared spatial element, the wall can become a vehicle for intimacy between neighbors. Scenarios for such sharing "through the wall" are discussed in the following section on program.

Program

The issue of program is two-fold, dealing on the one hand with building services that can be housed within the party wall and on the other hand with shared spaces designed for social encounter. The accommodation of services within the party wall is traditional and occurs in both plan and section (Fig. 6-4). Examples include shared plumbing risers between units (common in apartment stud-wall construction), shared chimney flues (common in masonry row-house construction), and shared ground-floor alleyways from rear yard to street (a tradition in early row-house construction but no longer common because of great expense). The light shaft, as an interruption of the party wall in nineteenth- and early twentieth-century tenements, is another example that is now obsolete. Modifications to and variations on these and other service ele-

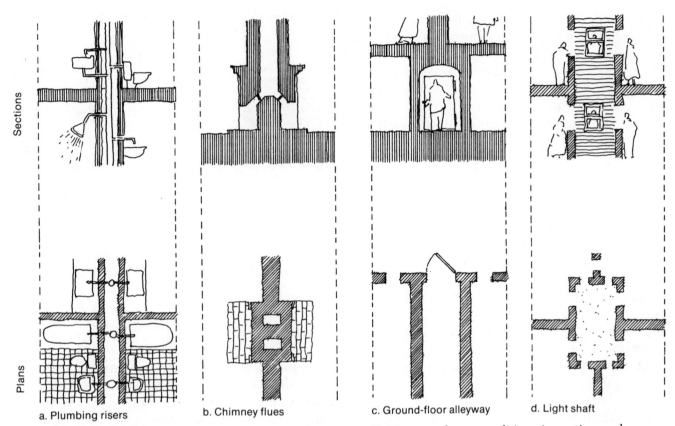

Sections

Plans

a. Plumbing risers   b. Chimney flues   c. Ground-floor alleyway   d. Light shaft

Figure 6-4. Precedents for shared features along the party wall. Top row shows conditions in section and bottom row shows conditions in plan.

ments are discussed further in the sections on structure and regulations.

The party wall also can be used to create shared spaces that respond to new social factors, particularly the changing composition of urban households. The growing number of single-person households and other nontraditional households suggests the need for a new housing model, here referred to as a "suite." The suite is shaped by the idea that households can be larger units with subgroups within them. Both the social configuration of these larger households and the physical configuration of the suites can be either vertical or horizontal in form (Fig. 6-5).

One vertical extension of the nuclear family is generational. It is not uncommon to find grandparents living with the family. The verticality in age has implications for housing configuration, where elderly, for instance, live on the ground floor, with other family members on the floor above. In such stacking of rooms, the floor may be a sort of horizontal party wall, where each unit has a sense of autonomy and privacy, yet meals

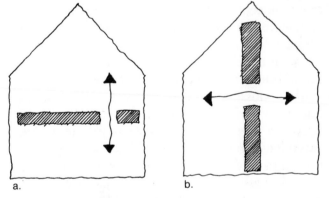

a.   b.

Figure 6-5. Vertical and horizontal models for shared features. **(a)** Vertical program modified by horizontal membrane: floor/ceiling; **(b)** horizontal program modified by vertical membrane: party wall.

may be shared on a level that straddles both realms.

A second type of vertical extension is the increasingly popular concept of the workplace in the home, in many ways a throwback to the old town model of "living above the store." Again the program may involve elements that straddle the two realms of workplace and house by modifying the floor/ceiling membrane. For example, an artist may live above a small commercial gallery and have a double-height studio space that connects both levels. Furthermore, such a program may modify the vertical versus horizontal distinction. The gallery, if it is shared by two adjacent units, is a bridge between the units, through the party wall.

Alternative households with a horizontal organization are more clearly aligned with the principle of symmetry that defines the wall. These households (like extended-family households) test the conventional definition of the dwelling unit with program configurations that are neither completely single family nor just communal. For example, two single mothers might have small adjoining units with some special shared space, the whole making up the larger unit. Similarly several artists might have individual lofts with a shared gallery space.

Such horizontal social structures are defined by the fact that the subunits are equal, and the suite is defined by the space that they all share. Within the suite, which is the grouping of sub-households plus a shared space, the smaller units retain a sense of autonomy and privacy. The challenge of accommodating such multiple households requires some modifications to our expectations for ownership, or in the case of rental housing, for clearly defined territories.

Many possibilities exist for such suites, including the previously mentioned examples, variations on the shared workplace in the home, extended-family households of the same generation, and single adult housemates. Each of these households could use a range of spaces within or along the party wall, which would be shared features of the otherwise autonomous small units. These spaces could respond to needs for service, entrance, work, storage, and light; and more ambitiously, for shared child space, kitchen, dining room, or workroom. What distinguishes such suites from the tradition of the communal house, where only the bedroom (if that) was private, is that in the suite there is a particular shared function that responds directly to the specific needs of that household. More generally, the proportion of private space to shared space is reversed

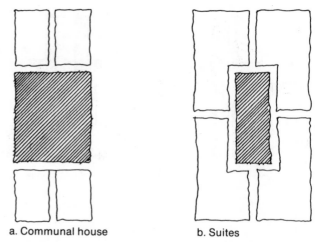

a. Communal house   b. Suites

Figure 6-6. Comparison of proportion of private space to shared space.

from the communal house, where most of the space is shared (Fig. 6-6).

Some of the elements mentioned above have precedent in more traditional housing design. For example, a shared entranceway is common in row-house design, where units are flipped as mirror images in plan to produce a certain image and scale on the street facade. But the suite, with an emphasis on function and lifestyle over image, suggests a more radical set of program interventions. Both the New American House and the Inner City Infill projects, discussed later in this chapter, give more specific solutions to the diagrammatic strategies discussed here.

Structure

The traditional party wall is a masonry bearing wall. The width of the row house, equal to the distance between bearing walls, was determined by the comfortable span for wood-joist floors—about 16 feet. Because the wall performs the double function of separating units and bearing the load of the floors, the wall is constrained by its structural function, and the resulting separation of the units must follow this structural line (Fig. 6-7a). (An exception to this is the previously mentioned alley that connects the rear yard to the street. This structural condition was complex and expensive, as the diagram shows in Fig. 6-4c.)

If the structural walls are turned 90 degrees—

that is, parallel to the street—the party wall no longer serves the load-bearing function. This frees the wall to adapt to the spatial configurations discussed in the previous section. The party wall then becomes a partition wall, already common in apartment house construction (Fig. 6-7b). In fact, the resulting form is a kind of hybrid between the traditional row house with masonry bearing walls and the apartment building with double-loaded corridors and fire-rated partitions dividing units. This structural hybrid of "house" and "apartment" closely parallels the programmatic hybrid between large household (suite) and smaller household (unit) already discussed.

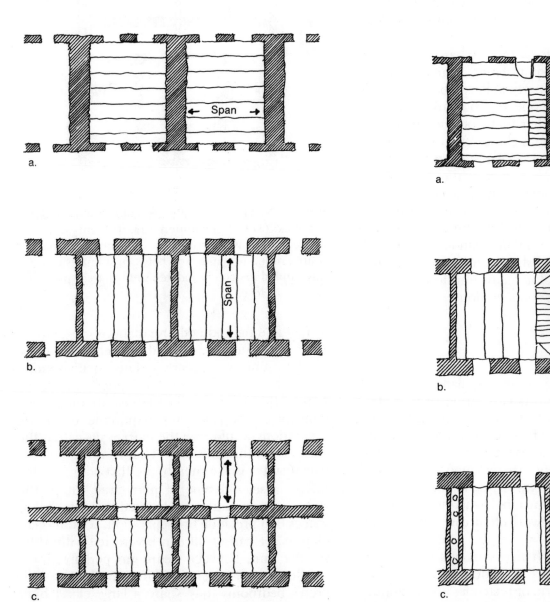

Figure 6-7. Structural implications of party walls. **(a)** Traditional framing, with party wall as load-bearing wall; **(b)** proposed framing, with load-bearing wall parallel to the street and party wall perpendicular to the street; **(c)** intermediate bearing wall for "deep" house.

Figure 6-8. Advantages in separating bearing wall from party wall. **(a)** Traditional stair framing with special joists to head off stair opening; **(b)** proposed framing with concrete plank omitted for stair; **(c)** plumbing risers between partition walls.

The freedom to turn the load-bearing wall parallel to the street is a result of contemporary construction technology. Hollow-core concrete planks can replace the traditional wood joists and can span a greater distance. A "shallow" house (such as the New American House) that is only about 24 feet deep requires only a single span. The bearing walls are the front and back walls of the house. A "deep" house uses a third bearing wall running down the middle, which gives a spatial and tactile quality to the interior rooms (Fig. 6-7c).

Spanning from front to back has other advantages. The stair, for instance, which normally runs parallel to the party wall, can be more easily framed by omitting one or two planks (Fig. 6-8). If the party wall rather than the floor surface is continuous, plumbing chases can run vertically without interruptions or bends and with great efficiency (Fig. 6-8c). Larger vertical zones for light, air, and shared stairways can be easily framed by introducing fragments of a load-bearing wall, still parallel to the street, as they are needed. Such structural innovations are all modest variations on existing construction practice yet open the way for many transformations of traditional housing configurations.

Regulations

Rigorous code and zoning regulations in effect nationwide, and particularly stringent in metropolitan areas, exist to protect the life safety and the quality of life of urban dwellers. Decisions and resulting enforcement of regulations often come as the result of extreme circumstances and even tragedy. Changes in regulations are difficult, and efforts must be patiently channeled through a dense network of bureaucratic specialists.

Rarely are such changes part of a larger strategy for innovations in housing. Yet subtle changes in the fabric of the codes and in zoning regulations do not necessarily threaten its logic or consistency, and these changes can support new design approaches that involve the transformation of the party wall. It is proposed here that these changes respond to the definition of the new housing type already discussed: the suite.

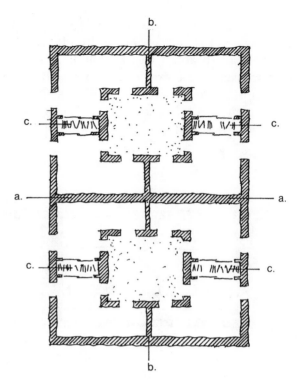

Figure 6-9. Hierarchy of party walls within a single complex. **(a)** Fire-separation walls; **(b)** party wall between units is interrupted to accommodate major shared room; **(c)** party wall between subunits is interrupted to accommodate minor shared space, such as a closet.

The zoning and code regulations currently in force are structured around the definition of the dwelling unit as a clearly defined spatial entity, whether in row-house or apartment configuration. If this definition is expanded to include the concept of the suite, the requirements for fire separations would free the party walls within the suites from this function. That is, if the wall between suites is the membrane that addresses life safety, a second type of party wall within the suite, between units, can be used to create shared spaces that preclude fire separation. A third "generation" of party wall can be created within the smaller unit, between bedrooms perhaps, for a smaller shared function. For example, two children's bedrooms may share a large closet built along the party wall. Thus a hierarchical relationship exists among the party walls themselves: some of the walls are purely spatial; some are tactile with the introduction of light, air, and materiality; and some provide the requisite and unequivocal fire separations (Fig. 6-9).

Although precedents for suites exist in building types such as dormitories and hotels, the potential has never been fully explored for more permanent housing. Dormitories usually are organized more like a communal house, where a larger proportion of the spaces are shared and only the bedrooms are private; the hotel suite, with two sleeping rooms on either side of a sitting room, assumes a temporary tenancy. The concept of suites requires cultural as well as architectural changes and the necessary modifications to existing code and zoning documents are complex.

Summary of Transformational Strategies

The issues of tactility, program, structure, and regulations serve to establish a dialogue between the normally independent concerns of culture and architecture. Relative to the design of the party wall, these four issues are as follows:

1. The party wall, when designed as a three-dimensional zone of material and light, becomes an active participant in the architectonic language of dwelling. When the wall is pierced, the qualities of material and light become especially evident.
2. The rising proportion of nontraditional households in urban neighborhoods suggests the need for creating a new housing type. This type, here called the suite, is a kind of hybrid between the traditional single-family house and the communal house, where the party wall becomes the zone for shared functions.
3. When the load-bearing walls are turned parallel to the street (and thus perpendicular to the party wall) the party wall is freed of its structural function. It can then respond to conditions of spatial sharing, service zones, and transparency suggested by program.
4. The concept of suites suggests a corresponding redefinition of the life-safety and quality-of-life requirements for dwelling units. A hierarchical set of party-wall types establishes a range of architectonic language from pure mass (fire separation) to pure space (shared rooms), which brings us full circle back to the issue of tactility.

TWO HOUSING COMPETITIONS

In recent years several national housing-design competitions have focused on the subject of innovative housing. Programs for these competitions emphasized issues of low cost, nontraditional family structure, modular construction technology, and the workplace in the home. In two such competitions I found the opportunity to test my notions of the party wall.

The New American House Competition

The New American House Competition was a single-stage event in 1984, open to designers, artists, and architects. The program called for six units of housing for middle-income, nontraditional professional households that would contain the workplace in the home. The challenge was to design a living unit and a workplace that together would equal not more than 1,000 square feet yet would preserve some separate identity between the two.

The following design, which won second place in the competition, was based on two concepts. The first concept was that the block of six units could be read as a single house, with a separate garden and garage. In this "large house" the ground level was devoted to the workplace, with two floors of dwelling above. Because of a slope in the site, the dwelling could be entered from the garden level, across a bridge to a raised porch.

The second concept was that the traditional party wall could be expanded to include several shared functions. Furthermore, unlike the traditional twin house, where one party wall separates two houses, the party walls on the two sides of one house could differ in character. Hence the shared aspects with the neighbor on one side could be quite different from those aspects shared with the neighbor on the other side.

Both the vertical and the horizontal types of shared space discussed in the section on program came into play. The floor/ceiling membrane between dwelling unit and workplace is opened to create a light well that connects these spaces. The party walls between dwelling units are thickened into zones that contain spaces and services to be shared between neighbors (Fig. 6-10).

As the plan developed one of these zones became "narrow" (6 feet) and the other one became "wide" (12 feet) (Fig. 6-11). On each of the three floors, different sets of functions occupy these zones, while the 10-foot zone between them belongs to the inviolable private space of each unit. Figure 6-12 illustrates the use of these wide and narrow shared zones.

The narrow zone at the second level is devoted to the entrance to the dwelling unit from both the garage and the garden. Chimney flues run up within this zone, framing a light well at the top story that gives cross-ventilation to alcoves in the bedroom and light to the entrance below. Within

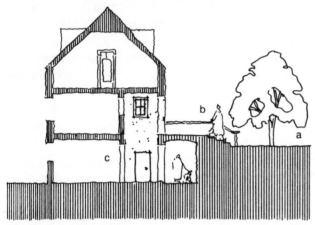

a. Raised garden level
b. Bridge over alley
c. Light court shared by dwelling and workplace

Figure 6-10. Diagrammatic section through New American House project.

the wide zone at the ground level is the shared entrance to the workplace, which continues as a light court above. This wide zone contains a shared kitchenette and a small bathroom within the workplaces, all the plumbing risers, and a shared porch at the kitchen level that extends toward the garage in the back. This zone also contains the stairs, kitchen, and bath for each unit, which are private but back to back.

Within each unit is a second-generation party wall between rooms. Replacing the traditional stud wall membrane is a system of wooden wardrobes between floor and ceiling. The wardrobes act as a thick but hollow (except when filled with clothes) separator. Although the space is not occupiable and therefore not actively shared, the wardrobes open on both sides and thus can be used from either room. Because they are movable the flexibility of use is increased and the interior plan can be continually modified to suit changing household needs.

The structural system for the New American House is the one described in the section on structural transformations. As the diagrams in Figure 6-9 show, the load-bearing walls are the front and back walls of the house, with concrete planks spanning between them. The party walls are partition walls supported on the concrete planks and are free to adjust to the plan configuration within each shared zone.

This New American House proposed transformations to the party wall on a small scale. Services—such as chimneys and plumbing risers—and small spaces—such as entranceways,

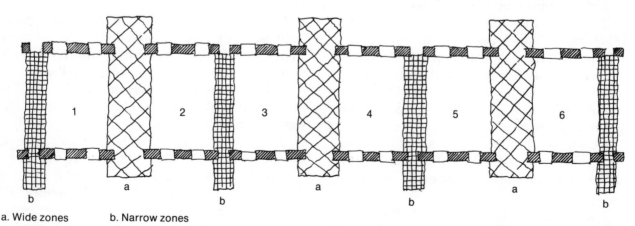

a. Wide zones   b. Narrow zones

Figure 6-11. Diagrammatic plan of the New American House, showing six units with wide and narrow party wall zones.

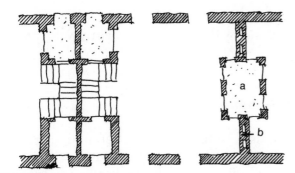

Third floor
a. Shared light court over second-floor entrances
b. Shared chimney flues

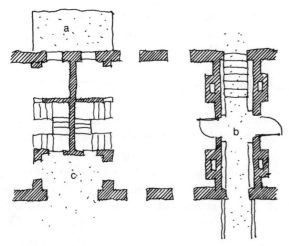

Second floor
a. Shared back porch, entered from kitchens
b. Shared entrances to dwellings
c. Shared light court above entrance to workplaces

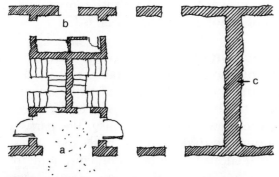

Ground floor
a. Shared entrance to workplaces
b. Shared kitchenette and half bath for workplaces
c. Thick party wall between workplaces

Figure 6-12. Diagrammatic floor plans of the New American House.

porches, and light wells—modify the linearity and opacity of the traditional party wall to involve each unit with its neighbor on either side. At the same time the essential privacy of the individual unit is maintained. These modifications to the party wall find expression on a larger scale in the Inner City Infill project.

Inner City Infill Housing Competition

The Inner City Infill Housing Competition was a two-stage event in 1985 and 1986, which called for 400 units of housing on five infill sites in Harlem, New York City. The following scheme was one of the four first-stage submissions premiated to the second stage, where it received an honorable mention.

The challenge of the competition was to design affordable housing in a wide range of unit types, from efficiency to four-bedroom, conforming to stringent New York City zoning and code regulations, in a mid-rise configuration of six to seven stories. The low- to middle-income population of Harlem that represents the potential residents comprises a large variety of household types, each of which presents a unique client profile for apartment dwelling.

The central concept for the design was the suite, as defined and discussed earlier. The suite, while considerably smaller than the urban block, and smaller than any of the infill sites themselves, is nonetheless larger than current dwelling units. In a difficult and dense urban neighborhood, the suite would encourage greater social cohesiveness and support among residents and would be a much more economical use of available space.

The suites were designed with the required programmatic density and site organization in mind, but also as generic spatial types that could accommodate specific types of nontraditional households. The resulting solution is a system of courtyards, raised one level above the street, that are shared by four duplex units that together form a suite. These courtyards are traversed two stories above the ground by bridges that provide circulation to shared raised porches, which lead, in turn, to four more duplexes. On the sixth and seventh floors, the suites are comprised of two units rather than four, with varied shared features.

Each of these suites is organized symmetrically around a party wall. In contrast to the New American House, the transformations of the traditional party wall are more definitive interruptions in the wall, creating large shared rooms. These rooms accommodate a function that is central to the aspect of sharing for that particular suite. Descriptions and diagrams of several program-specific suites follow. Although not all the unit types from the competition solution are included, these form a representative set of examples to illustrate the range of household types and functions addressed.

Single Parents' Suites

These suites of four units each are designed for four households headed by single parents. The units are organized symmetrically on either side of the raised porch, which leads to bridges across the courtyards and to the building's vertical circulation. These porches, although enclosed, face courtyards, and the windows can be opened in good weather. The entrance to each unit is through the kitchen, so that the four families can share the porch and children's play can be supervised while mothers are cooking. The porch also can be used for large dinners, such as a group meal at Thanksgiving or a children's birthday party. The porch is the single interruption in the party wall within this suite, which is otherwise a simple, symmetrical pairing of two units on either side (Fig. 6-13a).

Workplace-in-the-Home Suite

Similar to the single-parent suite, but with only two units, the workplace-in-the-home suite is designed for two small households, where one member of each is a partner in a small business. The office is entered from a single-loaded corridor, and, like the single-parent suite, faces a courtyard on either side. The office then leads to the respective units. The office, with a small bath and a closet, and the porch on the other side of

the private units are the shared elements positioned along the line of the party wall (Fig. 6-13b).

Artists' Suite

The artists' suite is located at ground level. Unlike the three examples already given, the shared element joins the units vertically (in section) rather than horizontally (in plan). A double-height gallery space that faces the street leads to four studio lofts beyond. The gallery, as the shared space, is an interruption in the floor/ceiling membrane (the "horizontal" party wall discussed in the section on program) (Fig. 6-13c).

Single Adults' Suite

The single adults' suite is designed for two working adults leading independent lives. The suite is located on the seventh floor and is entered from a stair leading up from the sixth-floor corridor. At the first landing the stair divides in two, leading to the two respective private domains separated by the party wall. On the other side of the suite, the party wall dissolves again into a common kitchen/dining area. This reverses the traditional apartment plan, where the living spaces are entered first and must be crossed to get to the privacy of the bedroom. The proportion of private space is greater than that in the traditional apartment yet the total area is comparable; thus the rent is not extravagant (Fig. 6-13d).

These suites and several others were designed to fit the module of the established site dimensions, the courtyards, and the structural system of masonry bearing walls parallel to the street. As with the New American House, the party walls are nonstructural partition walls that allow for more freedom in the plan configuration. In the Harlem scheme the modifications and transformations of the traditional party wall result in large rooms that respond to major aspects of program. Each of these rooms—the play porch in the single-parent suite, the office in the workplace-in-the-home suite, the gallery in the artists' suite, and the kitchen in the single adults' suite

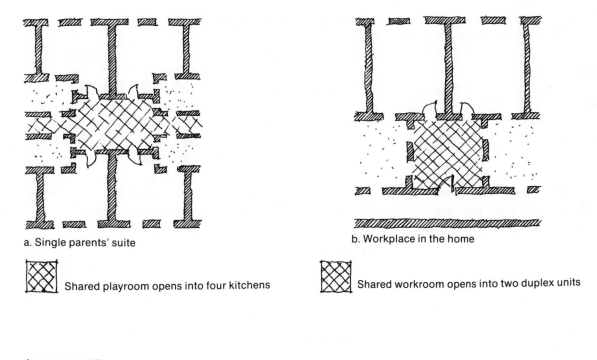

a. Single parents' suite

b. Workplace in the home

Shared playroom opens into four kitchens

Shared workroom opens into two duplex units

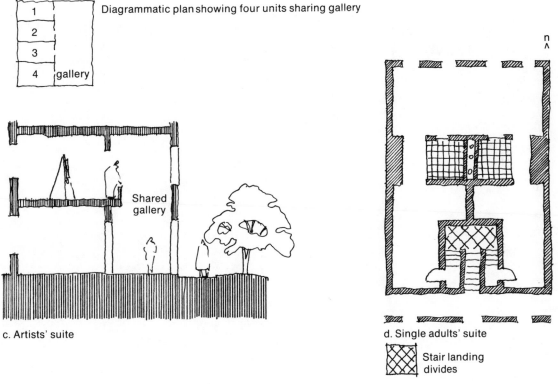

Diagrammatic plan showing four units sharing gallery

1	
2	
3	
4	gallery

Shared gallery

c. Artists' suite

d. Single adults' suite

Stair landing divides

Figure 6-13. Diagrammatic unit plans of the Harlem Inner City Infill housing project.

—establishes the identity of the particular suite. It is the suites, then, and not the subunits within them, that must respond to code and zoning regulations.

In many ways this design solution violated points of code with respect to fire safety. I believe, however, that the modifications discussed earlier, with the introduction of the concept of suites into the regulations, would allow such designs to meet objective requirements for life safety. The concept of the suite is introduced to provoke such change in the interest of designing more socially responsive housing.

CONCLUSION

These design strategies for transforming the party wall emphasize the synthesis of social and material issues in architecture. They suggest that the cultural dimension is not separate from the architectonic and that housing can be sensual as well as practical and even affordable. The simple, intuitive need to connect with one's neighbor is the essence of neighborhood, and in an urban context the party wall is the tangible and immediate source for this connection.

PART II

Housing for
Single-Parent Households

Chapter 7

Overview of Housing for Single-Parent Households

Sherry Ahrentzen

The single-parent family is an established household form in North American and Western European societies. It is, in fact, a traditional family form in the United States, with the proportion of single-parent families in 1970 equivalent to the proportion in 1870 (Seward 1976). Between 1970 and 1980 the proportion of single-parent households in the United States doubled; they now represent 21 percent of all families with dependent children at home, or 6.8 million families (USBC 1985).[1] Increases in the number of single parents also are reported in Canada, France, Great Britain, the Netherlands, New Zealand, Poland, Sweden, and the Soviet Union (see Anthony 1987).

Neither the proportion nor the number of these households is likely to diminish in coming years. Although the divorce rate is stabilizing, there is an upsurge in the number of families with never-married mothers. In 1985, 22 percent of all births were to unwed mothers, compared to 4 percent in 1950 (USNCHS, 1985); among black children born today, this figure is 60 percent. Of female-headed families, those that begin with out-of-wedlock births experience the most severe poverty and long-term welfare dependency.

Single-parent households are defined here as households consisting of only one parent and dependent children. While these families share some common experiences—such as reduced family income, a sense of isolation and loneliness, role overload, and inadequate access to public and social resources—there are important distinctions among them as well, a fact poorly recognized and addressed by researchers, policy makers, planners, and architects (for an exception see chapter 10). Gender is one significant distinction because it is tied to the availability of financial and social resources. In 1984 the median family income for a family with both parents and children was $29,730. For a family with a single male parent and children, the median income was $20,024. But for the female single-parent with children, the median income was $7,608 (Besharov and Quin 1987). Single-father families also are more likely to receive neighborly assistance and special treatment because of their "extraordinariness" (Greif 1985). The low incomes of single mothers, coupled with other insufficient social and financial resources, make the housing plight of single-mother households critical, especially in today's housing market. The chapters and cases in Part II focus squarely on low-income single-mother households with children.

Government bureaucracies and legislation typically reduce, instead of enhance, housing options for nontraditional families such as single parents. Ritzdorf (1986), for example, demonstrates how local planning departments, through zoning ordinances, make alternative living arrangements, such as home sharing among single-parent households, difficult and untenable. In addition single parenthood is considered and treated as a temporary and transitional stage of

143

life by many programs and agencies. This attitude too often results in housing programs and projects that are likewise considered temporary and transitory. Emergency shelters are available in many North American cities for immediate homelessness arising either from severe rental and economic conditions or from domestic violence. But these shelters are intended to be just that, not homes. They house families for a very limited time, usually less than a month.

But the problems of single parents do not typically disappear in a month, and single-parent households are not temporary. Three years is the median interval between divorce and remarriage for women 35 to 54, and this interval is increasing (Glick 1980). Approximately 30 percent of single parents remain single (USDHUD 1980). The problems these families face are not only immediate but also chronic. These problems result from minimal income and inadequate financial assistance; from demands on their time and energy to fulfill the financial, social, and domestic responsibilities of raising a family on one parent's income and resources; and from too-frequent violence and discrimination against women and the poor.

HOUSING ISSUES FOR SINGLE PARENTS

Problems single parents face are also the result of housing and neighborhood conditions. Housing may be unaffordable. Today's homes often are built for and marketed to the two-earner household. Homes that are affordable for single parents may be located in unsafe buildings and neighborhoods and may be distant from day-care centers, stores, or other services. Inadequate and unaffordable housing is a source of daily stress in the lives of single-mother families (Birch 1985). In many American cities the majority of homeless families are headed by female single parents (Hagen 1987; Hopper and Hamberg 1984). According to the 1981 National Housing Survey, of the 5,856,000 female single-parent households with dependent children, 14.7 percent live in dwelling units with some type of physical inadequacy, 6.2 percent are in crowded conditions, and 33.1 percent suffer a cost burden.[2] Single

mothers who rent live in even worse conditions (Table 7-1). Single parents are less likely than others to improve their cost burden conditions over time (Ahrentzen 1982). This becomes a compounded problem as excessive rent payments reduce the amount of household income available for food and other household expenditures (Weiss 1984).

Rather than creating housing forms that are an additional source of problems for single mothers, housing can be created to help ease some of the burdens already encountered in their daily lives. A number of planners, architects, nonprofit agencies, and local governments have begun to develop housing for single parents that is more than simply shelter for an "emergency." The terms *transitional* and *permanent* housing are frequently used to describe these new forms of housing. Transitional housing developments are those where single-parent families stay for a temporary but set period of time, usually limited to a maximum stay of 3 to 18 months. Such housing provides the time, services, and space for single parents to restructure and plan their lives before seeking permanent housing. Permanent housing is intended for unlimited tenure. In terms of physical characteristics, however, the differentiation between transitional and permanent is less clear. Many design features of transitional housing also are desirable in permanent housing for single parents. Permanent housing arrangements, however, assume a more stable financial condition and a longer stay, and hence they usually include larger units. Transitional housing is more likely to include space for social services.

Perhaps the most critical feature of all housing designed for these families is that the housing be affordable. Over 45 percent of female-headed families with children live below the poverty level, compared to 17 percent for all families with children (Besharov and Quin 1987). Poverty among female single-parent households has increased to such an extent that in 1981 the President's National Advisory Council on Economic Opportunity declared that if the proportion of the poor in female-headed families were to continue to increase at the rate it has over the previous 10 years, the poverty population in the year 2000 would be composed entirely of women and children (Rodgers 1986).

Creating affordable homes in today's housing market is a challenge. Frequently it is done by developing medium-density, multifamily residences with small apartment units. Smaller units may not be the most desirable living situation for families, but they may be the best available. Unfortunately housing discrimination, indirectly enforcing social norms of family living, makes it difficult for single parents to rent such housing. A national survey of renters and rental housing managers found that restrictions on families with children were prevalent (Marans et al. 1980). Managers often restrict the number of children sharing a bedroom, especially children of the opposite sex. A family with a boy and a girl, for example, would be excluded from 47 percent of all two-bedroom rental units. While such restrictions apply to both single-parent and two-parent households, the restrictions are particularly severe for low-income households trying to find a home that, although small, is at least affordable.

Single parents extensively use public and community services. However, because of their limited income, they typically do not own cars but depend on public transit to get to such services. In 1982 only 57 percent of female single parents had access to a car, compared to 89 percent of two-parent families (Klodawsky, Spector, and Rose 1983). Hence neighborhoods enriched with stores, public services, and employment opportunities are particularly desirable to these households, as is adequate public transit to get to those stores and services that cannot be reached by foot. Calthorpe's (1988) Pedestrian Pockets proposal addresses these concerns. An alternative suburban pattern of growth, the Pedestrian Pocket is a simple cluster of housing, retail space, and offices within a quarter-mile walking radius of a light rail system. By its clustering, the plan allows people a choice of walking, driving, or using mass transit. The pockets are typically 50 to 120 acres with a diversity of housing and commercial buildings. Similarly, mixed-unit developments and mixed-use zoning are design solutions that address the accessibility concerns of single parents.

Provision of child-care services is of primary importance to families with working parents. Unfortunately child-care services are seriously inadequate in North American communities. There is one day-care position open for every ten children who need placement. The average annual cost of day care for two children is $4,000, which is one-third the average working woman's salary (Gregory 1985). Fifty percent of single mothers with preschoolers work, which reflects the national norm for mothers. Yet one survey found that 74 percent of single mothers say they would work if child care were available and affordable (O'Connell and Bloom 1987).

For architects and planners one concern is the siting of day-care services. For single working mothers without access to cars, taking children to and from day care on public transit is an added burden to already pressured schedules and commutes. Placing day-care centers in office build-

Table 7-1. Inadequate Housing Quality in the United States (1981) (in thousands)

	All Households	All Female-Headed Households with Dependent Children	Female-Headed Households with Dependent Children Who Rent
Occupied Units	83,203	5,856	3,639
Substandard Units			
Physically Inadequate	7,749 (9.3%)	861 (14.7%)	669 (18.4%)
Crowded	2,489 (3.0%)	365 (6.2%)	285 (7.8%)
Cost Burden	12,899 (15.5%)	1,936 (33.1%)	1,510 (41.5%)

Source: Birch 1985.

ings and workplaces is one way to ameliorate this situation. The city of San Francisco recently passed an ordinance requiring newly constructed office and hotel buildings to incorporate day-care space in new structures. Day-care services located in residential areas also can address this concern.

Besides their need for private and public services, single parents often depend on social support—relatives, neighbors and friends—to cope with daily problems. Spaces in the neighborhood where neighbors can meet, talk, and watch over their children can be created: shared domestic facilities such as laundries, community rooms or buildings, courtyards, and play spaces. Certain single-parent families may need additional avenues of social support. Those leaving violent homes, for example, may require special psychological and social support services. Housing for single parents can include space for such services on site.

With one less adult in the home to assist in daily financial, domestic, and child-care responsibilities, a single parent's life is consumed by such obligations. In order to save time, single parents are more likely than their married counterparts to eliminate certain household jobs and are twice as likely to get help from outsiders (Michelson 1985). Design features that minimize maintenance and maximize convenience are useful for these households where time is a precious commodity.

Another essential concern of single-parent households is security, both within the dwelling and in the immediate surroundings. Opportunities that provide for informal surveillance on site by residents, well-defined play areas close to the residence, and a reduced number of entries to the site are some design treatments that can be used to enhance security. Parents and children leaving violent homes are particularly sensitive to relocating in a secure place. Since low-income housing developments often are located in high-crime areas, additional security measures are necessary.

Finally, it is important that single-parent households do not feel stigmatized by their housing. The image of a home affects not only how residents feel about their homes and themselves but also how others feel about them. By and large,

single parents do not want to live exclusively with other single parents. They want housing that largely reflects that of two-parent households of their same class and background (Anderson-Khleif 1981). In their design guidebook for medium-density family housing, Cooper Marcus and Sarkissian (1986) recommend several design features that enhance the image of multifamily housing by reflecting local prevailing middle-class norms: using locally acceptable building materials and providing private entries to units, for example.

Since the 1970s, sponsors and designers of housing developments for single-parent households have been striving to address their needs: affordability, safety and security, accessibility to services and neighbors, convenience of maintenance, and positive image. A brief overview of some housing developments for single-parent households is presented in the following section.

EARLY DEVELOPMENTS IN EUROPE

One of the most notable housing developments for single-parent families is the Huvertusvereniging, "Mother's Home," in Amsterdam, designed by Aldo van Eyck and completed in 1980 (Fig. 7-1). This government-sponsored building houses families "in transition": single parents, new immigrants, the temporarily homeless, and parents with irregular working hours. Infants awaiting adoption also reside there. Besides being transitional housing for up to 16 families, the Mother's Home also is a child-care center and an emergency shelter. The project was commissioned in 1973 and involved renovating a nineteenth-century building and adding a new wing to it on an infill site (France 1985; Hertzberger, van Roijen-Wortmann, and Strauven 1986; Strauven 1980; van Eyck 1984).

The Mother's Home follows the layout of the Israeli kibbutz, with separate living quarters for parents and children. The street-side volume of the house, where the parents live, is compatible in height and massing with the neighboring buildings: a multistory structure with windows and balconies facing the street. Behind this is a low two-story structure that is the children's wing. Warm, natural materials and bright colors were advocated by architect van Eyck to enhance

Figure 7-1. Huvertusvereniging, or Mother's Home, Amsterdam: *(Aldo van Eyck, Architect)*

the residential atmosphere: interior wood paneling, green bay windows, yellow staircases, and red metal frames on the roof terrace.

The children's wing includes five apartments, each with space for five children (Fig. 7-2).[3] Each apartment has a small kitchen, a living room with a veranda, a bedroom and a bath, and its own color scheme. All the apartments open onto an inner courtyard. The roof of this wing is a play space that is reached by a ladder from the courtyard.

Mothers have their own sleeping rooms in the renovated building but share among themselves the sitting areas and baths. Mothers with infants often have cribs in their rooms. Balconies off the sitting areas overlook the inner courtyard or the street.

Common areas for use by all residents include a dining room, a kitchen, and a counseling room. Administrative offices are downstairs in the renovated building. The dining room fronts the street. The kitchen and snack bar are accessible to all residents, although there is a kitchen and maintenance staff that provides meal and cleaning services.

The home is managed by an association of clients, staff, and outsiders. General management meetings are held monthly. Funding is provided by the Bureau of the Children's Judge, the Association for Child Protection, the Guardianship Association, and municipal social-service departments. Parents with incomes are asked to contribute also. Many social services are offered, including social and financial counseling, medical assistance, and child-care services. These services are provided with space in the building.

Other early housing developments for single parents are in Great Britain. A developer, activist, and single parent, Nina West developed several of these housing complexes (Strong 1975). Originally these started as conversions of small buildings into multiunit housing with day-care centers. West strongly believes that on-site day care is a critical housing component that enhances parents' opportunities for paid employment.

In 1972 with financial support from the government, West hired Sylvester Bone to design Fiona House in London (Fig. 7-3). This three-story building contains on each floor four private

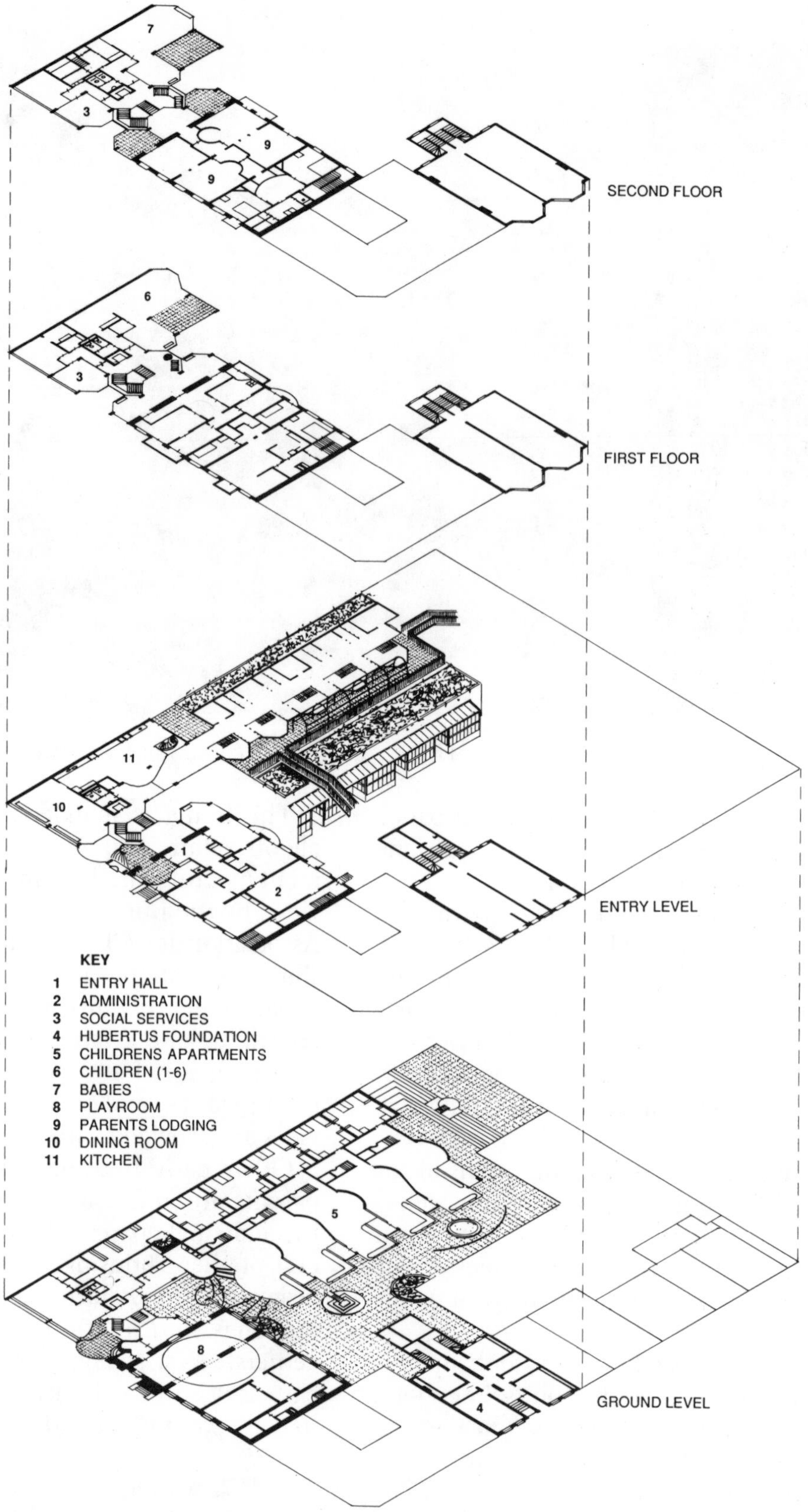

SECOND FLOOR

FIRST FLOOR

ENTRY LEVEL

KEY
1 ENTRY HALL
2 ADMINISTRATION
3 SOCIAL SERVICES
4 HUBERTUS FOUNDATION
5 CHILDRENS APARTMENTS
6 CHILDREN (1-6)
7 BABIES
8 PLAYROOM
9 PARENTS LODGING
10 DINING ROOM
11 KITCHEN

GROUND LEVEL

Figure 7-2. Mother's Home: exploded axonometric. (Fourth floor attic not shown, but it is similar in layout to third floor.)

dwelling units that share an interior corridor. With carpeting, and windows looking out from the apartment units, these corridors function as play spaces so that parents in the apartments can watch their children playing in the corridor. There also is a telephone and an intercom in the play area. The intercom system is linked to every flat so that parents can talk with children or other parents throughout the building. Most apartments have a kitchen, a bathroom, a screenable bedsit,[4] and a separate bedroom for the children; some have only a kitchen, a bathroom, and a screenable bedsit off the living room. The child-care center is in a separate building next to the residences. A single-story building, it accommodates 31 children.

West confronted considerable bureaucratic resistance to some of her design ideas, notably the inclusion of screenable bedsits that afford visual privacy of the mother's bedroom from the rest of the unit, particularly the living room. Since these would also allow privacy for the sexual lives of these women, some public officials objected to their inclusion in the design because, as one official put it, "it might encourage the mothers to sleep with men" (Strong 1975, 497). Despite such resistance, in a three-year period West had two homes under construction, one under conversion, and two homes completed. She undertakes the administration and management tasks of these buildings with two other persons and occasionally with professionals.

DEVELOPMENTS IN THE UNITED STATES

Warren Village in Denver is the first, and currently the largest, housing development for single

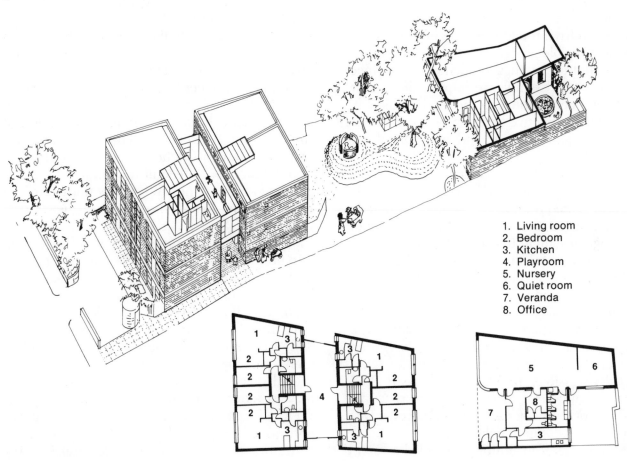

1. Living room
2. Bedroom
3. Kitchen
4. Playroom
5. Nursery
6. Quiet room
7. Veranda
8. Office

Figure 7-3. Fiona House, London: axonometric, floor plan of child-care center and floor plan of residence. (*Sylvester Bone, Architect*)

parents in North America. It was built in two stages. The first, Warren Village I, was completed in 1974 with 96 units and the second, Warren Village II, at another site in the city in 1984 with 106 units. Both were originally sponsored by the Methodist Church, although today they are run by two different nonsectarian, nonprofit organizations. Prospective tenants must meet several eligibility requirements: a single household head who is at least 18 years of age; children not older than 11 years at the time of enrollment; no more than four children per household; a source of income to pay rent (this is usually a government subsidy such as those available from Section 8); children must live with their parents; and residents must express a strong need and desire to reach personal development and financial goals. Residents typically stay for two years.

Both Warren Village I and II have on-site child care for children between the ages of 6 weeks and 12 years who live there or in the community. Together the child-care facilities for both sites are licensed for a total of 197 children. Residents are to set tangible goals for themselves when they move in and to use their residency time to meet these goals (for example, to improve budgetary, parenting, occupational, domestic, or child-care skills). This objective is supported by on-site counseling, job training, and educational services.

Warren Village I was financed under a Federal Housing Administration (FHA) loan. Since the FHA anticipated that the development might default, it insisted that the building construction and design resemble that used for conventional market housing for families. Warren Village II, building on the success of its predecessor, has more facilities and substantially more three-bedroom units.

At both sites there are one-, two-, and three-bedroom units ranging from 520 to 965 square feet each. Six units in Warren Village I are handicapped accessible. In Warren Village II there also are commercial spaces as well as space for training programs (for example, a classroom with computers for computer classes).

ABT Associates in Boston conducted a survey of residents of Warren Village I at the time of their enrollment and after leaving the housing development. While 47 percent of residents were employed at the time of entrance, 94 percent were employed two years after they left Warren Village. Even more striking is the finding that while 65 percent were receiving public assistance at the time of enrollment, only 6 percent were doing so two years after leaving the program. This type of supportive residence along with the requirements for residency contribute to these trends.

Since Warren Village I was built, other housing developments have emerged in the United States expressly for the residency of single parents. Table 7-2 lists several of these. Sparksway Common in Hayward, California, was designed by architects Mui Ho and Sandy Hirschen. It consists of 45 two-story townhouses, ranging from one to four bedrooms each. Units are clustered in groups of nine, arranged around courtyards to encourage social contact among neighbors and informal observation of children. A small on-site day-care center, a laundry facility, an office, and a board meeting room are housed in a central building. Residents, many of whom are single parents, maintain cooperative ownership in the development.

Ten sites have been developed by the Women's Development Corporation (WDC) of Providence, Rhode Island, as housing primarily for single-parent households. These developments involve new construction as well as rehabilitation, financed with federal support and local corporate co-sponsorship. WDC was started in 1978 by architects Joan Forrester Sprague, Katrin Adam, and Susan Aitcheson. Through workshops with single parents, they developed a design prototype that connects kitchen, dining, and living spaces so that playing, eating, cooking, and leisure activities could all occur in proximity to each other if desired (Fig. 7-4). Most apartments have three bedrooms to accommodate large families. In contrast to some of the other developments for single parents, WDC avoided placing shared spaces in their housing because they felt these spaces are difficult to maintain adequately. WDC also offers training and employment opportunities for women.

Another development for single parents is currently under construction. Willowbrook Green in Los Angeles, designed by Ena Dubnoff, is a housing development of 48 rental units (one,

Figure 7-4. Women's Development Corporation: prototype unit plan.

1. Kitchen / dining room
2. Den
3. Living room
4. Bedroom
5. Washer / dryer

two, and three bedrooms each) with child-care facilities for 60 children. The majority of tenants are expected to be single-parent families with some couples with children, elderly, and singles. It is located in an area of Los Angeles where 41 percent of the families with children are single-parent families.

Sponsored by the Los Angeles Community Development Commission and the Drew Economic Development Corporation, this development will help parents by providing on-site child-care facilities, spaces and services for counseling and job training, a location near public transportation and commercial facilities, and a central building with community rooms and offices (Figs. 7-5 and 7-6). To maximize security for women and children, all units face inward and entry is from a central courtyard. This inward focus also enables residents to watch children playing in the courtyard and facilitates neighborly contact. Walls around the site perimeter, courtyard, and private patios reinforce security. Although a low budget demanded a simple repetitive unit design, variety is given to individual units by the change of parapet profile, exterior stucco color, window arrangements, color of patio walls and gates, and entry gate trellis shape (Fig. 7-7).

Shared living spaces for single-parent house-holds are advocated by some architects and planners. Two proposed, but not yet built, housing developments for single parents recognize that shared living space may be appropriate for some families but not for others. Both the Vacant Lots design by Conrad Levenson and Marvin Meltzer and the Double House design by Lars Lerup propose residences with living spaces shared by two household units. Vacant Lots has family suites, each with two bedrooms, a bathroom, a kitchen-ette, a family room, and a terrace for the exclusive use of one household. But a living/dining room is shared by two suites (Fig. 7-8). Also in Vacant Lots there are self-contained one- and two-bedroom apartments with "swing" bedrooms between the apartments. These swing bedrooms are accessible to both apartments. Households can decide whether to share the swing bedroom or allow one household to use it exclusively. On the ground floor a recreational center is provided for resident teenagers (Fig. 7-9).

The Double House by Lars Lerup (Beers 1987) also is designed for single-parent families. Each family unit has a porch, a private yard, a bathroom, two bedrooms, and a kitchen. Shared between two family units is a large common room. Family units are arranged around a shared lawn or a courtyard with a day-care center at one end.

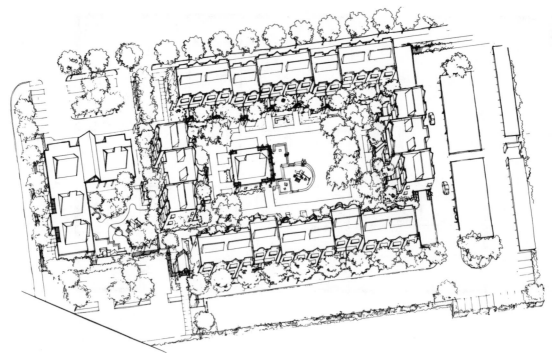

Figure 7-5. Willowbrook Green, Los Angeles: site axonometric. *(Ena Dubnoff, Architect)*

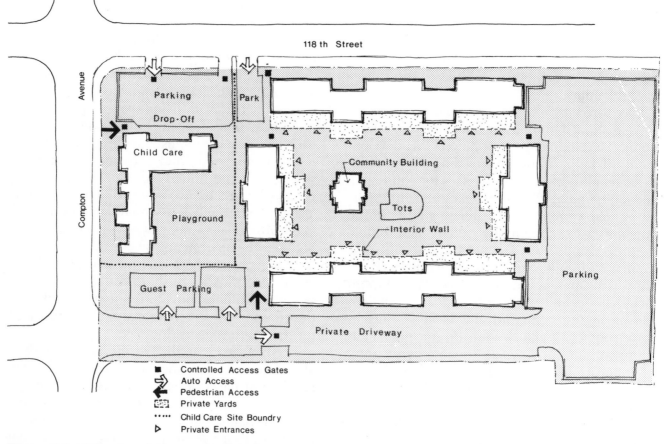

Figure 7-6. Willowbrook Green: site diagram.

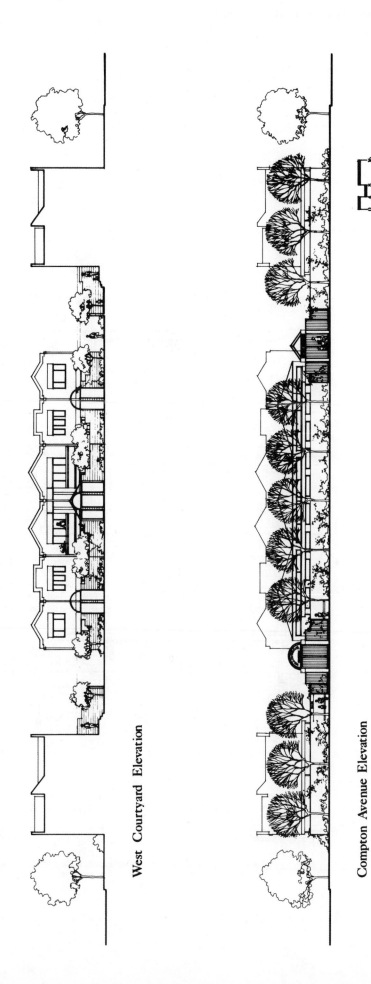

West Courtyard Elevation

Compton Avenue Elevation

Figure 7-7. Willowbrook Green: elevations.

153

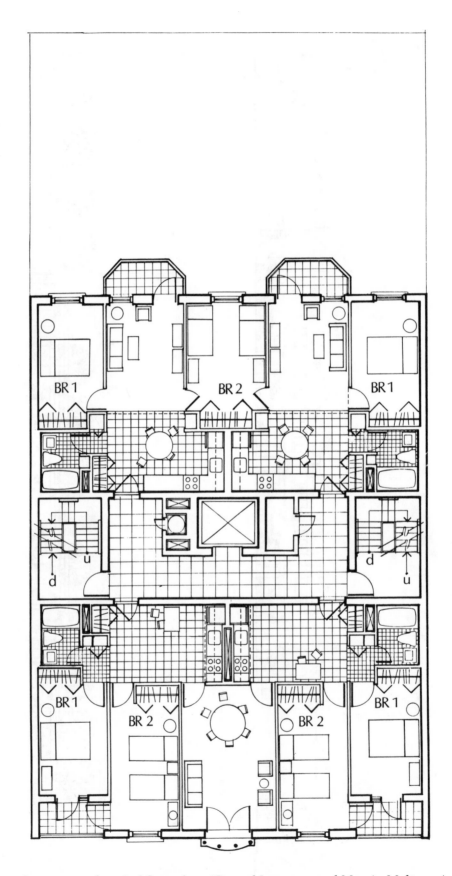

Figure 7-8. Vacant Lots proposal: typical floor plan. *(Conrad Levenson and Marvin Meltzer, Architects)*

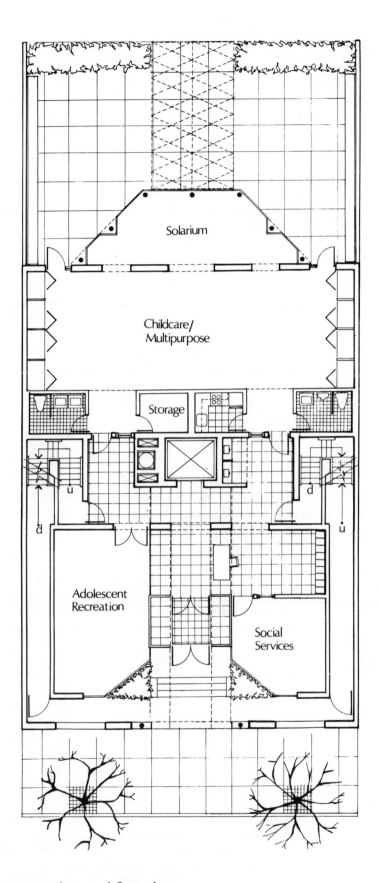

Figure 7-9. Vacant Lots proposal: ground-floor plan.

Table 7-2. A Partial List of Housing Developments for Single Parents in United States

Development	Description	Operation and Funding
Casa Rita 284 E. 151st Street Bronx, NY	Transitional residence for 15 single-parent families. Conversion of existing school. Includes laundry, shared kitchen and dining room, lounge, staff office.	Begun in 1986. Managed by Women-In-Need, Inc. Funded by New York State Homeless Housing Assistance Program and private grants.
County Street Residence New Bedford Child and Family Service 1061 Pleasant Street New Bedford, MA	Transitional residence for teenage single mothers and their children. Six apartment units. Counseling and educational services.	Begun in 1982. Managed by New Bedford Child and Family Service.
Elizabeth Stone House P.O. Box 15 Jamaica Plain, MA	Transitional and permanent residence for 20 women and their children. Two apartments for family childcare providers. Includes community rooms, laundry, conference space.	Begun in 1987. Founded and managed by Elizabeth Stone House, nonprofit organization.
The Haven Rockland Family Shelter 39 S. Main Street Spring Valley, NY	Transitional residence. 15 apartments; also shared bathrooms, kitchens, living rooms.	Begun in 1981. Part of Rockland Family Shelter for battered women. Nonprofit organization.
Horizon House 356 Boylston Boston, MA	Transitional residence for 6 single-parent families: private bedrooms and shared bathrooms, kitchen, living rooms. Vocational and social services.	Begun in 1985. Managed by Women's Industrial and Education Union.
North Hollywood Apts. Maud Booth Family Center 11243 Kittredge Street N. Hollywood, CA	Transitional residence. Ninety-five of 477 housing units set aside for single-parent families. Social services and child care.	Begun in 1970. Funded by Volunteers of America, United Way, Calif. Dept. of Education, fundraising and corporate funds.
One-Parent Family Facility 381/385/391 Virginia Avenue Lexington, KY	Transitional residence for 15 single-parent families. Consists of three apartment buildings. Child care, family services, health care, vocational training on site.	Begun in January 1986. Funded by County CDBG grant; Mayor's Office vocational training grant; low-interest loan from Kentucky Housing Corp.; HUD Section 8 rental assistance; Univ. of Kentucky counseling for parents and children; Tenant Services Board start-up funds and planning service.
Residence for Homeless Families 2136 Crotona Parkway Bronx, NY	Forty-two transitional and permanent residences. Conversion of existing structure to housing for single parents. Designed by Conrad Levenson. Includes social services, workshop space for teaching.	Construction started in 1988. Managed by Phipps Houses and Women-in-Need, Inc. Funding through New York City Dept. of Housing Preservation and Development, Capital Budget Homeless Housing Program; New York State Housing Trust Fund.

Table 7-2. *(cont.)*

Development	Description	Operation and Funding
Residence for Homeless Families 760–770 E. Tremont Bronx, NY	Twelve transitional and 13 permanent residences. Conversion of existing structure to housing for single parents. Designed by Conrad Levenson. Includes social services, workshop space for teaching.	Construction started in 1987. Managed by Phipps Houses, Inc. Funded by New York City Dept. of Housing Preservation and Development, Capital Budget Homeless Housing Program.
Residence for Homeless Women and Children 2248 Webster Avenue Bronx, NY	Transitional residence for 31 families. Conversion of existing structure. Includes congregate living units, manager's apartment, social service office, laundry, child-care center.	Construction started in 1987. Managed by Women-In-Need, Inc. Funding through New York City Dept. of Housing Preservation and Development, and Capital Budget Homeless Housing Program.
St. Francis Home 303 Madison Avenue Hoboken, NJ	Transitional residence. Mothers attend school or work full-time. On-site services. Child care provided.	Private donations.
Samaritan House 388 Prospect Avenue Brooklyn, NY	Transitional residence for 10 families. Conversion of existing structure for single-parent families. Includes staff quarters and offices, laundry, shared kitchen and dining room, recreation room, garden.	Begun in 1985. Managed by Christian Help in Park Slope. Private financing and private grants.
Second Step Housing Project 1717 Fifth Avenue San Rafael, CA	Transitional residence. Ten apartments accommodate 30 women and children. Individual counseling services and support group meetings.	Begun in 1983 by Marin Abused Women's Services as nonprofit corporation.
Shared Housing Project Catholic Social Services 2176 The Alameda San Jose, CA	Transitional residences. Existing structures with no physical changes. Each residence houses two families or family plus a single person.	Begun in 1980. Funded by CDBG, United Way, and Catholic Charities.
Sparksway Commons, Inc. Limited Equity Cooperative Housing Eden Housing, Inc. 1035 "B" Street Suite 201 Hayward, CA	Permanent residence. Forty-five apartments as an affordable limited equity cooperative. Designed by Mui Ho and Sandy Hirschen. Includes tot-lot, laundry, plans for Head Start Program. Residents exchange services, such as child care, auto repair.	Begun in 1984. Funded by County CDBG for land purchase; 30 years deferred note on entire project from Calif. Housing and Community Development Agency.
Warren Village Inc. 1323 Gilpen Street Denver, CO	Transitional residence of over 200 apartments in 2 complexes. Child-care centers and commercial space on site. Family and counseling services.	Begun in 1972 by United Methodist Church. Financial support from community-at-large, gifts, and grants.

Table 7-2. A Partial List of Housing Developments for Single Parents in United States *(cont.)*

Development	Description	Operation and Funding
Willowbrook Green Los Angeles, CA	Permanent residence. 48 units located near major employer. Designed by Ena Dubnoff. Includes common laundry, community room, child-care center, playground.	Construction started in 1988. Funding sources include Ford Foundation, Los Angeles Community Development, and Drew Economic Corporation.
Women's Development Corporation 861 A Broad Street Providence, RI	Permanent residences. One hundred units in numerous rehabilitated buildings and new construction.	Begun in 1979 to encourage involvement by women in design, building, and maintenance of housing. Funding through Section 8 Moderate Rehab Programs, loan from the NC Co-op Bank; mortgages obtained from Rhode Island and Ohio banks; City of Providence operating grant; charitable contributions.

Source: Adapted from State of New Jersey, Department of Community Affairs, 1987; Women's Institute for Housing and Economic Development, 1984, 1986.

OVERVIEW OF CHAPTERS

The following four chapters describe additional housing developments for single-parent households. Developing such housing involves reiterative planning and designing, negotiations with developers and community groups, time, and perseverance.

In "Two Prototypical Designs for Single Parents: The Congregate House and the New American House" Jacqueline Leavitt describes two housing developments that address one of the more critical constraints of single-parent living—restricted mobility. These developments, which she designed with architect Troy West, include housing sponsored by the Bergen County League of Women Voters and the winning design for the New American House design competition, Dayton Court. Both are intended to be permanent housing. Also both are intended to house other types of households in addition to single-parent families, but much of the program and design of each address the needs of single parents. Leavitt also shows the development of design ideas from one project to the next.

A progression in design ideas also is described by Joan Forrester Sprague in "Two Cases of Transitional Housing Development in Boston." She chronicles the involvement of the Women's Institute for Housing and Economic Development with the planning, design, and development of two housing developments for single parents. The design of the Abigail West Shelter, transitional housing in Boston, evolved from an earlier studio project for an architecture class. A subsequent transitional housing development, the Tree of Life, was initiated by the city of Boston. Although the goals of the two projects are similar, the cases provide some striking contrasts in their development and final design.

While the above chapters consider new construction, Passage Community, described by Christine Cook in "Passage Community: Second-Stage Housing for Single Parents," is a renovated building exclusively for low-income single-parent families in Minneapolis. A task force brought together by the YWCA of St. Paul to discuss housing problems of women in the Twin Cities area eventually generated a nonprofit organization to develop transitional housing. Many programmatic features of Passage Community were derived from Warren Villages I and II. An interesting aspect of the programming process was the development of profiles of three different types of single-parent families and their housing needs.

While the above projects were initiated and developed by outside groups, residents in the Toronto cooperatives described by Gerda Wekerle and Sylvia Novac in "Developing Two Women's Housing Cooperatives" participated in the programming and design of their housing. While these projects are not exclusively for single parents, they are particularly sensitive to the needs of such households. Many of the issues considered are those central to housing single parents—on-site child care, accessibility to services, shared spaces, and a focus on community life in the physical design.

These four chapters reflect some of the major concerns and difficulties inherent in developing housing for single parents. Community disagreement and resistance was especially prevalent in the Tree of Life project in Boston but was also a major factor in the siting of Dayton Court in St. Paul. Choosing which design features to eliminate when costs tighten is a major part of the development process in all these cases. A change in architects occurred during the design of both Abigail West in Boston and the Beguinage in Toronto. Space for on-site child care was advocated in most of the design programs, but it was cut in the construction of Dayton Court and Constance Hamilton in Toronto. Shared and service spaces range from common play and yard space (for example, Constance Hamilton and Bergen County housing) to community and job-training spaces (for example, Tree of Life and Passage Community), yet most of the sponsors and residents would have preferred more shared spaces and more service spaces. All the housing sponsors, however, acknowledge that such housing must accommodate the particular needs of single parents while still providing them with dignity and a sense of control.

ADDITIONAL INFORMATION.

Further information on the design and development of housing for single parents is provided in *Housing the Single-Parent Family: A Resource and Action Handbook* by the State of New Jersey (1987); *A Manual on Transitional Housing* by the Women's Institute for Housing and Economic Development (1986); and *Expanding Opportunities for Single Parent Families through Housing* by Cook et al. (1987).

NOTES

1. Different statistics result from alternative definitions of a single-parent household. The statistics cited are for those households consisting of single householders, male or female, with dependent children under the age of 18.
2. According to the National Housing Survey, physical inadequacy includes a problem with plumbing, with electrical or heating systems, or with kitchen or bathroom facilities. Conditions are classified as crowded when there is more than one person per room. A cost burden exists when a household pays more than 30 percent of income for rent, 40 percent of income for mortgage and maintenance, or 30 percent of income for maintenance on a non-mortgaged home.
3. Drawings of Mother's House and Fiona House were made by David Jaeckels. Drawings of Willowbrook Green were provided by Ena Dubnoff.
4. *Bedsit* is a British word for a combined bedroom and sitting room.

References

Ahrentzen, S. B. 1983. *Women and the Housing Process: A Look at Residential Fit, Adjustments and Constraints of Lower-Income Female-Headed Households.* Unpublished doctoral dissertation, University of California, Irvine. Ann Arbor: University Microfilms International.

Anderson-Khlief, S. 1981. Housing needs of single-parent mothers. In *Building for Women*, ed. S. Keller, 21–37. Toronto: Lexington

Anthony, K. 1987. *Initial exploration of the links between research in housing and divorce.* Paper presented at the Symposium on Changing Family Structures and Housing Forms (Sept. 17–19), Arc et Senans, France.

Beers, D. 1987. Redesigning the suburbs. *Image: Sunday Magazine of San Francisco Examiner* (July 12):12–18.

Besharov, D. J., and A. J. Quin. 1987. Not all female-headed families are created equal. *Public Interest* 80:48–56.

Birch, E. L. 1985. The unsheltered woman: Definition

and needs. In *The Unsheltered Woman: Women and Housing in the 80's*, ed. E. L. Birch, 21–45. New Brunswick, NJ: Center for Urban Policy Research.

Calthorpe, P. 1988. Pedestrian pockets: New strategies for suburban growth. *Whole Earth Review* 58:118–123.

Cook, C., M. Vogel-Heffernan, B. Lukermann, S. Pugh, and E. Wattenberg. 1987. *Expanding Opportunities for Single Parent Families Through Housing*. Minneapolis: Minneapolis/St. Paul Family Housing Fund.

Cooper Marcus, C., and W. Sarkissian. 1986. *Housing as if People Mattered: Site Design Guidelines for Medium-Density Family Housing*. Berkeley: University of California Press.

France, I. 1985. Hubertusvereniging: A transition point for single parents. *Women and Environments* 7(1):20–22.

Glick, P. 1980. Remarriage: Some recent changes and variations. *Journal of Family Issues* 1:455–478.

Gregory, J. 1985. Clerical workers and new office technologies. In *Office Workstations in the Home*, National Research Council of the National Academy of Sciences, 112–124. Washington, D.C.: National Academy Press.

Greif, G. L. 1985. *Single Fathers*. Lexington: D. C. Heath.

Hagen, J. L. 1987. Gender and homelessness. *Social Work* 32(4):312–316.

Hertzberger, H., van Roijen-Wortmann, and F. Strauven (eds.). 1986. *Aldo van Eyck*. Amsterdam: Stichting Wonen.

Hopper, K., and J. Hamberg, 1984. *The Making of America's Homeless*. New York: Community Service Society.

Klodawsky, F., A. Spector, and C. Hendrickx. 1983. *The Housing Needs of Single Parent Families in Canada*. Ottawa: External Research Program, Canada Mortgage and Housing Corporation.

Marans, R. W., M. E. Colten, R. M. Groves, and B.

Thomas. 1980. *Measuring Restrictive Rental Policies Affecting Families with Children: A National Survey*. Washington, D.C.: U.S. Department of Housing and Urban Development, Office of Policy Development and Research.

Michelson, W. 1985. *From Sun to Sun: Daily Obligations and Community Structure in the Lives of Employed Women and their Families*. Totowa, NJ: Rowman & Allanheld.

O'Connell, M., and D. E. Bloom. 1987. *Juggling Jobs and Babies: America's Child Care Challenge*. Washington, D.C.: Population Reference Bureau.

Ritzdorf, M. 1986. Women in the city: Land use and zoning issues. *Urban Resources* 3(2):23–27.

Seward, R. 1978. *The American Family: A Demographic History*. Beverly Hills: Sage.

State of New Jersey, Department of Community Affairs. March 1987. *Housing the Single-Parent Family: A Resource and Action Handbook*. Trenton, NJ: State of New Jersey Department of Community Affairs.

Strauven, F. 1980. A place of reciprocity: Home for one-parent families by A. van Eyck. *Lotus* 28:22–44.

Strong, S. 1975. Nina West homes. *Architectural Design*, 497–498.

USBC (United States Bureau of the Census). 1985. Money Income and Poverty Status of Families and Persons in the United States: 1984. *Current Population Reports*. Series P-60, no. 149. Washington, D.C.: U.S. Government Printing Office.

USDHUD (United States Department of Housing and Urban Development). 1980. *Housing Our Families*. Washington, D.C.: U.S. Government Printing Office.

USNCHS (United States National Center for Health Statistics). 1985. *Vital Statistics of the United States*. Washington, D.C.: U.S. Government Printing Office.

Chapter 8

Two Prototypical Designs for Single Parents

The Congregate House and the New American House

Jacqueline Leavitt

When making design decisions for housing for single parents, more insight is gained by comparing them with elderly households than with nuclear families. Both elderly and single-parent households experience a reduction in mobility, the former because of age and frailty and the latter because of the presence of children and the absence of a second adult in the house. This chapter reviews the issue of restricted mobility and examines the applicability of one design solution for single parents that has been tried with the elderly: congregate housing.

The discussion of mobility acts as a framework for understanding two of my designs for single parents and other nontraditional households. The early work, in collaboration with architect Troy West, for the League of Women Voters in Bergen County, New Jersey, began with the needs of single parents. Subsequently the design was tranformed into a congregate house for all generations. That work generated five principles for designing for single parents. Our more recent work, the design of the New American House (NAH), drew on those principles and provides an opportunity for evaluating them. Although it is too soon to do that completely—groundbreaking for the NAH has not yet taken place—this article

explains the reasoning behind the designs and provides a primer for introducing innovative ideas into housing and community plans.

DOMINANT IMAGES OF NUCLEAR FAMILIES, THE ELDERLY, AND SINGLE PARENTS

The dominant image of households in the United States is of nuclear families (Hayden 1984). This is widely considered to be the most desirable personal goal for adulthood, associated with marriage and children. The ideology surrounding the concept of the nuclear family imbues it with more than just the functions of reproducing and parenting. Being in a nuclear family is supposed to bring happiness, and this is linked to owning a single-family detached house. The most time-honored image of the nuclear family has been a commuter husband and a stay-at-home wife who maintains and nurtures the household. Economics has revealed this to be an anachronistic thought. If the nuclear family is to attain or at least to maintain a high standard of living, it is acknowledged that women need to work for wages. The most telling statistic documenting this has been the increasing number of mothers with children six years and younger in the labor force. If families live in the suburbs or cities without accessible mass transit, they need to have at least two cars. The adults need to move freely between their residences and workplaces; the wives, usually, need to add to their schedules the chauffering of children to sundry activities (Fox 1983).

Just as there have been adjustments in thinking about the lives of nuclear families, the concept of the elderly has changed over the past ten years. They are no longer viewed as a homogeneous group of people, aged 62 to 65 years and older. Rather there are differences in age groups —young-old, old-old, and frail-old—by marital status, location of residence, gender, and cultural and ethnic variations (Leavitt and Welch, 1989). Furthermore, research on the elderly is revealing that older people are not uniformly passive victims to changes in their environments (Leavitt and Saegert 1989). Rather they can initiate positive changes. The elderly tend to live in houses they own, although they suffer from reduced incomes in other ways. Their housing may be undermaintained and run down; they may shift their limited resources between housing and other necessities of life, such as food. Their range of activities becomes more confined. The older they get, the greater the likelihood is that their ability to move around is restricted because of increasing frailty compounded by a fixed income.

The lives of the majority of single parents are in stark contrast to those of nuclear families while they share some salient characteristics with elderly people. The typical single parent is more likely to be female, nonwhite, with a low income and few years of education and skills. The dominant ideology surrounding single parents is that they are deviant, or else single parenting is presented as merely a waystop on the road to marriage. Because of their low incomes, single parents are hard pressed to purchase services, such as child care, and instead need to make arrangements with relatives and friends. Without adequate child care they cannot pursue education that could lead to more lucrative employment. Life for them is not likely to be designer houses and home ownership but deteriorating

conditions in rental units. They are restricted in their movements and less able to move further away from their homes in order to find jobs or friends.

Thus single parents resemble nuclear families in that both groups have children. But in a more significant way, having to do with mobility, single parents more closely resemble the elderly. This bears on the designs I will discuss in this chapter. First, the term *mobility* is clarified as a point of departure for designers.

DESIGNING FOR MOBILITY

Mobility is defined here slightly differently from the way it is used in social science studies, which emphasize mobility "as a process whereby households adjust to dissatisfaction with their current housing" (Bartlett 1980, 3) because of changes in the life cycle, household standards, or locational changes (Ahrentzen 1985). This chapter defines *mobility* as the degree of freedom people have in moving about and between their residences, workplaces, public facilities, and commercial settings.[1] Lack of mobility may arise because of age and disability, but among single parents, there are added factors—the absence of another adult in the household and the presence of children. Solo parenting has ramifications for finding employment, developing a social network among adults, and carrying out daily tasks. Restricted mobility renders single parenting more difficult, particularly when it is accompanied by low income.

This definition of mobility has been used by some social scientists and planners. Alvin L. Schorr (1984) distinguished between city and block life in his criticism of urban renewal designs that wiped out neighborhoods. Policy makers originally conceived of urban renewal as a way of replacing what they considered to be blighted or slum neighborhoods. These areas usually were located near the commercial downtowns of older cities. Where urban renewal occurred, neighborhoods were rearranged physically and economically: high towers replaced small-scale dwellings, residential streets became high-speed routes for nonresidents, and higher-income residents displaced lower-income households. A vision of "city" life, where there were fewer face-to-face relationships with neighborhood merchants and friendships were not determined by geographical proximity, dominated "block" life. The block dweller became insecure, having lost a life that was familiar, manageable, and intimate. Block dwellers were more likely to be in poor households headed by women. They were unable to benefit from the city's resources in terms of jobs and services because they lacked either the income or the access to automobiles that would allow them to be more mobile.

When replanning Metro Toronto a group of women professionals met with 25 groups of women, including full-time homemakers, sole-support mothers, elderly women, and disabled women (Women Plan Toronto 1986). When the comments of all the women were analyzed, the paramount complaint was planned subdivisions without convenience stores nearby, thereby leaving them to their own resources for acquiring simple things such as an extra loaf of bread or a container of milk. The women also pointed to obstacles that prevented their moving about freely: escalators that do not allow easy access to people with strollers and parking garages that are isolated and lack security measures.

In research I conducted with environmental psychologist Susan Saegert (1989), we suggest a new way of thinking about housing for low-income people, tying it to community resources and calling it the Community-Household Model. A Community-Household exists when people, usually women, extend household skills—such as budgeting, house cleaning, and nurturing—to landlord-abandoned buildings and then to community redevelopment. To do so the community's resources must be accessible, whether they are schools, churches, child-care centers, or medical offices. Technical assistance from people within these institutions needs to be readily available. Building resources such as secure elevators and stairwells and barrier-free entrances need to be provided. One of the principles on which the Community-Household Model rests is mobility. Simply put, people cannot have access to resources without mobility. Problems of limited mobility affect single parents most particularly in relation to child rearing. Children need to get to

schools, play centers, child care, and doctors. The problem of restricted mobility is seen clearly when a child becomes ill. There are a few choices for the single parent: to stay home, to hire a babysitter for the day, to leave the child alone, to bring the child to someone else's house, or to bring the child to work. The economic consequences range from losing a day's pay to paying for child care. The psychological consequence is additional stress for the single parent who is having to cope with dividing her time between her needs and her children's needs.

Other aspects of mobility related to child care focus on the ease of finding and keeping a job. The lack of a driver's license and poor public transportation place constraints on job selection. Particularly for low-paid women, transportation costs can consume a large part of their salaries. Many single parents accept only part-time employment, thereby losing income and fringe benefits that in turn keep them in a precarious financial position. Others, when they can, try to find more suitable work arrangements, either in flexible hours or in jobs located near their homes. An example of how a single parent may capitalize on her restricted mobility and still provide for her children is found in the story of a community activist who started a neighborhood credit union. This allowed her to earn money without leaving the neighborhood.

Another aspect of mobility is movement in and out of a house or an apartment. Although there are enforceable regulations concerning barrier-free architecture, the term is typically applied to the disabled or the elderly. Yet the benefits may be more widespread. Pushing a baby carriage down a ramp is easier than using stairs; an adult with no handicaps may find a handrail in the shower useful. Reference books exist on barrier-free devices for the handicapped but ignore how these may be adapted for parents handling children, strollers, play equipment, and other sorts of packages (Robinette 1985).

There are two advantages in comparing the restricted mobility of single parents with that of the elderly. First, there is a longer history of designing special facilities for the elderly, particularly congregate housing (Chellis, Seagle, Jr., and Seagle 1982; Newcomer, Lawton, and Byerts 1986). The information generated by this history is instructive in designing for single parents. Second, understanding the concept of restricted mobility leads to the possibility of building facilities for activities and services into the residence and the community (Leavitt and Saegert, 1989; Wekerle 1985). Again this is a path that has been taken by advocates for the elderly.

Restricted Mobility and Congregate Housing

Given the restricted mobility that single parents face, one possibility is to concentrate settings for particular activities—such as child care, paid work, and socializing with adults—as close to home as possible. Some functions lend themselves to this more easily than others. For example, child care becomes a cost savings if shared with other households. Wage work conducted in the home reduces transportation costs. Proximity to other adults increases the opportunity for social encounters.

When considering these issues and keeping in mind the low incomes of most single parents, it is not difficult to move from these considerations to the idea of congregate housing. A word should be said about the term *congregate housing.* Congregate housing can be organized as long term and permanent or as transitional. There is some confusion about whether *congregate* refers to units, people, or services; noted gerontologist M. Powell Lawton has defined it as including all three. Swedish researcher Sten Gromark suggests that the naming is important to a conceptual and theoretical analysis.[2] In his work he describes *communality* as "social qualities usually associated with community life" that may be spontaneously or consciously organized into a housing commune (a few adults and children in a large apartment), a household group (a group of households sharing a common habitation including communal facilities, made up of about 10 to 25 households in informal cooperation), and collective households (with several collective service facilities). For many people the term *congregate* is used interchangeably with *shared* or *communal* housing (Chellis et al. 1982).[3] Whichever word is used, *congregate*, *shared*, or *communal*, the central idea is to provide housing with collective services. For the elderly the services usually are meals, social-recreational activ-ities, classes, transportation, medical care, homemaker services, counseling, and security.

In the United States the idea of residential environments with supportive services was first applied to the elderly and recognized by President Kennedy in 1963 (Chellis et al. 1982). The first congregate housing act was passed in 1970.[4] This was considered a truncated act because funds were provided for capital facilities but not for purchasing, preparing, and serving meals. In 1978 the Congregate Services Act was approved, providing a service subsidy. Although congregate housing has not been as widespread a solution to problems for the elderly as was once thought (Pynoos 1984), the concept can be meaningfully adopted as an option for single parents. Indeed, the idea of mixing single parents and the elderly in congregate housing informs the designs that will be discussed further.

There is one very important caveat about congregate housing: that is, to provide different levels of privacy. When people share housing they have to feel there are places where they can be alone. In congregate housing for the elderly, for example, service providers often have stipulated that each person have his or her own bedroom *and* bathroom. It is well-established that in the process of becoming a single parent, particularly if this is brought about by divorce, separation, or widowhood, housing accommodations worsen and the likelihood of finding privacy decreases. Poor housing may take the form of deteriorating conditions, a high proportion of income spent on rent, and overcrowding. Among racial and ethnic groups where single parenting is high, overcrowding also is high. Different levels of privacy in congregate housing for single parents may be the most essential component for a successful design.

SINGLE-PARENT OR INTERGENERATIONAL CONGREGATE HOUSING

My first opportunity to think about the relationship between the needs of single parents and design occurred in the fall of 1982 with a request from the Bergen County, New Jersey, League of Women Voters. The League had identified two types of needy households coming to their community advocacy housing center. One was the elderly, primarily women, whose mortgages were fully paid but who, because of age or income, lacked the physical mobility or capability to maintain their homes. The second group was single parents, also primarily women, who were unable to find affordable housing and/or landlords and managers willing to accept children. The League solicited help in preparing an annotated bibliography for single parents. Next, they organized a workshop for single parents, potential housing providers, bankers, designers, and planners. As one of their key speakers at the workshop, I drew on American and European examples of single-parent housing and housing designed with community facilities. Architect Troy West and I prepared a series of drawings prior to the workshop. One of West's earlier designs for affordable housing was expanded in concept to respond to issues of mobility, privacy, and low income; it ranged from 1,100 to 2,600 square feet. The appropriate design solution appeared to be a congregate house.[5] A new set of drawings was made, including a section, an elevation, a floor plan, and a framing plan. This set was sent to people who had registered for the workshop. An instruction sheet accompanied the drawings; the intent was to encourage people to draw their ideas directly on the framing plan prior to the workshop. This did not occur, but the idea remains a useful one for eliciting opinions from a potential user group. One possibility for accomplishing this is simply to ask people beforehand to draw freehand or write a description about what type of housing they would like.[6] A second possibility is to schedule enough time at a workshop to allow people to complete a drawing exercise.

A lively discussion took place at the workshop in response to our presentation and drawings. Although it is conjecture, some reasons for the success of the discussion may be traced to the recipients receiving the design package prior to the workshop (even if they did not notate it); the slide presentation, which presented options; and the "user-friendly" colored drawings, complete with a smiling sun.

Up until the workshop the design was expressly aimed at single parents. The two-and-a-half-story house, with basement, was intended for three to four single parents with six to seven children.

Our proposal was for new construction rather than for rehabilitation of an existing building. Rehabilitation should not be ruled out; the familiarity of the house type we used makes it easy to consider interior adaptation of a similar existing structure. Two of the four rooms on the main floor were designed as flexible rooms for paid work, such as giving music lessons or drafting. When the rooms were not in use for that, they would be available as social spaces where residents of the house could entertain and relax individually or in groups. Ensuring privacy and the easy conversion of rooms for different uses was provided by a separate entrance in one case and sliding doors in another.

The living room and kitchen, both on the first floor, were planned as congregate spaces. The bedrooms on the upper floors were the most private rooms in the house; they were designed to accommodate desks and, in some cases, cribs. Some of the bedrooms were shown with double beds, others with single beds. It is extremely useful to show furniture in drawings; this helps orient laypeople who are unfamiliar with reading drawings. The drawings themselves also may reveal underlying biases about single parents held by designers, developers, or planners in public and private agencies. With the bias visible, designs may be modified or changed to reflect the needs of single parents more accurately. Although it was not raised in any of our presentations, the treatment of beds and storage space was a problem identified by Nina West. West, a single parent, has successfully lobbied for single-parent housing in London, England. She felt that public officials tried to insert their moral views about acceptable behavior for single parents into their projects and drawings by not providing a screen in the "bedsit" and consistently showing a double wardrobe for a single adult.

Initially the main bathroom in our presentation was on the second floor, its facilities split—the bathtub/shower, toilet, and washbasin located adjacent to each other but separate—in order to permit a maximum number of residents simultaneous access. A half bathroom was located on both the main and loft levels.

A major change in the design occurred because of the age mixture of respondents at the workshop. The question of privacy, particularly for older residents, led to rethinking the use of

Figure 8-1. Single-parent house for Bergen County: section.

the basement. It was changed from a bedroom, a living room, and a bathroom to an accessory apartment (Gellen 1985) with its own kitchen but with easy access to the upstairs. This provided the option for older persons to maintain their discrete space but to be able to socialize and provide informal babysitting for other residents. Here, intergenerational housing means a mixture of ages from infants to the elderly. This residential configuration provides one response to what Lewis Mumford (1968) observed as the breaking up of the three-generation family within a single dwelling. Since the 1950s, the number of households has increased because adult sons and daughters leave home earlier to live on their own or with roommates, preparatory to marriage, and older widowed people maintain independent living arrangements rather than living with married children. In effect what can be created in the congregate house is a living arrangement for a three-generation nonrelated family (Fig. 8-1).

With more discussion it also became clearer that it would be difficult to house four single parents and six or seven children of varying ages in a single dwelling, primarily because of the noise and the lack of privacy. The workshop, and subsequent workshops, also revealed that the reso-

lution of many design problems varies with the social composition of the household, the ages and genders of children and adults, the attitudes toward sharing, the needs for privacy, and the exact uses of any of the work rooms and social rooms. For an intergenerational house to succeed, many thorny issues that develop whenever people live together need to be discussed in a planning period with the potential users.[7] An optimum goal is that discussions about activities in the house and attitudes of prospective residents guide design. It may not be possible to accomplish this. Often this planning stage is short-circuited and decisions about design are resolved with the sponsor or client. Even then, clarifying attitudes through identifying particular types of rooms and uses and then discussing attitudes and anticipated behavior are essential so that the designer and the client are aware of potential conflicts among residents. For example, assume a design decision is made that does not provide a bathroom for every bedroom. It will be necessary to probe for people's attitudes about sharing bathrooms in a screening process for prospective residents. In this way there is a greater likelihood that unrelated residents will live in harmony with each other.

One way to identify potential clients for innovative housing designs is to work collaboratively with an institution that is likely to have a high proportion of single parents. An example of this approach is in the Watts-Willowbrook area in Los Angeles, where 48 units of rental housing and a child-care facility for 60 children, designed by Ena Dubnoff, is nearing occupancy. The project, Willowbrook Green, began when an article about housing alternatives by Dolores Hayden was brought to the attention of administrators of the Los Angeles County Housing Agency. Subsequently the Charles R. Drew Post-Graduate Medical School set up an Economic Development Corporation, staffed by a full-time person, Brenda Shockley, who has managed the project from its inception and has acted as a liaison between Drew and the county. Occupancy by single parents is expected as residents will be drawn from the staff of Drew and the nearby Martin Luther King Hospital.

Alternatively once an institution is identified, a questionnaire can be used to elicit interest in sharing and living in a particular locality; subsequent planning meetings can be held to determine whether the institution and potential users are interested in pursuing the idea of congregate housing.[8] A continuing relationship between designers and clients is useful, but contracts rarely are made with designers or developers to modify or make changes after residents have occupied the building. As a result people often take matters into their own hands or adjust in one way or another (Cooper Marcus and Sarkissian 1987).

The intergenerational congregate house was never built, but it was awarded first prize in 1983 at a National House of Women exhibition sponsored by California State University at Long Beach. In addition, five design principles emerged from the work with the League and other groups, such as Parents Without Partners. These principles played a significant part in the thinking for the New American House competition.

First, a newly constructed house should be an integral part of the neighborhood to avoid calling attention to the different types of households living there. Research has shown that most single parents do not like attention drawn to them because of their marital status (Anderson-Khleif 1982). This suggests that infill housing is most appropriate. The house profile should fit in with the surrounding property in form and materials; exterior walls, for example, should reflect the materials used on surrounding properties. If an existing house is being rehabilitated, there is greater likelihood that it already fits into the context of the block; designers should be wary of changing the exterior in any substantial way. West and I worked with the idea of houses as opposed to apartments. However, there may be housing markets where large enough apartments can be built or rehabilitated without sacrificing privacy.

Second, private spaces are critical for the inhabitants. Given the definition of congregate housing, there are clearly rooms that purposely will be used by several people at the same time. Privacy may be found in those rooms, but this will depend on the daily schedules of residents. Privacy also may be found outside, depending on the size of the lot, the proximity to neighboring houses, and the landscaping. The bathroom facilities will be private. But the single place that will accord the most privacy will be the bedrooms. Designers should explore ways in which room configurations can lead to private nooks within bedrooms and also multiple uses of bedrooms. Developing L-shaped rooms and adapting loft spaces can create separate zones within a room. Other possibilities are designing built-in furniture to free other space in the room or nooks that can accommodate equipment such as computers, typewriters, or sewing machines. The congregate house was deliberately developed to angle the building from 30 to 90 degrees. At 30, 45, and 60 degrees, it was possible to create a greater feeling of privacy by not exposing the entire floor plan to view from the front door. At these angles it also was possible to have a greater sense of visual privacy even if there were other people engaged in activities "around the corner."

The third principle concerns encouraging a sense of community among people living in the house. In design terms this can be achieved by providing opportunities for social encounters; for example, a kitchen large enough to accommodate the entire household eating together, even if they do this on a quasi-regular basis. Another way is by ensuring the convertability of first floor rooms from work areas to social areas (Fig. 8-2).

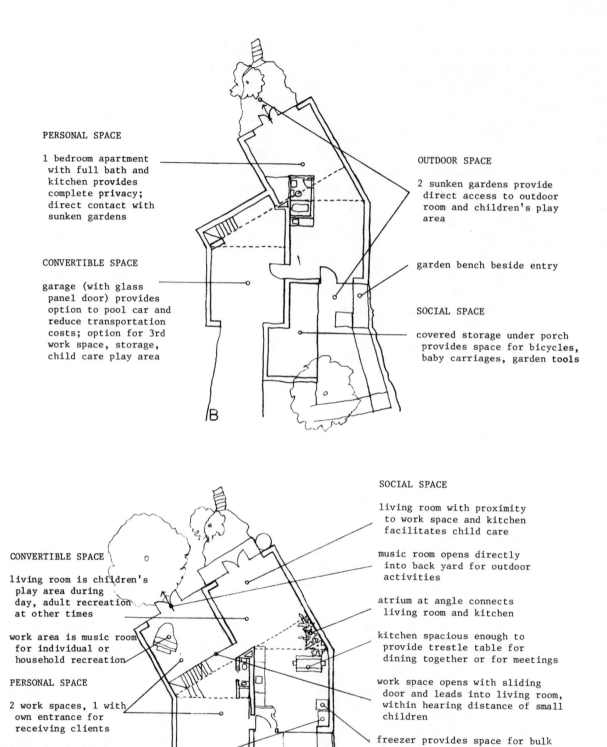

PERSONAL SPACE

1 bedroom apartment with full bath and kitchen provides complete privacy; direct contact with sunken gardens

CONVERTIBLE SPACE

garage (with glass panel door) provides option to pool car and reduce transportation costs; option for 3rd work space, storage, child care play area

OUTDOOR SPACE

2 sunken gardens provide direct access to outdoor room and children's play area

garden bench beside entry

SOCIAL SPACE

covered storage under porch provides space for bicycles, baby carriages, garden tools

SOCIAL SPACE

living room with proximity to work space and kitchen facilitates child care

music room opens directly into back yard for outdoor activities

atrium at angle connects living room and kitchen

kitchen spacious enough to provide trestle table for dining together or for meetings

work space opens with sliding door and leads into living room, within hearing distance of small children

freezer provides space for bulk buying to reduce food costs

porch overlook provides view of street activities

ramp provides access for handicapped, elderly, and small children

CONVERTIBLE SPACE

living room is children's play area during day, adult recreation at other times

work area is music room for individual or household recreation

PERSONAL SPACE

2 work spaces, 1 with own entrance for receiving clients

desk area in kitchen for household planning

Figure 8-2. Single-parent house for Bergen County: annotated floor plans.

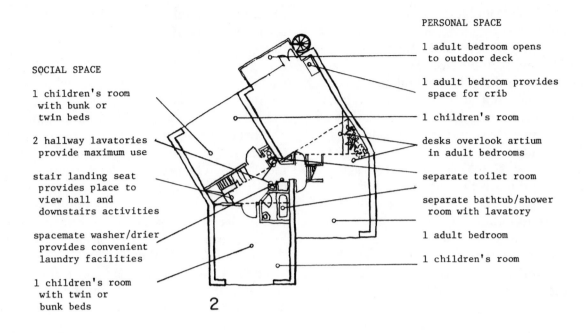

SOCIAL SPACE

1 children's room
with bunk or
twin beds

2 hallway lavatories
provide maximum use

stair landing seat
provides place to
view hall and
downstairs activities

spacemate washer/drier
provides convenient
laundry facilities

1 children's room
with twin or
bunk beds

PERSONAL SPACE

1 adult bedroom opens
to outdoor deck

1 adult bedroom provides
space for crib

1 children's room

desks overlook artium
in adult bedrooms

separate toilet room

separate bathtub/shower
room with lavatory

1 adult bedroom

1 children's room

2

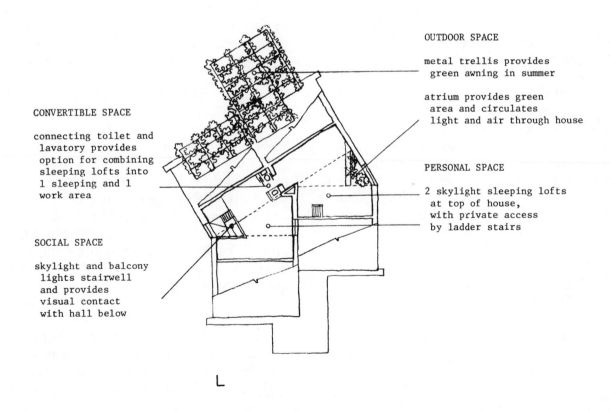

CONVERTIBLE SPACE

connecting toilet and
lavatory provides
option for combining
sleeping lofts into
1 sleeping and 1
work area

SOCIAL SPACE

skylight and balcony
lights stairwell
and provides
visual contact
with hall below

OUTDOOR SPACE

metal trellis provides
green awning in summer

atrium provides green
area and circulates
light and air through house

PERSONAL SPACE

2 skylight sleeping lofts
at top of house,
with private access
by ladder stairs

L

Figure 8-2. *(cont.)*

A garage also may double as a common utility room or a play space.

Fourth, to the extent possible, there should be maximum flexibility in the house over time. One way to accomplish this is to site buildings so that additions can be built at a later time. Alternatively the designer can consider the possibility of providing footings that can withstand adding stories to the structure of the house. This may prove to be costly and should be measured against other design and marketing decisions. A flat roof also will lend itself to adding stories later on. Perhaps the most important way to achieve flexibility and also to encourage a sense of community is to build several intergenerational houses on a block or in a neighborhood. This opportunity was provided by the New American House competition, and is discussed further in the next section.

Fifth, to the extent possible and when appropriate, self-help or self-management should be integrated into the designing, building, managing, and maintaining of the house. There are a number of different ways to organize management and maintenance operations. The most familiar is through a recognized agency that, for a fee, assumes these responsibilities. But there are other options that involve varying degrees of self-management. At least one proposal suggests that opportunities should be made available for single parents to self-manage; the benefits are that they can acquire social skills through group process and assertiveness training through making suggestions and reaching decisions about their housing and service needs.[9] There also are ways in which residents who contribute to management and maintenance can be awarded points, perhaps linked to lower costs per month.

THE NEW AMERICAN HOUSE COMPETITION

In 1984 a one-stage competition for the New American House (NAH) was announced. Planning for the competition had started two years earlier.[10] The sponsors of the competition were the Minneapolis College of Art and Design in the Whittier neighborhood of Minneapolis and the National Endowment for the Arts, Design Arts Program, through an application to the Minneapolis-based Dayton-Hudson Foundation.[11] Key to the entire project has been Harvey Sherman, a single parent who perceived the needs of other single parents and an architect who made the connection between needs and built form. He took the lead in the program development stage and his on-the-spot presence has been extremely critical in subsequent design changes and implementation. The program's advisors included people from the Twin Cities development and architectural community, including Rodney D. Hardy, vice-president of the Minneapolis-based Sienna Corporation. Hardy became a partner in the development of the project.

The competition program called for six prototypical units of urban infill housing, expressly for nontraditional households, on about a third of an acre, each individual unit not to exceed 1,000 square feet, with space exclusively dedicated to wage work. The initial program announcement read: "The intent of this competition is to generate and disseminate innovative concepts for the design of urban housing units which will accurately reflect the needs of nontraditional, professional households." The program stated that the types of households being considered were the following: "Single-parent families, two-income families, unrelated young adults sharing a single residence, adults without children at home and retired, active adults . . . which are emerging to replace the traditional nuclear family."

The units could be grouped as two and four, three and three, or as six row houses. The intent was to produce prototypical units adaptable to any urban infill site; identical unit plans could be rotated 45, 90, 180, or more degrees or flipped to provide a mirror image; end or corner units had to be identical to other units. The program requirements specified what should be counted in the square footage. In the work-space area, for example, communal waiting rooms or reception areas serving more than one unit were not permitted. While there was information about the climate of the area, there were no specific requirements for energy conservation or for cost estimates. Although the program provided sample scenarios of who could live in each unit, registrants were free to write their own scripts.

The Winning Design

Our winning design was based on a row-house concept with six contiguous buildings (Fig. 8-3). Each of the six units fronts the major street with its more public workplace side (workplace or work space refers to paid work). The work spaces, 199 square feet each, are places where people conduct business, whether it is an artist's studio or a lawyer's office or whether it is adapted for a community service, such as a child-care center. In section movement (Fig. 8-4) from the street brings the person to the work space first; adjacent to it is a half bathroom. The work space overlooks the inner court. This inner court may be handled in several ways; open or closed, with clear panes or solar panels. The work space is connected to the more private two-and-a-half-story residential zone by a one-story linear kitchen with windows overlooking the inner court. The kitchen leads to the living room, which also has access to the court. Stairs in the living room lead to the second- and third-floor sleeping areas, a full bathroom, and another half bathroom. The main entrance to the residential space is from the rear alleyway. Carports for the residences are in the rear, along with access for the handicapped.

The flipping of one end unit results in a double unit, labeled building E in the site plan. The flipping permits the last combined unit to become a single-parent or intergenerational house with a child-care center. This unit has the flexibility of having either one or two kitchens; the ground-floor residential area can be converted into an accessory unit, housing two single parents and an older person, or any combination thereof. The work space, now double the size, can become a child-care center for the group of six buildings as well as for the block and the neighborhood. The combined front yards can be a play area for the child-care center; similarly the enlarged inside court can function this way. Unit E's household organization is identical to that of the single-parent house described earlier but the site plan and section are different. Although the design of the NAH is not congregate housing, it nonetheless fulfills four of the five principles learned in developing the single-parent house: creating a fit with an existing neighborhood, ensuring privacy, en-

couraging a sense of community, and providing flexibility. Even the fifth principle, self-management, can be accommodated in the formation of the residents' association to oversee the maintenance of common spaces. Each of the four principles will be discussed in turn.

The fit between a house for single parents and the surrounding community was accomplished by fulfilling the program's call for infill housing. Subsequent steps in implementation furthered this idea when the St. Paul Heritage Preservation Commission successfully argued for exterior cladding that was compatible with the surrounding buildings. Privacy also is attained by meeting the program's requirement for six units, each of which is self-sufficient with its own bathrooms and kitchen. Encouraging a sense of community is achieved by providing for the sharing of public spaces where casual neighboring may occur in informal ways. Placing the one-story workplace on the street would allow people passing by to stop or simply to nod hello to those in the workplace, thereby fostering more community interaction.

Flexibility is made possible by flipping the end unit, and it is achieved in a number of other ways as well. First, the beauty of the row house lies in its potential for expansion in either the front or the back. Because there is a front and a rear yard and the building is not built to the street or lot line, outdoor rooms can be created through trellises or partial enclosures. Alternatively, in one unit, the carport was fully enclosed to provide a soundproof room for the rock musician son of a single parent. Attention also has been paid to child care in the home. Loft areas on the third floor overlook the second floor, where children's rooms can be located, and windows in the kitchen, living room, and work room overlook the inner court, where children can play. Depending on children's ages, folding gates will be necessary at the foot of stairs to different levels. The rear yards become places for children to play away from the street, and neighbors can chat over the knee-high planters separating one house from another.

An earlier drawing included more aspects of congregate housing by combining the interior courtyards and not connecting each residential

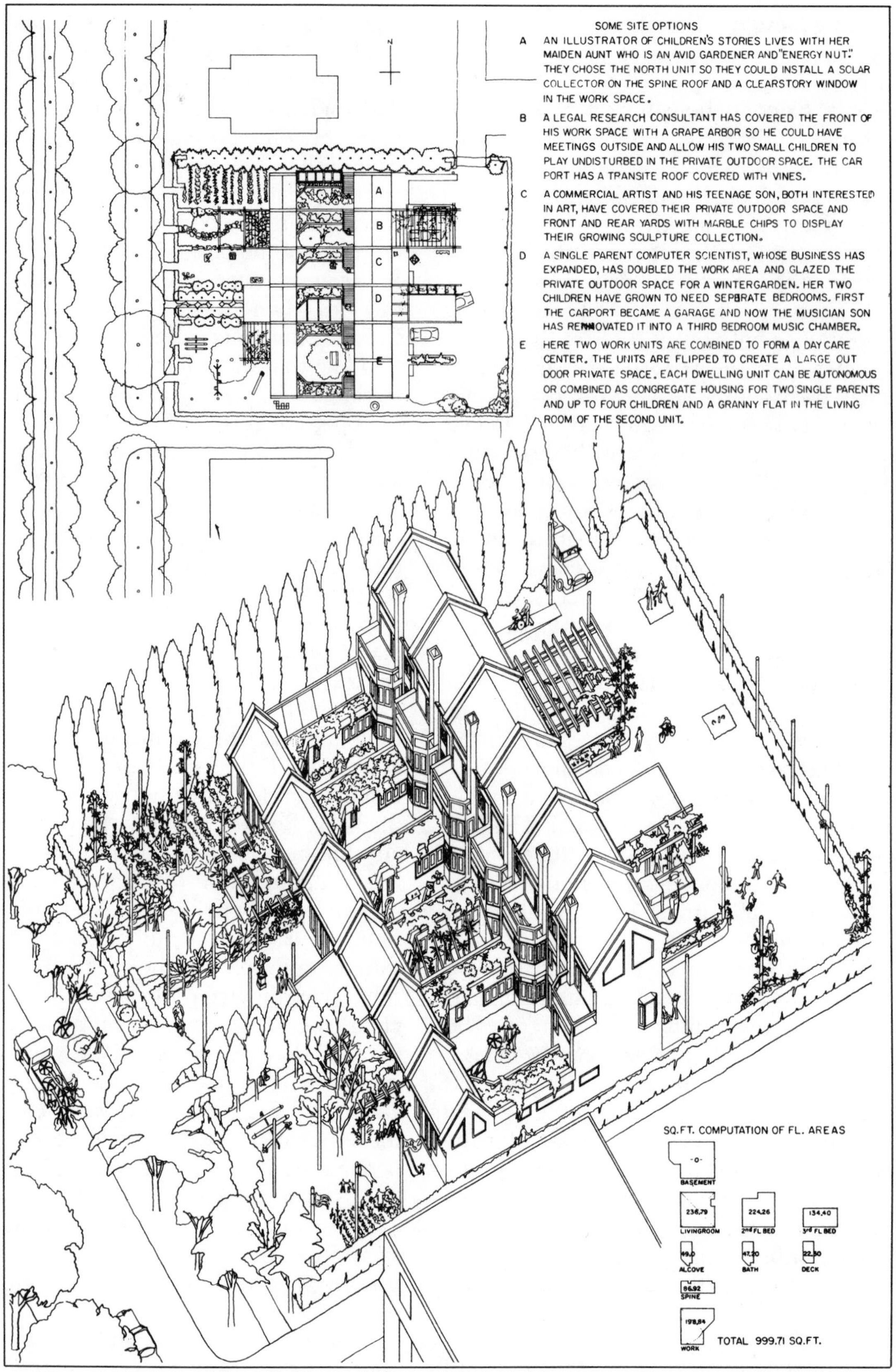

SOME SITE OPTIONS

A   AN ILLUSTRATOR OF CHILDREN'S STORIES LIVES WITH HER
    MAIDEN AUNT WHO IS AN AVID GARDENER AND "ENERGY NUT."
    THEY CHOSE THE NORTH UNIT SO THEY COULD INSTALL A SOLAR
    COLLECTOR ON THE SPINE ROOF AND A CLEARSTORY WINDOW
    IN THE WORK SPACE.

B   A LEGAL RESEARCH CONSULTANT HAS COVERED THE FRONT OF
    HIS WORK SPACE WITH A GRAPE ARBOR SO HE COULD HAVE
    MEETINGS OUTSIDE AND ALLOW HIS TWO SMALL CHILDREN TO
    PLAY UNDISTURBED IN THE PRIVATE OUTDOOR SPACE. THE CAR
    PORT HAS A TRANSITE ROOF COVERED WITH VINES.

C   A COMMERCIAL ARTIST AND HIS TEENAGE SON, BOTH INTERESTED
    IN ART, HAVE COVERED THEIR PRIVATE OUTDOOR SPACE AND
    FRONT AND REAR YARDS WITH MARBLE CHIPS TO DISPLAY
    THEIR GROWING SCULPTURE COLLECTION.

D   A SINGLE PARENT COMPUTER SCIENTIST, WHOSE BUSINESS HAS
    EXPANDED, HAS DOUBLED THE WORK AREA AND GLAZED THE
    PRIVATE OUTDOOR SPACE FOR A WINTERGARDEN. HER TWO
    CHILDREN HAVE GROWN TO NEED SEPARATE BEDROOMS. FIRST
    THE CARPORT BECAME A GARAGE AND NOW THE MUSICIAN SON
    HAS RENNOVATED IT INTO A THIRD BEDROOM MUSIC CHAMBER.

E   HERE TWO WORK UNITS ARE COMBINED TO FORM A DAY CARE
    CENTER. THE UNITS ARE FLIPPED TO CREATE A LARGE OUT
    DOOR PRIVATE SPACE. EACH DWELLING UNIT CAN BE AUTONOMOUS
    OR COMBINED AS CONGREGATE HOUSING FOR TWO SINGLE PARENTS
    AND UP TO FOUR CHILDREN AND A GRANNY FLAT IN THE LIVING
    ROOM OF THE SECOND UNIT.

SQ. FT. COMPUTATION OF FL. AREAS

- 0 -
BASEMENT

236.79
LIVINGROOM

224.26
2nd FL BED

134.40
3rd FL BED

69.0
ALCOVE

47.30
BATH

22.30
DECK

86.92
SPINE

198.84
WORK   TOTAL 999.71 SQ. FT.

Figure 8-3. New American House: site plan and axonometric.

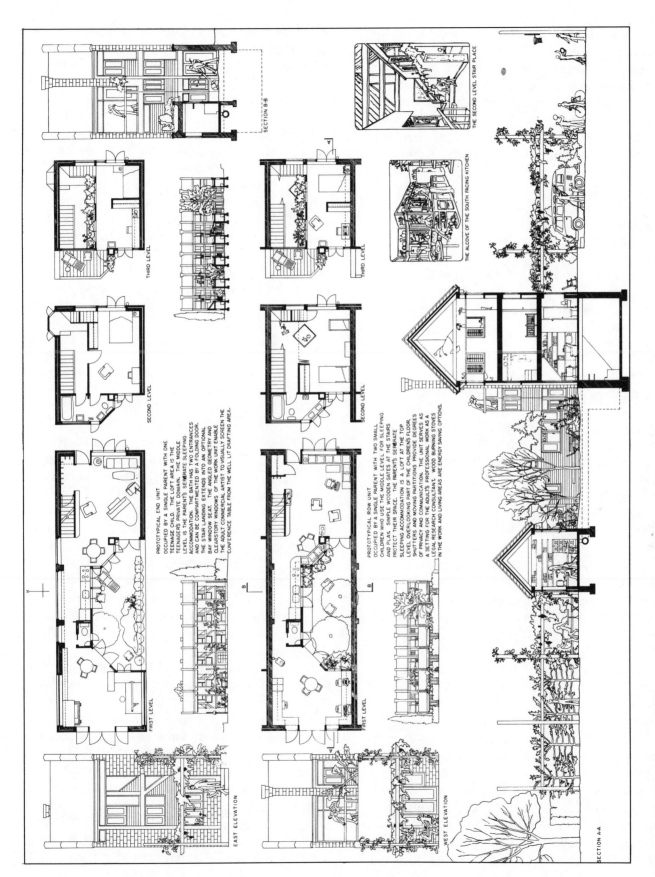

Figure 8-4. New American House: section and floor plans.

173

area to a work area by a kitchen spine. When the answers to questions about the competition were published, it became clear that each work space had to be directly connected to its own residential space. Nonetheless, it is easy to imagine the possibilities of combining some or all of the individual inner courts and, depending on the residents, reducing the size of individual units, even eliminating some of the kitchens. A group of friends might, for example, buy three or four units and share one complete kitchen, retaining a minimum kitchen space in each unit.

As the implementation phase unfolded, some design ideas had to be modified, others changed or scrapped completely. At each stage design and development decisions had to be made that affected the innovations generated by the competition program.

Getting the New American House Built

Negotiations for implementation were begun in October 1984 with Rodney Hardy and Harvey Sherman, who are now the developers of the project. The original site for the competition had not been secured, and it was realized that any new site would require reworking the design.[12] Hardy, Sherman, West, and I toured the immediate Whittier neighborhood and other parts of the Twin Cities looking at potential sites.

In March 1985 a second site was found in adjacent St. Paul, where there was more vacant and affordable land. The land at this second site was owned by the St. Paul Housing Redevelopment Authority (HRA). The orientation of this site and its configuration in relation to adjacent property meant that the original drawings for the NAH had to be modified. The drawings were subsequently submitted for approval to the City of St. Paul. St. Paul, like many other cities, has an elaborate planning process for land-use development; neighborhood residents and other interested parties are given the opportunity to debate the worth of all proposed projects. The community planning process requires a presentation, first before the neighborhood planning district and then before the Board of the District Planning Council;

only then is a recommendation sent to the City. After receiving this the staff—the Department of Planning and Economic Development also is the staff for HRA—presents a report to the City Council. The City Council also is the Board of the HRA.

In July 1985 a proposal for "townhouses," for the second site, based on our winning design, was submitted to the Summit-University District 8 Planning Council and the Department of Planning and Economic Development for consideration. The developers tried to garner political support. G. Richard Slade, president of the Minneapolis College of Art and Design, wrote a letter that described the project to George Latimer, mayor of St. Paul. Mayor Latimer expressed interest in the project's prototypical and demonstration aspects, but he was in no position to support it above any other schemes for the site. On August 8, 1985, the City Council chose to award the site to a developer for housing for the developmentally impaired.

A third site was found. In early 1986 two contiguous sites at the corners of Dayton Avenue and Dale Street were identified and proved to be the most propitious. Sherman began to gather the pieces needed to package and process the project, which was now called Dayton Court (the developers took the name Dayton Court Associates). This site also is in District 8. Because of the increased size (25,840 square feet), it was possible to project 12 units instead of six. A new site plan massed two rows of six row-house units, separated by a 30-foot courtyard and turned 90 degrees to the east-west street, Dayton Avenue. Refining the site plan and units became a critical step in the implementation process.

From the time West and I were announced as winners of the competition in 1984 to almost three years later when Dayton Court received recommendation for final developer status from the District 8 Board at the end of March 1987, there were at least 26 different steps that had to be taken. These included different review and approval processes. Also there were meetings with the city, negotiation of contracts, soil tests, and preparing construction documents. Half the site was owned by the HRA and the other half by a private party who initially acted as the project's contractor. Negotiations had to occur to assemble the site. The two lots are in a designated Heritage Preservation District known as the Historic Hill District. Sherman had to request the building permit through the St. Paul Heritage Preservation Commission. In June 1986 the Heritage Preservation Commission voted favorably on the project, but only after changes had been made regarding compatibility with the surrounding buildings, including the change from stucco to lapsiding with a cedar wainscot on the exterior. Half of the property was zoned multifamily, but part had to be rezoned from B-2 to RM-2. The rezoning is handled by the Department of Planning and Economic Development's staff, but Sherman had to present other variance requests before the Zoning Board of Appeals for their approval. The zoning variances involved the narrow floor plan, long configuration, and higher density, which affected the number of permitted zoning rooms,[13] off-street parking spaces, and side yard setbacks. In July the Board of Appeals approved changes including reducing off-street parking requirements from 1.5 to 1.25 spaces per unit. In December 1986 the developers had to request another variance to allow an increase in rooms and a decrease in parking spaces per unit from 1.25 to 1.0.

There were innumerable other meetings and telephone calls with the U.S. Department of Housing and Urban Development, the St. Paul Departments of Human Rights and Planning and Economic Development, and private mortgage companies. Applications were submitted for an environmental review, a fair housing marketing plan, an affirmative action plan to recruit female and minority employees, federal guaranteed mortgages, and construction- and end-loan financing. These efforts took many months, but the tasks required in expediting a project are linear, overlapping, and sporadic. They often involve waiting until one set of forms has passed over to another desk in another office or agency before being able to proceed; meanwhile other tasks in a different agency move forward. Delays of another kind also may be caused by how neighborhood residents react to changes in initial plans or to modifications as a design becomes more refined.

Fitting into the Community

The first principle derived from the intergenerational congregate house was to fit into the neighborhood; the earlier discussion on the NAH described how an infill program met this requirement. But any physical program reflects social issues as well. Implementing the NAH illustrates what fitting into the community means from a physical and social perspective: the congruence of these two aspects revolves around costs. The longer it took to find a site, the more the development cost. With rising costs it became increasingly unlikely that some of the nontraditional households would be able to afford the units.

By June 1986 the contractor estimated that construction costs were higher than previously anticipated. The selling price for the NAH had also become exceedingly critical to the residents on District Council 8. The Dayton-Dale site is on the edge of a predominantly black area, and community members of the District 8 Planning Council were concerned about gentrification. In 1980 the District had the highest percentage of blacks in St. Paul, 44 percent; the median income of $16,066 was the second lowest in the city. On one side of the site is one of the wealthiest areas in St. Paul. Some District Council 8 members perceived that conditions were becoming ripe for higher-income white residents to move into the area. A high percentage of the District's existing units are rental; there is a mixture of large, older single-family houses and apartment buildings. Many of the larger single-family houses have been converted to duplexes or apartments. Six- to twelve-unit apartment buildings have been converted to condominiums. There was other new and costly housing in the area. Although the District Council had given prior approval to go forward with the NAH concept, Sherman had to appear before a newly reconstituted District 8 Planning Council to gain their approval. After voicing their objections the new District 8 Council voted to turn the project down.

The New American House competition had always been intended to be market-rate housing with units sold to individuals like any other subdivision. The project is being developed with private financing; the value is approximately 1.2

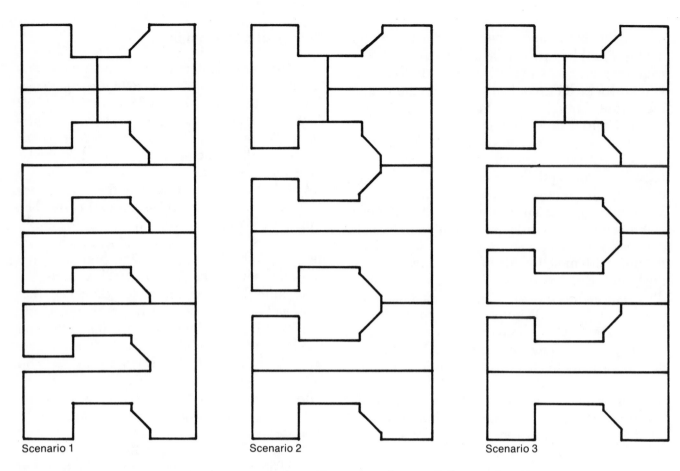

Scenario 1   Scenario 2   Scenario 3

Figure 8-5. Three scenarios for the New American House, now known as Dayton Court.

million dollars with no city assistance. Soon after the competition, a selling price in the mid-$70,000s was casually discussed, although the developer and designers understood that was only a ballpark figure. When the design modifications were made and the costs calculated, the figures had increased into the $80,000s. In a presentation to the District 8 Planning Council, Sherman reported that the cost of units in the Dayton-Dale project of $87,500 was very near the average selling price in that neighborhood. Eight units sited directly across from the project had sold for $75,000 to $88,500 in 1983, when interest rates were higher. Community representatives did not think these cost comparisons were a good enough response.

The community's concerns had to be addressed if the project was to move ahead. By early September 1986 some hard decisions had to be made by the developer about the redesign of the inner courts and reduction of costs in general.

When trying to achieve cost reductions, Sherman suggested three possibilities and conferred with West and me separately (Fig. 8-5). The closest of these to the original design (Scenario 1) laid out five units in row-house fashion, with the northernmost sixth unit flipped. In another scheme (Scenario 2) two enlarged courtyards were provided, with all units now being paired side to side. The end units have their own inner, but not completely enclosed, courts: the unit at the northern end of the site opened to the garages and the southern end to Dayton Avenue. The third possibility (Scenario 3) is a combination. In all schemes two additional small units were formed from the combined work spaces of the two northernmost units, for a total of 14 units.

The final scheme is most similar to Scenario 2. Each of the two rows of townhouses is laid out in a north-south orientation, separated by a mews (Figs. 8-6 and 8-7). One alternative for a more formal entrance is under a trellis leading to the mews. The entrances to the units are from the mews and into the shared or individual courtyards. In addition there are more formal entrances to the residential portions of the larger units that border the east (Dale Street) and west edges of the site. There are 14 units in four house types (two one-bedrooms; four two-bedrooms; six three-bedrooms; and two duplexes) (Fig. 8-8). The single most important cost innovation has

North

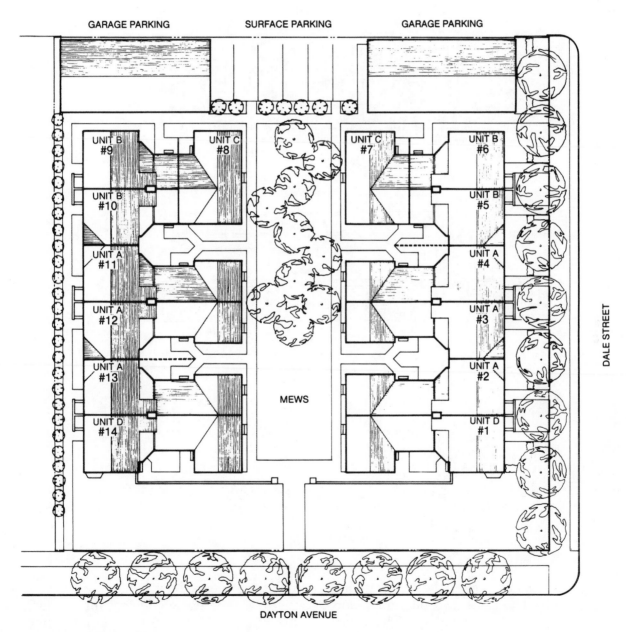

Figure 8-6. Dayton Court: site plan.

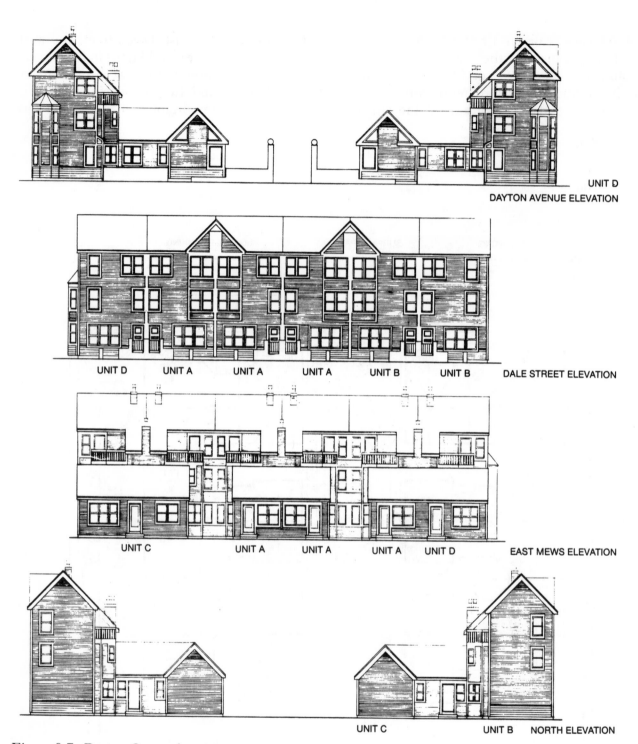

UNIT D
DAYTON AVENUE ELEVATION

UNIT D   UNIT A   UNIT A   UNIT A   UNIT B   UNIT B   DALE STREET ELEVATION

UNIT C   UNIT A   UNIT A   UNIT A   UNIT D   EAST MEWS ELEVATION

UNIT C   UNIT B   NORTH ELEVATION

Figure 8-7. Dayton Court: elevations.

been the creation of two of the northernmost units (Unit C). These are two one-story, one-bedroom units (Unit C), each of which has a base selling price of approximately $37,500.

The two units (Unit D) fronting Dayton Ave-

nue have been subdivided to provide duplexes of 1,485 gross area square feet for a selling price beginning at $109,000. This permits a number of options. A person with moderate income may rent the efficiency apartment of 310 square feet

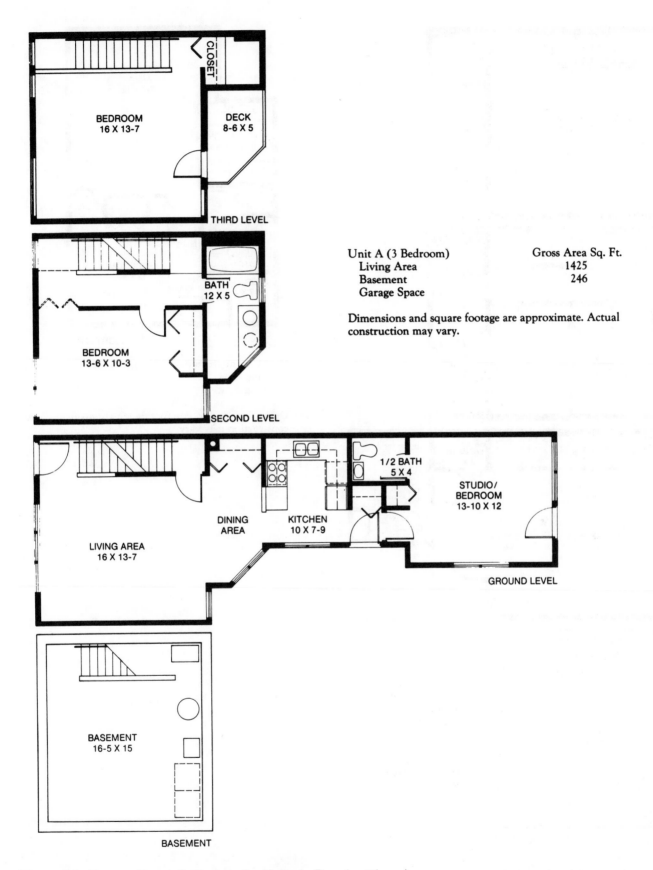

Figure 8-8. Dayton Court: floor plans for Units A–D. *(continues)*

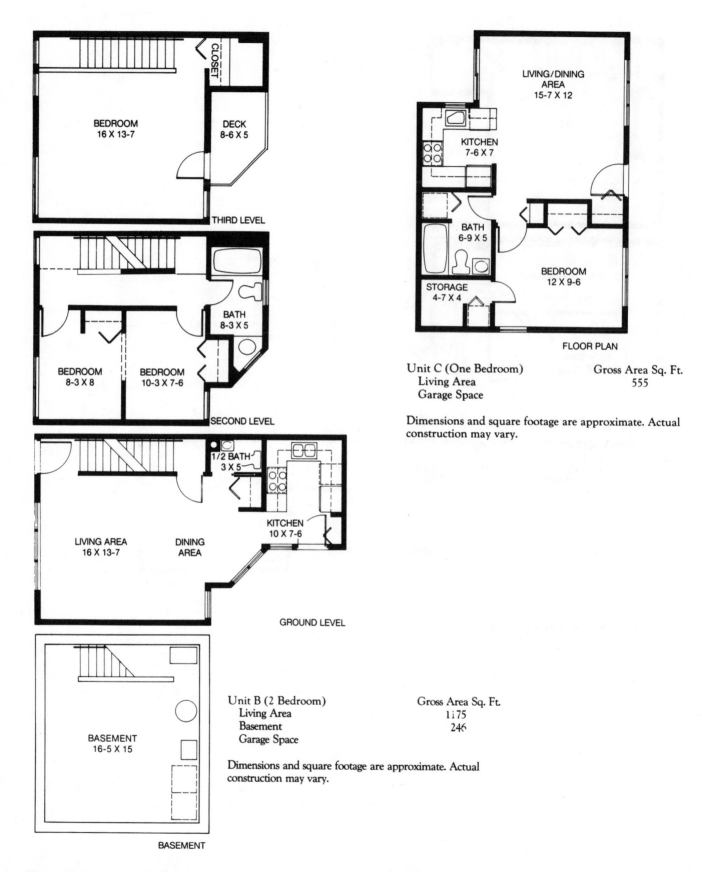

Unit C (One Bedroom)   Gross Area Sq. Ft.
   Living Area   555
   Garage Space

Dimensions and square footage are approximate. Actual
construction may vary.

Unit B (2 Bedroom)   Gross Area Sq. Ft.
   Living Area   1175
   Basement   246
   Garage Space

Dimensions and square footage are approximate. Actual
construction may vary.

Figure 8-8. Dayton Court: floor plans for Units A–D.   *(cont.)*

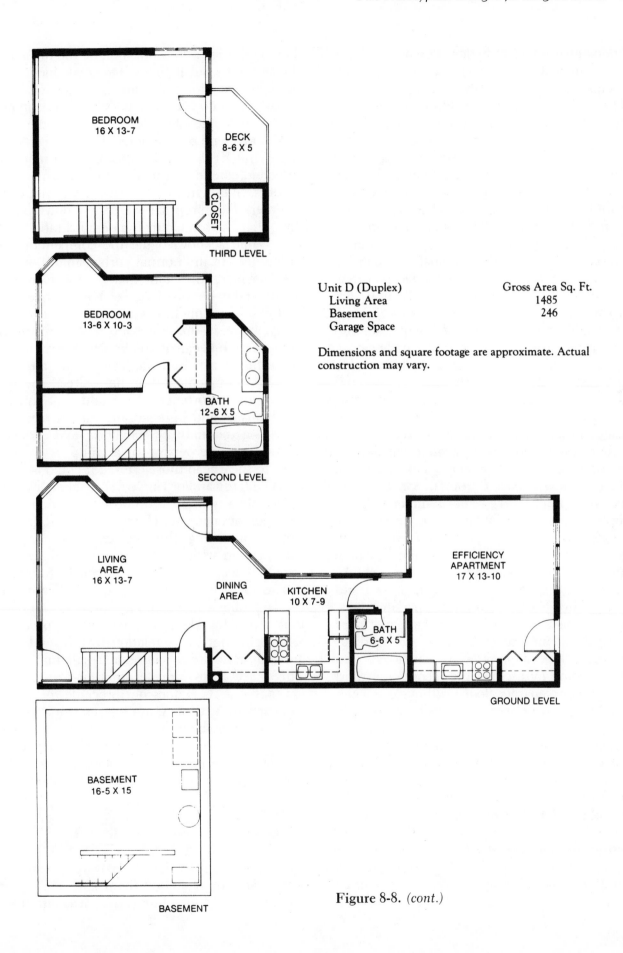

BEDROOM
16 X 13-7

DECK
8-6 X 5

CLOSET

THIRD LEVEL

BEDROOM
13-6 X 10-3

BATH
12-6 X 5

SECOND LEVEL

Unit D (Duplex)	Gross Area Sq. Ft.
Living Area	1485
Basement	246
Garage Space	

Dimensions and square footage are approximate. Actual construction may vary.

LIVING
AREA
16 X 13-7

DINING
AREA

KITCHEN
10 X 7-9

BATH
6-6 X 5

EFFICIENCY
APARTMENT
17 X 13-10

GROUND LEVEL

BASEMENT
16-5 X 15

BASEMENT

Figure 8-8. *(cont.)*

contained within each duplex. The owner of the duplex can realize income from this apartment, reducing his or her monthly housing costs.

The majority of units are the basic unit plan adapted from the original competition entry by West and me. There are six three-bedroom units (Unit A) at 1,425 square feet each for a base price of $91,500; the option of an extra half bath raises the price somewhat. (The exact cost of options cannot be predicted at this time because this will be affected by interest rates and delays in construction.) The ground-floor level shows a studio/bedroom, which in the original competition entry was the work space. The adjacent three-story units, each with two bedrooms (Unit B), are 1,175 square feet with a base price of $77,500. They can be finished as three bedroom units with an extra half bath, at a somewhat higher cost. Garages and other options are available at additional cost. At the time of this writing, the construction cost per square foot of living area (unfinished basements are included at one-half the actual square footage) is projected to be $46.

Other design changes from the original entry were influenced by a number of factors related to climate. Fully enclosed courts, for example, would have made snow removal difficult. Quite early the developer stipulated that freestanding garages, rather than carports, were needed in order to market the houses in a climate where winter can last as long as five months. Ten enclosed garage spaces are provided, in two end groups of five each, as well as six parking stalls. The loft space between the second and third floors was deemed to be costly if the buildings were to be braced properly for windload. This was overcome by treating the second and third floors as two separate floors, although a wider second-floor corridor was created in order to bring in more light. The option of a two-story loft space is available for those able to pay for it.

This discussion of costs and design changes brings us back to the original program. The original program required exclusive space for paid work attached to the residential unit. This was interpreted by the winning designers as a way of meeting the needs of the restricted mobility of single parents. In addition, the winning design showed how two work spaces could be converted to child care, a pressing need for single parents.

The final design does not include the flipping of the end units (see figure 8-3) to create indoor and outdoor space for child care. The two sets of interior courts do offer this possibility. It is important to note the obstacles to creating the child care and single-parent house in the original design (Unit E). In an effort to obtain funding for the child care and units for lower-income single parents, Sherman wrote a brief to Mayor George Latimer. That proposal was turned down on the basis that Dayton Court is a demonstration project. While acknowledging the competition and differences from "normal" urban infill housing, Latimer made the point that Dayton Court has to succeed in the open market.[14] It is conceivable that child care might occur in the one-bedroom units and/or in the efficiency apartments in the duplexes. Child care is an idea that Sherman supports; his presence in the Twin Cities area and his role in implementation have already been of enormous importance. The nature of funding mechanisms and bureaucratic turf in regard to providing community facilities and housing means that one person (or a group) is going to have to spearhead those efforts. It could be Rodney D. Hardy and/or Harvey Sherman in concert with residents when the houses are under construction or occupied. Hardy has offered the possibility of selling the project to a nonprofit organization with a track record in delivery of social services, such as the Episcopal Church.

The ability to convert some units into duplexes is compatible with the original design. The space that was set aside as the paid work space was rethought, not in its relation to the residential area but in its use as additional residential space. This space helps provide different-size units at lower prices. This does not preclude the use of work spaces in Unit A; in plan the work space is labeled studio/bedroom. The New American House can be seen as a kit of parts comprised of the kitchen, court, and residential area and a work area that can be converted to a rental unit.[15]

Lessons from the New American House

The New American House provides several lessons. Paramount among them is that it is very difficult to introduce innovative ideas into housing development. There is no place for the faint of heart or those who desire immediate gratification in this process. Under the current house-building system in the United States, there are lengthy time lags between conceiving, designing, obtaining approvals for, constructing, and occupying houses.

A second lesson is that an intended group of buyers (or renters), such as nontraditional households, may be unable to afford innovative housing. It is highly unlikely that low-income single parents are going to live in the New American House. Housing even in the high $30,000 range is unaffordable. (The estimated mortgage payment for the one bedroom unit will be about $268 per month.) That might be within the means of a better-paid single parent but, depending on the number of children in the household, the unit might be too small. Costs will vary with the interest rate and this price quotation does not include taxes, insurance, and association fees. The only way in which the poorer single parent can afford the New American House is either through a subsidy, such as skewed rents, or through a housing trust fund or other types of government (or private foundation) sources. Alternatively it is possible that a small part of the market for the New American House may be two unrelated adults and their children who opt to share the duplex. As stated earlier Sherman and Hardy have tried to find other ways to subsidize the child care and the units for lower-income single parents. In order for this to occur in other projects, this task requires someone devoting full-time effort to achieve only this component. Such a person would identify funding sources for child care and housing subsidies, and groups who would support these types of services for single parents.

That a full-time person is needed to accomplish this is illustrated by obstacles raised in another setting. In March 1987 I was a jury member for a third-year architectural review at California Polytechnic State University at Pomona. The program was an "electronic cottage" of 500 to 700 square feet with on-site amenities, including child care. When I pointed out that single parents were primarily low-income women with children, a marketing man on the jury simply stated: "That's not the market." Indeed it is not. Thus at the same time as changes are occurring regarding marital status, child rearing, and work location, designs are being promoted to address these issues but a large segment of the "new" households cannot afford these innovations. For most private developers, interest in serving lower-income single parents will occur only when there is the carrot of government assistance. But in addition to identifying those financing sources, a full-time person is also needed to identify the "hidden" market of single parents who may be able to share costs for facilities that are designed with this purpose to begin with.

Given these two lessons regarding time and money, there are three others that are more positive. One concerns the competition itself. The competition program did not require a cost breakdown, perhaps understanding that whatever the cost, some of the emerging new households would not be able to afford to live in the dwellings designed. But the exercise permitted the ideas to be discussed, and it encouraged creative minds to address the problems at least on the design level. As a competition it appears to have been quite successful, both in terms of the number of entrants (1,200 programs were mailed to registrants and 346 submissions represented the work of over 600 people) and the subsequent uses of the program. Anecdotal evidence suggests that the program for the competition was used or adapted in schools of architecture for student projects. In 1984 *Progressive Architecture* called it the most "socially relevant" competition.

In addition, the location of the competition in the Twin Cities area provides a remarkable opportunity and perhaps a model for strategizing about how to select supportive settings for innovative design ideas. There is a strong and active women's community, and Dayton-Hudson is one of the most community-conscious foundations in the United States. In 1986 the Minneapolis/St. Paul Family Housing Fund awarded $25,000 to the Minnesota Association of Women in Housing and the Center of Urban and Regional Affairs (Cook, Vogel-Heffernan, Luckermann, Pugh, and Wattenberg 1987). The award is to produce a set of guidelines for new construction and to retrofit existing housing and neighborhoods for single-parent families. There also are limited equity cooperatives that have been organized in the

Twin Cities. The Housing Fund has sponsored three developments, for a total of 47 three-bedroom units for single parents at a maximum rent of $400 a month, to be converted into cooperatives within a five-year period.

The lesson to be drawn from this is that cities with encouraging environments for innovative projects are likely to have active women's groups, community-minded foundations, public agencies with a proven record of funding innovations, and universities, colleges, hospitals, or other institutions with a history of activity around social issues. Coordinating or building on the work of any one of these types of organizations may lead to more success than trying to introduce new ideas in cities where none of this infrastructure exists. This does not mean that efforts should not be made in other places, but that difficult as it is to get the NAH implemented, it is far easier to do when there are the types of institutions that are to be found in the Twin Cities. Alternatively issues around housing and social services for single parents can be promoted through national advocacy groups and federal legislation, much as the elderly have done through organizations such as the American Association of Retired Persons, the Gray Panthers, and political sponsors.

A third lesson, on affordability and innovation, is still ongoing and is embedded in the development process itself in the private market. The history of Dayton Court may give a good indication of what can and cannot be introduced in the way of innovative ideas when there is no governmental assistance, such as "write downs" for land or site preparation.

CONCLUSIONS

This chapter began with a discussion comparing the restricted mobility of the elderly with that of single parents. From there the concept of congregate housing for single parents was described. Many of the ideas developed for the single-parent congregate facility, which was later broadened to include intergenerational households, were applied to the NAH competition. But the program for the competition had to be modified if it was to be built at all. In particular, the needs of lower-

income single parents cannot be met in the private market. Efforts to solicit subsidies from the City of St. Paul were met with the response that the NAH has to demonstrate that it can meet the needs of nontraditional households through the market. This type of reasoning is tautalogical insofar as low-income single parents are not in the market to begin with. Thus the concept of restricted mobility is not completely demonstrable in this project. The most likely residents of Dayton Court will not be households restricted to the block level; they probably will be households that can choose to function at both the city and the block level.

Nonetheless the building of the NAH will allow the testing of some ideas to see how they work. There will be an opportunity to evaluate what types of households are attracted to Dayton Court, how the inner courts and front and back yards are used, how the duplexes and efficiency units work, whether sharing takes place, whether there is sufficient privacy, whether neighbors visit and children play with each other, what the informal networks are, who takes care of children and adults when they are ill, whether working at home is satisfactory, how people personalize their spaces, and what relationships are made within the neighborhood.

The developers have voiced a marketing concern about the perceived relative attractiveness of city versus suburban life. Suburban living has regained its popularity in the Twin Cities area, particularly with the availability of lower interest rates. While this may be true, it does not preclude the possibility of people wanting to move back to the city, especially those who are divorced, separated, or widowed. Studies have shown that the optimum environments for single parents and the elderly are denser areas with ready access to goods and services[16] (Rothblatt, Carr, and Sprague 1979; Wekerle 1985; Wekerle and MacKenzie 1985). While the NAH cannot serve the needs of low-income single parents, it will still be possible to find out whether a more supportive environment has been created for moderate- or higher-income single parents and other nontraditional households, such as the elderly. In addition there will be a clear message about which nontraditional households are left out.

NOTES

1. This formulation benefited from collaborative work with Susan Saegert and is drawn from our book *Housing Abandonment in Harlem: The Making of Community-Households* (1989).
2. Sten Gromark,"Communal Living and Habitation," an English summary from *The New Housing Question*, an unpublished dissertation, School of Architecture, Chalmers University of Technology, Göteborg, Sweden, 1986.
3. See Elaine M. Brody, "Service Options in Congregate Housing," in Chellis et al. (1982). I suspect that one reason for the difficulty in "naming" is because of the socialization process in the United States, where a private house is considered to be the optimum living arrangement. Planning, with its zoning ordinances, confirms this by systematically according private detached houses the highest use, prohibiting other types of uses in an R1, or residential use, zone.
4. This brief history is drawn from Marie McGuire Thompson, "Enriching Environments for Older People," in Chellis et al. (1982).
5. Responses from over 800 readers to a *Ms.* magazine survey, prepared by Susan Saegert and myself, lead me to think that people will respond favorably to this type of exercise. One optional request was the following: "Draw your ideal house (floor plan) and/or neighborhood." Even people who could not draw responded either by writing what they would like or by drawing anyway. A large proportion of the drawings were annotated.
6. For a fuller discussion of the congregate facility, see Jacqueline Leavitt, "The Shelter-Service Crisis and Single Parents" in Eugenia L. Birch (ed.), *The Unsheltered Woman: Women and Housing in the 80's* (1985), New Brunswick, NJ: The Center for Urban Policy Research, 153–176. Also see Mary Lou Petitt and Peggy Huchet, *Housing the Single-Parent Family: A Resource and Action Guidebook* (1987), Trenton, NJ: Department of Community Affairs, Division of Housing and Development.
7. For a discussion of preplanning for moves by the elderly, see Elizabeth W. Markson, "Placement and Location: the Elderly and Congregate Care," and Louis E. Gelwicks and Maria B. Dwight, "Programming for Alternatives and Future Models," in Chellis, Seagle, Jr., and Seagle (1982).
8. We met with the New Jersey Institute of Technology and did develop a questionnaire, but this project did not move forward.
9. In correspondence with the author, Enid Gamer —coordinator, Child and Adolescent Services, South Norfolk, Massachusetts, Area Office, Department of Mental Health—suggested that using self-help in the planning and construction stages of single-parent housing is a positive way of overcoming isolation.
10. The original grant application to the National Endowment of the Arts was submitted in May 1982, initially rejected, resubmitted at the end of 1982, and approved in June 1983. The competition officially began in January 1984.
11. The five-person jury was unusual in its inclusion of David Stea, an environmental psychologist; James Wines, a sculptor, president of SITE Projects, and chair of the Department of Environmental and Interior Design, Otis Parsons School of Design; and three architects: Michael Brill, who in addition to his practice as president of BOSTI, Inc., in Buffalo, New York, is on the architecture faculty at The State University of New York at Buffalo, Thomas H. Hodne, Jr., and Cynthia Weese.
12. The original site was owned by the Minneapolis Community Development Agency, and they proceeded with a local architect to construct five houses.
13. Zoning rooms are calculated differently from merely counting the number of rooms; zoning rooms must conform with the zoning ordinance. For St. Paul the definition of room is as follows:

> For the purpose of determining lot area requirements and density in a multiple-family district, a living room, dining room, or bedroom equal to at least 80 square feet in area. A room shall not include the area in kitchen, sanitary facilities, utility provisions, corridors, hallways, and storage. Plans presented showing 1, 2, or 3 bedroom units and including a "den," "library" or other extra room shall count such extra room as a bedroom for the purpose of computing density.

> In RT-2 Townhouse, RM-1 Multiple-Family, RM-2 Multiple Family, and RM-3 Multiple Family Districts, for the purpose of computing the permitted number of dwelling units per acre, the following room assignments shall control: One Bedroom = 2 rooms, Two Bedroom = 3 rooms, Three Bedroom = 4 rooms, Four Bedroom = 5 rooms.

Plans presented showing 1, 2, 3, or 4 bedroom units and including a "den," "library" or other extra room shall count such extra room as a bedroom for purpose of computing density. Efficiency apartments shall have the same room assignment as a one bedroom unit.

14. Communication between Harvey Sherman and Office of the Mayor, June 8, 1987.

15. The potential creation of accessory units as rental property has been built into other projects. The most important element is providing for connections to utilities at the time of construction. In some cities building inspectors are reported to be "looking the other way" when certifying the property as a single-family residence.

16. Another question may be whether there is a market for row houses, which are largely undifferentiated from each other in their facade and treatment. The site plan and the interior courtyards do offer a variety of experiences, which may offset this.

References

Anderson-Khleif, S. 1982. *Divorced But Not Disastrous: How to Improve the Ties Between Single-Parent Mothers, Divorced Fathers, and Children.* Englewood Cliffs, NJ: Prentice Hall.

Ahrentzen, S. 1985. Residential fit and mobility among low-income, female-headed family households. In *Housing Needs and Policy Approaches: International Perspectives,* eds. W. Van Vliet, E. Huttman, and S. Fava, 71–87. Durham, NC: Duke University.

Bartlett, S. 1980. Residential mobility and housing choices of single-parent mothers. Unpublished paper submitted to MIT, Department of Urban Studies and Planning (Sept. 26).

Chellis, R. D., J. F. Seagle, Jr., and B. M. Seagle. 1982. *Congregate Housing for Older People: A Solution for the 1980s.* Lexington, MA: Lexington Books.

Cook, C., M. Vogel-Heffernan, B. Lukermann, S. Pugh, and E. Wattenberg. 1987. *Expanding Opportunities for Single Parents through Housing.* Minneapolis/St. Paul: Family Housing Fund.

Cooper Marcus, C. and W. Sarkissian. 1987. *Housing as if People Mattered: Site Design Guidelines for Medium-Density Family Housing.* Berkeley, CA: University of California Press.

Fox, M. B. 1983. Working women and travel: The access of women to work and community facilities.

Journal of the American Planning Association 49 (Spring): 156–170.

Gellen, M. 1985. *Accessory Apartments in Single-Family Housing.* New Brunswick, NJ: Center for Urban Policy Research.

Hayden, D. 1984. *Redesigning the American Dream: The Future of Housing, Work, and Family Life.* New York: W. W. Norton.

Lawton, M. P. 1976. The relative impact of congregate and traditional housing on elderly tenants. *The Gerontologist* 16:237–242.

Leavitt, J. Forthcoming. Homelessness and the housing crisis. In *Homelessness: The National Perspective,* eds. M. Robertson and M. Greenblatt. New York: Plenum Press.

———. 1985. The shelter-service crisis for single parents. In *The Unsheltered Woman: Women and Housing in the 80's,* ed. Eugenie Birch, 153–176. New Brunswick, NJ: Center for Urban Policy Research.

———, and S. Saegert. 1989. *Housing Abandonment in Harlem: The Making of Community-Households.* New York: Columbia University Press.

———, and M. B. Welch. 1989. Older Women and the Suburbs: A Literature review. *Women's Studies Quarterly.*

Mumford, L. 1968. *The Urban Prospect.* New York: Harcourt, Brace & World.

Newcomer, R. J., M. P. Lawton, and T. O. Byerts. 1986. *Housing an Aging Society: Issues, Alternatives, and Policy.* New York: Van Nostrand Reinhold.

Petitt, M. L., and P. Huchet. 1987. *Housing the Single-Parent Family: A Resource and Action Guidebook.* Trenton, NJ: Department of Community Affairs, Division of Housing and Development.

Pynoos, J. 1984. Setting the elderly housing agenda. *Policy Studies Journal* 13 (Sept.):173–184.

Robinette, G. O. 1985. *Barrier-free Exterior Design: Anyone Can Go Anywhere.* New York: Van Nostrand Reinhold.

Rothblatt, D. N., D. J. Carr, and J. Sprague. 1979. *The Suburban Environment and Women.* New York: Praeger.

Schorr, A. L. 1964. *Slums and Social Insecurity.* Washington, D.C.: U.S. Department of Health, Education, and Welfare.

Wekerle, G. R. 1985. From refuge to service center. *Sociological Focus* 18:79–95.

———, and S. MacKenzie. 1985. Reshaping the neighbourhood of the future as we age in place. *Canadian Woman Studies* 6:69–72.

Women Plan Toronto. 1986. *Shared Experiences and Dreams.* Toronto: Mimeograph.

Chapter 9

Two Cases of Transitional Housing Development in Boston

Joan Forrester Sprague

Close to 350,000 women in the United States, along with their children, were sheltered as the result of domestic violence in 1986.[1] These and many other women, through housing displacement or family changes, need housing as well as jobs. More and more families, particularly those headed by women, are homeless. As documented by the United States Conference of Mayors, 90 percent of all homeless families in Boston, Hartford, New Orleans, Norfolk, Philadelphia, and Saint Paul are headed by women.

The shortage of affordable housing, coupled with the need for an integrated system of supports to help women become economically self-sufficient, has generated a new type of housing: transitional housing bridges the gap between emergency shelter and permanent affordable housing. Its components generally include residency for a period of six months to two years as well as child care and assistance in job development and life planning. The result is a new kind of mixed-use development.

This chapter describes the origins, design, and realization of two transitional housing developments in Boston. One of the projects was begun in 1984 by Abigail West Shelter, a women's group.[2] The other, the Tree of Life, was initiated in 1986 by Mayor Raymond L. Flynn. The goals of the two projects were similar.

Both projects are examples from a spectrum of transitional housing initiatives that were assisted by the Women's Institute for Housing and Economic Development in Boston during the period that I was its executive director. The two developments reflect a chronology in the work of the Women's Institute. The Women's Institute was established in 1981 by women professionals—an attorney, a banker, and myself, an architect. Its purpose has been to stimulate, advocate for, and assist in the development of real-estate projects that benefit low-income women and their families by providing technical assistance in strategic planning, feasibility, design, financing, and community education.

For nonprofit organizations the Women's Institute has offered education about the development process at the same time that it has provided services. Groups with limited resources have been enabled to own and manage buildings by reducing their risks through strategic planning. Services have included project analysis and financial feasibility; preliminary architectural design; preparation of construction and operating pro formas (the detailed financial projections necessary for financing); loan strategies and negotiations with lenders; and consultation on the selection of other members of the development team—lawyers, architects, and contractors.

For government agencies, the Women's Institute has provided information about innovative real-estate development and associated services that can benefit low-income women and children. It has brought together private-sector groups and individuals to create community-based projects responding to governmental initiatives.

In 1984 many groups, particularly nonprofit sponsors of shelters, saw the crucial need for transitional housing. At the time, however, few models existed. Because this was an area of need and because transitional housing is unique in taking a comprehensive view of housing, child care, and economic self-sufficiency, the Women's Institute began to focus its development program in this area. The program's goal was the development of transitional housing for 100 or more families in Massachusetts on behalf of sponsor groups that wanted to own and manage this new housing type.

That goal was met through a number of projects assisted by the Women's Institute. The largest of these initiatives are described in this chapter. The Women's Institute's assistance to sponsors and its 1986 publication *A Manual on Transitional Housing*, the first on this subject, have increased understanding of the development and design of transitional housing. Particularly in Boston, we are now past the question "What is transitional housing and should it be built?" Instead the question is "Where and how?"

ABIGAIL WEST SHELTER

When Abigail West Shelter approached the Women's Institute for assistance in 1984, its goal was to acquire one or more of Boston's "triple-deckers," typical wood-frame buildings with three apartments stacked one above the other. West Shelter, an alternative therapeutic program for women in emotional distress, battered women, and their children, owned just such a building in Boston.

Their shelter accommodated the therapeutic program for women and children, but increasingly the staff found that the residents' progress toward better lives was thwarted because post-shelter housing was not available and a continuing, transitional level of support was necessary. The residents' anxiety about finding affordable housing blocked their path toward a positive vision of the future.

Strategy discussions regarding goals for transitional housing took place between the Women's Institute and West Shelter. The shelter altered its initial idea of acquiring a triple-decker. At that time Boston's real-estate market was tightening, and good triple-deckers that came on the private market were swiftly purchased, often at $100,000 or more. West Shelter did not have the funds to move as quickly as the private market demanded. The Women's Institute suggested the possibility of a larger project through the substantial rehabilitation of a building or new construction.

The Women's Institute and West Shelter worked together to define their complementary roles in the development process. West Shelter had two primary areas of responsibility: to formulate the design criteria to meet their social service goals and to raise capital for the project. The Women's Institute's responsibility was to teach West Shelter about the development process, to secure site control, to prepare the financial package, and to negotiate loans that would allow the transitional housing goal to be realized. At West Shelter's request the Women's Institute also translated the program criteria into an architectural program and a preliminary design.

West Shelter began to look for a site in 1984, at the beginning of Raymond Flynn's first mayoral term. It was a time of change in the city's priorities. Previously city-owned properties had been auctioned to the highest bidder. Under Flynn developers were selected through an advertised Request for Proposal (RFP) for each property. Priority was given to projects that would provide affordable housing, particularly those sponsored by nonprofit community-based groups. The new city policy designated developers to whom property was sold for as little as one dollar to make projects feasible, with the possibility of additional loans from the City to fill funding gaps.

West Shelter and the Women's Institute staff toured Boston with lists of city-owned properties, identifying the best possible sites for the project. The new commitment to increasing the stock of affordable neighborhood housing led city officials to take a special interest in early preparation of a Request for Proposal (RFP) for an 18,800-square-foot vacant parcel of land in Roxbury that West Shelter wished to acquire. The Women's Institute prepared the application for developer designation, including a basic site plan showing the proposed allocation of apartments, preliminary pro forma development, and operating budgets. These were submitted with the joint credentials of the West Shelter and the Women's Institute.

City agencies looked favorably on the proposal, and a series of meetings was held with the local nonprofit organizations, the neighborhood residents, and the city's development office staff. Discussions in these meetings addressed community questions about the proposed project and the city's property designation process prior to formal developer designation.

Process for West Shelter Design

The design process for the West Shelter transitional housing began under special circumstances. At about the same time that the potential city site had been identified, Women in Architecture, a group of graduate students and staff members at the Massachusetts Institute of Technology, requested a design studio that addressed women's special needs. I was asked to teach this studio, and chose to focus on transitional housing.

The 15-week architecture studio provided an opportunity to explore new approaches to housing for low-income women and children with women students of diverse racial and ethnic backgrounds. The city-owned property that we identified as a possible site for the West Shelter project was one of the site choices for the studio. Members of West Shelter acted as clients and reviewed alternative architectural forms for their project. The student work was a step in the development process whereby the West Shelter staff learned about architectural possibilities and defined their program.[3]

Studio work began with sketches of the images of conventional housing compared with the new images for transitional housing. This was followed by a two-week generic design exercise: the cluster design of housing for 50 families—with related child-care, counseling, and enterprise spaces—and the design of an ideal site. Through the generic study the full spectrum of levels of privacy for both interior and exterior space was explored, ranging from separate apartments to a scheme more closely approximating a dormitory (Fig. 9-1).

Each student then selected a particular client program and translated the housing and support service needs into physical form, giving special attention to the following:

- private and shared living space
- child-care or elderly day-care, counseling, and/or business space
- economical use of space and means of construction
- flexibility for accommodating families of varying sizes
- an architectural setting for a changing community in which personal support is a primary issue

The goal of the studio was the development of useful prototypes for the West Shelter client, as well as for two other client groups who were planning transitional housing. Each student was encouraged to take a personalized approach to her design. Statements by two students reveal differences in approach.

Penny Hungle concentrated on the sense of home and family. Her design focused on the metaphoric "womb": the collective child-care center, kitchen, and community living space in the building, with clusters of bedrooms, the classrooms, and the offices forming the "protective skin."

She described the spatial organization this way:

> The major internal access of the building occurs along the south side so that the large outdoor collective/play area is visually accessible from many points within the building. Light serves to clarify this internal movement; residents move along the path of light to other collective areas bathed in light. Living spaces are located in three-bedroom clusters with each three-bedroom cluster sharing a kitchen, collective space, and living room/flexible space. These larger collective/play spaces and smaller more intimate private living rooms provide a variety of experiences in response to user needs.

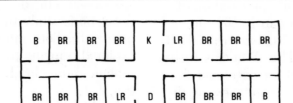

A dormitory scheme is most appropriate for single women. If children are included, doors *between* bedrooms can give some family privacy. Bathrooms in this scheme must be compartmentalized.

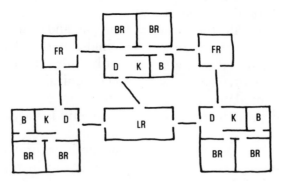

In this innovative approach, each family can have a mini-apartment with their own bedrooms, bathroom, and kitchen/dining area, sharing living space with other families. Flexible rooms (FR) can provide additional bedrooms for larger families or temporary private living or study spaces.

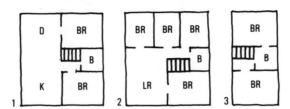

A shared house can provide community living space on one floor and the community kitchen/dining space on another floor. Or it might have more than one kitchen and living area.

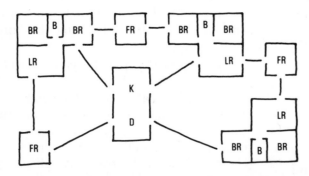

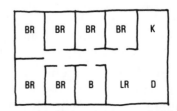

Using an alternative approach, each family can have a bed-sitting apartment, including bedrooms, bath and living space. These bed-sitting apartments share the kitchen/dining space. Flexible rooms (FR) can also be included here.

A shared apartment can include up to six bedrooms housing two or three small families. With that number, a compartmentalized bathroom is necessary.

Figure 9-1. Spatial diagrams of alternatives for shared and private spaces. These diagrams, the result of MIT studio analyses, were prepared for *A Manual on Transitional Housing* (1986).

Another student, Gail Sullivan, proposed a spatial alternative that balanced private and shared space in a townhouse model that she described this way:

Each woman and her children or two single women were provided with a private unit—not quite a full apartment—including a large kitchen/gathering place, two or three bedrooms and a bath, as well as a full 'outdoor room'—a patio or balcony. Three such units share a formal living room, family room and another small room as well as a roof garden.

The design responds to the transitional nature of the residence by providing 'flexible' rooms— which are between private units and which can be linked to them for use as additional bedrooms, depending on the family size. Shared spaces on one side, private on the other, split at half-levels, provide continuity between the larger shared areas and the private spaces. The public functions at either end of the site, bounding the residential areas, increase a sense of security and protection for the residents.

After analyzing the range of possibilities, from shared congregate housing to private apartments proposed by students, West Shelter chose shared apartments of three or four bedrooms for the transitional residents. Two women and one or more children would occupy each unit, creating a "buddy" system whereby mutual support would be created. At the same time each private apartment would foster more independence than did the shared house that the families were leaving.

Other spatial and program criteria were developed as well. The maximum number of women to be served would be 20, or a few more if a high percentage of the residents were single women. This dictated ten shared apartments. In addition to planning for "buddies" in each apartment, each apartment entry would share a stair hall with another apartment on the same floor, creating the next level of partnership.

The organization of apartments around these stairways fulfilled other criteria. Long institutional hallways were avoided, and apartments looked out on both the front and the back of the building. The resulting sight supervision of both front and back yards contributed to security, an issue that was a priority for residents whose prior lives might have included domestic violence. Se-

curity dictated other design decisions—such as a large, fenced back-yard play space and the choice of a single, locked entrance to the transitional housing apartments. Exits from fire stairs would be alarmed so that entrance through these auxiliary doors would not be possible.

In addition to security advantages, the single entrance was planned to encourage community cohesion: all residents passed through community rooms or program offices on the way to their apartments. The pairs of shared apartments branched out from the entry. The ten apartments served by two stair halls created clusters of five shared apartments, each housing ten families.

When the analysis of zoning requirements indicated that 14 apartments were allowable on the site, West Shelter voted to increase its program to include four apartments for permanent residents. These apartments, accessible from a separate building entrance, were designated for functions that would enhance the transitional program: two apartments would be designed for occupancy by a licensed family child-care provider, one apartment designed for a permanent resident who would have some building maintenance responsibilities, and one designed as a shared permanent residence for single women (Fig. 9-2).

Instead of a conventional pitched roof, a sloped mansard was designed to decrease the perceived height of the three- and four-story building and to create alternating sloped and vertical walls at the top of the building, producing a more residential scale. It would also offer a more intimate residential space for the top-floor bedrooms, each of which had a skylight. Other bedrooms had single windows that, with the double windows of the living room and kitchen areas, created a rhythm of openings in the exterior facade. The first-floor windows were shielded with decorative iron grilles for security.

West Shelter Realization

The financial package was based on income that included the Chapter 707 state housing subsidy allocations linked with Department of Social Services program funds for staff. (Massachusetts is

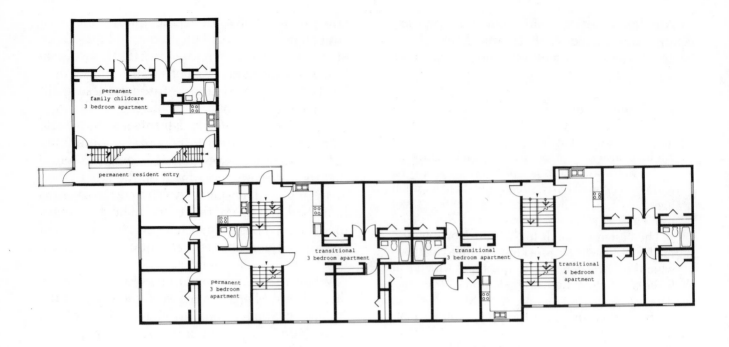

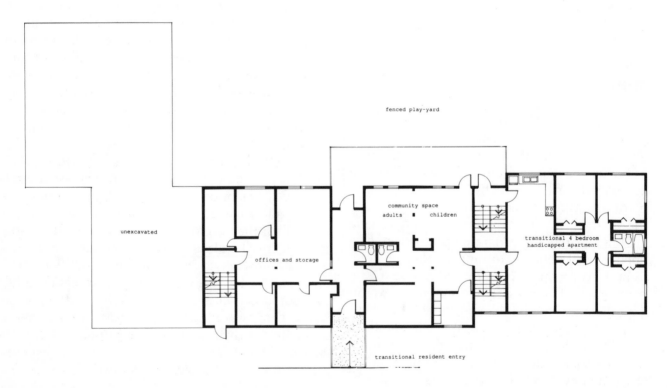

Figure 9-2. West Shelter preliminary scheme: plans of entry-level floors. Plans take advantage of the sloped site. Permanent residents enter their apartments one floor above the transitional housing entry. Permanent and transitional residents use separate stair halls. Each apartment overlooks the front and back yards of the building.

unique because it has its own rental subsidy program, which is similar to the now-discontinued federal Section 8 rental subsidy program for construction. The linkage of the state rent subsidies to operating funds for social services was an additional state innovation that supported the development.)

The financial self-sufficiency of the project was planned by balancing subsidized rental income with the expenses of loan paybacks and building operation costs. Capital fund raising and gap financing made up the difference between income and expenses. West Shelter raised approximately 15 percent of the total development costs from foundation grants and donations. Loans for what ultimately became a million-dollar project included gap financing from the city of Boston, a low-interest loan from the Boston Community Loan Fund, and long-term mortgages from the Massachusetts Land Bank and the Massachusetts Thrift Fund (a consortium of savings and loan institutions), with bank financing for the construction period. This combination of funding from state, city, and private sources gives clear indication of a political environment that, despite limited resources, supports innovative housing for special needs.

An overriding goal for the project was an economical construction cost. Although the preliminary designs by the Women's Institute had been based on conventional construction, the consulting architect's cost estimator suggested that if factory-built modular units were used the construction costs would be substantially lower than if the project was conventionally built at the site.

In accordance with this advice, the building was redesigned by Comunitas, the architecture firm of record that had been retained for the project. Modular construction, consisting of factory-built wood-frame "boxes" 14 feet wide, up to 54 feet long, and 8½ feet high became a component of the design (Fig. 9-3). A number of companies in New Hampshire and Vermont had become specialists in this kind of construction. Drawing on a labor pool of semiskilled workers who earned less than on-site carpenters, and using factory methods, these "boxes" could be manufactured to special design specifications. The modular units, fully finished with kitchens and bathrooms in place, would then be delivered on trailers to

the site, where they would be lifted and stacked by a crane. Exterior siding along with roofing, electrical, and plumbing connections would be installed at the site.

Some modular housing had already been constructed in Boston, and the results were good. With housing construction becoming more and more expensive, state agencies were interested in supporting innovative construction methods that could demonstrate lower construction costs. The proposed innovative construction method of manufactured housing and its economical approach was a primary reason for its attractiveness to long-term mortgage lenders.

Research was done to identify the best manufacturer and contractor for the project. The decision was made to work with a Vermont company that had been attracted by state funds to build a major branch plant in the Orange/Athol area of Massachusetts, an area with a very high unemployment rate.

The design of West Shelter for modular construction differed from the designs of other modular townhouse apartments that had been built. The latter typically have their entries along the short end of the box, with each living unit limited to the 14-foot dimension that could legally be transported along a highway. The West Shelter design took an approach similar to the one-story single house, where the long side of the box forms the exterior wall. This allowed for a larger apartment on one floor and more opportunities for windows. The modular design retained the basic plan layout and the mansard roof of the original design.

Because it was a multifamily apartment building, West Shelter's fire standards were more stringent than for smaller, more conventional projects. Work with city and state regulatory agencies was intensive. In addition much legal work was done to define the separate yet interdependent responsibilities of the manufacturer, the owner, and the general contractor who was in charge of completing the construction once the boxes were stacked on the site. Finally, the financing was in place, and the building permit was issued in September 1986. Then came the shock.

The modular manufacturer was experiencing difficulties. In the Orange/Athol area, the 17 per-

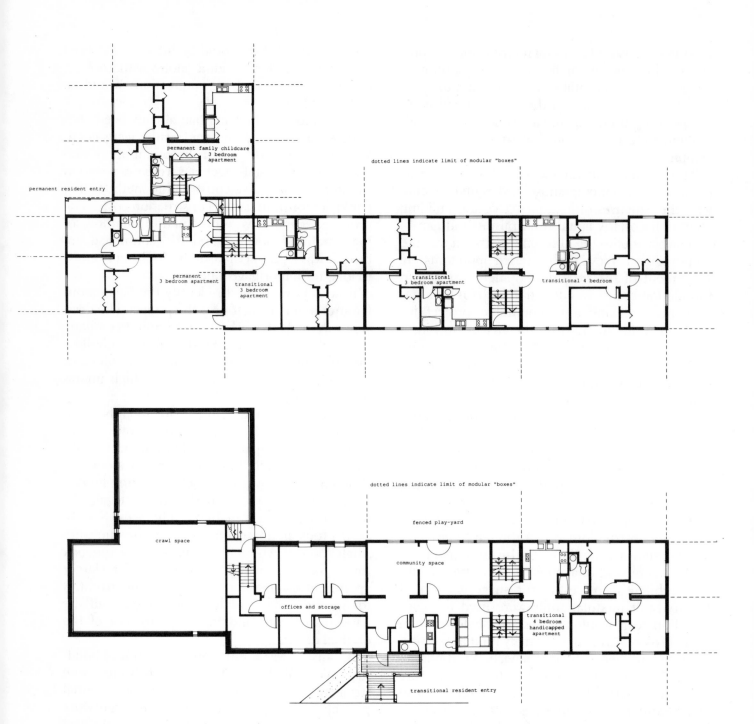

Figure 9-3. West Shelter modular scheme: plans of entry-level floors. Redesign for modular construction brought some changes to the entry-level floors along with a decrease in the total square footage. The permanent resident stair hall was consolidated with a transitional resident stair hall. One apartment lost its view of the back yard. The dotted lines show the outline of each modular "box."

cent unemployment rate of skilled construction laborers, had diminished to 6 percent, and the labor pool needed training. The plant manager and the chief executive officer of the company had been replaced, and the company decided to limit manufacturing to standard models that were simpler for their limited production capability.

Despite the fact that a shift in construction methods would require extensive revisions as well as additional cost, West Shelter decided not to pursue another modular manufacturer. After having been involved in the long design and planning process, the group became independent of the Women's Institute in their project management decisions. After the Women's Institute renegotiated terms of the loan that allowed for an increase in construction costs for on-site construction, West Shelter chose to enter into a design-build agreement with a contracting company. Their choice was partially based on their assessment that this approach would allow construction to begin before winter set in.

This design-build approach was not recommended by the Women's Institute because the bid price for architectural services and construction costs was higher than other bids that were obtained. Moreover, the design-build contract provided no checks and balances on the contractor with regard to design changes and quality control. The contractor's aim was to make his profit and to bring the project in on time at the required cost. Design refinements are often compromised in this kind of situation. In addition the contractor could not provide a performance bond that was required by the bank construction lender.

The Women's Institute saw its role as protecting the project from financial risk as well as ensuring the design quality of the project. The West Shelter choices appeared risky; legal advisors warned of the Women's Institute's liability for a project in which the sponsor's choice was questionable. As a result, in November 1986, the Women's Institute regretfully terminated services to the project. The construction broke ground in May 1987. Changes to the original design included elimination of the mansards and replacement with a pitched roof. The building was completed late in 1987.

TREE OF LIFE

In 1986, at just the time that West Shelter had been scheduled to break ground on its modular construction project, another transitional housing initiative was being formulated. Unlike the West Shelter grassroots leadership, this project began in the highest office of the City of Boston.

Mayor Flynn's concerns about the growing problems of homelessness have made him a national spokesperson on this issue. As an advocate he often had visited shelters and was aware of the changing profile of the homeless population. His administration's statistical research had estimated 200 female heads-of-household and their children living in emergency shelters, hotels, and motels in Boston. Women and children represented 90 percent of the homeless family population. In a rare leadership move on behalf of these disadvantaged families, the mayor asked the Director of the Boston Redevelopment Authority (BRA), the city's planning and urban renewal agency, to propose a project responding to the needs of this population.

The BRA director located a large and attractive city-owned site on which housing might be built to serve a significant segment of this population. Transitional housing was chosen to provide families with a way out of homelessness. The site was located in the South End neighborhood, close to downtown Boston, where the BRA owned a number of undeveloped parcels. The South End, despite recent gentrification, is well known today as well as historically for its diversity of racial, ethnic, and income groups.

Adopting the model of Warren Village in Denver, Colorado, the largest and oldest transitional housing development in the United States, BRA planners and architects designed a transitional housing complex for 101 female-headed households and their children. They called it the Tree of Life.

A report issued by the BRA for neighborhood and social-service community meetings described the project this way:

> The current development proposal calls for the construction of a housing facility with a total of 76 units . . . including 41 two- and three-bedroom family apartments of 1,200 gross square

feet (GSF) each, and 35 congregate living units of 800 GSF each. This development would also include a 4,000 GSF day care center for children of house residents that could be operated and maintained as a separate entity. Additional space would be allocated for resident staff, administration services, and common areas. Most of the project's social services would be located off-site [Fig. 9-4].

In addition, the report proposed 10,000 square feet of ground-level retail space, 32 rented parking spaces for residents of the community, 25 additional units of transitional housing on an adjacent street, and 8 units of market-rate condominiums.

The plans, perspectives, and financing strategy were presented to the South End community at several neighborhood meetings amidst consternation and anger. Although hostile community reaction is not unusual for housing proposals that involve low-income women and children, the negative reaction to the Tree of Life was extreme. Boston has had a long history of community struggle with city government, well described in *Common Ground* (Lukas 1985), which details the history of development in the South End along with its chronology of the fight against school busing. The press was fascinated by the BRA proposal and the outcry. Many stories appeared in both daily and weekly papers. Television reported angry neighborhood meetings. One newspaper headline read, "South Enders Plot Suit Over Tree of Life Plan." These articles added to the general confusion by describing the project as a massive shelter for battered women.

The proposal was attacked on many levels. Private real-estate promoters in the community formed the Dumping Ground Committee, determined to block a project that they saw threatening the South End's hot ($200-per-square-foot) condominium market. To them the proposed transitional housing was yet another undesirable project, lumped with the prison and the garbage-processing plant that had been proposed for the South End. Housing advocates criticized the project for being too large and institutional. Neighborhood leaders objected to a proposal that

had not included community participation in the planning process.

At the first community meeting the mayor said, "My job is not to come out to tell people what they want to hear. My job is to address unmet social needs." Months later, after the proposed project had been substantially reduced in size and revised through a community planning process, he joked, "Nobody at that meeting thought the project was a good idea except for my daughter, and I had just bought her a hot fudge sundae."

To save the Tree of Life project, the mayor set up a two-part process: one part was led by the Women's Institute; the other part was led by Michael Taylor, the City's Commissioner of Elderly Affairs.

Between October 1986 and March 1987, the Women's Institute was retained by the city to refine the original proposal. Recommendations were solicited from Boston's social-service and nonprofit community to redefine and improve the proposal. This process began through informal meetings and continued with a questionnaire that was mailed to approximately 150 nonprofit and social-service organizations in Boston. Those on the mailing list were asked to distribute copies to any others who might wish to respond.

Approximately 50 agencies responded. Informal planning meetings and telephoned recommendations led to two all-day planning workshops in the South End. Approximately 20 persons attended one or more of these sessions. Four basic questions were addressed at this planning session:

1. Who should be served by the Tree of Life?
2. What kind of housing is needed?
3. What social services and child care are desirable?
4. What is the recommended management structure?

Material from the planning sessions was consolidated with prior responses in an interim report sent to those participating in the process. Suggestions on the interim report and further discussions led to amplification and some additional refinements.

During the same period that the Women's In-

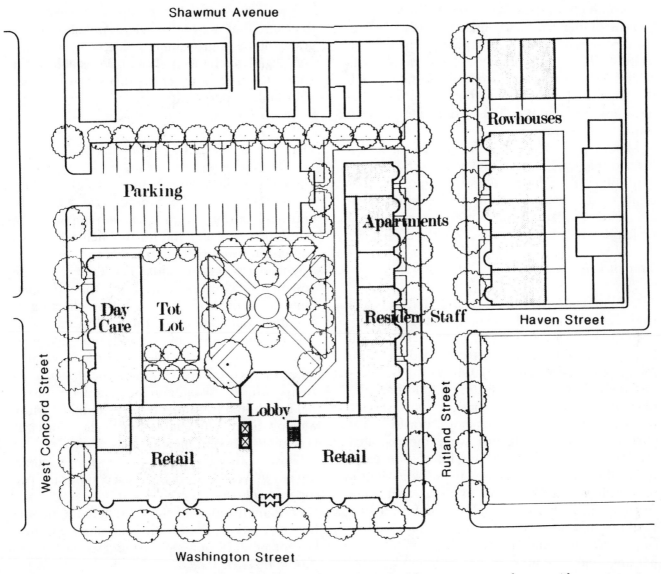

Figure 9-4. Tree of Life preliminary scheme: site plan. One large building was proposed to provide apartments and child care for transitional residents as well as to provide retail space. A single main entrance gives access to all the units. Outdoor play space is adjacent to on-site parking; market-rate condominiums are located on an adjacent street.

stitute was working with the social-service community, Commissioner Michael Taylor worked with community residents to elicit their recommendations for the project. The Commissioner had formerly headed a social-service agency in a neighborhood adjacent to the South End. He had narrowly lost a race for the City Council in the South End in 1983, but he still had strong ties there.

Many informal meetings were held in houses in the neighborhood. Residents suggested better

integration of transitional housing in the neighborhood through a scattered-site approach, creating a plan that would allow greater anonymity for the transitional housing residents. Most community residents validated the need for this kind of housing, but they were concerned about the scale of the initial proposal. They wanted a mix of low- and moderate- and market-rate permanent housing as they had suggested for the other city-owned parcels in the South End.

The results of the collaborative planning process conducted by the Women's Institute and by Commissioner Taylor formed the basis for a revised proposal that was presented by the BRA in March 1987. The community and newspapers rallied behind the new proposal. Residents felt that they had been heard, that the process had been fair, and that it represented the best in community collaboration.

The support of the housing advocates, social-service agencies, and some neighborhood residents offset the continued opposition of the real-estate speculators and luxury condominium owners. As a result the project moved forward in a scaled-down, more carefully considered version.

Tree of Life Design

The Women's Institute's report that resulted from consultation with the nonprofit community presented suggestions to the mayor in several areas. Some of the points were consolidated from the questionnaire responses. Others, such as recommendations on size, clustering, and finer details, drew on the experience of social-service providers in the all-day workshops. For the most part the recommendations were incorporated into the final BRA guidelines for the development of the parcel. Summary items from the report follow, with notation of items that were further adjusted (for example, reduction in the total number of transitional housing units, omission of commercial space, and an increase in parking requirements).

Program Goals

The Tree of Life should serve women with children and pregnant single women who are homeless and are screened for motivation toward life improvement.

A diverse racial, ethnic, and age mix of women 17 to 55 years of age, with preference for homeless Boston residents, is suggested.

Each woman should define for herself, with peer and counseling assistance, a contract for her 6-month to 2-year period of residency.

The suggested goal of the Tree of Life program is to provide a sound foundation for continued, independent life improvement.

A program evaluation component is suggested to ensure that not only residents but also the program will be improvement focused.

A legal mechanism should be established to guarantee that housing on this site will remain affordable in perpetuity.

Density and Design

Up to 60 families (later reduced to 36) should be accommodated in the Tree of Life transitional housing for optimal program development, for economies of scale, and for the inclusion of permanent housing on the proposed site.

Housing for transitional residents should be designed in clusters of no more than 10 apartments in a row-house arrangement reflecting the architectural character of the South End.

Each townhouse, including community space, a handicapped-accessible apartment, and a fenced back-yard space, should be designed for an age, ethnic, racial, and life-experience mix.

Transitional housing clusters should be within walking distance of each other to allow for easily accessible program meetings.

Clusters should be designed to give residents privacy as well as to encourage a community peer support network.

Permanent housing should reflect the population diversity in the South End, and opportunities for homeownership on the Tree of Life site should be encouraged.

An evaluation plan should include a 5-year assessment of the transitional program and city-wide need to determine whether some of the transitional units should be changed to permanent units.

Social Services and Child Care

A comprehensive social-service program, developed in collaboration with existing agencies, should provide services both on-site and off-site.

Child-care facilities built on the site should be large enough to accommodate the number of children expected at the Tree of Life and, if possible, also to provide for children from South End neighborhood families.

Children's development is an important focus of the program and should be coordinated with the existing child-care services in the neighborhood, providing after-school and drop-in services.

It is probable that most children will be of preschool and lower elementary school age, reflecting the predominance of those currently homeless.

Commercial Space

Commercial space (omitted from the final plan), located on Washington Street, should be preleased to ensure its immediate occupancy.

Commercial tenants should be selected for functions that will be assets to the Tree of Life program and that also will provide necessary neighborhood services.

Parking and Open Space

Very few if any of the transitional residents will have cars and therefore two parking spaces should be allocated for each transitional cluster (increased to .7 per apartment).

Outdoor community space reflecting the character of the neighborhood should be included for transitional and permanent residents.

Management

The board of directors for the Tree of Life should be composed of social-service providers and others from the business and neighborhood community, including those who have experienced low-income single parenthood.

The physical plant of all buildings should be managed by a high-quality, private housing management company.

Program management of the transitional housing clusters should be done by a counselor/facilitator working in collaboration with the residents of each cluster. A staff of three can centrally coordinate for a number of transitional clusters, thereby reducing operating costs.

The child-care program, contracted with an experienced child-care agency, should coordinate services with other local child-care organizations.

Tree of Life Realization

In response to the Women's Institute's report and the suggestions of neighborhood residents, the planners and architects at the BRA prepared a new architectural scheme for the mayor (Fig. 9-5). Unlike the large apartment building with a central entrance in the original proposal, the new scheme had a series of Victorian-style brick townhouses, reflecting the architectural character of the South End. A transitional residence housing nine families was located on each of the four streets at the proposed site. The transitional townhouses appeared identical to the other moderate- and market-rate townhouses on the site (Fig. 9-6). A day-care center was located on an area of the site where a restricted building height was recommended by the neighbors. Parking was buried on the level below the townhouses to expand the number of available spaces at the same time that it created a maximum amount of open space on the site.

In an innovative development approach, the BRA linked the construction of transitional housing on the South End site to a prestigious commercial downtown development site owned by the BRA near the Boston Common. This Parcel to Parcel Linkage RFP was advertised in June 1987, with applications from developers due in November. The developer of the downtown Park Square site was required to include 90 units of housing (36 transitional units, 24 moderate-income condos, and 30 market-rate condos) and child-care space on the South End site as part of the total development.

The RFP stated that:

> a portion of the economic value created by a mixed use development comprised of office, residential, and retail space at Park Square will be used to leverage the development of [the South End parcel] homeownership and transitional housing. . . . A special feature of the project is that it addresses the need for a critical social ser-

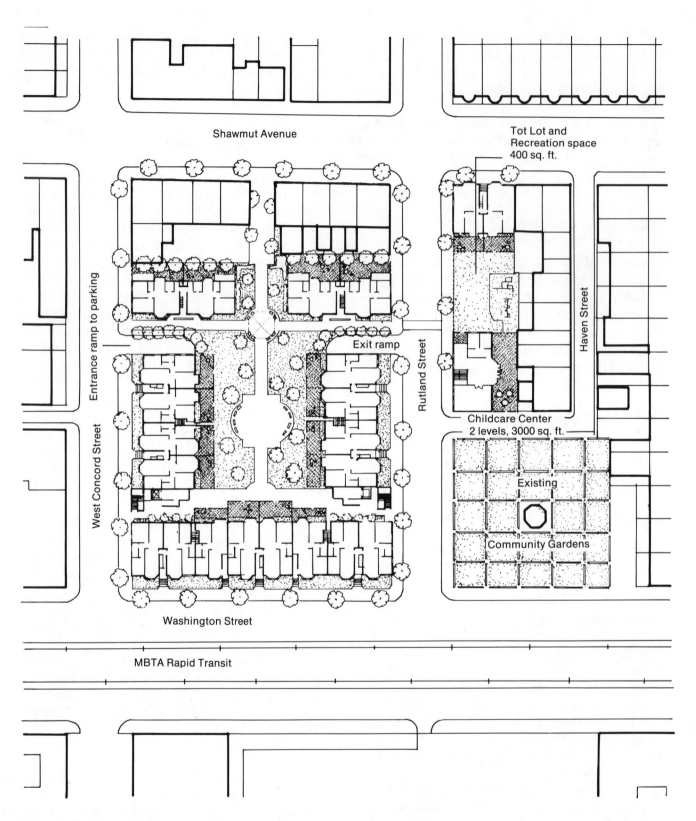

Figure 9-5. Tree of Life revised scheme: site plan. Townhouses built above underground parking have back yards bounded by a shared outdoor space. One townhouse on each street is designated for transitional residents. Similar adjacent townhouses contain market-rate and moderate-income condominiums. Child-care center is located on an adjacent plot.

Figure 9-6. Tree of Life revised scheme: perspective. Townhouses maintain the character and scale of the adjacent neighborhood. The four transitional townhouses are scattered anonymously throughout the development appearing identical to the buildings for permanent residents.

vice program, transitional housing. As federal and state resources to meet the needs of poorer residents are constrained, Boston must rely on innovative programs such as the parcel to parcel linkage to fill the funding gap.

To explain the motivation for the city's approach, statistics were included in the RFP:

During the last decade, the number of female-headed households nationwide rose dramatically. Whether through divorce, separation, widowhood, or teenage motherhood, an increasing number of women found themselves as the sole provider for their families. In 1980, 30 percent of Boston's families were headed by single women; 63 percent of those families had children under the age of 18. At a time when women are emerging as major family providers, the number of

women and children living in poverty is also growing. *In Boston, 37 percent of the families headed by women live at or below the poverty line; for women with children under the age of 18, the percentage is an astonishing 53 percent.* Various economic factors contribute to the plight of these families, including the shortage of affordable housing in the city; lack of job experience; a shortage of adequate childcare; and reduced welfare benefits.

The need for transitional housing also was clarified in the RFP:

The characteristics and needs of Boston's homeless individuals and families are varied. The facilities and services required to meet the needs of homeless people are also diverse. Emergency shelters serve the vital function of providing immediate assistance to homeless people. Most shelters, however, are not designed to provide follow-up services for long-term stabilization. Homeless people need the continual support and training afforded by transitional housing to become self-sufficient providers for themselves and their children. Emergency shelters and long-term facilities complement each other; both are needed to deal with the crisis of homelessness in this city.

The financial goals of the competition for designated developer were described this way:

Proposals which incorporate funding toward the cost of social service programs will be preferred. This funding would help defray the costs of providing daycare, job training, health care and other services for women in the transitional housing program. In addition, proposals that include the creation of a capital improvement fund for any extraordinary operating expenses for the transitional program are encouraged.

The developer was offered these alternatives:

To develop both sites and convey the transitional housing units to a nonprofit corporation on a turnkey basis; to form a joint venture to develop one or both sites whereby the developer contributes gap financing and technical assistance to develop the transitional and affordable units; or any other arrangement that . . . in the Authority's view, achieves the intent and objectives.

The RFP described the community planning goals and guidelines. It called for traditional row houses that appear no different than other South End row houses and the moderate- and market-rate units in the development. The architectural style was detailed, the recall of traditional details encouraged through the size, shape, sills, lintels, and arrangement of windows as well as the inclusion of bays, bows, oriels, turrets, and stoops.

During the bidding period the Women's Institute was retained to provide additional detailed information to the competing developers and to contribute to the review of the results. Through the innovative linkage competition more private developers learned about and participated in the development of transitional housing. Over 50 developers, including several national firms, took

out the development kit. Four development teams submitted complete proposals in November and presented their schemes at community meetings in December. In January 1988 two of the developers were selected by the BRA to work together on the project. Shortly thereafter, drawing on suggestions from the community, the mayor appointed a board of directors to oversee the realization of the transitional housing.

The four developers' applications contained surprising variations, given the detailed requirements of the RFP. The selected scheme, however, most closely fulfilled the guidelines. The variations may be attributed to difference in philosophies of social-service providers and consultants on each of the development teams. Basic differences concerned congregate versus private apartments and attitudes toward safety and security.

Competition Variations

Although private apartments were specified in the guidelines, two developers proposed congregate housing instead. This deviation from the guidelines suggests a social-service approach oriented toward a close community in which interpersonal and parenting skills are stressed. A shared environment encourages peer support and pooling resources. Household tasks can be done cooperatively and traded off, giving more time to single parents for job development and life improvement. Sharing also provides an informal basis for spontaneous cooperation in babysitting.

There are other arguments for sharing. Some see it as integral to the definition of "transition," connecting permanence with "being on your own." Some who maintain this perspective feel that residents of transitional housing are disinclined to move on to nonsubsidized housing if they live in a private, comfortable apartment, although little evidence exists to support this disincentive concept.

Private apartments give residents experience in independent living. Potential conflicts that may arise from possible conflicting parental habits and lifestyles among residents in a shared housing environment can be reduced through private

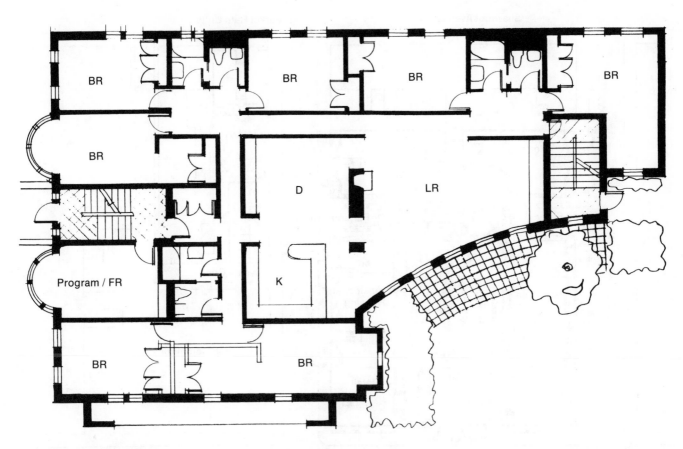

Figure 9-7. Urban Renaissance scheme: floor plan of transitional congregate apartment (*Notter, Finegold, and Alexander, Architects*) The two- and three-bedroom suites in this congregate scheme include private compartmentalized bathrooms. The bedroom suites and a program space/flexible room (reached from the entry hallway) surround the large dining/kitchen/living space.

apartment accommodations. Without skilled assistance in conflict resolution at a congregate housing site, a poor program reputation and a high vacancy rate could result despite critical housing needs. Financial instability of a project caused by vacancies can lead to problematic use of space over time. These risks may have influenced the BRA to reject the congregate housing proposals.

The developers' attitudes toward safety and security were reflected in their proposed location of transitional units on the site and also in the pedestrian traffic planning.

One of the congregate designs, submitted by Urban Renaissance, included two apartment blocks at the back of the site with a unique dining/kitchen/living area as the spatial focus for the bedrooms (Fig. 9-7). This living area also formed a sheltering arc around the outdoor children's play space. Located at the back of the site, the congregate units are protected by the homeowners' row houses and neighborhood stores facing the major thoroughfare (Fig. 9-8). Pedestrian traffic is encouraged on the surrounding streets at the same time that the courtyard is protected from outsiders.

In contrast, the Pavilion team concentrated private transitional apartments at the corners of the site, accenting a major pedestrian walkway through the center of a terraced courtyard (Fig. 9-9). The two other proposals, distributing transitional townhouses throughout the site, also diverged in their approaches to use of the courtyard. One encouraged heavier street traffic by bringing cars into the central space and the other provided the option of closing off the courtyard with gates, protecting this space for residents only.

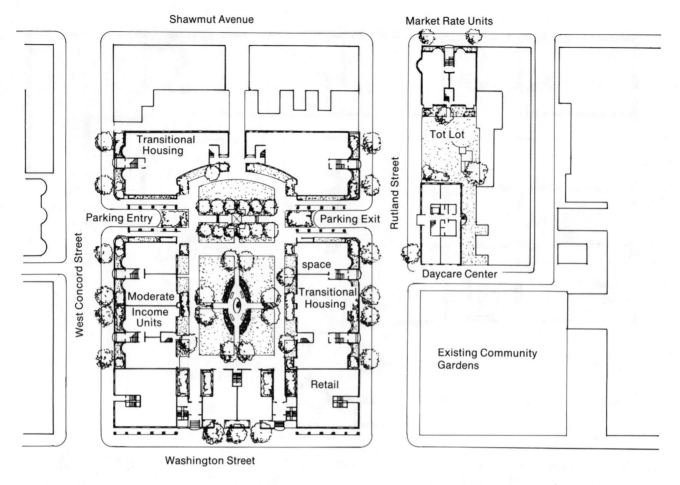

Figure 9-8. Urban Renaissance scheme: site and ground-floor plan. The children's play space at the back of the site is defined by the curved wall of congregate suites. Entry into the garden space is controlled, with no through pathway.

The two developers selected to work together by the BRA offered particular development benefits: the Pavilion Partnership offered to set up an endowment for the transitional site with a local foundation. The South Park Partnership, chosen to do the transitional site, most closely followed the RFP guidelines. The latter development team also was unique among the competitors in its inclusion of minority and women, companies as collaborative owners of the development. This fulfilled another of the mayor's goals for Boston: raising the number of women and minorities involved in the city's projects.

The two selected development teams were given 60 days to prepare a joint proposal. Completion of the South End site is projected in 1989, prior to the completion of the linked Park Square site.

COMPARISONS AND LESSONS

West Shelter, through its social-service work, had an intimate knowledge of program specifics, calling on the Women's Institute for architectural concepts and financial packaging that leveraged city, state, and private resources. For the Mayor's Office and the BRA, the Women's Institute provided the link to the social-service community, facilitating the programmatic and design guidelines.

These allied but different roles demonstrate the kind of teamwork that is necessary for developing transitional housing. Overlaps in expertise strengthen the team. Collaboration and working through differences are essential if the team is to survive. Clear contracts are necessary even between groups with closely tied perspectives and

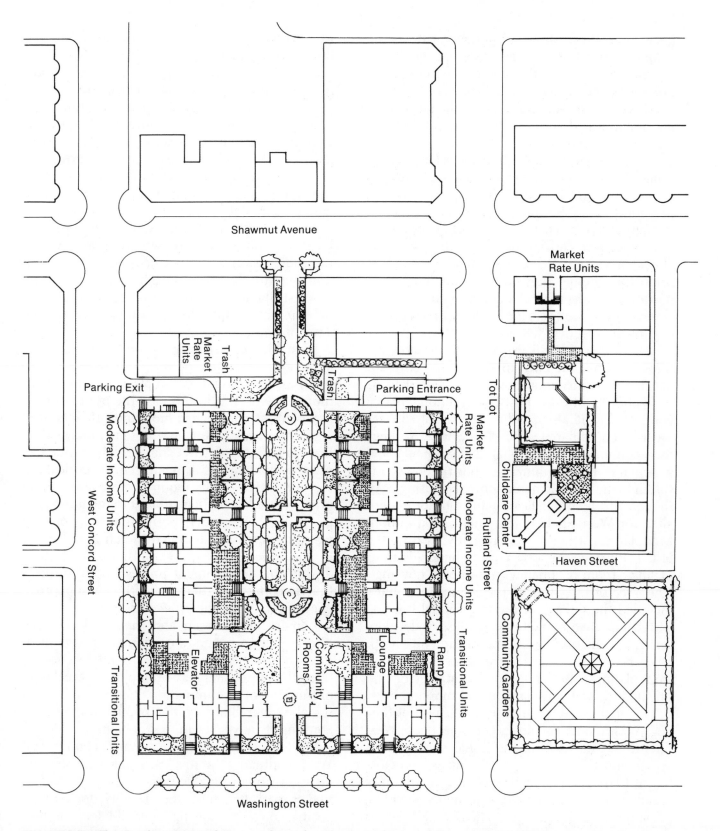

Figure 9-9. The Pavilion Limited Partnership scheme: site and ground-floor plan *(Childs Bertman Tseckares and Casendino, Architects)* The oval-shaped garden and pedestrian pathways in the center of the block are at a lower level than the back yards of the townhouses. This gives private outdoor space to the residents and at the same time encourages the public to circulate through the garden area.

goals. The West Shelter experience caused the Women's Institute to reevaluate and clarify its contract procedures. Particularly when capacity-building and education are elements of technical assistance, contracts must be explicitly defined and reconfirmed at different stages in the development process.

Developing transitional housing is like all real-estate development in its most general terms. As a project proceeds it can change in subtle and profound ways. Some of the changes can strengthen the project. In other instances important objectives can be lost along the way. It is always necessary to keep in mind the highest priorities, whether they be size, functional composition, architectural character, or costs, so that necessary trade-offs can be made within a context of explicit objectives.

At a time when it is expensive to develop any housing at all, the containment of the costs for developing transitional housing is central to its realization. Not only must construction costs be controlled, but also funding for social services must be coordinated. The West Shelter strategy for economy included shared apartments and a scheme for minimizing construction costs through the use of manufactured housing. (Although this technological saving did not materialize for West Shelter, it is still a good option. Modular construction was recently used by the H.E.L.P project in New York to build 200 units of single room occupancy, transitional housing.) The Tree of Life strategy for financial feasibility included the linkage of the transitional housing with a lucrative market-rate real-estate development, which subsidizes some of the costs. Both projects were supported by funds for complex up-front planning. Both depended on state, city, and private financial participation and support.

The final projects are of similar scale, yet they began with smaller and larger objectives. West Shelter expanded from the initial concept of 3 apartments to housing for 24 families: two clusters of 10 transitional families sharing community spaces and four permanent apartments providing backup functional services. The original goal for the Tree of Life of 101 transitional housing units and 8 market-rate units with child-care and commercial space diminished to 36 transitional apartments and a child-care center, with an expansion

to 24 moderate-income and 30 market-rate permanent housing units.

Both schemes are planned with clusters of nine to ten families as optimal for a community of peer support. Space for group meetings and counseling functions are integrated with the housing. Both have provision for child care: West Shelter by including apartments for permanent residents who are licensed child-care providers, the South End site by including a group child-care center. Both programs are designed to refer residents to job development functions in off-site locations, dispersing program functions within the wider community. Both combine permanent housing with the transitional housing. In the case of West Shelter the number of transitional units predominate, while the opposite is true for the Tree of Life.

West Shelter began from the bottom up, the Tree of Life from a top-down initiative. It is generally assumed that those in places of power have more control. But in this case the bottom-up effort of West Shelter had more individual control over the development and design process than the mayor's top-down initiative. The latter had more visibility and was open to more critical observation. Its visibility required more attention to process and the participation of many more people in the community. Both projects involved a planning team and enrolled the efforts of many in the wider community. Both required shifts during the development process; both affirmed that maximum participation from a supportive community helps the project's progress.

Low-income women and their children face discrimination in the housing market as individual renters. Negative neighborhood reaction to transitional housing may exemplify an escalation of this kind of discrimination. The economic and social vulnerability of the population requires community advocacy in their behalf.

Strategic planning was necessary in both cases. West Shelter did this in a less visible way, steering its way through the openings in the system. The mayor, with his automatic visibility, took a bold position on size, allowing for a fall-back, compromise position. The optimal size for transitional housing is debatable. With so many women and children in need, and with development planning so complex and therefore expensive, there is a natural impulse to want to serve greater numbers.

One of the South End neighborhood's fears regarding the original size proposed for the Tree of Life was that the density of transitional families would lower neighborhood property values. Yet the size was based on the success of the first transitional housing development of Warren Village in Denver. Since its establishment in 1974 in a mixed neighborhood of large Victorian houses and apartments, one of the most expensive highrise condominiums in Denver was built across the street.

For both cases described here, residential architectural character was a goal. Accenting residential design qualities and clustering families in peer support modules can provide a basis for combining economies of scale with a supportive environment.

The challenge of size also can be addressed through developing a stronger connection between transitional and permanent housing. Like the final proposal for the South End site, clusters of apartments creating a community of peer support can be integrated into larger, permanent housing developments. Alternatively some transitional apartments may become permanent housing for occupants over time. This approach is being implemented by the Women's Institute's ongoing assistance to a development team comprised of the Family Service Association of Greater Boston and the Boston Citywide Land Trust. These transitional apartments will become limited-equity cooperatives, providing permanent housing when residents reach a stage of greater stability in their lives.

As homelessness in the United States has increased, the need for transitional housing has increased as well. Once a family becomes homeless, a period of transitional residency is generally needed before the family can make it on their own. The function of transitional housing is critical; its form is still being defined by the many projects springing up around the country. There is much still to be realized and evaluated.

NOTES

1. Personal communication (September 1987) from the National Coalition Against Domestic Violence, Washington, D.C.
2. Abigail West Shelter is a fictitious name. The events detailed here are those of a real project, but a pseudonym has been used to respect the privacy of the group.
3. A more complete description of this studio work, student designs, and discussion appears in Sprague (1985).

References

Boston Redevelopment Authority. 1987. *Parcel to Parcel Linkage, Project 2: Park Square and Transitional Housing*. Boston: Boston Redevelopment Authority.

Lukas, A. 1985. *Common Ground*. New York: Random House.

Sprague, J. F. 1985. Transitional housing planning and design: Practice and education by women for women in the USA. *Ekistics* 310:51–55.

United States Conference of Mayors. 1987. *A Status Report on Homeless Families in America's Cities*. Washington, D.C.: U.S. Government Printing Office.

Women's Institute for Housing and Economic Development. 1986. *A Manual on Transitional Housing*. Boston: Women's Institute for Housing and Economic Development.

Chapter 10

Passage Community
Second-Stage Housing for Single Parents

Christine C. Cook

Existing housing options and neighborhoods fail to address the needs of low-income single parents and their families. They typically lack programs and support services targeted to the specific needs of single parents and their children. Passage Community, located in Minneapolis, Minnesota, responds to the needs of women and children by providing a secure, supportive, and affordable housing environment. Passage is second-stage, program-centered housing designed to serve low-income single mothers who want to build a new life for themselves and for their children—one of social, psychological, and economic self-sufficiency.

Passage Community is located in an inner-city neighborhood where many single parents reside. The building is a three-and-one-half-story, extensively renovated apartment building (Fig. 10-1).[1] It has 17 units and includes one handicapped-accessible unit, a child-care facility, community rooms on the second and third floors, a laundry, out-of-season storage space for each household, and indoor and outdoor play spaces. The units range in size from one to three bedrooms. The three one-bedroom units rent for $150 per month, including heat. Seven two-bedroom units were made available to women with Section 8 existing certificates. The seven three-bedroom units have Section 8 moderate rehab subsidies attached to them. Women waiting for Section 8

certificates were given priority for the three-bedroom units. Fair market rents, based on HUD guidelines, are charged for the two- and three-bedroom units.

Women's Community Housing (WCH), incorporated in 1984 as a nonprofit housing developer, planned and developed Passage Community. The board of WCH is composed of women from diverse backgrounds, but they have in common a desire to develop housing that adheres to a basic principle of empowerment and self-determination for resident families. The board of directors views housing as a vehicle for residents to attain self-defined goals, as a means of achieving self-sufficiency. Passage Community reflects these goals and values.

Passage is not emergency or crisis housing but is for women who are leaving a situation of crisis. Residents are able to live in Passage Community for periods of six months to two years, or more. During that time the executive director works with individual residents to assist them in attaining self-defined goals, using individual and community resources. The executive director and a housing assistant are responsible for building management. There also is a full-time assistant child-care director. Because the residents of Passage Community are to be self-directed, none of the staff lives on-site. The philosophy of WCH has been to provide for women decent housing that does not rob them of any control over their own lives.

Renovation of the building for Passage Community began in January 1986, and the first residents moved in July 1, 1986. To be selected to live in Passage, applicants have to have low incomes, be eligible for a Section 8 rental subsidy, and be willing to (1) identify goals (in the area of education, employment, on-the-job training, or upgrading present skills) and make continuous progress toward them and (2) take an active part in activities such as support groups, resident meetings, and workshops. In addition no children over the age of 12 years may reside at Passage Community. The restriction on teenagers living in Passage is modeled after Warren Village, a housing development in Denver, Colorado (Warren Village 1985). According to Warren Village planners, teenagers require special programming and additional space, supervision, and staff, which are cost prohibitive for a small housing development. After deliberation, the WCH board decided to avoid these costs in the first development, Passage, but to consider lifting age restrictions in housing they develop in the future.

PLANNING AND DEVELOPING

Most of the current board members of Women's Community Housing met each other when they served on a task force of the YWCA of St. Paul. The task force, brought together to assess the current use of the eight-story YWCA facility, provided a forum for discussing the particular housing needs of women in the Twin Cities metropolitan area. Members of the task force had expertise in different housing and support services, but all shared the belief that existing housing alternatives had failed women and children. They felt that the formula for successful housing lay not only in providing safe and affordable housing but also in linking support services with housing to help women define and implement their personal goals. About one year after the formation of the YWCA task force, members formed a nonprofit housing development company to develop housing that would provide the services needed by single-parent families in transition.

The women identified as having the greatest need for housing were displaced homemakers

Figure 10-1. Passage Community: front facade.

and single mothers from battered women's shelters, chemical-dependency centers, and other crisis situations. From agencies throughout the Twin Cities, members of the task force gathered data that indicated these women had particularly limited housing options and would be a potential clientele for "second-stage," or transitional, housing. In addition, because there were existing networks for these populations that could act as referral agencies, it was felt that transitional housing opportunities would both be welcomed by the community and have a ready clientele.

The identification of the population to be served was an important part of the development process. WCH board members recognized that the women and children targeted would be coming from crisis- and stress-filled lives. They would be economically vulnerable and in need of services tailored to them. Decisions regarding site location, design, and support services, as well as identifying funding sources for support services, rested on careful consideration of the population to be served.

Building Community Consensus

Building community consensus was an important ingredient in the successful completion of Passage Community. The members of the WCH board recognized that developing housing to meet the needs of single-parent families requires "community consensus." Toward that end Women's Community Housing and the Minnesota Association of Women in Housing (MAWH) joined forces in a community awareness campaign in 1983. Since MAWH is a nonprofit organization that addresses the particular concerns of women who work in the housing industry, it was a likely partner in the building of community consensus. Their meetings offer a forum for networking and provide information on topics related to development, finance, management, and the consumption of housing.

A slide presentation, "Housing Is a Woman's Issue," was developed by WCH and MAWH board members; it included a short slide show and statistics on the problems women encounter when seeking safe, decent, and affordable housing. Both housing and women's groups were tar-geted. This groundwork and later meetings with foundations and key local policy makers paved the way for Passage Community.

During the consensus building process, a plan for second-stage housing began to take shape. Key among the considerations were (1) that the support program component of Passage Community be developed simultaneously and in conjunction with the housing design and management, (2) that the building design facilitate the goals of the program, and (3) that both housing and services support the goal of the empowerment of women by providing opportunities for self-determination and self-direction. Other guiding principles evolved that have since been detailed in a report entitled, *Expanding Opportunities for Single-Parent Families through Housing* (Cook et al. 1987). The development and design of Passage Community attempted to realize the following guiding principles. The housing should:

- Empower the residents, allowing them to take control over their lives.
- Provide a stimulating yet safe and stable environment for single-parent families.
- Be developed holistically; that is, it should consider the interdependency of location, design, support services, management, and finance.
- Respond to the needs of single parents and their children, as a group and as individuals.
- Provide opportunities for neighboring and encourage the development of strong neighborhood networks.
- Not segregate families by marital status, race, income, lifestyle, or other socioeconomic characteristics.

Finding a Site

Two years elapsed between the establishment of the YWCA task force and the founding of Women's Community Housing. In 1984 WCH began to search for an existing building and/or site in St. Paul and Minneapolis to realize the board's vision for second-stage housing. During this time the intentions of WCH were made clear to the community through newspaper articles and a brochure explaining the housing philosophy and program being proposed. When Women's Community Housing incorporated, they established their purpose as the "utilization of the skills and knowledge of women to expand the housing opportunities currently available to women and their families" (Women's Community Housing 1986). Three objectives were identified: (1) to develop new housing models that meet the needs of specific types of women and to demonstrate their effectiveness; (2) to demonstrate the need for integration of support services, such as day care, into housing; and (3) to demonstrate the importance of housing location within the neighborhood and the larger community.

In the fall of 1984, the housing director of the Whittier Alliance, a community development agency in Minneapolis, approached the board of Women's Community Housing with a potential site for the proposed transitional housing: a vacant, three-story apartment building that was close to shopping, public transportation, and educational institutions for adults and children (Passage Community Resident Handbook 1986). The building was in need of substantial rehabilitation and was in danger of being condemned. The roof leaked and frozen water pipes had burst, causing interior damage.

An agreement was made with the Whittier Alliance to act as the developer for WCH. Whittier Alliance garnered additional community support for the transitional housing envisioned by WCH and initiated a capital fund drive for acquiring the building. Whittier Alliance oversaw the development process.

Securing Funding

With an initial loan from the Greater Minneapolis Metropolitan Housing Corporation (GMMHC) and a grant from the Minneapolis Foundation, WCH obtained an option on the building in the Whittier neighborhood and hired Val Michelson and Associates to prepare a design feasibility study.

Additional funding necessary to develop Passage Community and to support the program and program staff came from a variety of sources. Private foundations and Hennepin County provided

start-up program grants. Loans and foundation grants provided the $1.5 million needed to rehabilitate the units and mortgage the building (Table 10-1).

On-going fund-raising efforts are necessary to keep Passage Community open. A professional fund raiser is employed to raise $125,000 to continue the day-care and other programs. Because of early difficulty in finding single mothers who had Section 8 certificates or who could afford the market rent of $427.00 per month at Passage Community, a request has been made by WCH to the Minnesota Housing Finance Agency for a grant of $211,745. The grant would reduce the current mortgage loan and permit rents on the two-bedroom units to be lowered to $225 per month. It is expected that the grant will be funded and that the rent reduction will help stabilize the finances of Passage Community.

Between January and July 1, 1986, a series of announcements, mailings, and information meetings alerted the community to Passage Community—the concept, the availability of new units for single-parent families, and so on. Most initial applications came through agency referral; some came by "word of mouth" or from

Table 10-1. The Financing of Passage Community

Funding Sources	Costs
Project Development	
Foundations	$185,000
GMMHC	31,000 (seed loan)
Family Housing Fund	156,000 (loan)
Minneapolis Community Development Agency	425,730 (loan)
Mortgages from:	
Meritor Mortgage	342,500 (construction)
Minnesota Housing Finance Agency	422,000 (long-term)
TOTAL	$1,562,230
Programs	
Hennepin County	$ 30,000
Honeywell	10,000
TOTAL	$ 40,000

newspaper advertisements. Nearly 100 women applied for residence at Passage Community. Initial applications were reviewed for income eligibility by the executive director and several WCH board members. Names of applicants who met the criteria were placed in a lottery, pooled by eligibility for a one-, two-, or three-bedroom unit. Applicants selected were interviewed by members of the board of directors of Women's Community Housing and selected by the executive director based on their interest and understanding of the program components of Passage Community.

NEIGHBORHOOD CHARACTERISTICS AND HOUSING DESIGN

The Whittier neighborhood was chosen as the site for Passage Community after evaluating many other places. As a site for housing single parents it has many strengths. First and foremost, Whittier is a central location with good public transportation. City buses, providing access to downtown Minneapolis and to other areas of the city, can be boarded one block from Passage. For residents with automobiles on-street and off-street parking is available close to the building.

Another important consideration when choosing Passage Community's location was that Whittier's neighborhood organization and housing development corporation, the Whittier Alliance, with whom WCH developed Passage Community, is a strong and visible force in the surrounding area. Some sites that were considered early on met with community resistance. On the other hand Whittier Alliance's housing director, who knew of WCH and their search for a site, approached the group with a potential building for Passage. The Alliance was receptive to locating second-stage housing in their community.

The neighborhood is residential in character and provides a convenience store, fast-food restaurants, and a full-service grocery. Passage is within walking distance of a park, a children's theater, and the Minneapolis Museum of Art. A number of community schools, public schools, and adult education and training programs can be found in the Whittier neighborhood or are accessible by public transportation. Potential employment opportunities for adults exist nearby.

In some ways the Whittier neighborhood, however, falls short of the ideal. Although Whittier Alliance is implementing a plan to reduce crime in the area, it is still one of the less safe neighborhoods in Minneapolis. According to Passage Community residents, the fear of crime and the quality of the neighborhood schools are the two most disturbing features of the neighborhood. Passage Community is at the intersection of two streets that have heavy vehicular traffic. Fortunately the L-shape of the building provides a protected play space behind the building, which also is fenced in.

The building design of Passage Community is program centered. The architect, Mary Vogel-Heffernan, a former YWCA task force member and experienced in the design of shelters for battered women, used her knowledge about the needs of single mothers to arrive at the final solution.

The needs of the residents, both women and children, were the driving force to which the design responds (Vogel-Heffernan 1985). Vogel-Heffernan focused on four issues that she felt were especially important when responding to the needs of women and children (Cook et al. 1987).

Psychological Security and Physical Safety

The housing should both be secure and feel safe. Plant materials, pedestrian pathways, siting, lighting, and sight lines from the housing should contribute to the safety of the housing.

Community and Privacy for Children and Adult Residents

The design of the housing should foster privacy for individual members of the family and for the family unit. At the same time the design should provide opportunities for sharing and mutual support among families, potentially fostering the development of a sense of community.

Connection to Outdoors

Because children need to be outdoors daily, housing for families with children should provide a direct connection to the outside. Preferred ways to provide this connection include a private patio, a porch, or a deck.

Quality Construction Materials

The housing provided for single-parent families should withstand the extra demands energetic children put on an environment. Materials should be durable and require little maintenance. The building should be climatically sensitive, well insulated, and energy efficient.

Figures 10-2, 10-3, and 10-4 show the floor plans of the basement level, ground floor, and the two upper floors at Passage Community. The redesign of the building's interior and exterior provided for security, privacy, community, and connection to the outdoors. The building's entry is controlled by a security system. The call buttons to each apartment permits tenants control over building access. Fencing to surround all public sides of the building was eliminated from the final plan due to the cost. However, the backyard play spaces are fenced in. Because the child-care center is available to neighborhood children, a separate outdoor entry is provided for their use so they do not enter the other areas of the building.

Both residents' needs for privacy and community were considered in the building redesign. Individual units, with complete kitchen and bathroom facilities, are provided. Community spaces on the second and third floors were intended for a variety of uses—a space for group meetings, an indoor play space for children, a gathering place for families, and a place where common meals might be eaten. Community space on the first floor, originally intended for resident use, is used as office space because the area on the ground floor that was to have been offices was converted into a two-bedroom unit.

Recently the executive director locked the community spaces because some residents complained to her that neighbors were failing to comply with the rules. The residents' handbook governs the use of these spaces, stating that "residents should ensure that their children and visiting children leave these areas clean and tidy after use. Children are to be supervised or checked periodically, as the parent is responsible for any damages incurred. Common areas' playtime for children is from 9:00 A.M. to 8:00 P.M. to avoid disturbance of other residents" (Passage Community Resident Handbook 1986). The director's position is that residents must cooperate with each other when taking responsibility for the community spaces. Now, unless the space is reserved by a resident or until residents present a cooperatively developed plan for the use and policing of the community spaces, the rooms will remain locked at all times.

Connection to the outdoors is achieved for some residents by enclosed porches on the north and east sides. Porches are to be added on the south and west sides when economically feasible. A yard for use by residents is available at the back of the building. Insulation was added to the walls and roof, existing windows were replaced with insulated windows, and outdoor play spaces were made to face south in an effort to respond to the Minnesota climate. There also is a sheltered deck for play during the "mud" season (Vogel-Heffernan 1985). Protected areas indoors, intended for children's play during the long winter season, were provided on the second and third floors.

Special care was taken to lessen the burden of child care and to accommodate the particular needs of children by providing child-care and common play spaces on each floor. Stairways have child-size handrails in addition to adult handrails. Stair towers are closed off by doors so children can move easily from their apartments to the common space with minimal parental supervision. Outdoor play spaces are visible from hall windows, and the outdoor play space is accessible from the child-care facility and the stair towers.

Office space for the executive director and the property manager is located on the first floor, in spaces originally intended as community space. Unfortunately the first-floor office space does not have access to a bathroom, so the director must go downstairs to use the bathroom on the ground floor, in the child-care area. The child-care director has a small "cubby" on the ground floor in

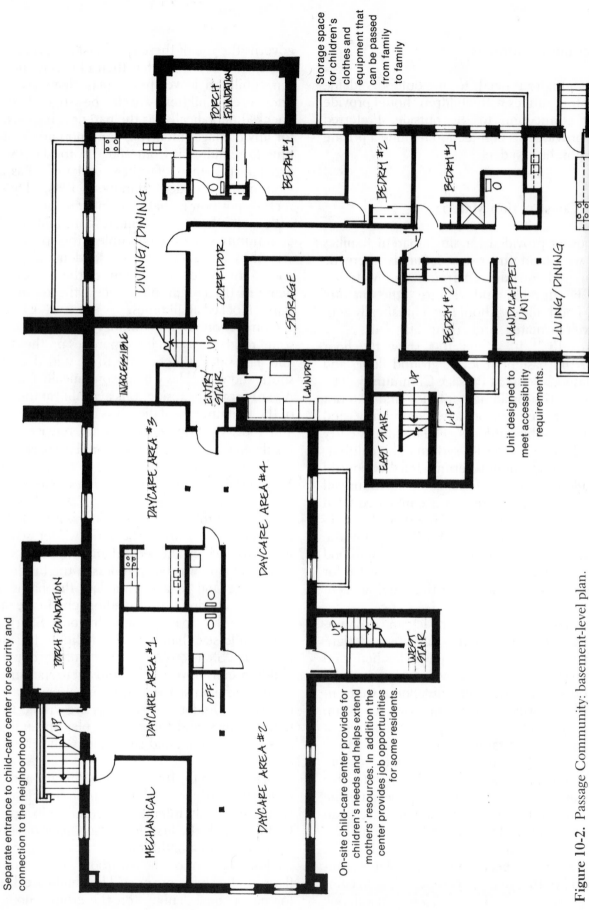

Separate entrance to child-care center for security and connection to the neighborhood

Storage space for children's clothes and equipment that can be passed from family to family

On-site child-care center provides for children's needs and helps extend mothers' resources. In addition the center provides job opportunities for some residents.

Unit designed to meet accessibility requirements.

PORCH FOUNDATION

DAYCARE AREA #1

DAYCARE AREA #3

OFF.

DAYCARE AREA #2

DAYCARE AREA #4

MECHANICAL

UP

WEST STAIR

UP

LIFT

EAST STAIR

UP

LAUNDRY

STORAGE

ENTRY STAIR

UP

INACCESSIBLE

CORRIDOR

LIVING/DINING

PORCH FOUNDATION

BEDRM #1

BEDRM #2

BEDRM #1

BEDRM #2

HANDICAPPED UNIT

LIVING/DINING

214

Figure 10-2. Passage Community: basement-level plan.

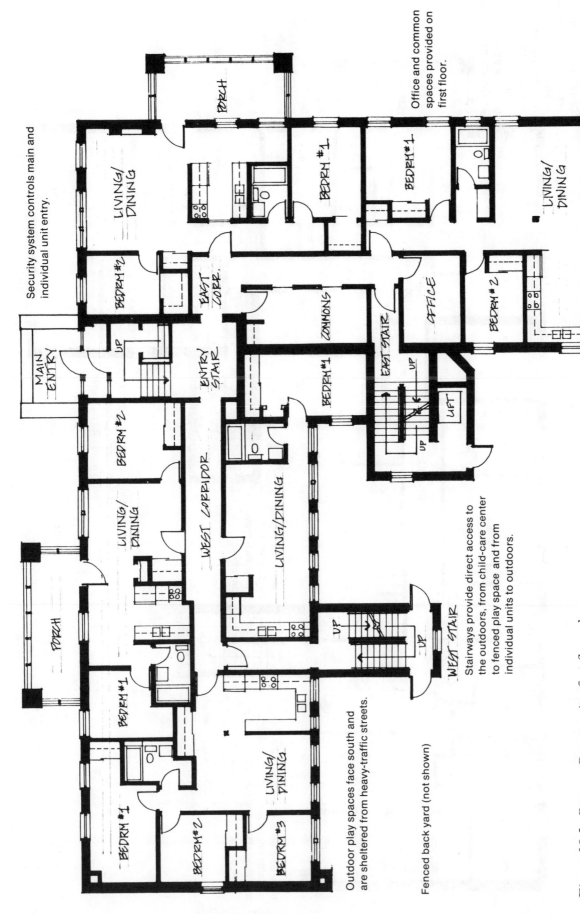

Security system controls main and individual unit entry.

Office and common spaces provided on first floor.

Outdoor play spaces face south and are sheltered from heavy-traffic streets.

Fenced back yard (not shown)

Stairways provide direct access to the outdoors, from child-care center to fenced play space and from individual units to outdoors.

Figure 10-3. Passage Community: first-floor plan.

215

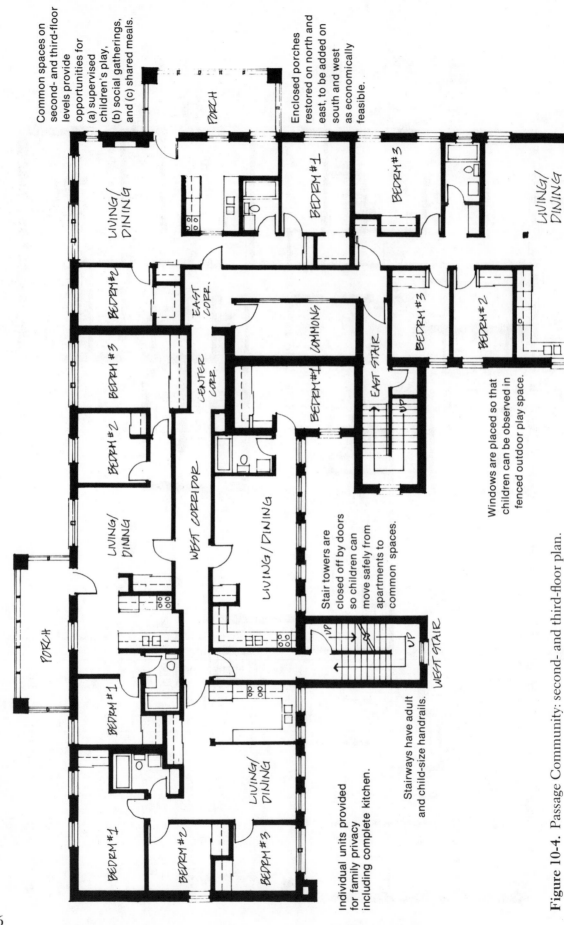

Common spaces on second- and third-floor levels provide opportunities for (a) supervised children's play, (b) social gatherings, and (c) shared meals.

Enclosed porches restored on north and east, to be added on south and west as economically feasible.

Windows are placed so that children can be observed in fenced outdoor play space.

Stair towers are closed off by doors so children can move safely from apartments to common spaces.

Stairways have adult and child-size handrails.

Individual units provided for family privacy including complete kitchen.

PORCH

LIVING/DINING

BEDRM #2

BEDRM #3

BEDRM #2

EAST CORR.

CENTER CORR.

PORCH

BEDRM #4

BEDRM #3

BEDRM #1 COMMONS

EAST STAIR

UP

BEDRM #3

BEDRM #2

LIVING/DINING

LIVING/DINING

WEST CORRIDOR

LIVING/DINING

UP

UP

WEST STAIR

BEDRM #1

BEDRM #1

BEDRM #2

BEDRM #3

LIVING/DINING

Figure 10-4. Passage Community: second- and third-floor plan.

216

the day-care center. The spaces allocated to the child-care staff and the office of the executive director are small. This has been a noted inconvenience. The architect hopes to remedy the problem in the future by converting the two-bedroom unit on the ground level to offices for the executive director, property manager, and child-care staff. This would free the first-floor area for its intended purpose: a community room.

The architect for Passage Community is not entirely satisfied with the final product. Vogel-Heffernan believes that the design decision-making process broke down and that some decisions were made by the developer and contractor without regard for, or understanding of, the intended residents. She feels, for example, that the vinyl flooring in the kitchen and the kitchen cabinets are not of sufficient quality and that the use of flat paint, instead of semigloss, throughout the building was not an appropriate choice for families with small children. Vogel-Heffernan feels that the developer wanted, and received from the WCH board, too much control. She fought against the conversion of the first-floor community space into office space. The developer, however, convinced the board that in order to make "the numbers work," an additional two-bedroom unit on the ground floor was needed.

It also is the architect's contention that WCH did not always get its money's worth because the contractor was not asked to bid on alternative items that at first did not seem financially feasible. For example, due to a better loan arrangement than originally expected, there was money for additional items. However, because the contractor's original bid did not contain these items, the contractor was able to charge WCH for change orders. This raised the cost of these items. Wood baseboards were added as a result of the new monies; they were not bid on initially, and so a change-order fee was charged.

Some special features intended for the building were cut due to cost constraints. An intercom system between apartments, to allow monitoring of units or children when adult residents are absent from the apartments, was eliminated in the final plan. A children's garden in the back yard and fencing surrounding the building were eliminated as well. The ventilating system was downscaled to save money. Vogel-Heffernan fears that the long-term costs that will be born by WCH will exceed the cost of buying a better ventilating system at the time of the building's renovation.

The architect's recommendation to the WCH board for future developments is not to relinquish so much power to the developer. In fact, plans are being made to create a WCH staff position of housing developer. This full-time staff member would pursue funding leads, select sites for transitional housing, and oversee the development of new transitional housing units for WCH.

SUPPORT SERVICES AND MANAGEMENT

As with the design of Passage Community, the support services and management components respond to residents' needs. Safe and affordable housing and on-site child care are services needed by all potential single-parent residents. However, it was not possible to predict ahead of time the additional support services needed by residents. Programs are implemented as requested by residents or at the executive director's discretion. Residents attend monthly business meetings to discuss building, group, and individual needs and concerns. The meetings often are followed by guest speakers in the areas requested by residents.

The director is the crux of the support-service and management component of the program. The responsibilities of the director are key to the long-term success of Passage Community. She is mentor, role model, and community liaison for the residents of Passage.

The director currently assists residents in finding needed services on an individual basis. The residents are encouraged to define and identify their own needs and be self-directed when finding solutions to individual and family problems. The program takes advantage of existing services and referral programs to meet individual women's goals. Consequently the executive director is "many things to many people." Initial observation suggests precautions must be taken to reduce her duties and give her more assistance.

Although steps were taken to distribute her responsibilities by changing the position of housing assistant from part-time to full-time, the shortage of funds to pay the assistant (who has been working full-time on the promise of payment) has only added to the director's stress.

Most residents indicate they are satisfied with the management and rules governing Passage Community (Cook 1986). A residents' handbook is nearly complete. It contains information on the history and background of Passage Community, tenant roles and responsibilities in the program, general policies and rules and regulations, telephone numbers of many agencies and services, information on how to get things fixed, and other household hints. It is modeled after the handbook of Warren Village in Denver, Colorado (1985).

EVALUATION OF THE FIRST YEAR OF OCCUPANCY

Residents of Passage Community are committed to making changes in their lives and have chosen to be part of a mutually supportive shared community. The first adult residents of Passage Community range in age from 18 to 43 years. They are a racially and ethnically diverse group. All the residents are pursuing or planning to pursue additional education or job training, or they are currently employed. Twenty-eight of the first residents are children—17 boys and 9 girls, ranging in age from 3 months to 10 years.

According to a survey conducted in the fall of 1986, the first residents are expecting many things from Passage Community (Cook 1986). They applied for residence in order to take advantage of the on-site child care, reasonable rents, and the building's perceived security, and to pursue goals in a positive environment. The individual goals residents have for themselves and their children are diverse. They want to pursue education or additional training in electronics, accounting, fashion design, data entry, word processing, media production, sociology, and human services. In addition the residents indicated they want more information about existing community programs and about topics ranging from parenting, self-assessment, and incest to budgeting and buying a car and a house.

According to residents safety was the issue that needed the most attention in their old neighborhoods. They felt unsafe in their former neighborhoods and thought that they were noisy, poorly maintained, and in need of more recreation areas. Substandard housing—needing improvements in security, sanitation, plumbing and energy-related items—also was cited as a problem in residents' previous locations.

"Out of pocket" rents ranged from $34 to $430 per month for the twelve respondents; three had Section 8 certificates and two received General Assistance. Residents indicated that they had gone without adequate food, transportation, and essential furniture during the past year. Most received food stamps and food donations at community centers. Some had gone without heat, adequate housing, a telephone, and child care while they worked.

Problems encountered in obtaining child care were primarily due to cost. Five families had not used child-care services prior to coming to Passage Community, and six others used day-care centers. Most previous child-care arrangements of residents were located close to home. Weekly fees ranged from free to $50. Only three families received child-care subsidies.

Before coming to Passage Community, six of the residents were looking for work. Low pay, inadequate transportation, and inadequate and insufficient skills were major barriers to finding suitable employment. Only one resident received child care, paid vacation, and sick and personal leave as part of her benefits package. Nine residents were on AFDC (Aid to Families with Dependent Children), and three received earnings from wages. All the residents are expecting to increase their wage-earning capabilities through additional education and training over the next two years.

The first year of Passage Community has been difficult. Financial problems have resulted partially from a freeze in child-care subsidies and from the eviction of several tenants. In addition the two-bedroom units, at the market rent of $427 per month, usually are not affordable without Section 8 certificates. They have been difficult to fill. The executive director helped to staff the child-care center after one staff member resigned. Consequently she was unable to focus as completely as she would have liked on the current residents and on finding prospective residents for the vacant units. The child-care center runs at a loss.

Financial difficulties in the child-care center have forced a closing of the center that board members and staff hope is only temporary. The cost of operating the center was calculated on the assumption that residents would be receiving individual subsidies (Title XX or special needs subsidies) and that, because the child-care charter permits neighborhood children to use the center, it would never be underutilized. Unfortunately Title XX funds have been frozen and none of the residents can afford to pay the actual cost of child-care delivery, which ranges from $70 to $99 per week per child, depending on the age of the child. The executive director is pursuing funding and management alternatives, hoping to reopen the center in the near future. Understandably the closing of the center has created tension at Passage Community; for residents it seems as if a major benefit of residing in Passage Community is threatened.

Evaluation of Passage Community is progressing in three phases. The first phase is an assessment of each resident's success in achieving self-defined goals. This evaluation of the progress of the residents toward their goals is being measured by entry and exit surveys and by interim reports prepared by the executive director. The interim reports help the director identify programming priorities and needs among residents. The second phase is an evaluation of the housing and the program as a model for housing, day care, and service for single parents. This post-occupancy assessment will involve evaluation in five areas: location, design, support services, management, and finance.

In the last phase the executive director will conduct follow-up interviews to determine the program's long-term effectiveness when assisting single-parent families. In addition it will be important to detail the characteristics of the women for whom Passage Community does not work as a housing/program solution and who abbreviate their stay. Only baseline data has been collected to date.

RECOMMENDATIONS FOR FUTURE DEVELOPMENTS

Four years elapsed between the formation of the YWCA task force in 1982 and the day the first resident moved into Passage Community in July 1986. There were many times when it appeared that Passage would never move off the drawing board. A great deal of persistence, dedication, and undaunted zeal were required to bring the project to fruition. The efforts by board members were voluntary and time consuming. Until funding can be found to hire a housing development director to identify available sites, secure base funding, and assess project feasibility, it is unlikely that Passage Community will be duplicated. In addition state monies for development of alternative housing and federal monies for Section eight subsidies have dried up. Limited availability of child-care subsidies makes the provision of on-site child care next to impossible and suggests that the next development by WCH may not include on-site day care. For future developments WCH board members also think a good alternative to managing the child care themselves may be leasing the on-site space to an experienced child-care provider. Securing staff and financial management would then be left to their supervision. Based on their experience with on-site child-care provision, the WCH board will be expanded to include someone more knowledgeable than current members about children's services and child-care delivery.

Although there seems to be no formula for developing alternative housing for single-parent families, a recent report entitled *Expanding Opportunities for Single-Parent Families through Housing* attempts to provide funders and non-profit agencies with guidelines for providing housing for this population. The report details strategies for developing new housing and for retrofitting existing housing and neighborhoods to meet the needs of single parents and their families. Three of the five authors of the report are members of the Women's Community Housing board of directors. Their experience as early YWCA task-force members and their participation in planning Passage Community shaped the recommendations.

Experience with Passage Community program

development suggests there are at least three populations of women for whom housing opportunities are needed. (Emergency housing for the homeless and crisis housing for battered or chemically dependent women are not discussed in the report.)

The single parents comprising the first group are leading stress-filled lives; are emerging from crisis; have under- or undeveloped management and coping skills; are economically vulnerable; and are in need of services tailored to meet their needs and the needs of their children. Adults and children in this group are in need of intense, tangible support services, such as income, employment, job training, vocational education, child care, and health care. In addition this group needs "soft" social services—counseling and assistance with child-development techniques, abusive situations, self-esteem, and family stress. For the most part, housing responding to the needs of this group will have to serve very low-income families, many of which will be on public assistance or marginally employed.

The families of the second group are able to organize themselves with little assistance. Single parents in this group seek out cooperative living arrangements as a means to avail themselves of peer support. They need and invite communal living situations in which they can network with women whose experiences have been similar to their own. Single parents in this group are low-income, primarily employed (working poor) adults. They need access to some "soft" support services.

The families of the third group identified in the report place high value on privacy and self-sufficiency. They require good up-to-date information and access to information networks. For the most part this group will be employed and low-to-moderate income. These families need temporary assistance to maintain current owner status or assistance to enter into homeownership.

Recommendations on the neighborhood, design, management, support service, and financing of housing to accommodate the needs of single parents also are identified in the report (Cook et al. 1987). The neighborhood and design guidelines are summarized below.

The housing should be sited:

- Where strong formal or informal neighborhood associations and/or networks exist. (Where they do not exist tenants should be encouraged to organize.)
- Away from areas that pose a continual threat to women and children (light or heavy industry, bars, crime-ridden areas).
- In neighborhoods where police surveillance is regular and response to complaints is quick and sympathetic. (In neighborhoods where this is not the case, neighborhood associations, management, and/or concerned others need to take steps to gain the help and cooperation of police.)
- To protect children from vehicular traffic.
- Where pedestrian bridges, bike paths, walkways, and other means to avoid heavy traffic are well maintained, well lighted, and easily accessible.
- Near quality, affordable child care (if child care is not on-site).
- Where public transportation is available within walking distance and where bus routes include a variety of service and employment centers.
- Where alternative schools and training opportunities are available to school-age children, teenagers, and adults.
- To provide potential employment opportunities for single parents and teenagers.
- Within walking/biking distance of recreation opportunities for adults, teens, schoolagers, and tots.
- In neighborhoods with many community and support services that are accessible by foot, by public transportation, and by automobile.
- Within walking distance of one full-service grocery store.
- In neighborhoods that consist of people with varied socioeconomic and demographic characteristics.
- To give families an opportunity to live in neighborhoods where they currently reside and to live in neighborhoods of their choosing.
- In "receptive," well-maintained neighborhoods and in neighborhoods that are not crime ridden.

The following criteria should be considered in the design of housing for single-parent families:

- The form of the building(s) is compatible with other buildings in the neighborhood.
- The building is extensively lighted, including building exteriors, interior pathways, car parking areas, children's play areas, neighborhood sidewalks, streets, bus stops/shelters.
- The siting and configuration of the building allow residents surveillance over the site—the immediate

exterior, children's play areas, parking lots. The building is sited to reduce security problems.

- Planted materials (1) do not create security problems, (2) are environmentally/seasonally appropriate, (3) are durable and low maintenance, (4) are nontoxic.
- Pathways are adequate for children's wheel play, are slip resistant, drain adequately, and avoid steep elevations.
- Fencing is placed to enhance security, accommodate snow shoveling, and surround play spaces for children five years and under.
- Outdoor spaces are provided for adults that permit leisure activities, outside work on cars, gardening and surveillance of children's play.
- Outdoor spaces are provided for families, including organized game areas and picnic areas.
- Play areas for tots, grade-school children, and teenagers are provided.
- Areas for children's play have the following characteristics: a variety of defined areas for different play activities; year-round outdoor play area; small children's spaces close to the building; protection from wind and cars; child-safe surfaces; proper drains.
- Areas for teenagers have the following characteristics: visual privacy; location away from parking and driveways; bicycle racks, 1 per 4 units.
- Entries are individual, secure, easy to negotiate while carrying a child. A waiting bench is provided that is large enough for an adult and several children.
- Entry doors are not heavy to open and provide overhead protection from the weather.
- Building has an intercom system with buzzers to individual units, community rooms, and offices; has a fire alarm panel.
- Common hallways have the following characteristics: shared with few units; durable materials on walls; low-pile floor covering; sound-deadening ceilings; natural light and ventilation; lights powered by two different circuits; durable lights; fire doors with magnetic holders; places provided for information and resident's displays.
- Stairways have the following characteristics: no long runs of stairs; deep treads and low, closed risers; low railings for children in addition to adult railings; balustrades spaced six inches on center or less; stair width that allows use of standard child gate; gates at top and bottom of stairs; if carpeted, low pile.
- Accessible play space is provided indoors, adjacent to units. This play space is visible from the interior of units; allows for child, family, and adult activities;

is sound insulated; is lighted naturally; is accessible to the outdoors and a public toilet; has storage for coats, play and meeting equipment.

- Laundry connections are available in individual units. Common laundry areas are conveniently located; provide play space for children, shelves, and lockable storage spaces; walls are enamel painted or vinyl covered.
- Building storage for toys and out-of-season clothing has shelves, rods for hanging clothes, and space for large equipment items.
- Exterior garbage containers are durable, quiet, spill and kick proof, have a light lid, are accessible to adults and children. Dumpster areas have a solid wall and gate and a concrete slab in pick-up areas.
- Office space provided for staff is large enough for a small group meeting, has an adjoining half bath, storage for resource materials, and lockable filing cabinets.
- Living rooms are near to the unit entry; accessible to outdoors; accommodate more than one furniture arrangement; provide storage and display space. Placement of doors in living area reduces traffic through the area.
- Color scheme accommodates various furnishings, colors, and patterns.
- The kitchen has the following characteristics: accommodates high chairs and serves as play space for children and several people preparing food; impedes traffic through the "work triangle"; task lighting over the work area; operational window with view to play spaces; work space on either side of range/oven; range/oven ventilation fan, light, and grease shield; range controls located at the rear; storage areas for food and equipment accessible to older children and inaccessible to younger children; rounded edge counter tops and 180-degree openings on cabinet doors; wall-mounted telephone outlet; hard floor surfaces; semigloss enamel paint on walls and ceilings, and wood or vinyl-base floors.

The neighborhood guidelines focus on five major issues: safety and security; service availability; interaction among socioeconomically and demographically diverse populations; neighborhood maintenance; and community receptivity to single-parent housing. Six key issues are addressed by the design recommendations: the homelike quality of the housing; the scale, density, and arrangement of the units; the community and privacy; the safety and security; the indoor and outdoor connection; and the quality of the residential environment.

A final caveat is offered: each housing development undertaken to serve nontraditional households should be unique. Unlike speculation housing for middle-income households, second-stage housing targeted to low-income single parents and their children is difficult to mass produce. It requires careful resident selection and a matching of the resident population to specified program and support services. And second-stage housing has a purpose beyond traditional housing development. It aspires to economic, social, and psychological empowerment of its residents.

NOTE

1. Karen Eid, a senior in the architecture program at the University of Minnesota, is responsible for Figures 10-1 to 10-4.

References

Ahrentzen, S. B. 1983. *Women and the Housing Process: A Look at Residential Fit, Adjustments, and Constraints of Lower-income Female-headed Households*. Ph.D. dissertation. Irvine: University of California.

Birch, E. L. 1985. *The Unsheltered Woman*. New Brunswick: Center for Urban Policy Research.

Cook, C. 1986. Passage Community—an evaluation. St. Paul, MN: Report for Women's Community Housing.

———. 1987. Housing in the community: evaluating the alternatives for single-parent families. Paper read at Annual Conference of the American Association of Housing Educators (Nov. 2–7). Newport, Rhode Island.

———, M. Vogel-Heffernan, B. Lukermann, S. Pugh, and E. Wattenberg. 1987. *Expanding Opportunities for Single-Parent Families Through Housing*. Minneapolis: Minneapolis/St. Paul Family Housing Fund.

Leavitt, J. 1984. The shelter plus issue for single parents. *Women and Environments* 6:16–20.

———, and S. Saegert. 1984. Women and abandoned buildings: a feminist approach to housing. *Social Policy* (Spring):32–39.

Minnesota Housing Finance Agency. 1985. Female-headed family households in Minnesota: An analysis of housing and household characteristics. St. Paul.

Passage Community. 1986. *Passage Community Resident Handbook*. Minneapolis, MN: Women's Community Housing.

President's Commission on Housing. 1982. *The Report of the President's Commission on Housing*. Washington, D.C.: U.S. Government Printing Office.

Vogel-Heffernan, M. 1985. Feasibility study and cost estimate of the building located at 17 East Twenty-fourth Street. Design program presented to Women's Community Housing, Minneapolis, MN.

Warren Village. 1985. *A Community for One-Parent Families—Handbook*. Denver: Warren Village.

Wekerle, G. R., R. Peterson, and D. Morley, (eds.). 1981. *New Space for Women*. Boulder: Westview Press.

Women's Community Housing. 1986. Brochure. Minneapolis, MN.

Chapter 11

Developing Two Women's Housing Cooperatives

Gerda R. Wekerle
Sylvia Novac

In recent years an opportunity for Canadian women to sponsor and develop housing projects for themselves has been provided under the Canadian Non-Profit Housing Program. Case studies of two women's housing cooperatives show that when women develop their own housing, their concerns with community are reflected both in the physical design of the housing and in the social design of decision making and community life. This chapter describes how two groups of women in Toronto, Canada, developed and manage their own housing.[1]

While not targeted solely to single-parent families, these co-ops were planned to meet the needs of single mothers. They provide affordable, secure housing units in a community supportive of women and children that also offers women a safe environment in which to heal and grow. Thus they meet some of the fundamental housing needs of single mothers while they also accommodate the needs of other sole-support women.

DEVELOPING WOMEN'S COMMUNITIES

In the growing literature on women's housing, there is an emerging debate on the relative merits of improving the distribution of affordable housing to women or providing appropriate housing design that incorporates supportive services, such as child care or enterprise space within the shelter envelope. On the one hand authors such as McClain and Doyle (1984) argue that women should not be defined as a special-needs group but should be provided with sufficient income and financing to compete in the housing marketplace. The extension of their argument is that housing targeted specifically for women, or certain classes of women, stigmatizes them and does not ultimately meet their needs. On the other hand feminist writers, primarily within the planning and design fields (Hayden 1984; Leavitt 1985), argue that conventional market-built housing is inadequate in responding to women's housing needs. Hayden makes the compelling argument that standardized and traditional housing forms are based on assumptions about the nuclear family and a wife at home. Recent changes

223

in family composition and women's increasing participation in the labor force have created needs for new housing with greater attention to the physical design and the incorporation of support services within the shelter component.

Within the past few years, numerous designs for such housing have elaborated possible solutions including West and Leavitt's proposal that permits sharing between single parents and seniors (Leavitt 1984) and their prize-winning proposal for the New American House competition where living space incorporates opportunities for work-at-home and neighborhood-based child care (see chapter 8). Hayden's (1981) proposal for the redesign of a typical suburban neighborhood (HOMES) is larger in scale and demonstrates how spaces for neighborhood-based employment, child care, and transportation, as well as communal living, might be carved out of a typical suburban neighborhood of single-family homes on large lots.

While these proposals have been provocative and widely discussed, there are few North American examples of housing specifically designed, developed, and controlled by women that would allow us to evaluate the relative importance to women housing consumers of basic shelter, affordability, design responsive to changing lifestyles, and community elements. In Canada women's groups have used the federal Non-Profit Housing Program to produce cooperative housing projects developed by and for women since the early 1970s and increasingly in the 1980s. These are significant demonstration projects that allow us to examine some of the issues raised in the literature concerning housing for women.

THE CANADIAN NON-PROFIT HOUSING PROGRAM

Established in 1973 under Section 56.1 of the National Housing Act, this program has been used extensively to develop nonprofit cooperative housing projects; between 1979 and 1985 approximately 30,000 housing units were developed across the country (Hannley 1986). Under this program community-based groups initiate the development of a "modest" housing project and apply for financial assistance to provide not-for-profit housing for low-income households. This nonequity form of collective ownership provides residents with greater security of tenure and greater control through democratic decision making and self-management than is the case for rental housing.

The actual development of cooperative housing projects was placed in the hands of nonprofit community groups. They were eligible for development cost-assistance grants and 100 percent mortgage insurance from the federal government through the Canada Mortgage and Housing Corporation (CMHC). Each co-op received a substantial financial subsidy that covered the difference between monthly amortization costs at the market rate of interest and an interest rate of 2 percent. Housing costs for units were set at the low end of the market compared with market rents in the adjacent community. Designed to provide moderate-cost housing, Maximum Unit Prices (MUPs), based on land and construction costs, were established for each city and region. To keep projects within budget, potential housing sponsors have had to make difficult choices and compromises over site locations, construction materials, amenities, and interior space. This affected most co-op housing projects but particularly small women-sponsored projects where initial expectations of space for communal services and a quality housing environment often are quite high.

Since its beginnings the program has indirectly favored housing sponsorship by existing community organizations with members who have a common interest, as the often-lengthy process of developing a housing project requires cohesive sponsoring groups. Co-ops have been developed by unions for their membership, such as the co-op developed by the International Ladies Garment Workers Union; by church groups, including several Orthodox Jewish congregations; by ethnic groups, as, for instance, co-ops developed by the Czech, Chilean, and Vietnamese communities; and by organizations of artists and disabled people. There is no count of how many thematic co-ops have been developed nationally, although people in the co-op housing sector describe them as a minority of all nonprofit co-ops, which generally are targeted to a cross section of the community.

Within this context women's community groups obtained funding to develop housing cooperatives for an all-women membership. While this was novel to CMHC, the federal housing agency, potential sponsors of women's housing in Vancouver, Quebec City, and Toronto argued that a women's housing cooperative was no different from a Chilean co-op or one limited to practicing artists. In the case of the two women's co-ops described in this chapter, the sponsors proposed that only adult women could be members of the co-op with rights to vote in elections, sit on the board of directors, and participate fully in policy making and decision making. They were concerned that women retain control of decision making in the co-ops since experience in more broad-based co-ops showed that women members did much of the committee work but were underrepresented as presidents or vice-presidents of the organizations (Co-operative Housing Federation of Toronto 1985). The arguments were accepted after legal opinions established that these co-ops could obtain an exemption from the provincial Human Rights Code.

Nonprofit housing cooperatives across Canada attract women residents: approximately 25 percent of all households are single-parent households. Both affordable housing and stable community supports are fundamental for single-parent families that are likely to move with greater frequency after separation and divorce, largely because of affordability problems. A disruption such as repeated moving adds stress for adults and children alike at a time when they require a new base of security. Several aspects of housing co-ops address the needs of single mothers in particular: affordability, security of tenure, and a neighborly environment that promotes mutual support among members.

Developing the women's housing co-ops has involved attention to several key concerns: affordability, security of tenure, user participation or development input, livability and housing quality, creation of a supportive community, and empowerment through self-management and democratic decision making. The two Toronto women's housing cooperatives described in this chapter each developed its own approach to these issues.

TWO WOMEN'S HOUSING COOPERATIVES

In the early 1980s two women's housing cooperatives were developed in Toronto. Constructed in 1982 and designed by Joan Simon of Simon Architects, the Constance Hamilton Co-op is a 30-unit stacked townhouse project with an attached 6-bedroom transitional house for single women. The Beguinage, a 28-unit stacked townhouse project designed by Phil Goldsmith of Quadrangle Architects, was occupied in 1985.

As part of a larger study of ten women's housing projects in eight Canadian cities (Wekerle 1988), Joan Simon and Gerda Wekerle conducted a post-occupancy evaluation of Constance Hamilton and the Beguinage between September 1985 and October 1986. The study had two objectives: first, to document the development process in each project through interviews with sponsors, architects, and housing officials; second, to interview residents about their experience of living in these housing environments, utilizing a 90-item interview schedule generally taking two hours to complete. Response rates in the two co-ops were high—89 percent in the Beguinage and 67 percent in the Constance Hamilton.

The Constance Hamilton Cooperative obtained one of the last sites in the Frankel/Lambert development in the west central area of Toronto (Simon and Wekerle 1985). This 23-acre industrial site had been redeveloped by the City of Toronto Housing Department to accommodate four nonprofit cooperatives, a nonprofit housing project owned and managed by the City Housing Department, a seniors complex, and owner-occupied row houses. The Constance Hamilton site is 1,900 square meters—a tight site that restricted both the configuration of the building and the outdoor open space. It overlooks a small community park.

The building form consists of three-story stacked townhouses of concrete block (Fig. 11-1). Each unit has a door at ground level, a requirement of the City of Toronto's design guidelines for all projects in this development. The co-op has 30 units: 10 one-bedroom units, 16 two-bedrooms, and 4 three-bedrooms. In addition there is a two-story unit of six bedrooms with a shared living room, dining room, and bathrooms, which

Figure 11-1. Constance Hamilton Cooperative. *(Simon Architects)*

was designed to accommodate, for up to one year, homeless single women referred by women's hostels. While this unit was initially managed by the co-op, now it is run by a full-time counselor who is on the staff of a women's hostel.

Each unit has either a private balcony or a small outdoor area adjacent to the unit. All two- and three-bedroom units have a private basement area, accessible from within the unit, that is used for storage, private laundry facilities, or an indoor play area for children in bad weather.

Communal spaces were limited by both the tight site and the funding formula, which provides funding primarily for the shelter component of the housing and limits funding for nonresidential use to 15 percent of capital costs or 20 percent of floor area. A communal courtyard at the center of the building is heavily used for small children's play and for sitting and communal celebrations in the summer months.

A laundry room is located at grade overlooking the small park. In the basement there is a small meeting room that accommodates four persons comfortably and an office for a part-time

co-op coordinator who does the bookkeeping, handles inquiries and applications, and coordinates maintenance.

The Beguinage was offered a site that had been cleared for urban renewal in the early 1970s. Conditions on the use of the site limited redevelopment to some form of nonprofit housing. The site was in two parts, separated by half a block of private housing, on a busy arterial street at the eastern edge of Toronto's downtown core. Because the site was split into two parts, it would be more difficult to develop a cohesive community. From the point of view of the co-op sponsors, the site had other drawbacks as a place for a women's co-op: it was adjacent to a massive post-war highrise public housing development and close to the city's skid row.

The Beguinage was a modified turnkey project: the co-op purchased the land and the developer carried the interest charges during construction and was liable for meeting building requirements and correcting deficiencies. Although the developer hired the architect, the agreement with the co-op stipulated that the architect, Phil Goldsmith of Quadrangle Architects, was working for them. The project consists of 28 units on two properties within the same block. The form is stacked townhouse construction with brick siding and stucco on the ground floor and wood siding on the second story (Fig. 11-2). There are 13 one-bedroom units, 12 two-bedroom, and 3 three-bedroom units. Each unit has either a large private balcony or a fenced yard at ground level. Townhouse units have direct access to the street; one-bedroom units share small vestibules (Fig. 11-3).

There is no communal outdoor space that could accommodate all co-op members for summer barbecues or celebrations, and the indoor meeting room is small. A coordinator's office, a workshop/storage room, and one laundry room for the entire complex are the other shared spaces.

Both the Constance Hamilton and the Beguinage share certain characteristics: the small size of the co-op; the emphasis on private dwellings; the minimum amount of communal space; and the lack of other services on-site, such as child care or business space.

User Participation in Co-op Development

A unique feature of the Non-Profit Housing Program is the institutionalization of user participation and grass-roots control through two key elements. First, a community group interested in establishing a co-op is provided with start-up funds to undertake needs studies and to pay for preliminary professional assistance. If the project proceeds, these development costs are included in the capital costs of the project. Second, the program initially provided funding for the establishment of local resource groups or housing consultants to assist community groups in taking projects from the idea stage to final completion.

Resource groups developed expertise in all stages of the development process: dealing with government officials, filling out applications, and hiring architects and construction companies. These resource groups paid special attention to member education and organized sessions for board and committee members on financial management and the day-to-day operations of the co-op.

For women's organizations the existence of re-

Figure 11-2. The Beguinage. *(Philip Goldsmith, Quadrangle Architects)*

source groups has been particularly important. In our two case studies, founding members had limited or no experience with property development. Being able to rely on the technical expertise of resource groups allowed them to pay special attention to quality-of-life issues, the implementation of their vision into a built form, the identification of user needs, and the incorporation of supportive elements.

Maintaining control of the development process was a key concern for both co-op groups. The Constance Hamilton Cooperative was initiated at a series of meetings in 1979, where representatives of various women's hostels working on the Metro Toronto Department of Social Services (1979) Long-Term Housing Committee discussed the concept of forming a structure that could acquire and run long-term housing for women. City of Toronto alderman Janet Howard proposed using CMHC funding to form a housing cooperative for women. A voluntary board of women, many of them professionals in the social-service field, incorporated the Constance Hamilton Co-op.

A major objective of the Constance Hamilton group was that women be in charge of the project and sit on the board, so that they could maintain direct control of the design and development process rather than leaving major decisions on these matters to a resource group. The board interviewed half a dozen architects and chose Joan Simon because she had experience in working with users in a community setting. She was the only architect interviewed who showed alternative kitchen designs and discussed how users actually live in housing. She emphasized energy conservation and quality materials that would save on long-term maintenance costs. Her approach to programming was to conduct interviews with potential residents and to utilize post-occupancy evaluation studies of the first residents who moved into the project.

The experience of developing this first Toronto women's housing co-op informed the development process of the second women's co-op. The Beguinage development group included a carpenter who had been active on the Constance Hamilton Board and a ten-person board of women active in the Toronto women's community. A core group met regularly for four years

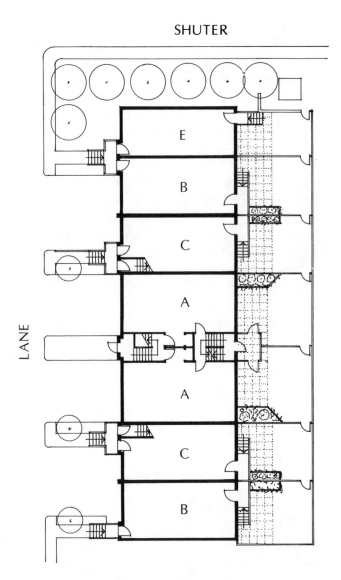

Figure 11-3. The Beguinage: site plan.

and was actively involved in searching for a building site. They hired a resource group, the Cooperative Housing Federation of Toronto, to assist them with their task. The initial goal was to restore a stately downtown building. But funding an affordable inner-city building within the budget allowed for nonprofit co-ops proved impossible. After half a dozen buildings were considered and rejected, the board was ready to dismiss the project when it was offered an inner city site on land assembled for urban renewal in the 1970s. Even though the location on the edge of skid row was not ideal, the group accepted the site.[2]

SHUTER

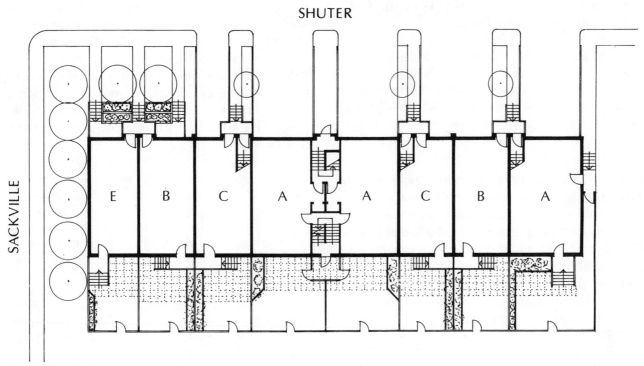

Figure 11-3. *(cont.)*

Despite an early commitment to working with a feminist architect who had prepared initial working drawings for several potential sites, this site was available only as a turnkey operation, whereby the owner of the land had already pre-selected the architect and prepared initial plans. With the assistance of the resource group project officer, the board negotiated with the developer and his architect to decrease the density of the site to 28 units from almost twice that number of units. Through many meetings with the architect, the board established priorities and preferences.

In both projects maximizing user control over design and site decisions was an important objective for the founders, despite the years of volunteer work required. The resource groups that act as housing consultants specifically for cooperative housing projects made it feasible for these inexperienced women's groups to sponsor and develop housing according to their own dictates. However, the unavailability of appropriate and affordable building sites, particularly close to the downtown area where many women prefer to live, acts as a crippling constraint on new housing development.

Design for Livability and Housing Quality

For both of these women's housing cooperatives, the ultimate goal was to make affordable housing available quickly and within budget; design innovations, which might express a women's culture and community through physical form, were secondary. However, each group fought for certain features that it felt would contribute to members' quality of life: high-quality materials, energy-conservation features, and unit designs that would accommodate a range of households. They were hampered by Non-Profit Housing Program's emphasis on building modest housing. Each of the sponsoring groups found it had to make trade-offs to come in under the maximum unit prices. At both projects electric heating was installed rather than gas because it was less costly to install even though it is more expensive to run. At the Beguinage the group wanted bigger units, better finishes, better-quality windows, and heat-recovery units, but the funding constraints did not allow for these added features.

The use of quality materials and long-term maintenance and durability were key concerns for the developers of both the women's co-ops.

Joan Simon discussed the attitude of the Constance Hamilton Co-op Board:

> The board was very concerned with the habitability of the units. If we were working for a private developer, attention would have frequently been on gimmicks and trim rather than basic quality. The board wanted to maximize living space and make houses better for people to actually live in.

This involved structural decisions, such as using concrete-block walls, good-quality wood windows that would not leak, and more insulation than required. Detailing included in the initial tender allowed residents to upgrade their housing and make additions in the future. This included detailing of the front doors of units so that a vestibule could be added. For the women's hostel unit, a roof garden also could be incorporated in the future.

After the building was occupied, the Constance Hamilton residents experienced considerable problems with sound transfer between the units and condensation in the attics due to the tight seal of the building. Subsequent retrofitting involved improving attic ventilation, adding another layer of drywall between the units, blowing insulation into the space between units, and insulating and boxing in bathroom pipes.

Special attention was paid to aural privacy for the Beguinage project. To eliminate sound transmission, a common problem in stacked townhouse projects, the architect of the Beguinage stayed with simple forms and simple unit separation: the party walls line up, unit separation is as simple as possible, and interleafing provides sound separation. Over the wood floors and between the units there are ¾-inch Gypcrete floors. A sound consultant advised on wall treatments: block wall construction with cement over one side to make a solid surface; 1-foot by 2-foot strapping on both sides and insulation to create an air chamber. Stairs are of extra heavy construction and are hung from floor to floor without touching the walls and creating vibrations. Extra care also was taken in plumbing installations by using rubber gaskets to separate plumbing from hangers and to make enclosures tight.

For energy conservation 2-foot by 6-foot construction was used for external walls, with extra insulation and sealing; insulated basement walls and wood windows were installed instead of cheaper, more conventional aluminum windows.

An objective of the co-op founders was to provide units that would meet the needs of a broad range of women. In the Constance Hamilton project, there are seven different unit designs (Figs. 11-4 and 11-5). Joan Simon commented on this variety:

> We designed units to suit a large number of lifestyles: 2–3 women sharing, multi-generational families, two single parents, etc. I split the living areas and put the living room on one floor and the dining room and kitchen on another so that both social spaces could be used at the same time. This meant the kitchen moved to the front of some units. The Board wanted dining kitchens and not separate galley kitchens. The plan allows for a linear kitchen on one end of the dining room. The entrance to the units is often in the kitchen. Almost all the men in the approval process commented on this, while all the women who looked at the plan thought it was sensible. There is also a toilet in the laundry room for kids in the park, which had to be deliberately designed.

Attached to the co-op but completely separate is a six-bedroom transition house for single women. Large bedrooms and private balconies permit privacy; the kitchen and living areas are shared.

At the Beguinage architect Phil Goldsmith mixed three types of units: a core of six one-bedroom units in a central block that is like a walk-up apartment building; standard two-story townhouses with street access; and units stacked above the townhouses. To facilitate the sharing of units, the board insisted on same-size bedrooms, rather than the conventional "master" and "junior" bedrooms. Achieving this small modification met with some resistance from both CMHC and the architect because conventional housing usually differentiates status within the family by size of bedroom. Six units have two master bedrooms of the same size (Fig. 11-6).

It is not common practice for nonprofit housing cooperatives to provide child care on site; for example, 70 percent of Toronto area co-ops do not provide any form of organized child care (Cooperative Housing Federation of Toronto

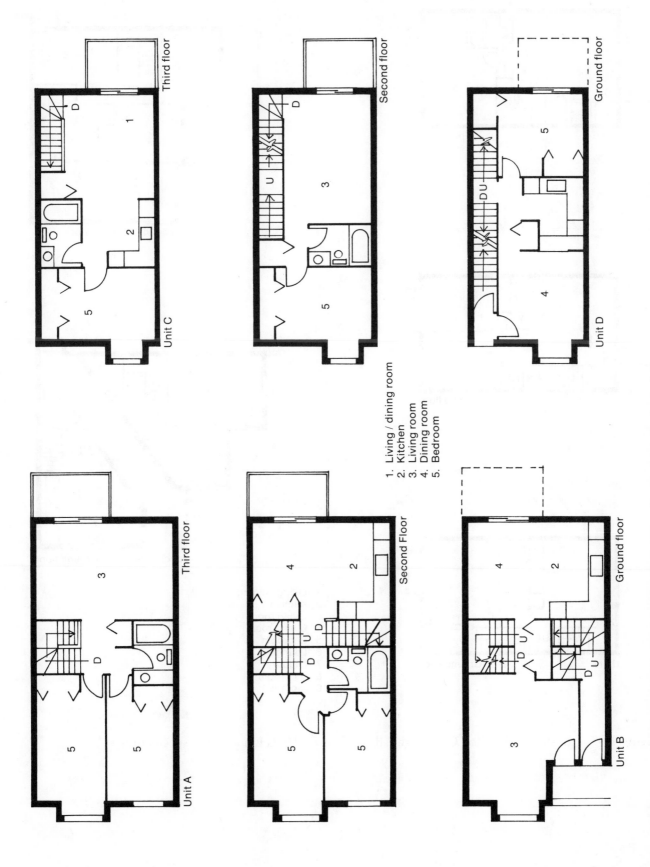

1. Living / dining room
2. Kitchen
3. Living room
4. Dining room
5. Bedroom

Third floor

Unit C

Second floor

Unit D

Third floor

Unit A

Second Floor

Ground floor

Ground floor

Unit B

Figure 11-4. Constance Hamilton Cooperative: floor plans for Units A, B, C, and D.

231

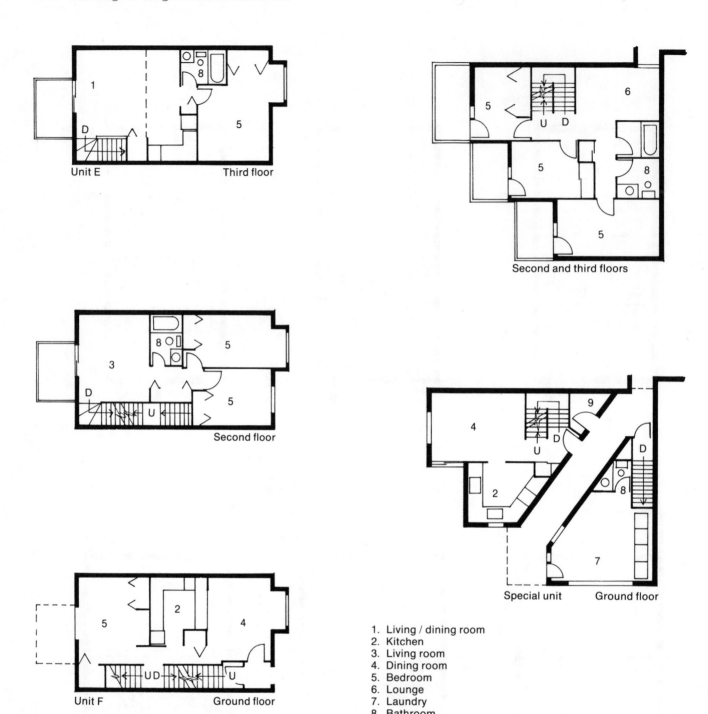

1. Living / dining room
2. Kitchen
3. Living room
4. Dining room
5. Bedroom
6. Lounge
7. Laundry
8. Bathroom
9. Storage

Figure 11-5. Constance Hamilton Cooperative: floor plans for Units E and F and special unit.

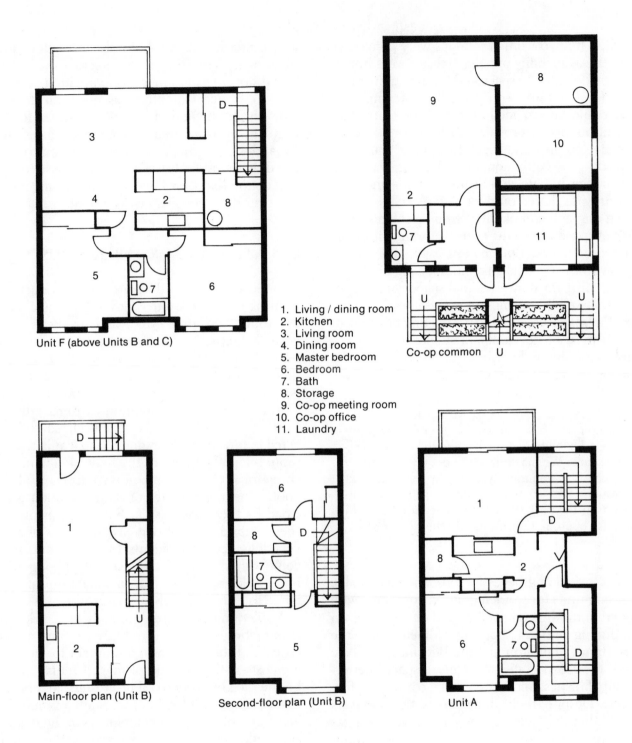

Unit F (above Units B and C)

1. Living / dining room
2. Kitchen
3. Living room
4. Dining room
5. Master bedroom
6. Bedroom
7. Bath
8. Storage
9. Co-op meeting room
10. Co-op office
11. Laundry

Co-op common

Main-floor plan (Unit B)

Second-floor plan (Unit B)

Unit A

Figure 11-6. The Beguinage: floor plans for Units A, B, and F and co-op common.

1985). The two women's co-ops were concerned with the availability of child care but were unable to provide it due to space and funding constraints that limited the amount of nonresidential use that could be provided on site.[3] The Constance Hamilton Co-op provides no formal child care, but the co-op is adjacent to a small park that provides play equipment and a wading pool. The Beguinage has no child-care facilities and does not provide shared outdoor play space.

An ongoing complaint of co-op residents is the lack of space within the projects for meetings and shared activities. Both co-ops expressed frustration with the CMHC guidelines, which limit capital funding for nonresidential space with the result that small housing projects do not have the meeting space essential to transacting normal co-op business or developing a supportive community. Joan Simon described the dilemma faced by the Constance Hamilton Co-op:

> To make the co-op work, we needed space for the co-op members to get together. There is not much flexibility in a small co-op to build a meeting space. We maximized the use of the laundry room as a community room by keeping it at ground level, so as to be able to supervise children in the park from there. The laundry room is also opposite the entrance to the women's hostel.

The overriding necessity to provide affordable housing units for women quickly, combined with program funding constraints and an emphasis on producing modest housing, forced both the Constance Hamilton and the Beguinage to scale back their expectations for more space, better-quality finishes, and more energy-conserving features. Despite their initial goals the sponsors found that the program would not cover the costs of constructing communal space to accommodate child care or enterprise space that could be used for work-at-home businesses, an idea that had been discussed by the Constance Hamilton Board. Nevertheless sponsors were able to obtain approvals for minor changes not standard in conventional residential building: kitchens that open to living rooms and the placement of living rooms and dining rooms on different floors of the dwelling at Constance Hamilton; same-size bedrooms

and a superior standard of noise insulation at the Beguinage. The innovative integration of transitional housing for single women with a co-op at the Constance Hamilton has not been duplicated. Although these are minor victories for the users, in a process that frequently sacrifices quality and space, these changes have contributed not only to residents' satisfaction but also to their perception that they have some modicum of control over their housing environment.

CREATING AFFORDABLE HOUSING

Women are attracted to nonprofit cooperative housing by the low entry fees to become a member (often less than $100) and by the housing costs that either are somewhat lower than market rents or are further subsidized to rent-geared-to-income levels. Many seek a subsidized rent-geared-to-income unit. The federal Canadian Non-Profit Housing Program required that at least 15 percent of units be subsidized and targeted to low-income residents who would not pay more than 30 percent of their adjusted family income for shelter. Each co-op controls a "subsidy pool," and the manner of its distribution is decided by the membership. Some co-ops provide "deep subsidies" that decrease the rents of a few very low-income residents to 30 percent of income; others distribute the subsidy among many households and provide a small amount of assistance to a larger number of residents.

A dilemma is caused by high land prices in major cities, such as Toronto, rising construction costs, and the program requirement to set housing costs at the low end of market rents (relative to the neighborhood). This results in housing costs that are still too high for many women. For instance, some founding members of the Beguinage could not afford to live there. At the Beguinage, housing payments in 1986 were $430 to $450 for a one-bedroom unit (compared with an average cost of $800 for a market unit), $650 for a two-bedroom unit, and $720 for a three-bedroom unit (heating costs and parking are extra). Of the 28 households eight are on permanent subsidy ranging from $100 to $600, per month. In addition the co-op has found it necessary to provide two households with emergency subsidies as residents lose their jobs, are employed only part-time, or encounter unusual circumstances. Housing charges are somewhat lower at the Constance Hamilton, which was completed 3 years earlier: $390 to $401 for a one-bedroom unit, $540 to $578 for a two-bedroom unit, and $610 for a three-bedroom unit. Six units are subsidized through the co-op's internal subsidy pool; two additional units are provided a rent supplement that reduces the housing cost to 25 percent of residents' income by the provincial rental assistance program (OCHAP); and the residents of the six-bedroom communal transitional housing also receive provincial rent supplements that reduce rent to 25 percent of income.

Approximately one-third of all the households in the two co-ops receive a direct subsidy to lower their housing charges. Of those households with children, 69 percent receive a direct housing subsidy. Women's low incomes make it difficult for them to support themselves financially; responsibility for children usually necessitates financial assistance, and subsidized housing is one way of meeting this need. To give some idea of the financial situation of the women interviewed, an average of 32.9 percent of individual gross income was spent on co-op housing charges. (The housing charge covers only what the co-op collects to cover the mortgage and management costs; it does not include utilities or parking.) This percentage of income was being spent on housing despite the fact that more than one adult was sharing costs in 16 of the 42 households (38.1 percent), and that the housing charge for 12 of the households (31 percent) was subsidized to some degree. This percentage of subsidized units is slightly lower than those found in Toronto co-ops at large (Schiff 1982) and is a function of both government funding agreements and the co-op's discretion regarding the spread of its subsidy pool. Women, because of their lower incomes, are more likely to require deep subsidy, which would reduce the number of subsidies available within a co-op. The waiting lists for household subsidy are consistently long, with preference going to current members whose insecure and low incomes necessitate intermittent support. Despite the low-end market rents paid by the remaining residents, they still present an affordability problem for several of the women.

WHO LIVES IN WOMEN'S HOUSING CO-OPS?

Single parents in particular have been attracted to the nonprofit and cooperative housing project developed under the federal Non-Profit Housing Program. Nationally 25 percent of the residents living in these projects are single parents, most of them women (Klodawsky, Spector, and Hendrix 1983). In Metropolitan Toronto 20.4 percent of all households in a survey of 37 housing cooperatives were single parents (Schiff 1982). Of the 45 women interviewed in the Beguinage and the Constance Hamilton, 18.2 percent and 40 percent, respectively, were single mothers. A demographic profile for each of these housing projects follows.

In the Beguinage the mix of households is 8 (36.4 percent) women living alone, 7 (31.8 percent) women living with friends or partners, 4 (18.2 percent) single mothers with at least one child, and 3 (13.6 percent) couples with at least one child. All the adult residents are female, and four of the households include two children; otherwise there is one child. Individual incomes range from $4,000 to $36,000, with an average of $15,740, and the range of formal education is from grade 9 to Ph.D., with 11 of the women having a university degree (44 percent). The youngest member was 22 years of age, the oldest was 50 years, and the mean age was 33 years.

For the Constance Hamilton the mix of households is 8 (40 percent) single mothers with at least one child, 5 (25 percent) women living with friends or partners, 6 (30 percent) women living alone, and 1 (5 percent) couple with at least one child. Except for one husband all the adult residents are female, and four of the households have two children; the rest have one child. Individual incomes range from $3,000 to $26,000, with an average of $17,750, and the range of formal education is from grade 12 to doctoral candidate, with nine of the women having a university degree (45 percent). The women range in age from 25 to 50 years of age, with a mean age of 36 years.

This demographic profile of the residents of the two women's housing co-ops shows a fairly wide range of income ($3,000 to $36,000) reflecting the low-to-moderate socioeconomic mix fostered by co-op advocates and the funding arrangements of the federal government housing program. These residents also display a broad range of formal educational achievement (grade 9 to Ph.D.), with a very high percentage having university degrees (44.4 percent). This is a higher level of education than is found among housing co-op members in metropolitan Toronto, where 25 percent were reported to be university graduates (Schiff 1982), and it is much higher than in the population at large. Yet there is no reflection of this high level of academic achievement in the income level of the women, and their occupations are singularly difficult to stratify because of the discrepancy between the levels of work responsibility and the remuneration. Several of the women work within the arts world (theater and film), and several work in feminist organizations (for example, shelters) for fairly low pay. For instance, the director of a small community-based social-service agency has a high degree of responsibility but an annual income of $22,000. The socioeconomic mix of co-ops allows women to live in close proximity on the basis of shared values and choice, regardless of their income.

Single parents are attracted by the income mix of co-ops, preferring them to large, income-segregated public housing projects. Single mothers seeking affordable housing frequently resist considering public housing projects, despite their affordability, out of fear for themselves and their children. One of our respondents with two school-age children rejected public housing because of the lack of opportunities for her children to know adults active in the labor force, with interesting jobs—people who had not given up hope. She pointed out the variety of employment experiences among her co-op neighbors.

Seeing women in a variety of roles also was highlighted as another desirable model for children. All the single mothers in both the Constance Hamilton and the Beguinage had positive feelings about their respective co-ops as a place to raise children. Except for some concerns expressed about the neighborhood around the Beguinage, all the mothers felt that their children were in a safe environment. The fact that other adult co-op members knew the children and would provide extra supervision was cited by several women as an example of how the co-op pro-

vides a supportive, caring environment for children. The informal babysitting networks also are much appreciated by mothers and nonmothers alike.

WOMEN EXERCISE CONTROL

Nonprofit housing cooperatives, by their very nature, combine two objectives: meeting residents' shelter needs and aiding members in exercising control over their own housing. Residents have a direct say in issues and, in the process of doing things for themselves, can make the housing their own. They initiate the co-op, buy the land or buildings, hire the architect and resource groups, negotiate with CMHC for funding, and define how their needs might be met. Co-op members have given careful thought to decision-making structures, to questions of participation and hierarchy, and to selection criteria for members. In the ongoing management of their co-ops, women are involved in hiring and supervising staff, financial planning, and maintenance. Evaluated against Arnstein's (1969) "ladder of citizen participation," these two women's co-ops achieve the highest rung of the ladder—participation in terms of actual redistribution of power. Residents have the power to set priorities, to establish alternatives, to choose among options, and to change goals and objectives as the situation changes.

Participation takes several forms. Since both co-ops in our study are relatively small, they have not hired a professional property manager, and the tasks normally undertaken by a manager are the responsibility of residents. The Constance Hamilton Co-op chose to re-allocate funds budgeted for a property manager to its subsidy pool. Both co-ops have a maintenance committee, staffed by resident volunteers, that carries out inspections of all units annually to assess their condition and all basic maintenance. Members do minor repairs, such as changing washers or locks, and tend the grounds. Although hiring a property manager would eliminate this workload, it also would require a rent increase. All co-op residents are expected to participate on one of several committees composed of five to six women each (for example, board of directors, membership committee, finance committee, maintenance committee, and newsletter committee) and to attend general membership meetings.

Board members from the Constance Hamilton discussed the problem of board directors burning out after a few years of intense involvement and the tendency in a small co-op of a small proportion of the members to rotate on and off the board. After almost five years it is becoming difficult to find members willing to take on board responsibilities and there is continuing pressure on active members to maintain their involvement. Not everyone has the skills or inclination to be on the board, and this is cause for concern about the future leadership of the co-op. The Beguinage has not had time to develop a reliance on a limited number of members, but this problem does appear to be exacerbated in small co-ops.

Participation in co-op management is promoted as a benefit for members, an opportunity to learn new skills, usually out of necessity. In our study, skill development was reported as a gain by 66.7 percent of the women. The type of skills gained primarily included social and negotiating skills and administrative skills (that is, budgeting, finances, and property management).

Social and negotiating skills had much to do with "resolving our housing situation differently," as one woman stated. Working collectively to solve problems, to resolve conflicts, and to make decisions is a new challenge for the majority of the women, and the need for patience was mentioned more than once. On the other hand, one resident, who is a board director, cautioned against romanticizing the opportunities in co-ops for women to develop a sense of competence and new skills.

A realistic appraisal of the empowering opportunities and potential for skill development in these housing co-ops would focus on the likelihood over time of successful matches between the needs and assets of individual members and those of the co-op. The necessity for members to take on full responsibility for co-op management and the decision-making process allows these women to experiment with styles that suit them and their feminist principles.

CREATING A SUPPORTIVE COMMUNITY

Creating a supportive community of women was the explicit goal of both women's housing co-ops. According to Jean Woodsworth, chair of the founding board of directors of the Constance Hamilton Co-op, one of the initial objectives was to create an environment where women might obtain support from other women to make changes in their lives, especially after divorce or the death of a spouse. It was to provide security of living arrangements and the possibility of community life. This has occurred. Co-op residents put out a monthly newsletter, sponsor workshops, and organize several yearly celebrations. Child care and exchanges of services are arranged informally. In general the women's co-ops provide a housing environment that is also a supportive community, where residents know one another, friendships form, and a level of mutual aid develops that is more intense than usually is found even in other housing co-ops. A sense of community is one of the most frequent reasons given by residents of the Constance Hamilton and the Beguinage for moving into their co-op. In response to the question "Why did you choose to move into a housing co-op?" almost all the women reported seeking a sense of community.

When they were asked to name the types of activities that they share in the co-op, all but one respondent reported at least one activity, and some residents participated in as many as ten— including social, participation, and exchange activities. The participation activities included those formal, organized activities that are part of the management structure of a housing co-op. Social activities included those carried out on a voluntary basis with other members of the co-op, generally within the physical setting of the co-op: barbecues, sports, parties, coffee klatches, dinners, and socializing across back yards. These activities usually were not formally organized and involved a variable number of other residents. Barter between co-op residents formed the basis of the exchange category. These typically combined social and exchange activities, such as potluck dinners and barbecues, but also included babysitting, professional services, or sharing assets, such as cottages or cars. The greatest number of shared activity types were primarily social (reported by 77.3 percent of the women), while 70.5 percent of residents engaged in formal co-op activities, and 36.4 percent practiced exchange or barter. The high level of participation in formal co-op management for these two co-ops is greater than in metropolitan co-ops at large (64.1 percent according to the Schiff survey, 1982) and may be due to a stronger commitment to direct involvement and/or the small size of the co-op (requiring proportionately more work of members).

The Constance Hamilton and the Beguinage were particularly attractive to women who were actively seeking units in the co-op sector and who valued aspects of cooperative living. Many of the residents knew other residents or the founders or had some affiliation with the women's movement prior to moving in, so that living in a women's housing co-op was particularly attractive to them.

When asked what they had given up in moving to the co-op, the majority (59.2 percent) said they had not given up anything. Some mentioned a few things: loss of time (mentioned by the president of the co-op), neighborhood security, large furniture that would not fit in the units, space, and privacy. But they all said they had gained something and spoke repeatedly about shared values, reduced isolation, mutual support, and opportunities for participation and control. Besides the appreciation of the general security and support, the friendships, and the sense of community, there was strong appreciation by lesbian women of a space where they were accepted and their behavior no longer stigmatized. For these women the benefits of co-op tenure are augmented by the attractiveness of a women's community.

Of the relatively few negative comments regarding life in the co-op, most addressed aspects of the neighborhood (noisy neighbors) and some the design of their units (too small). What the women liked least about the co-op also was linked to the structure of the community—the sometimes lengthy decision-making process, development of factions, and having to accept and implement the views of the majority. The requirement to cooperate and contribute means that individuals have to learn new tolerance for differences and new skills in negotiation.

The self-management component of these housing co-ops demands that at least some members become involved in the formal activity of running the co-op. A high level of social and exchange activities is not mandated, but many co-op residents choose to interact with fellow members in these ways. Residents of these women's co-ops emphasize the sense of community that is created by working and socializing together. If emotional support were counted as an additional form of social activity, the level of mutual sharing by the women in these co-ops would be unusually high. The fact that this level of interaction also results in some tension and struggle speaks to the women's commitment to cooperative living, despite their widely different backgrounds.

SECURITY OF TENURE

Given a history of limited housing choice, women find security of tenure and freedom from worry about arbitrary eviction a powerful attraction. In a nonprofit housing co-op, as in homeownership, there also is the expectation that housing costs will go down when the mortgage is paid off. For women who cannot expect rising incomes over time or substantial retirement incomes, this is an incentive to seek out and stay in co-ops over the long term. When asked about their future plans, most of them expected to move from the co-op at some time in the future, but a few expressed a very strong intention to live in the co-op indefinitely. These latter women are, without exception, living on very low incomes, usually with social assistance, and may reasonably see few options open to them. The co-op is the best housing situation to which some women can aspire.

Many of the women expressed a desire to have a residential environment similar to the co-op whenever they decided to move. Some of them hoped to obtain a house, a few specifying a desire for owner occupation, attributing to that tenure the benefits of security, control, freedom, and financial investment.

Women with very low incomes (usually single mothers) are among the most enthusiastic supporters of the co-op program, hoping to live out their lives in their co-ops. However, changes in family composition can affect a resident's right to live in a particular unit (two-bedroom units generally are not allocated to singles) or to retain a subsidy. Several women mentioned the likelihood of future changes in their household composition; some feel secure in the co-op because preference is given to current members for available units of appropriate size. Other members are concerned about having to leave their units when children are grown and move out—because of either the occupancy rules, which would necessitate moving to a smaller unit, or the possible loss of their subsidies.

Perhaps the most emotionally-charged aspect of security of tenure in women's co-ops revolves around the issue of who is eligible to be a co-op member. Both of the women's housing co-ops limit their membership to women only. One allows only female adults, while the other allows adult males who live with women members. The Constance Hamilton was the first women's co-op built in Toronto, and there have been on-going debates within the co-op on the issue of adult males in the co-op. While males can live in the co-op, the by-laws specify that only adult women can be full voting members. This means that male spouses, grandfathers, or adult sons are disenfranchised. The co-op also loses the skills and participation of these males.

At both the Constance Hamilton and the Beguinage, some women have male children who will never be allowed to become members of the co-op with full voting rights and responsibilities, although they can live with their mothers in the co-op indefinitely. If the member mother of an adult male dies, the son would lose his right to reside in the unit, which is not the case in other co-ops. Since both of these women's co-ops are relatively new, it remains to be seen whether the policy of gender-restricted membership is retained over time. If not, some members fear that women's accessibility to, and control of, their housing will be diminished and threatened.

CONCLUSIONS

The cooperative housing program was intended to provide affordable housing for people with low and moderate incomes, creating within each project a socioeconomic mix of residents. Members of the women's co-ops we studied display a wide range of characteristics in terms of level of formal education, employment status, and income. Even middle-class women have relatively low incomes, making the affordability issue paramount for most residents. The social mix results in a factory worker from a small rural community with a high-school education living next to a woman with a Ph.D. who works in government administration and who has lived in many other countries. Despite their differences, what all these women have in common is their desire to live in the supportive security of a community of women. Almost all the women had previously rented their housing, and many had experienced discrimination and threats to their security of tenure. They put a very high value on the security of tenure provided by cooperatives, along with the ability to control their housing. When asked what advice they would give to other women like themselves who needed housing, support for cooperative housing as a solution was almost unanimous. As a form of housing tenure and community-based organization, co-ops are very well-appreciated by the women in this study.

In the face of limited options, the residents downplayed the significance of the location of these co-ops because getting into women's housing co-ops was their primary goal. However, both housing co-ops are located downtown, near transit, and in established neighborhoods with a reasonable range of accessible services—all very important to single mothers who are not very likely to own a car. Given escalating and prohibitive land costs in the downtown area, their location represents a coup, despite their somewhat marginal sites; most urban co-ops are forced to take marginal sites because they cannot compete with private developers in a tight housing market. The vehicles for cooperative housing development are community-based groups who may have had no prior experience with such an undertaking, but are assisted by nonprofit local resource groups. It is this community-level approach and tailored assistance that make it possible for women's groups to develop viable cooperative housing projects.

What stands out in residents' design preferences are two factors: design for diversity and maximum consumer value. Although both projects are small in scale, a wide variety of unit designs is available. This variety comes from an explicit philosophy which recognizes that women cannot be treated as a homogeneous group, but that their needs vary with age, household composition, and lifestyle preferences. As an application of their consumer knowledge in the domestic economy, the residents' focus on qual-

Table 11-1. Comparison of the Beguinage and Constance Hamilton Co-ops

	The Beguinage—The Toronto Women's Cooperative (1985)	Constance Hamilton Cooperative (1982)
Developer	Tom Schwartz—Quetico Developments.	Bradsil.
Architect	Modified turnkey project—Philip Goldsmith, Quadrangle Architects.	Joan Simon, Simon Architects and Planners.
Funding	Start-up of $10,000 for original feasibility study; $65,000 for final proposal from CMHC's 56.1 program, $1.6 million capital budget from 56.1 program.	$12,000 start-up funds from City of Toronto for membership development coordinator's salary. $2,330,000 from CMHC 56.1 program.
Construction	New construction of stacked townhouse, row construction of block wall construction with wood siding.	Three-story stacked townhouses new construction, concrete block; 7 different unit types.
Size	Twenty-eight units on two properties within the same block: 13 in west building; 15 in east building; 13—1 bedrooms; 12—2 bedrooms; 3—3 bedrooms.	Thirty units: 10—1 bedrooms; 16—2 bedrooms; 4—3 bedrooms; 6-bedroom communal house.
Housing Costs (1986)	1 bedroom—$430–$450 2 bedroom—$650 3 bedroom—$720	1 bedroom—$390–$401 2 bedroom—$540–$578 3 bedroom—$610
Subsidies	Eight units ranging from $100–$600 per month provided from co-op's subsidy pool.	Eight subsidy units: 6 units subsidized through internal subsidy pool; 2 units subsidized down to 25% of income by provincial rent supplement program (OCHAP); 6-bedroom communal house subsidized by OCHAP rent supplement.
Sponsors	Ten-person voluntary board of directors of women drawn from Toronto women's community.	Five-member voluntary board of directors drawn from social service field, municipal politician, lawyer.
Services	Co-op coordinator employed 12 hours per week; bookkeeper works 10 hours per week; small meeting room and workshop; 1 laundry room.	Co-op coordinator paid for 25 hours per week to deal with enquiries, rent collection, subsidies, bookkeeping, coordinating committees. Full-time counselor for communal house who is staff person of Nellie's Hostel for Women. Laundry room, small meeting room, coordinator's office.

ity of materials and energy conservation translates into getting the best value possible in housing construction. For architects and builders these women were "tough customers" with high expectations, struggling to maximize their very limited budgets.

Although cooperative housing tenure is grounded in a self-management model that promotes community involvement, it is sometimes a struggle to design communal space to support group activities. Funding limitations force trade-offs between private space and communal space. The Constance Hamilton group decided to accept minimal private outdoor space in favor of a communal courtyard. The Beguinage group opted for private outdoor space and lacks communal space for the high number of social and group activities. In each of the co-ops, the lack of communal space is decried by residents. In larger housing cooperatives of 50 to 100 units, there is sufficient funding for a larger meeting room. A recently constructed high-rise women's co-op has incorporated child-care space. The difficulty of including these shared spaces lies in a funding formula that is targeted to shelter individual households at minimum standards and little else. Resource groups also have not provided leadership in educating co-op groups about options such as space for work-at-home occupations and the incorporation of commercial space that might produce revenue for the co-op.

The residents of the Constance Hamilton and the Beguinage are successful in managing their own housing developments. The self-management model of cooperatives works, albeit at a high cost in terms of input from already busy women. Compared with the practice of condominium owners who typically use professional management and maintenance services, co-op housing members have a very high level of management involvement, with some attendant pluses. There are opportunities for women to learn new skills and thereby gain experience and confidence. On-going assistance is available from the resource groups that offer workshops and courses in financial management, property maintenance, newsletter production, membership issues (such as maximizing participation), and board of directors' responsibilities. Hired part-time coordinators provide some continuity as

members rotate responsibilities, and they relieve members of some tasks, such as bookkeeping and responding to new applicants. Within the co-op model there is a range of self-management options that extends from complete control and implementation by residents, who do all the work themselves, to purely directional decision making by members, with implementation carried out by paid staff or contractors. The women's co-op groups lean toward a high level of member participation in order to save money and to garner the rewards of direct self-involvement.

Although the goal of providing affordable shelter for women is of major importance, the incorporation of space for community activities and services also is a high priority for some women. The cooperative model can facilitate the development of such housing by making the following changes: increasing the funding base to accommodate both private and communal space, providing more direct housing subsidies, and allowing funding flexibility to provide a service such as neighborhood day care on-site.

The federal Non-Profit Housing Program has provided an opportunity for community-based groups to develop housing projects with a high level of participation in the development process, the recruiting of members, and the on-going management. Women's groups have made use of this opportunity to provide housing that addresses their own needs and ideals and that remains under their control. Although the provision of adequate affordable housing was a predominant goal, the developers and residents of these two women's co-ops also have sought to create communities supportive of their varied circumstances. Resident's satisfaction with their co-op is very high overall, with great emphasis placed on the sense of community they have fostered.

NOTES

1. The research reported here was supported by CMHC's Part V External Research Grant Program and the Social Sciences and Humanities Research Council. These federal agencies are not responsible for the approach or interpretation of results.
Joan Simon, Associate Professor of Consumer

Studies, University of Guelph and a partner in Simon Architects, collaborated in the initial design of this research and participated in the site visits. Her untimely and sudden death in November 1986 has been a great loss to the project. In our many discussions about the projects we visited and about her experience as architect of the Constance Hamilton Co-op, she communicated her keen interest in issues of building community in residential environments and in the crucial importance of residents' participation in management. We hope we have done justice to her concerns in this chapter.

A study of this type relies on the assistance and participation of many people. Foremost, we are grateful to the residents of the Beguinage and the Constance Hamilton co-ops, who gave generously of their time despite hectic schedules and heavy time commitments. Initial founders, current board members, coordinators and members of co-op resource groups all willingly answered our questions and provided us with insights into the process of developing and building a housing co-op. Claude André deserves special thanks for his painstaking attention to supervising coding and data entry.

2. CMHC policies favored new construction as a higher maximum unit price was allotted for new construction than for renovation of existing buildings. In Metropolitan Toronto, high land costs, especially in the city, excluded the conversion of many existing buildings to co-ops. New construction also was favored because it did not entail evicting existing tenants—a measure that was seen as politically embarrassing to the federal housing agency at a time when the supply of affordable rental housing was shrinking.

3. The construction of child-care spaces attached to nonprofit housing projects is being examined by an interministerial committee of the Ontario provincial government. In May 1988 the Ontario Ministry of Housing announced three demonstration projects in the province where child care will be incorporated into nonprofit housing projects. Whether capital costs for child care should be borne by the Ministry of Housing or funded from the Community and Social Services budget—which currently funds other day-care centers, including those in schools—is the subject of great debate.

References

Arnstein, S. 1969. A ladder of citizen participation. *Journal of the American Planning Association* 35:216–242.

Co-operative Housing Federation of Toronto. 1985. Co-op questionnaire results. Toronto: CHFT.

Hannley, L. 1983. The new federal co-operative housing program. *Canadian Housing* 3(1):14–17.

Hayden, D. 1981. What would a non-sexist city be like? In *Women and the American City*, eds. C. Stimpson et al., 170–187. Chicago: University of Chicago Press.

———. 1984. *Redesigning the American Dream*. New York: W. W. Norton.

Klodawsky, F., A. N. Spector, and C. Hendrix. 1983. *The Housing Needs of Single Parent Families in Canada*. Ottawa: CMHC.

Leavitt, J. 1984. The shelter plus issue for single parents. *Women and Environments* 6(2):16–20.

McClain, J., with C. Doyle. 1984. *Women and Housing: Changing Needs and the Failure of Policy*. Toronto: James Lorimer.

Metro Toronto Department of Social Services. 1979. *Long Term Housing Needs of Women*. Toronto: Metro Toronto Department of Social Services.

Schiff, M. 1982. *Housing Co-operatives in Metropolitan Toronto: A Survey of Members*. Ottawa: The Co-operative Housing Foundation of Canada.

Simon, J., and G. Wekerle. 1985. *Creating a New Toronto Neighborhood: The Planning Process and Residents' Experience*. Ottawa: CMHC.

Wekerle, G. 1988. *Women's Housing Projects in Eight Canadian Cities*. Ottawa: CMHC.

PART III

Single Room
Occupancy Housing

Chapter 12

Overview of Single Room Occupancy Housing

Karen A. Franck

Single room occupancy (SRO) housing offers private furnished rooms for short- or long-term rental.[1] Until very recently this type of housing was considered substandard by virtue of the small rooms and the absence of private kitchens and baths, despite an earlier tradition of similar single-room accommodations that were widely accepted. Today, with the lack of low-cost rental housing in urban areas and the severe problem of homelessness, the advantages of well-managed and well-maintained SRO housing have again become apparent.

As a general category SRO housing has included a variety of housing types: lodging houses, boarding houses, rooming houses, residences for single men and single women, and, most recently, SRO hotels. These types vary in building form, form of ownership, type of occupants, and availability of meals and other services. The definitions of the different types also vary, historically and regionally. However, the basis of the SRO housing model in all its variations is that residents occupy single furnished rooms and share certain spaces and facilities including bathrooms and kitchens (although in a few cases private bathrooms or individual kitchen units are provided). Thus, unlike conventional apartments, the individual rooms are not complete, self-sufficient dwelling units, and spaces and facilities usually located within the private unit are shared with other residents. However, in the ma-

jority of SROs *sharing* means only joint use, much as it does in a hotel for transients. Unlike in the shared house model, coordination and frequent social interaction between residents are not expected in most SROs. Residents are free to choose the degree of interaction they wish to pursue and, in fact, this choice is one of the social advantages of the SRO housing model. This choice allows for a high degree of independence and autonomy, conditions that many SRO residents appreciate.

Formerly, services in SRO hotels often included a 24-hour desk clerk, linens, and housekeeping. Some SRO housing continues to provide these services, and today almost all renovated and newly built SROs provide kitchen facilities, either in each room or in a common space. By virtue of the cost savings derived from shared bathrooms, shared kitchens, and the relatively small but furnished rooms, SROs are more affordable than complete apartments. When well managed and well maintained, they offer low-income single people and couples, of all ages, the opportunity to live in clean, safe housing that is often conveniently located in downtown neighborhoods. And when social and health services are available on-site or nearby, SROs also allow frail elderly, handicapped, and mentally disturbed individuals to live outside of institutions and lead independent lives.

245

RISE AND DECLINE OF SINGLE ROOM OCCUPANCY HOUSING

The United States has a long, but almost forgotten, tradition of SRO housing starting with lodging houses in the seventeenth century. The term *lodging house* can be found in the earliest building regulations for American cities, referring to single rooms rented out for residence in a building that was neither an inn nor a hotel. Sometimes what was rented was simply a bunk, a hammock, or a place on the floor (Schneider 1986). The term *lodging house* is still used in building codes, although its definition varies from one city to another and may include other similar housing types, such as rooming houses. In Brookline, Massachusetts, the local building code still requires lodging houses to have live-in managers and prohibits drinking in common areas (Fig. 12-1).

In the nineteenth century, with the growth of employment opportunities in urban areas, a great variety of SRO-type accommodations developed, offering acceptable forms of housing for lower- and middle-class singles and sometimes couples. What was common to all versions of these accommodations was the provision of single furnished rooms or suites and at least some housekeeping services; many also provided meals. The boarding house was a privately owned house offering private furnished rooms, a socializing and entertaining space (the parlor), and a dining room with meal service. It catered primarily to clerks, merchants, artisans, and the whole

Figure 12-1. Former lodging house in Brookline, Massachusetts. These two buildings, which were single-famly houses in the 1800s, were converted to a lodging house in the 1900s. In 1985 they were renovated by Pine Street Inn to serve as SRO housing for homeless people.

spectrum of the emerging middle class. In the twentieth century the rooming house gradually replaced the boarding house and served somewhat poorer individuals; it provided no social spaces and no meal service. In many cities rooming houses consisted of several floors of rooms above ground-floor commercial spaces (Groth 1986). Some of these rooming houses later became SRO hotels. Lower-cost lodgings, where people rented places to sleep on the floor, were called flophouses.

Poor people in the nineteenth century often rented spaces in tenement cellars, back yards, and inner rooms of apartments; these spaces were sometimes called lodgings. Following housing reform directed at the deplorable conditions in tenements, reform groups established "model lodging houses" for poor working men and women; these often included social spaces and meal service. The Mills Hotel (Fig. 12-2), designed by Ernest Flagg and built in New York City in 1897, housed 1,500 poor and single working men around two covered courtyards. The rooms were very small; showers were in long rows in the basement. There were two lobbies and meal service (Groth, forthcoming). The Municipal Lodging House in New York housed 7,000 men in dormitories and provided showers, dining room, laundry, and health-care facilities (Mostoller 1985). Low-cost hotels with housekeeping services but no meals and no social spaces other than the lobby also served as long-term housing for single working and retired men.

Professional single men could find accomodations in rather elaborate residences that were built as commercial ventures; sometimes these were called residential clubs. One example is The Shelton; built in New York City in 1923, it featured a wide range of amenities and social spaces, including a lounge for entertaining ladies, a restaurant and grill, a library, a reading room, a stenographer's room, outdoor terraces, and an infirmary.

Municipal lodging houses also were established for women. Various religious and charitable organizations sponsored more elaborate hotellike residences for working women in the nineteenth and twentieth centuries and simpler accomodations for poor women. In New York City in 1933, there were a total of 51 residences for women,

Figure 12-2. Former Mills Hotel, New York City. Built as a "model lodging house" in 1897, it became a SRO hotel and then was converted to luxury condominiums in the 1970s.

although few of these provided accommodations affordable to women in the lowest wage-earning group (Ford 1936). Places such as the Markell Evangeline Residence in New York, owned and managed by the Salvation Army, catered to business and professional women as well as to office workers (Fig. 12-3). As in the residences for professional men, many of the rooms had private baths but none had kitchens.

It was most likely after World War II that the term SRO emerged to refer to many kinds of single room occupancy housing: low-cost residential hotels, rooming houses, lodging houses, and the renting out of rooms in private apartments. With an influx of single, low-income workers into cities, apartment buildings and hotels for travelers, including some formerly luxurious ones, were converted to SRO hotels, adding to the ex-

Figure 12-3. The Markle Evangeline Residence, New York City. Opened in 1930 it continues to provide furnished rooms with private baths and meal service for business and professional women as well as for students and elderly women.

isting stock of low-cost hotels and rooming houses (Fig. 12-4).

Just when SRO hotels emerged as the latest version of housing for low-income singles, after World War II, single-family detached houses began to increase in number and affordability, and the nuclear family of a married couple with children became the idealized, prototypical household. All types of hotel dwellers were increasingly viewed as deviant and undesirable simply by virtue of their marital status and the building type they inhabited (Minkler and Ovrebo 1985). The power of the intertwined images of the nuclear family, the single-family house, and the apartment that should approximate it as closely as possible rendered single people residing in hotels virtually invisible to those involved in urban redevelopment (Groth, forthcoming).

The social stigmatizing of hotel dwellers was matched by a legal stigmatizing of the hotels.

New York City codes, which had been modified in the 1940s to encourage the renting out of rooms in private apartments, were changed again in the 1950s to restrict the creation of rooming units in apartments, rooming houses, and hotels (Hamberg 1984). In 1949, federal minimum property standards defined an acceptable dwelling unit as containing a complete bathroom and kitchen. This criterion classified all SRO housing as substandard, thereby preventing the use of federal funds or mortgages for their rehabilitation as residential projects. Banks also were loathe to give loans to owners of SROs for their renovation or repair. This lack of financing contributed to the physical deterioration of SRO buildings and to their increasing disreputability.

After World War II, many SRO hotels began to deteriorate in physical condition, management quality, and housekeeping services, and they began to house a more vulnerable population. On the West Coast in 1942, Japanese families

Figure 12-4. The Bush Hotel, Seattle. Built in 1915 as a hotel for travelers, it became a SRO hotel; was renovated in 1981 and now includes SRO units, retail spaces, and social service spaces.

who had owned, managed, and lived in SRO hotels that they maintained very well were forced to relocate. Their hotels fell into the hands of speculators who allowed them to deteriorate. In the 1950s many owners of SRO hotels began to disinvest and no longer maintained adequate security or living conditions in their buildings. The economic prosperity of the 1950s allowed many single working people in cities such as Chicago to move to other more expensive accommodations (Hoch and Slayton forthcoming). In New York City, SROs became home to a greater number of alcoholics and former mental patients (Shapiro 1971) but did not have the services or facilities to meet the needs of these residents. In other cities as well, the population of SROs came to include more elderly people and former mental patients. Often SROs that were not well maintained or managed became centers for a wide range of antisocial activities, including drug dealing and victimizing of residents and staff. Other SRO

hotels, however, continued to be well managed, safe buildings and were accepted by the surrounding neighborhoods. And residences for single working women (not usually called SROs), such as the Barbizon in New York and the Civic Center Residence in San Francisco, continued to be well managed and well maintained, and constituted a respectable form of housing through the 1960s and 1970s.

The perception of SRO residents as deviant, simply by virtue of their single status and place of residence, and the classification of the SRO building type as substandard made it difficult, if not impossible, for policy makers and others to recognize that residential hotels might be a valuable source of low-cost housing or might support a preferred way of life for some people. Therefore the possibility of preserving or improving hotels to allow people to remain housed in adequate conditions or to continue a preferred lifestyle was completely disregarded in urban redevelopment programs, despite some suggestions to the contrary (Groth, forthcoming). Indeed, the housing needs of low-income single people were largely ignored in housing reform after World War II, and much of the housing that had been developed for this population over the course of a century was lost.

When residential hotels were located in areas slated for urban renewal, they were systematically destroyed or converted. This was the case in the West Side urban renewal area in Manhattan (Shapiro 1971) and in San Francisco, where the Yerba Buena urban renewal project demolished 4,000 SRO units in the early 1970s (National Trust for Historic Preservation 1981). Between 1975 and 1979, 17.7 percent of the 32,214 SRO units in San Francisco were lost in the renovation of the Tenderloin neighborhood, where ten SRO buildings were converted to tourist hotels (Hartman 1982, cited in Kasinitz 1986). In many cases those people displaced by the destruction of SROs did not qualify for the low-income housing that was included in urban renewal areas because they were single but not elderly or handicapped.

In other cases SRO hotels were in the path of expanding institutions. Before 1971, on the Upper West Side of New York, such expansion caused the conversion or destruction of 19 of 31 hotels in the vicinity of educational institutions (Shapiro 1971). More recently SRO hotels have been lost to gentrification, sometimes encouraged by local tax incentives or federal, low-income housing programs. In New York City, the J-51 tax abatement program gave landlords property tax abatements as incentives to renovate their buildings. Once the program was extended to include SRO buildings, the number of lower-priced hotels decreased, from 298 buildings to 131 between 1975 and 1981. And 89 of the 167 buildings that dropped out of the lower price range were closed or converted to another use, including luxury apartments (Kasinitz 1986). The Longacre and the Barbizon in New York, formerly women's residences, were converted to luxury apartments for both sexes (Bader 1986). Other philanthropic organizations, including the YMCA and the Salvation Army, sold their residences for single men and single women to developers. In 1986 there

were 13 women's residences in New York (Bader 1986), whereas in 1933 there had been 51 (Ford 1936). In San Francisco, SRO hotels were converted to apartments under the Section 8 moderate rehabilitation program, a program intended to provide housing for low-income residents but that, at the time, required complete kitchens and baths in all apartments.

The loss of SRO housing through these different forms of urban redevelopment has been considerable. Between 1976 and 1981 San Francisco lost an average of 1,200 SRO units each year (Minkler and Ovrebo 1985). Between 1968 and 1980 Los Angeles lost 2,195 SRO units, or 31 percent of the SRO housing stock, in the skid-row area (Silvern and Schmunck 1981). Seattle lost 15,000 SRO units in the 1960s and 1970s, and Portland lost 1,345 units (Kasinitz 1986). Chicago lost 22,603 units between 1973 and 1984 (Community Emergency Shelter Organization 1985). Estimates for New York indicate a loss of 110,000 SRO units since 1970, a decrease of 87 percent of the total stock (Baxter 1984). Estimates for the country as a whole suggest that one million rooms were converted or destroyed between 1970 and 1980 (Alter et al. 1986).

HOMELESSNESS

The recent rise in homelessness is attributable, in part, to this severe loss of SRO housing through urban renewal and gentrification. Many of those who use emergency shelters lived in SRO hotels prior to coming to a shelter. Conversely the preservation and renovation of existing SROs, as well as new construction based on the SRO model, with the incorporation of social-service programs when needed, present one solution to the current problem of homelessness among single people and couples without children.

Estimates of the number of homeless people, both single persons and families, vary tremendously from 250,000 to 3,000,000 (Erickson and Wilhelm 1986). In November 1983 the Department of Health and Human Services estimated that two million Americans might be homeless. Based on four different types of information, the

Department of Housing and Urban Development (HUD) estimated that on an average night in December 1983 or January 1984, 250,000 to 350,000 people were homeless nationwide (HUD 1984).

This is considered by many to be a very low estimate, and the methods HUD employed to reach it, and their definition of homelessness, have been severely criticized (Hartman 1986; Hopper and Hamberg 1984). In 1984 HUD defined the homeless as those people who have no permanent shelter and whose nighttime residence is a public or private emergency shelter or a public or private space that is not intended to be a shelter, such as a train station. Others have defined the homeless to include persons living on a short-term basis in SRO hotels or motels. Still others have recommended that the homeless be defined as anyone not assured of a month's sleeping quarters that meet the minimum health and safety standards (Caro 1981). Whatever definition is used there is no doubt that homelessness is severe, widespread, and increasing. Along with an increase in the total number of homeless people is an increase in the proportions of young adults, children, and women who are homeless. In 1985, estimates indicated that the average age is 34, that single women make up 13 percent of the homeless, and families 21 percent (U.S. Government Accounting Office 1985).

Four causes of homelessness typically are given: a severe shortage of affordable housing, rising unemployment, deinstitutionalization of mental patients, and tighter restrictions for disability benefits (Hopper and Hamberg 1984). Additional causes of homelessness among women are domestic violence and abuse (Stoner 1986). And drug abuse, particularly crack addiction, is another cause of homelessness among men and women. What distinguishes today's situation from earlier poverty is the current absence of affordable housing (Hopper and Hamberg 1984). The loss of rental housing units in urban areas has been massive, and that loss is experienced most severely by the lowest-income renters (Adams 1986). As many as one-half million lower-rent units are lost each year.

Parallel with the changes in the types of housing available for low-income singles are changes in the kinds of people who are in need of housing. Schneider (1986) and Hoch and Cibulskis (1985) have traced historical changes in the population of people who have no permanent address and live in hotels, in shelters, or on the street. Four phases can be distinguished. During the first phase, after the Civil War until the Great Depression, a great many male workers traveled the country doing seasonal work. These were hoboes whose social culture, mobility, and independence gave them a kind of dignity and political influence that is not characteristic of today's homeless population (Hoch and Cibulskis 1985). More important, those men could and did work for wages, and with those wages paid for the shelter that was appropriate for their way of living.

The second phase, the Great Depression, rendered many people completely homeless: that is, they could afford no shelter whatsoever. This resulted in large-scale federal interventions including shelters, insurance programs, and work projects. During the third phase, after World War II, economic prosperity reduced the numbers of homeless and the development of suburban living reduced their visibility. The homeless were primarily older single males on marginal employment or meager pensions (Schneider 1986). The population also included single male alcoholics.

The homeless of the fourth phase, the 1980s, are different from these earlier "skid-row" residents in many respects (Hoch and Cibulskis 1985). Skid-row residents were overwhelmingly white, middle-aged and elderly males living alone while the "new homeless" include more women, more minority members, more younger people, and more families. Mental illness, alcoholism, and drug abuse figure as prominent problems among today's homeless. These people are not hoboes, vagrants, or exclusively alcoholics; they are desperately poor victims of both economic and physical problems (Hopper and Hamberg 1984). They cannot afford to pay for any housing that is presently available. In earlier times the "homeless" often could afford the low-cost, minimal housing that was then available in the form of SROs and flophouses, but much of this housing has now been systematically destroyed or converted.

ADVANTAGES OF RENOVATING OR DEVELOPING SRO HOUSING

Poorly managed, poorly maintained, and unsafe SRO hotels are not an acceptable solution for housing homeless people, even though they do meet the most essential shelter needs. The horrendous conditions of hotels where homeless families are housed in New York City testify to what can happen when physical and social conditions are allowed to deteriorate completely (Stimpson et al. 1984). Given that high-quality management and maintenance are possible (see chapter 14), there are significant advantages in substantially renovating existing SROs or developing new ones. Prime among these advantages are affordability and convenience.

Given the reduced size of each unit and the sharing of kitchens and baths, the cost of rehabilitating and subsidizing SRO hotels is significantly lower than the cost of providing and subsidizing conventional apartments for single people. In 1980 replacing 1,000 SRO units with studio apartments with private kitchens and baths under HUD's Section 8 Rehabilitation program would have cost 50 to 100 million dollars for initial construction, with additional millions for rent subsidies. Rehabilitating 1,000 hotel rooms would have cost only five million dollars and would have required little or no ongoing subsidies (National Trust for Historic Preservation 1981). The Portland Redevelopment Commission reports that renovations to provide Section 8 apartments for single individuals or couples cost $40,000 per unit, while the rehabilitation of four hotels to provide SRO units cost between $4,000 and $13,000 per unit (Greer 1986). The owner of an SRO hotel also may receive revenue from leasing ground-floor commercial space.

For potential residents SROs provide the least expensive housing on the private market and in nonprofit or limited-profit housing. Researchers in Chicago found that the monthly rents of survey respondents in SROs, which had not been renovated, averaged $161 a month (Community Urban Shelter Organization 1985). Research conducted by this author in 1984 and 1985 indicated that monthly rents in renovated hotels ranged from $75 to $212 in Denver, San Francisco, and Seattle. Rents for units in hotels in Portland, Oregon, renovated under the Section 8 moderate rehabilitation program were limited to $203 a month in 1984. In comparison rents in conventional federally assisted apartments in Portland started at $475 (Greer 1986). In addition to having low rents, SRO housing requires no expenditures for utilities or for furniture and up-front costs are at a minimum—typically, a small security deposit. The location of SROs in neighborhoods that have other low-cost facilities further contributes to their affordability.

Existing SRO hotels in downtown, or near downtown, locations are highly convenient, allowing residents to be near public transportation, sources of employment, and a wide range of commercial facilities and social services that urban centers provide. Often the neighborhoods where SROs are located contain services and facilities that are particularly useful to SRO residents, such as low-cost restaurants, used-clothing stores, and sources for finding day labor, but these will remain only if steps are taken to preserve the neighborhoods as well as the SRO buildings (Minkler and Ovrebo 1985).

The traditional services of SROs (central location, desk clerks, and security and housekeeping services) make the building type a preferable alternative to public housing or institutionalization for those residents who depend on such services (National Trust for Historic Preservation 1981). In-house health and social services, or a good referral system to such services, allow the frail elderly, the handicapped, and other vulnerable residents to stay out of institutions (Levy 1968; Felton et al. 1981). Such an arrangement is invaluable in social and economic terms. (For additional social advantages of SRO housing, see chapter 15.)

POLICIES AND PROGRAMS FOR PRESERVING AND RENOVATING SRO HOTELS

Recently legal steps have been taken in several cities to stem the loss of SRO units. San Francisco followed its 1979 moratorium on SRO destruction with a 1981 SRO ordinance making it unlawful for an owner to convert or demolish a residential hotel unit unless the city had granted a permit (Werner and Bryson 1982). New York City finally instituted a moratorium in 1985 and, through the Mayor's Office on SRO Housing, enforces that moratorium.

The city of Portland, Oregon, has pioneered in the preservation, renovation, and quality management of SRO hotels. In 1978 a nonprofit organization, the Burnside Consortium (now called Central City Concern), was formed to coordinate services and to advocate solutions to neighborhood problems in the Burnside neighborhood, where many SROs are located. Central to its mission was the improvement and maintenance of hotels as a source of low-cost housing. Under the leadership of Andy Raubeson, the Consortium embarked on a program of hotel management and maintenance, a program for leasing hotels, and its first renovation project. Since then the Consortium has developed a manual for the maintenance of SRO hotels, has renovated several hotels, and has purchased some as well.

Portland, Oregon, also became the first city to persuade Congress and HUD to allow SROs to be eligible for federal housing assistance and was the first city to receive a Section 8 demonstration grant. In 1982 the Portland Development Commission invited interested developers and nonprofit organizations to submit proposals under their SRO/Section 8 Demonstration Program. The program was designed to rehabilitate SRO rental units that were substandard; provide financial assistance as an incentive to renovate such buildings; provide to the owner rental income that would repay the rehabilitation costs, meet monthly operating expenses, and allow a reasonable profit on the owner's investment; and provide rental subsidies to low-income residents. Tenants who qualify for rent subsidies pay 30 percent of their income toward rent; the Portland Housing Authority pays the remainder directly to the hotel owner. The maximum monthly rent allowed by HUD under this program began at $203 a room, including utilities, and can be increased annually by only a fixed amount.

In 1981 Congress amended the Section 8 program to permit the use of Section 8 Moderate

Rehabilitation funds for SROs in other cities as demonstration projects. The Stewart B. McKinney Bill, enacted in 1987 in a comprehensive effort to deal with homelessness, allocated 35 million dollars for the rehabilitation of SRO hotels with the use of the Section 8 Moderate Rehabilitation program to subsidize rents. HUD then requested proposals for SRO renovations, setting a maximum of $14,000 per SRO unit in rehabilitation costs; 25 such proposals were funded. This represents a significant reversal from the earlier federal view of SROs as substandard housing and from the earlier use of federal urban renewal funds to destroy or convert them.

Building on the prior work of the Skid Row Development Corporation in Los Angeles, the Los Angeles Redevelopment Agency established the SRO Housing Corporation in 1984 with the goal of renovating and operating 1,110 units within three years. Under the directorship of Andy Raubeson, the SRO Housing Corporation has purchased 11 hotels in the skid-row neighborhood of Los Angeles. Five of them have been completely renovated; four others have been substantially renovated, and work on two more will be completed in 1989. The SRO Housing Corporation has sponsored many other projects in the area, including a job fair, clean-up campaigns, a food-distribution program, and the construction and maintenance of a local minipark.

In New York City the SRO Loan Program makes federal block grant money available to hotel owners at 1 percent interest. Between 1983 and 1988, 1,222 units were restored under this program, either through the development of vacant units or the improvement of occupied ones, at a cost of 21 million dollars. Additional funds have been used for SRO renovation in New York through the city's Capital Budget Homeless Housing Program and the state's Homeless Housing Assistance Program. In Chicago, New York, Seattle, San Francisco, Denver, and other cities nonprofit organizations have sponsored the renovation of particular hotels and often oversee their management. In Chicago several for-profit developers are purchasing and renovating SRO hotels, and in San Diego for-profit developers are building new SRO housing (Kadden and Goldberg 1988).

THREE CASES OF SRO HOUSING

Recently the most frequent form of "new" SRO housing has been SRO hotel renovation either by nonprofit or for-profit owners, often with public financing. The Florence Hotel in Los Angeles is an example of SRO hotel renovation by a nonprofit organization. The SRO housing model of single furnished rooms and shared facilities is now being used in other situations as well: in the renovation of deteriorated apartment buildings (The Heights in New York City) and even in new construction (University Gardens in San Diego). The latter two cases illustrate possible variations in the ownership and financing of SRO housing. The Heights is owned by a limited partnership between a private developer and the for-profit subsidiary of its not-for-profit community sponsor. The Heights received public and private financing. While the owner and sponsor of University Gardens is a private developer, it also has received public and private financing.

The Florence, in the skid-row neighborhood of Los Angeles, was the first SRO hotel to be purchased and renovated by the SRO Housing Corporation, a semipublic, nonprofit group formed by the Los Angeles Community Development Corporation to buy and improve SRO hotels. Located on "Thieves Corner," formerly known to be the highest crime corner in the city, the Florence was in extremely poor condition in 1985, with only one shower and one toilet operational. The building was completely renovated (Fig. 12-5). All mechanical systems were replaced. The existing structure of rooms and baths was retained as much as possible to control costs and to provide as many individual rooms as possible (Fig. 12-6). Most of the rooms are 120 square feet, with the front rooms slightly larger at 130 square feet. On the second and third floors, rooms and baths were replastered and repainted, and new fixtures were installed. One ground-floor commercial space was converted into a community lounge, a kitchen, and a dining space, totaling 1,170 square feet (Fig. 12-7). Eight units on the ground floor were designed for handicapped residents. The facade was cleaned, and the entire front of the ground floor was rebuilt with the installation of windows for the lobby.

Some commercial space on the ground floor was kept and is leased to a grocery-store operator as a convenience to residents in the Florence and other nearby hotels. The previous tenant also was a grocery-store owner, who paid $1,500 a month. SRO Housing evicted him because he refused to stop selling alcoholic beverages. The present tenant pays only $100 a month with a lease covenant prohibiting the sale of alcohol.

The renovation, producing 61 units, cost $1,190,300 or $19,513 per unit. The purchase and renovation of the hotel was entirely supported by a low-interest loan from the Los Angeles Community Development Corporation, which was financed with tax increment proceeds. Rents range from $158 to $194 a month and $25 extra for double occupancy. Before the renovation rents were $180 to $200 a month with a 100 percent increase for double occupancy.

Most of the residents receive income from Social Security or General Relief. About three quarters are men. Ages range from 20 to 60 and over, with half being under 40. About half of the residents have a history of substance abuse. Should a resident's use of drugs or alcohol cause too many housekeeping or other problems and the resident make no effort to change, the resident is evicted. There is a live-in manager, an assistant manager, and a maid. Maintenance is provided by SRO Housing Corporation's central maintenance staff. The hotel also is one site for the Corporation's Project Hotel Alert, which serves meals to elderly residents of the area seven days a week. Residents can receive counseling, referrals, assessments of needs, and advocacy for entitlements to benefits from social-service staff at another, nearby hotel under programs put in place by SRO Housing Corporation and funded by other agencies.

The Heights, in the Washington Heights neighborhood of New York City, was converted from an abandoned apartment building containing 20 apartments to SRO housing of 55 rooms (Fig. 12-8). The Heights project was initiated by the Committee for the Heights Inwood Homeless (CHIH), a nonprofit group concerned with establishing permanent housing for the homeless (Baxter 1984). Each of the four floors above the ground floor has 12 rooms of 120 square feet each, three complete baths, a kitchenette, and a

Figure 12-5. The Florence Hotel, Los Angeles. *(Photo: George Gray)*

lounge that looks out onto the street. Each private room has a clothes closet but no sink, unlike most SRO hotels. (The cost of new plumbing required for individual sinks in each room would have exceeded the maximum cost allowed for a Section 8 moderate rehabilitation subsidy.) The ground floor contains a community kitchen and dining room, two small offices for the director and the desk clerk, seven additional rooms, and two bathrooms. The basement contains a recreation room, a laundry room, an office for service staff, and bathrooms. One basement room, originally intended to be an emergency shelter for

homeless women, is now being used for storage until the shelter is established (Fig. 12-9). There is a small garden in the back. Furniture for the building was donated by the Pierre Hotel (Fig. 12-10).

The total construction cost was 1.1 million dollars or $20,000 per unit. Residents pay one third of their income for rent, which ranges from $96 to $217 per month. Almost one third of the cost of the project was financed by private investors who contributed the equity capital needed by CHIH to create a limited partnership. The investors receive some tax savings based on operating

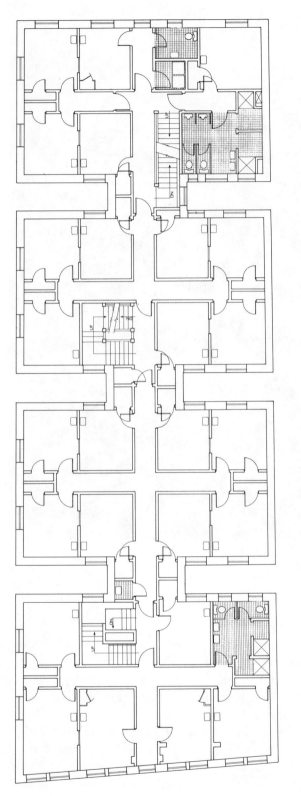

Figure 12-6. The Florence Hotel: second-floor plan. (*Urban Innovations Group, Architects*)

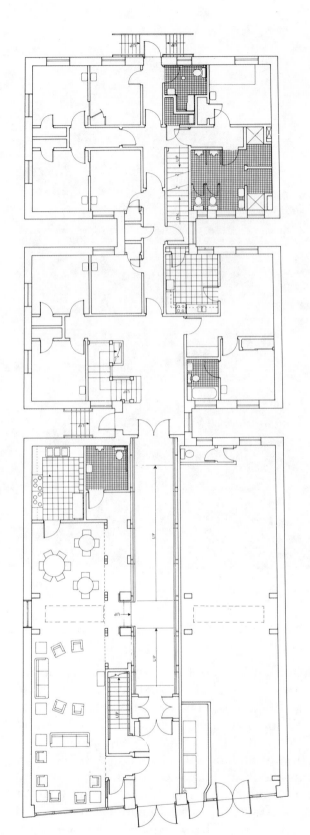

Figure 12-7. The Florence Hotel: first-floor plan.

Figure 12-8. The Heights, New York.

losses, mortgage interest, and depreciation. Additional grants and loans were provided by private foundations, the New York City Community Preservation Corporation (a consortium of 23 banks), the New York City Department of Housing Preservation and Development, and the New York State Division of Housing and Community Renewal. Rents are subsidized by the Federal Section 8 moderate rehabilitation program. Technical assistance was provided by the Community Service Society of New York (CSS) and the entire project was directed and coordinated by Ellen Baxter, who is employed by CSS. The Heights is thus the result of private financing, public subsidies, and the coordination and support of several nonprofit groups.

Fifteen rooms are reserved for individuals with a history of mental-health problems and the City Department of Mental Health provides funding for three full-time staff members to care for these residents. A desk clerk is on duty around the clock; the shifts rotate among a number of residents who take responsibility for maintaining security, operating the intercom system, following fire safety precautions, handling all visitors, and dealing with management crises when management staff are absent. There is no live-in manager, and there is no staff present on weekends or in the evenings. Members of the tenants' association, along with the director and the service staff, interview prospective tenants.

All residents were previously homeless, living on the street or in shelters. The building is carefully integrated in terms of age, race, and gender, with some mentally and physically disabled residents as well. Many of the residents are not accustomed to living in such close proximity with people different from themselves in age, gender, or race, but friendships, romances, and cliques have formed nonetheless, making The Heights a close knit community. The most serious problem the project has encountered is crack and heroin use, but under the close monitoring by the tenants association, management, and service staff, drug users have become more cautious in their behavior and some have left. The combination of on-site service staff, management, and tenant involvement make The Heights an unusual example of SRO housing (Baxter 1986).

University Gardens will be completely new SRO construction in the Hillcrest neighborhood of San Diego, next to a highway (Fig. 12-11). The sponsor and owner is Jackson and Associates, a for-profit developer who, like other developers in San Diego, turned to SRO housing partly because of the city's moratorium on the construction of conventional apartments. The seven-story building with underground parking will contain 151 rooms, ranging from 160 to 240 square feet each, the latter for handicapped residents. All rooms will have private bathrooms with showers (Fig. 12-12). Private telephones will be available for installation for a deposit. There will be a community kitchen on every other floor and a laundry room on every floor. Additional common spaces include a community room, with board games and a large-screen TV, and a barbecue and picnic area. Residents will be able to rent televisions, refrigerators, and microwave ovens from the management to place in their rooms.

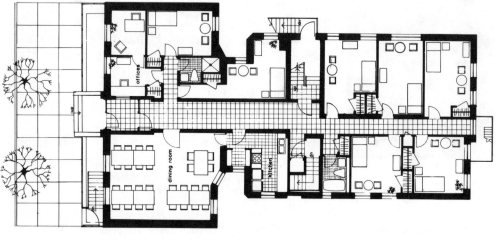

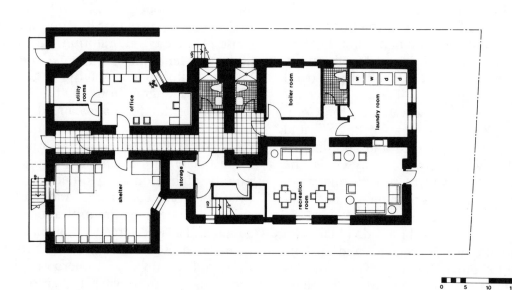

TYPICAL (FLOORS 2-5)

FIRST FLOOR

CELLAR

0 5 10 15

Figure 12-9. The Heights: floor plans. *(Conrad Levenson, Architect)*

Figure 12-10. The Heights: fifth-floor lounge.

The construction is expected to cost $30,000 per unit. The City of San Diego provided a half-million-dollar loan to the developers with the agreement that 20 percent of the units would be for low-income residents. These residents will be eligible for the lowest rent of $225 a month. The rest of the financing was private. The market rents will range from $300 to $350 a month. Good maintenance and good security are high-priority objectives. There will be a live-in manager and a 24-hour desk clerk at the single entrance to the building where security cameras will be installed. The developer is planning for a population of retired people and stable working people in low-paying jobs who have no serious alcohol or mental-health problems. The developer recognizes that these two groups of potential residents are often unable to afford the upfront costs and the monthly rents for conventional apartments and may prefer new SRO housing to other shared living arrangements.

Advertised as an "SRO hotel" and providing quality housing with some amenities for some of those people who cannot afford conventional apartments, University Gardens indicates a rediscovery and a modification of the SRO hotel as an acceptable and viable housing type in the private market.

Figure 12-11. University Gardens, San Diego: perspective. *(Jackson and Associates)*

185 square feet

229 square feet

1. Living / sleeping room
2. Bathroom
3. Sink
4. Minirefrigerator
5. Desk
6. Television
7. Adjustable shelves

Figure 12-12. University Gardens: floor plans of typical units.

OVERVIEW OF CHAPTERS

The following three chapters offer design and management recommendations for future renovation or new construction of SRO housing. In chapter 13, "The Design of a Single Room with Furniture for a Residential Hotel," Michael Mostoller views SROs from the perspective of how a single room is used for most daily functions and the consequent implications for the design of such a room in SRO housing. Drawing on his own historical and contemporary research, Mostoller presents a design analysis and the resulting design prototypes for an SRO room and its furniture.

In chapter 14, "A Look at SRO Hotel Residents with Recommendations for Management and Design," Mary Burki describes the types of residents who typically live in SRO hotels and their particular needs, focusing on the more vulnerable and needy residents. She draws on that analysis and her own experience renovating and managing SROs to present recommendations for planning, managing, and designing SRO hotels. Burki, like Mostoller, offers a view of what SRO housing is and what it can be.

In chapter 15, "The SRO Hotel: A Rediscovered Housing Type for Single People" Karen Franck describes nine cases of renovated SRO hotels, including ones that house a mixture of residents, ones targeted for the elderly, and ones occupied primarily by young or middle-aged, self-sufficient individuals. She discusses the design and management implications of these and other cases for future renovation and new construction of SRO housing.

ADDITIONAL INFORMATION

For a discussion of the current need for SRO housing with a socioeconomic history of SRO housing in Chicago, see Hoch and Slayton's *New Homeless and Old: Community and the Skid Row Hotel* (forthcoming). Additional insights into the design of SRO rooms, furniture, and common spaces can be found in Liu's *San Francisco Chinatown Hotels* (1980). The *SRO Development Handbook* by Church et al. (1985) has information on SRO housing design and development, and the *SRO Housing Management Handbook* (Central City Concern 1983) contains detailed guidelines for management and maintenance. Information on particular cases of renovated SRO hotels can be found in *Rehabilitating Residential Hotels* (National Trust for Historic Preservation 1981) and in Greer's *The Search for Shelter* (1986).

NOTE

1. Some of the material presented in this overview was gathered as part of a research project, "Recent Social and Spatial Innovations in American Housing," conducted by Karen A. Franck and funded by the National Science Foundation (Grant CEE-830721-13). I am grateful to Conrad Levenson for providing the drawings of The Heights and to the Urban Innovations Group for the drawings of The Florence Hotel.

References

Adams, C. 1986. Homelessness in the post industrial city. *Urban Affairs Quarterly* 21:527–549.

Alter, J., A. Stille, S. Doherty, N. F. Greenburg, S. Agrest, V. E. Smith, and G. Rain. 1986. Homeless in America. In *Housing the Homeless*, ed. J. Erickson and C. Wilhelm, 3–16. New Brunswick, NJ: Center for Urban Policy Research.

Bader, E. J. 1986. The company of women. *City Limits*. March: 22–27.

Baxter, E. 1984. *Interim Progress Report: The Development of a Community Based Housing Model for Homeless Single Adults*. Report to the Ittleson Foundation, New York.

———. 1986. *The Heights: A Community Housing Strategy*. New York: Community Service Society of New York.

Caro, F. 1981. *Estimating Numbers of Homeless Families*. New York: Community Service Society.

Central City Concern. 1983. *SRO Housing Management Handbook*. Portland, OR: Central City Concern.

Church, W., S. Galbreath, and A. Raubeson. 1985. *Single Room Occupancy Development Handbook*. Portland, OR: Portland Developmental Commission.

Community Emergency Shelter Organization and Jewish Council on Urban Affairs. 1985. *SROs: An Endangered Species: Chicago's Single Room Occupancy Hotels.* Chicago: Community Emergency Shelter Organization.

Erickson, J., and C. Wilhelm. 1986. Introduction. In *Housing the Homeless.* ed. J. Erickson and C. Wilhelm, xix–xxxvii. New Brunswick, NJ: Center for Urban Policy Research.

Felton, B., S. Schuman, and A. Adler. 1981. Single room occupancy hotels. In *Community Choices for Older People*, ed. M. P. Lawton and S. Hoover, 267–285. New York: Springer.

Ford, J. 1936. *Slums and Housing.* Cambridge, MA: Harvard University Press.

Fulton, W. 1985. A room of one's own. *Planning* (Sept.):18–20.

Groth, P. Forthcoming. Non-people: A case study of public architects and impaired social vision. In *Architect's People*, ed. R. Ellis and D. Cuff. New York: Oxford University Press.

———. 1986. "Marketplace" vernacular design: The case of downtown rooming houses. In *Perspectives in Vernacular Architecture II*, ed. C. Wells, 179–191. Columbia, MO: University of Missouri Press.

Greer, N. 1986. *The Search for Shelter.* Washington, D.C.: American Institute of Architects.

Hamberg, J. 1984. *Building and Zoning Regulations: A Guide for Sponsors of Shelters and Housing for the Homeless in New York City.* New York: Community Service Society.

Hartman, C. 1986. Testimony on a report to the secretary on the homeless and emergency shelters. In *Housing the Homeless*, ed. J. Erickson and C. Wilhelm, 150–155. New Brunswick, NJ: Center for Urban Policy Research.

Hartman, K. 1982. *Displacement—How to Fight it.* Berkeley, CA: Legal Services Anti-displacement Project.

Hoch, C., and A. Cibulskis. 1985. Planning for the homeless. Paper presented at conference "Housing Research and Policy in an Era of Fiscal Authority" (June) in Amsterdam.

———, and R. Slayton. Forthcoming. *New Homeless and Old: Community and the Skid Row Hotel.* Philadelphia: Temple University Press.

Hopper, K., and J. Hamberg. 1984. *The Making of America's Homeless.* New York: Community Service Society.

Kadden, D., and A. Goldberg. 1988. Shelter for the poor: SROs can work. *The Neighborhood Works* 11 1:16–19.

Kasinitz, P. 1986. Gentrification and homelessness. In *Housing the Homeless*, ed. J. Erickson and C. Wilhelm, 241–252. New Brunswick, NJ: Center for Urban Policy Research.

Levy, H. 1968. Needed: A new kind of single room occupancy housing. *The Journal of Housing* 25:572–580.

Liu, J. K. C. 1980. *San Francisco Chinatown Residential Hotels.* San Francisco: Chinatown Neighborhood Improvement Resource Center.

Minkler, M., and B. Ovrebo. 1985. SROs: The vanishing hotels for low income elders. *Generations* 9:40–42.

Mostoller, M. 1985. A single room: Housing for the low income single. In *The Unsheltered Woman*, ed. E. L. Birch, 191–216. New Brunswick, NJ: Center for Urban Policy Research.

National Trust for Historic Preservation. 1981. *Rehabilitating Residential Hotels.* Washington, D.C.: National Trust for Historic Preservation.

Schneider, J. 1986. Skid row as an urban neighborhood, 1880–1960. In *Housing the Homeless*, ed. J. Erickson and C. Wilhelm, 167–189. New Brunswick, NJ: Center for Urban Policy Research.

Shapiro, J. H. 1971. *Communities of the Alone.* New York: Association Press.

Silvern, P. J., and R. Schmunk. 1981. Residential hotels in Los Angeles. Paper presented at conference "Residential Hotels: A Vanishing Housing Resource" (June 11–12) in San Francisco, California.

Simpson, J. H., M. Kilduff, and C. D. Blewet. 1984. *Struggling to Survive in a Welfare Hotel.* New York: Community Service Society.

Stoner, M. 1986. The plight of homeless women. In *Housing the Homeless*, ed. J. Erickson and C. Wilhelm, 279–294. New Brunswick, NJ: Center for Urban Policy Research.

U.S. Department of Housing and Urban Development. 1984. *A Report to the Secretary on Homelessness and Emergency Shelters.* Washington, D.C.: U.S. Government Printing Office.

U.S. General Accounting Office. 1985. *Homelessness: A Complex Problem and the Federal Response.* Washington, D.C.

Werner, F., and D. D. Bryson. 1982. A guide to the preservation and maintenance of single room occupancy (SRO) housing. *Clearing House Review* (Apr.):999–1009.

Chapter 13

The Design of a Single Room with Furniture for a Residential Hotel

Michael Mostoller

Single adults with little income have traditionally relied on various types of single room housing for their permanent residence. Most recently this housing has taken the form of single room occupancy (SRO) hotels, but over the last 20 years a large proportion of these hotels has been lost through urban renewal and gentrification. The remaining hotels often are in need of renovation and improvement in order to accommodate their low-income residents in any reasonable manner. New facilities, based on some variant of the SRO model, are needed to house displaced and poor single people of all ages. This chapter provides guidance for these efforts by chronicling the research and design of a prototype single room, with furniture, for residents of SRO accommodations.

This chapter is based on two studies conducted by the author. The first, the Parkview study, was part of a larger project to provide architectural and other services to existing SRO hotels; the project was coordinated by the Columbia University Community Services program and funded by the State of New York.[1] The second study was conducted with the Vera Institute of Justice to create a model SRO hotel in New York City, and was funded by the National Endowment for the Arts. The earlier research of John Liu (1980) and

Mary Comerio (1982) in San Francisco's Chinatown provided both a model to follow and a challenge to delve into similar issues in New York City with its varied population and larger hotels.

The designs for a prototype room and furniture were developed through an interlocking set of investigations. These included historical research on building and furniture types that could stand as precedents; contemporary research on inhabitants of SRO hotels in New York City; the articulation of a particular design philosophy; and detailed analysis of different room and furniture alternatives. Each of these investigations is described in turn.

HISTORICAL RESEARCH

The historical research identified earlier types of single room accommodations and earlier items of furniture that could be used in contemporary SRO rooms.

Historically single room accommodations were developed by a variety of agents (Mostoller 1985). One generator of such housing has been the private sector. In the nineteenth century the boarding house was an important housing form when industrialization created a vast increase in the

263

number of single workers living in cities. The boarding house provided a small-scale setting, meals, and space for social activity. In the first quarter of the twentieth century the boarding house was supplemented by rooming houses and then by residential hotels in denser parts of the city. There also were hotels that accommodated the lowest-paid workers. The price of a room at each type of hotel varied considerably, allowing for a broad spectrum of residents to be housed. The services provided ranged from lobby desk service and linen to amenities rivaling those at a live-in private club. Sanitation facilities also varied from facilities for each room, to facilities for each suite, to facilities shared by a group of rooms. In the better hotels the furnishings usually included a bed, a dresser, an easy chair, and a table or a desk. Often a sink was provided in each room. While boarding houses generally were three- to four-story row houses, the hotels were fireproof elevator buildings.

In addition to hotels owned privately by landlords was a series of facilities developed by the government and by charitable organizations. Among these were men's and women's municipal lodging houses. In the most minimal ones, cubicles rather than rooms were provided, with a simple pallet and a stand. These buildings were large, elevator-equipped structures. Philanthropic organizations also offered single room occupancy accommodations. While the sponsor often was the YMCA or the Salvation Army, Ford's 1936 study reveals an impressive range of sponsors, building sizes and types, and social services and amenities. In many of these a homelike atmosphere was promoted as a solution to the homelessness of the new urban migrant or immigrant.

types reveals the variety of accommodations that provided private furnished rooms to serve a working population. The rented rooms and their furnishings met the needs of their poor and mobile inhabitants who possessed few, if any, household goods. The sharing of sanitary facilities increased economy while social spaces, hotel-like services, and sometimes meals met additional needs. The mix of rooms, facilities, and services varied widely; at present single people have much less choice—condominiums or public shelters, with very little in between.

The historical analysis of furniture from different periods and locales revealed general types suitable for life in a single room as well as particular examples that could meet the needs of economy, strength, and durability—characteristics deemed essential for long-term use in residential hotels. The analysis of precedents suggested additional criteria important to the design of each piece.

The captain's chair was one precedent. Its basic form is hundreds of years old. It is strong and durable yet also light enough to be easily moved (Fig. 13-1). It can serve as an armchair for reading, watching television, or socializing; it can be pulled up to a table or desk whereas a larger, upholstered chair could not. It has interesting curves that provide visual pleasure. It can be seen from either the front or the back, thus allowing for choice in its placement. One can see through it, which is a very important quality in small spaces. All these characteristics indicated that the captain's chair was a proper solution to the problems inherent in living in a small space, and these attributes became criteria for the design of a similar chair.

The light, wood side chair is a very flexible item, easy to move and to use for a variety of events. The tavern table, a sturdy wood table with a drawer, was identified as a multipurpose piece that could serve as a desk or a table for meals. Armoires with storage behind doors and also in drawers became another important precedent.

Figure 13-1. Captain's chair from nineteenth century.

For more general purposes the breakfront with open shelves below and doors above provides for exposed and hidden storage.

These pieces have a long history. Some emerged as early as the sixteenth century to meet the needs of everyday life in European culture and remained essentially unchanged for many years. According to Edward Lucie Smith (1985, 755ff):

> . . . certain pieces of furniture, because of their essential practicality and usefulness, began during this period to achieve definitive forms which they were to retain for many years. Skilled but unsophisticated country craftsmen, usually joiners rather than cabinet-makers, repeated the same designs again and again, without changing them much, because they had been found to be best for a particular purpose. A good deal of furniture thus escaped from the influence of fashion and, however unconsciously, responded only to the principle of fitness for use.

This same principle applies today.

Paintings and other depictions of everyday interiors in earlier times were also sources of information about furniture. In a simply furnished garret at the turn of the nineteenth century, which is the home and workplace of a milliner, we see a set of interesting objects, particularly those for storage (Fig. 13-2). On the near left is a bureau with a mirror and shelf above it; beyond the canopied bed is a tall wardrobe. Both could be used today. A chest, a box, and a basket complete the storage repertoire. The woman has been ironing on a folding table. Here are two items to add to our list of precedents—the storage containers and the folding table.

Chests also appear in the second vignette, where the most prominent item is the built-in bed with a canopy to conserve heat (Fig. 13-3). One chest for clothes and blankets is under the window; another chest is at the foot of the bed. Two simple wood chairs with rough seats complete the setting. The pot and toilet seat lend an air of sixteenth-century reality to this room, which, without them and the canopy, resembles many residential hotel interiors of today.

Vermeer's sixteenth-century interiors reveal the potential beauty of these simple pieces. His paintings not only display typical and timeless

furniture for our selection but also depict them so completely that the furniture seems to come alive as much as the silent beings they surround and support. A bench, a table, two chairs, and a framed picture beside a window form a world unto themselves (Fig. 13-4). The pillows and carpets add a festive touch. The musical instrument, sheet music, carafe, and glass indicate the richness of a life that is otherwise presented with profound austerity. These qualities of Vermeer's rooms brought another, more qualitative matter to the fore: the potential symbolic meaning of furniture in people's lives. All items can become invested with personal value as a consequence of long use, associations, or personal habits. To enhance the potential for symbolic meaning, the furniture must be well made and long lasting and should give visual delight.

Shaker design demonstrated the possibility of fusing furniture design with interior room design while also maintaining the furniture as discrete pieces. Shaker work of the early nineteenth cen-

Figure 13-2. "The Unforseen Accident" by Louis Darcis, 1801: mezzotint after a painting by Nicolas Lavreince. (*Source: Plate 128*, An Illustrated History of Interior Decoration *by Mario Praz, Longanesi & C.*)

Figure 13-3. Engraving of Emblem XIII by Johannes de Brune, Amsterdam, 1624: from Emblemata of Zinne-werck. (*Source: Plate* 72, An Illustrated History of Interior Decoration *by Mario Praz, Longanesi & C.)*

tury shows sound construction, economy of line, and visual openness. In these respects the furniture shows a great improvement over the heavier, bulkier pieces of earlier periods. Shaker furniture also was mass produced.

Shaker chairs were so light that when not in use they could be hung from wall pegs. The Shaker pegboard solved many storage problems and helped create a serene sense of order. The Shakers even put pegs on objects that hung from the wall so that other objects could be hung from them. The hanging shelves are particularly elegant and ingenious. Other pieces exhibit the same care and adaptability. The deacon's desk, with its folding writing surfaces, and the bureau, with drawers on two sides, show how simple modifications create a much more useful piece.

The lap desk shows how a small, simple box could be substituted for a much larger piece of furniture (such as the grand secretary of the same century).

The Shaker room also is worthy of study (Fig. 13-5). All pieces are light and easily movable, except the sets of cupboards and drawers, which are built into the walls. The pegboard was continuous.

Ideally, a Shaker dwellingroom for Brother or Sister was to contain little more than one candlestand, two beds on rollers easily movable, several large windows for light and ventilation, two straight chairs, one lamp, one table, one broom and several clothesbrushes, one small iron woodburning stove for heating, one or more built-in cupboards and sets of drawers, one woodbox with dustbrush, one small hanging mirror, one simple carpet . . . and of course wall pegs. [Sprigg 1975, 64]

Placing the two chairs by the stove created a social space where the two inhabitants, separated yet joined by the table, could talk, work, read, or study. Items to clean the room were also included.

Shaker design added another dimension to our historical analysis by revealing an acute attention to finish and detail. One such detail appears on the washstand (Fig. 13-6). To most of us the washstand looks very much like a dresser, with handles. These are towel bars. The washstand was indeed a dresser on which one washed in a bowl, using water from a pitcher. In those days washing took place in the bedroom, much as it does today in residential hotels.

Other details that served as inspirations were the many varieties of drop-leaf table construction and the various ways in which furniture was decorated. The painted chest in Pennsylvania Dutch culture shows a transformation of the most simply constructed and inexpensive piece into a treasure handed down from generation to generation. Decoration served here as a way to personalize and to add value to something simple, a principle that should not be forgotten.

This historical review identified types of furniture, specific examples, and design criteria for pieces suitable for single room occupancy accommodations. It also generated a reassuring feeling that long-enduring but sometimes-forgotten design solutions could continue to meet everyday needs.

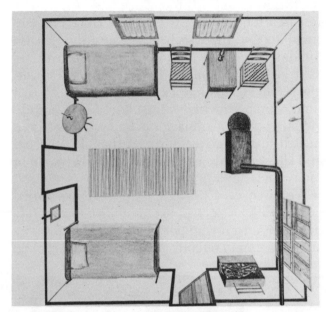

Figure 13-5. Double room for Shaker Sisters: plan perspective. *(Source: From* By Shaker Hands, *by June Sprigg. Copyright © 1975 by June Sprigg. Reprinted by permission of Alfred A. Knopf, Inc.)*

Figure 13-4. "Girl Drinking with a Gentleman" by Jan Vermeer: from Kaiser-Friedrich Museum, Berlin. *(Source: Plate 95,* An Illustrated History of Interior Decoration *by Mario Praz, Longanesi & Co.)*

Figure 13-6. Washstand from nineteenth century.

CONTEMPORARY RESEARCH

The historical review of buildings and furniture was accompanied by documentation of rooms and furniture in single room occupancy hotels in New York City. This research generated many issues to be considered in developing prototypes for furniture and for room size and layout. The research focused on the Parkview Hotel on Central Park North, which is a five-story elevator building originally built as a tenement with 32 apartments for families. It was converted to single room occupancy use around 1940. At that time the apartments were subdivided into individual rooms opening onto hallways that connected four or six rooms to a shared bathroom and kitchen. This arrangement is fairly typical of many such buildings in New York.

We discovered that the hotel residents varied widely with respect to age, employment, family ties, and need for support services. This diversity also was seen in tenants' use of their SRO rooms.

Some residents used them for a wide range of activities, as a complete house, while others used them only for a few activities. Of the two types of use, the use of the room as a miniature house with all its many activities was the source of the most fruitful information for design.

Mr. P. was a long-term Parkview resident who spent most of his time in his room. Sixty-two at the time of our research, Mr. P. had lived at the Parkview for about 10 years. During his working years he had been a professional musician playing tenor saxophone in big bands that toured the country. He was divorced from his wife, who was living on the West Coast, and had a son whom he rarely saw. He was confined to a wheelchair. Mr. P.'s room served as bedroom, kitchen, and sitting room. He read the newspaper regularly, was highly interested in world events, and was an avid baseball fan. He rarely went outside and was often alone in his room, but he was in the habit of leaving his door open and other hotel residents sometimes dropped by to visit. He had as many

Figure 13-7. Mr. P. eating a meal at his desk.

Figure 13-8. Another view of Mr. P.'s room.

pieces of furniture as the space would allow, along with many photos and many personal objects that kept alive the experiences of his earlier years, including an upright piano that he would play sometimes. He had homemaker care and ate in his own room, most often at the desk. A view of his room shows him eating a meal at his desk, which also serves as his bedside table (Fig. 13-7). There also is a comfortable chair, and next to it is a TV with a fan and a photograph on top of it. On the dresser behind the TV, are more photos, flowers, food, medicine, and personal papers.

The armchair and desk are placed near the window and the remaining furniture against the walls. Mr. P. placed many of his personal items on a decorative architectural molding (Fig. 13-8). We carefully noted this happenstance provision of a place for things (a found Shaker peg rail). We also were struck by the placement of a statue next to a framed photograph of Michelangelo's *Pietà*, a crucifix, a picture of Jesus praying, and a

photograph of Coretta Scott King. These and other possessions, located in different places throughout the room and intentionally kept in sight at all times, are evidence of a "display aesthetic." Other items in the room included several lamps, a radio, a telephone, clothes hanging on hangers from the molding, two side chairs, and more personal items. Mr. P.'s room is very small (94 square feet) and, while his furnishings are needed, they fill up the room so that it is cramped. More space is required for both functional and visual reasons: to allow for room to move around and to create a greater feeling of spaciousness.

Mrs. H. is one of several elderly single women for whom the hotel is a stable home. She had lived in the Parkview since 1954. Born in North Carolina, she was orphaned before her sixth birthday. She worked on a farm and later as a domestic in North Carolina and Virginia. After moving north with her husband, she continued to do housework. Her husband died when she was 56. Her adopted son lives in downtown Manhattan, but although they are on good terms, they do not see each other often. She visits her hometown in North Carolina once a year and occasionally sees a nephew who lives in the Bronx.

A religious woman, Mrs. H. rarely leaves the hotel except to go to church once every two weeks. Her close friend, 87-year-old Mrs. E., has a room on the same hall, and the two socialize frequently. Mrs. H. also is an active participant of a recently formed social and support group for elderly tenants in the Parkview. Mrs. H. is proudly self-reliant. A neighbor carries groceries and laundry home for her, but Mrs. H. says she does not rely on the hotel management for anything. She does hand washing in the sink of the shared bathroom and cooks in the shared kitchen. She prefers eating in her own room, where she has a refrigerator. Her 12-foot by 16-foot room has a window with southern exposure onto Central Park. By the window are two chairs where she and a guest can enjoy the sunlight and the view.

The room is filled with furniture, most of which Mrs. H. owns. The bed is placed in the center of the room, organizing the room functionally into a living-room area between it and

Figure 13-9. East wall of Mrs. H.'s room.

the window and a dressing and storage area between it and the door. Opposite the bed, on the west wall, are two focal, functional objects—the television and the sink. Both have other objects on top of them, personal photographs on the TV and medicines and glasses on the sink.

This mixing of disparate objects, which in larger accommodations would be in separate rooms, occurs almost everywhere in Mrs. H.'s room in spite of her zoning strategy. The mixing, along with the forced proximity of the disparate items, creates a tension in the room. If one observes closely the north part of the room, one sees juxtaposed in her glass door cabinet, plates, cosmetics, artificial flowers, cooking utensils, food, silverware, and a wig. Some of these items, and those in the metal storage cabinet, are taken down the hall and used for cooking and washing. They are placed here for convenient access for

these functions. Her towel is placed next to the door for the same reason.

In other cases the mixing of objects creates a delightful sense of functional and symbolic order. In a kind of tableau on the east wall next to her bed, Mrs. H. placed a crucifix and family portraits at the top and balanced them, underneath on either side, with two extremely functional objects, a flyswatter and a dustbroom (Fig. 13-9). Surrounding these items are objects bearing written words, forming a "frame" of prayer, homily, and helpful medical instructions. Mrs. H.'s sewing and correspondence lie on a bedtable below. It is clear that for Mrs. H., her room is her home and her home is her room—a place for her to live and to assert her own values through her possessions.

In many ways Mrs. H.'s room served as a model for our room designs. Aspects we considered positive included the zoning into two functional areas with the bed at the center, geometrically and functionally. The social area was near the light and the view while the functions relating to the tasks of life—health, cleanliness, and dining—were near the entry. Her room also gave us a feeling of hope. Her room was a house. It was large enough. It was organized and cheerful. That it was a long rectangle with the door and window on the short, opposite ends gave it amplitude and direction. Yet the problem of storage of the many and disparate items, in and out of sight, was not resolved. Mrs. H.'s room underscored the need for careful attention to storage needs.

DESIGN PHILOSOPHY

The philosophy adopted in our analysis and design for a single room and furniture for residential hotels consisted of a general orientation toward the problem and several more specific objectives and principles. The general orientation was based in part on the tradition in modern architecture of attempting to understand daily life and providing for it economically so as to create a better life for all. This tradition is best expressed in the work of Le Corbusier who, more than any other architect in the twentieth century, was concerned with the rationalization of life in the home, believing that the good city is based most fundamentally on the home.

> No decisions or enterprises, evolution or revolution, postulation of a theory of life . . . can be sound and healthy unless they are based upon a human unit, a cell, that is biologically good in itself (in conformity with the individual's needs). . . . Before undertaking my researches into the Radiant City, I had already satisfied myself to the point of certainty that a human 'cellule' of 14 square meters [140 square feet] per inhabitant would provide the basis for calculations that would lead to the expansion and flowering of men's lives in a machine age. [Le Corbusier 1967, 143, 144]

This emphasis on standard requirements rationally derived from investigation of the actions, but not the feelings, of daily life can result in functional but soulless environments. To avoid this, the functional orientation must be coupled with a sensibility for the feelings of human satisfaction provided by the solicitude of home, with a way of designing that enhances the experiences of a person "at home, comfortable in that home, happy in that home" (Le Corbusier 1967, 143). Therefore, we searched for solutions that would meet the objective of a rationalized dwelling but that would also support the occupant's feelings of satisfaction derived from being at home. We attempted to fuse objectivity with affect.

Our efforts were strongly influenced by the recognition that the inhabitants would be members of a forgotten, almost outcast population. We sought to advance designs that would enhance the occupants' feelings of self-esteem and would indicate to them that they are valuable people. We sought designs that would allow the occupant to identify with the pieces of furniture, encouraging him or her to experience a sense of dwelling rather than transiency or homelessness. A textured environment that possesses decorative and symbolic elements and that projects warmth and complexity would aid in these endeavors.

Feelings of permanence also would be strengthened by living in a complete, workable environment where there is a place to store winter blankets, to put a mop and bucket out of sight, and to hang up a bath towel, washcloth, or dish towel unobtrusively. The room and the furniture should allow the simplest of things to occur with grace and ease because the details of life have been thought out. Many of the design results are simple and down to earth. Esoteric or fashionable design has no place here. We found the design of simple, universal rooms and items of furniture to be more appropriate, and much more difficult, than the creation of designs for complex functions or for exotic individual tastes.

We also sought to create a design that would encourage participation in life beyond the room itself, through observation or engagement with others. The room and its furniture should promote the use of the space for publicity when others are present and for privacy when alone. A "hearth" for conversation could invite engagement with a guest; a window seat where one might sit watching the street or yard could encourage observation of the world outside.

These philosophical goals were augmented by

general objectives and specific guidelines that grew out of the research, our general orientation, and prior and concurrent work on low-income housing. Economy was the first general objective since a modest budget could be expected in residential hotel situations. Economy also had to include concerns for durability. The rooms would be subject to heavy use by their occupants. One solution in economic terms would have been to design very inexpensive furniture that could easily be broken. Indeed, such furniture is marketed internationally. However, these underdesigned pieces would not fulfill any of the goals of our philosophical orientation. Therefore the pieces were designed to last. Efficiency was another requirement. When you eat in the same room in which you sleep, when you entertain in the same room in which you work, when you clean the one room in which you have placed all your possessions, when you decorate for the holidays the same room in which you brush your teeth and wash your hands, things must work together in an orderly way.

Finally, high visual quality in finish, shape, and sturdiness was a way to enhance a sense of personal worth and the feeling of being at home. Visual quality and unity between pieces of furniture also would help in providing a sense of order among a lot of items in a small space. The furniture and room as arranged by the inhabitant should provide a sense of visual order and should promote as much feeling of spaciousness as possible.

Three principles contributed to the achievement of these objectives. First, the furniture and the room should allow for flexible and multiple uses. A single, specialized use for each piece of furniture would be impossible; no single room could accommodate all the pieces required. Multiple use also would lead to economy and efficiency. Second, the room and pieces should allow for alternative arrangements of furniture. Pieces should be usable and visually pleasing in a variety of positions and locations. The shape and size of the room should also allow for a variety of furniture arrangements. Third, the room should be designed for the particularly heavy demand for storage, which is produced by the reduction of all functions of life to a modest-size single space.

ROOM STUDIES

With these objectives and principles in mind, the creation of a prototypical room was undertaken. However, before the room and specific furniture could be designed, prototypical pieces of furniture had to be selected. Six pieces were assumed to be essential to daily life in even the most modest of circumstances:

1. Bed—for rest and sleep and also for many other activities, such as sitting, reading, eating, and watching TV.
2. Wardrobe—for clothes storage.
3. Table—for eating and working.
4. Chair—for sitting at or away from the table.
5. Stand—for storage of personal items.
6. Sink cabinet—for personal and environmental cleanliness routines; necessary when bath facilities are shared.

Then a series of room sizes and shapes was developed to help answer the following design questions:

1. What would a minimum room size be, given that the room should accommodate the six basic pieces of furniture without becoming overcrowded, cramped, or oppressive?
2. What room shapes would easily and discreetly promote the zoning of activities in the room?
3. What room shapes would allow for alternative arrangements of furniture?
4. What organizational, operational, and visual problems arise when the furniture is arranged in rooms of different sizes and shapes?
5. What uses or activities do the basic furniture pieces leave unresolved?
6. What relationships emerge, between pieces of furniture placed next to each other, that call for redesign of the room or the furniture?

Once a series of room sizes had been posited to answer these questions, furniture was placed in them and each room size was evaluated. In all the alternative rooms studied, the door is located at the top of each plan and the window at the bottom. This arrangement was adopted because it is the most typical and logical in hotel room layouts. The sink has been placed near the door.

This facilitates efficiency of use relative to the use of shared bathroom facilities down the hall and keeps the remainder of the room clear for other furniture and other functions.

The Eight-Foot-Wide Room

When the basic furniture pieces are placed in the 8-foot by 8-foot room, in either of the two room configurations shown, the room becomes filled with furniture (Fig. 13-10). There is almost no room to move about and use of the furniture will be severely constrained because of the proximity of the pieces to each other.

The 8-foot by 10-foot room allows for somewhat more space in which to move about and provides more space between the pieces of furniture. In the 8-foot by 10-foot room two basic layouts emerge as generic patterns: (1) placing the bed lengthwise in the room and (2) placing the bed crosswise in the room. Given this first decision on the location of the bed, the next largest object, the wardrobe, is placed either on the side wall or against the back wall. This room, while severely restricted in size, does allow for a minimum level of comfort and could be the minimum size acceptable under emergency conditions.

The 8-foot by 12-foot room generates a greater feeling of spaciousness. More important, the 2-foot increase in the long dimension allows for a new arrangement of furniture: placing the bed in the center of the room and the wardrobe on the same side. Using this third generic pattern, space is created for an additional piece of furniture—an armchair, for example.

The Ten-Foot-Wide Room

The basic furniture arrangements that are possible in the 10-foot by 8-foot room are similar to those possible in the 8-foot by 10-foot room (Fig. 13-11). The 10-foot by 10-foot room, however, accommodates all three generic furniture arrangements: with the increase in room width, the bed can be placed either perpendicular or parallel to the wall. Placement of the bed in the middle of the 10-foot by 10-foot room can organize the room into a social-work area by the window, a

dressing or storage zone along the top wall, and a bed zone in the middle of the room. The bed zone can function as part of the social zone in the daytime and as part of the dressing and hygiene zone when required.

This zoning organization also is evident in the 8-foot by 12-foot scheme when the bed is placed in the middle of the room, lengthwise against the wall. This tripartite zoning, proceeding from the door across the room to the window, creates an internal order to the room that is commendable. No new furniture arrangements emerge as the room is increased in size to 10-feet by 12 feet although this increase in size does allow for a larger bed and more space between pieces of furniture.

Two conclusions can be drawn from the room analyses described so far. First, a long rectangular room has several advantages over a square room. The 8-foot by 12-foot room, with less square footage than the 10-foot by 10-foot or the 10-foot by 12-foot room, can accommodate all three generic furniture arrangements and the orderly zoning of activities. Furthermore, the long parallel walls create a visual axis directed toward the window and an organizational axis for locating the furniture. The visual axis and the organizational axis together create a sense of coherence to the furniture arrangements. The visual focus on the window and the spatial armature of the rectangular space coincide with the tripartite zoning, lending another level of order. In contrast the squarer room provides neither a visual nor a functional focus and leaves between pieces of furniture many oddly shaped leftover spaces that cannot be put to good use. These spaces also tend to give the room a disorganized air.

Second, the placement of certain pieces of furniture in proximity to other pieces can support particular patterns of activity that we have called "rotational use"; *rotational* refers to physical and temporal rotation. Some pieces of furniture are used for different functions over the course of the day. When they are placed in close proximity, parts or sides of the same piece can be used for different purposes. For example, the table is generally used during the day for working or eating. If it is placed next to the bed, it can be used at night as a nightstand. The table can thus be used from one side during the day and from the other

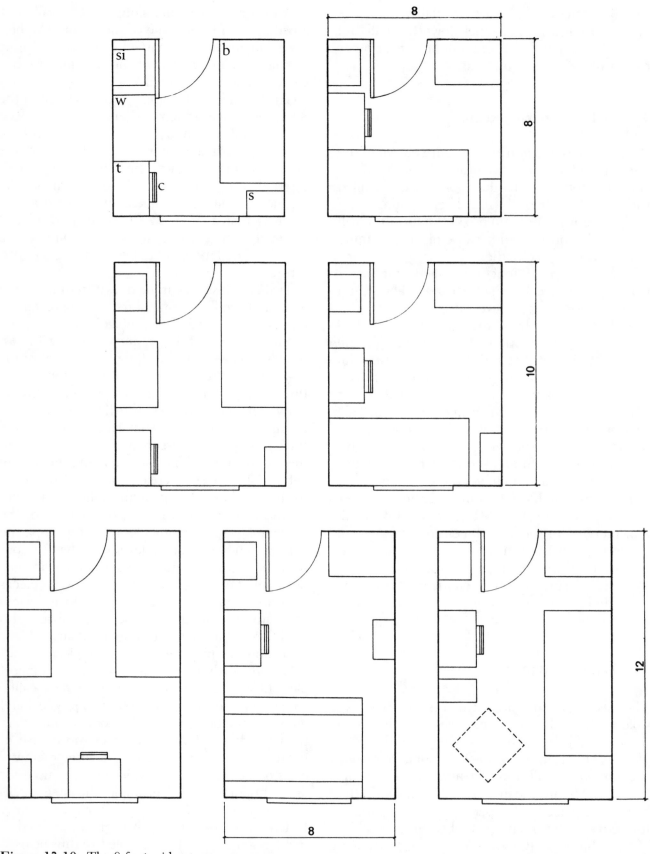

Figure 13-10. The 8-foot-wide room.

Figure 13-11. The 10-foot-wide room.

side at night. If the table is placed between the bed and an armchair that is used for reading, it can also function as a shelf. The table is not only multifunctional; it is used in a rotational manner both temporally and physically. The bed is another example. At night it is used for sleeping, yet it often acts as the pivot piece for various activities and for the furniture on either side of it. It can be a place to sit and talk, a place to work, or a place to lay out clothes or other belongings. It, too, is a rotational-use object. In fact, all pieces were designed in accordance with the idea of rotational use.

The Twelve-Foot-Wide Room

In the investigation of the 12-foot-wide room, no new opportunities for furniture arrangement or for zoning emerged (Fig. 13-12). Increasing the width adds square footage without improving functional efficiency or creating another functional zone. Although the larger size increases the feeling of spaciousness, it creates the problems inherent in the square room that were mentioned earlier: lack of visual focus, no organizational axis, and leftover chunks of space. The 12-foot-wide room achieves no more with its square footage than the 8-foot by 12-foot room, which, with minimum square footage, provides for alternative furniture arrangements and creates visual order and coherent zoning.

The Eight-by-Sixteen Prototype Room

The 8-foot by 12-foot room was developed into the recommended prototype by increasing its long dimension by 4 feet. This prototype room provides an area of 128 square feet (Fig. 13-13). Two plan variations illustrate the possibilities of furniture placement. One depicts the bed in the center of the room against the wall; the other depicts the bed in the corner farthest from the window. The six basic pieces of furniture are shown. With the increase in length, there is room for additional furniture, such as a storage piece (in both plans) and an additional armchair and table (in one plan).

The 4-foot increase in length improves all

aspects considered in our analysis. It accommodates various furniture arrangements comfortably. Also in the long room, large pieces of furniture, notably the bed, can be placed at different distances from the window and the door. In the square room the variety of relationships between the bed and the window, or the bed and the door, is much more limited. The long room thus allows for more clearly differentiated zones of front, middle, and back. This zoning possibility increases the sense of scale and the possible homelike feeling of the room. The long walls also provide a strong organizational axis for arranging the furniture, and with the focus on the window, they emphasize the rectangular volume of the room. Coupled with a view out the window, this perspective effect adds a feeling of spaciousness.

Several additional features are delineated in the elevations of the room to increase practicality and to prevent damage. The baseboard is increased in height to protect the wall and a chair molding, often found in houses of the past, helps protect the walls and creates visual interest. A peg rail at head height, like the Shaker rail, will allow the occupant to hang up possessions such as clothes, pictures, bags, and momentos. The chair molding and the peg rail also organize the room visually, reinforcing the visual axis towards the window and providing a crisp, orderly background for use by the occupant. Also, even if there is little furniture and the occupant has few possessions, the room will not feel empty.

The room height shown is 9 feet 3 inches because a vertical dimension taller than the present convention of 8 feet is recommended. The 8-foot height, ubiquitous even in luxury apartments today, is too low for extended living in one relatively small room. A higher ceiling will do much to increase the feeling of spaciousness.

This prototype room is an attempt to create a maximum/minimum accommodation, that is, to meet the inhabitant's needs within economic constraints. Increasing the width, if the budget allows, to 10 or 12 feet would certainly be acceptable. The prototype was applied to an existing situation at the Cecil Hotel in Harlem as part of the model hotel developed by the Vera Institute of Justice. The rooms there are 11 feet by 12 feet. (It also should be pointed out that rooms in the Parkview and the Cecil have ceilings over 9 feet high.)

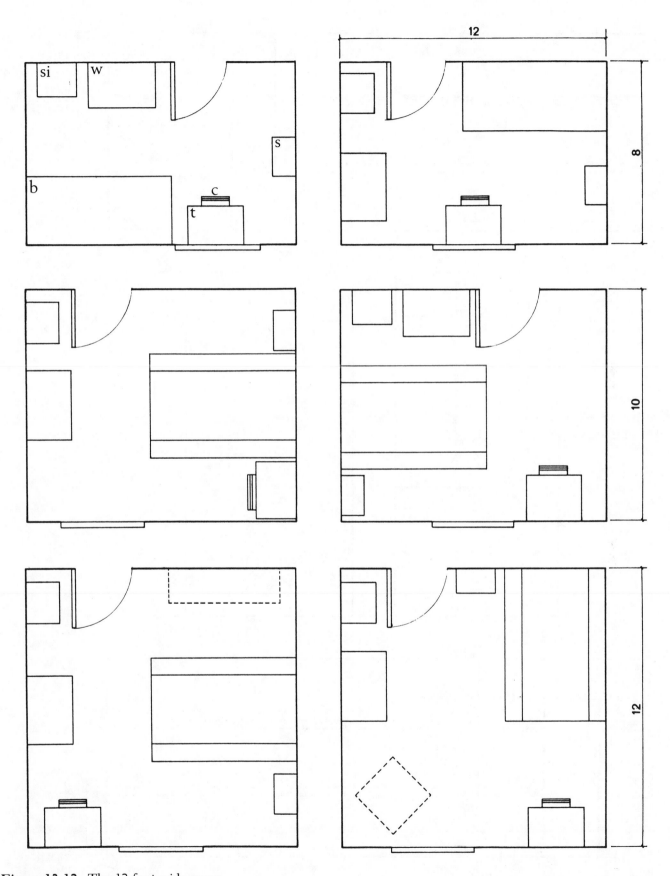

Figure 13-12. The 12-foot-wide room.

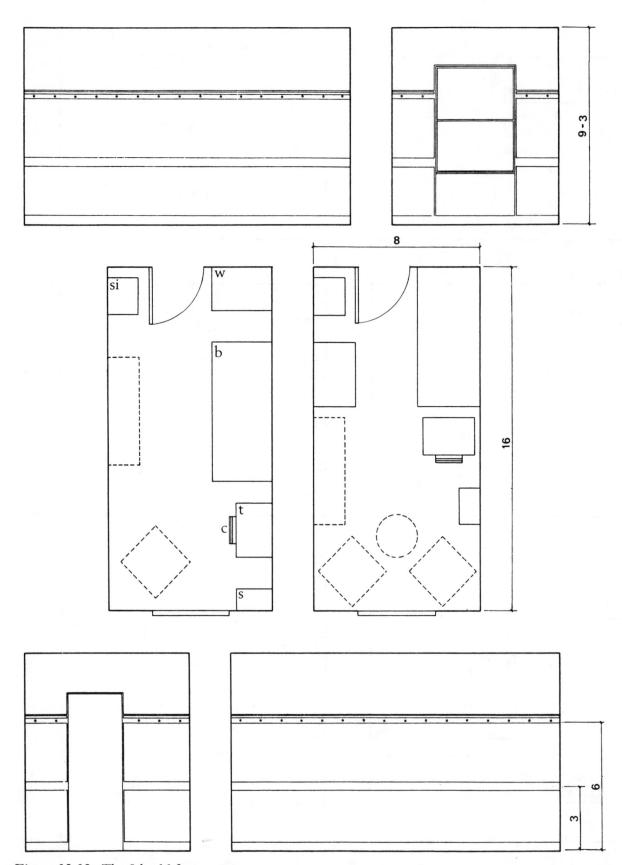

Figure 13-13. The 8-by-16-foot prototype room.

The prototype room is a result of our search for a rationalized standard allowing for mass replication. This search is part of the tradition in modern architecture that is concerned with meeting human needs in mass society, which is perhaps the greatest legacy of the pioneers of architectural reform of the 1920s and 1930s. The creation of a rationalized standard, augmented by our research into historical precedent and the documentation of current circumstances and coupled with imaginative design born of empathy, provides a model for the design process.

FURNITURE DESIGN

During the room analysis each piece was reconsidered for multiple and rotational use, for opportunities for use in alternative arrangements, and for the need for storage for the functions the piece accommodates. Specifications for each piece of furniture were then written and drawn.

The bed was designed first (Fig. 13-14). The importance of the bed has been noted several times. It is the largest piece of furniture and dominates the room visually and functionally. It is used for many different activities over the course of the day, and is the most important symbol of home, generating feelings of comfort, status, and habitation itself. It is, for all of us, a house within the house, our ultimate personal place. For these reasons any ideas of eliminating it through design, such as hiding it like a sofa bed or placing it in the wall like a Murphy bed, were rejected. The bed we designed provides space for long-term storage between the floor and the mattress. It provides a headboard for linen storage on the front and for personal items on the top and side. A simple surface decoration was introduced to create a sense of value and scale. The decoration is based on a square, circle, and triangle, the simplest decorative shapes. Small open circles serve in place of hardware to open the drawers and doors.

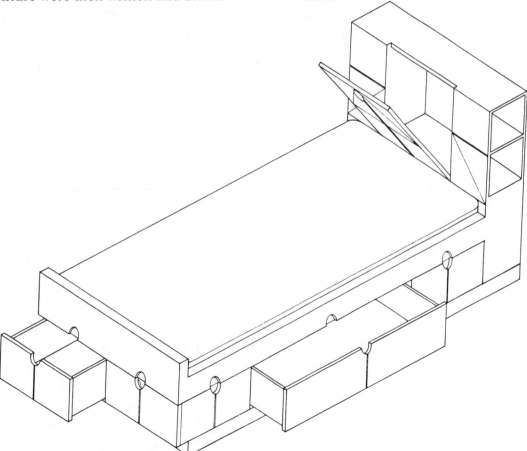

Figure 13-14. The large-scale pieces: bed, wardrobe, and sink/broom closet. (*continues*)

In designing the wardrobe we followed several basic propositions (see fig. 13-14). Both shelves and drawers were provided to accommodate the range of apparel and possessions anticipated. The shelves in particular are multifunctional and can house books, clothes, or hygiene materials. Hanging rods were attached to each side for hanging towels, washcloths, skirts, pants, or wet clothes washed in the sink. A well, several inches deep, is provided on the top to accommodate long-term storage. The decorative grid of 9-inch squares is applied to the lower sides and to the front. This simple motif establishes the value of the piece.

The third important item for living in a single room is the sink. When one room is a person's home, the shared bathroom, kitchen, and laundry must be supplemented in each room by the element common to them all—the sink. The sink will be used for personal hygiene, for washing clothes, and for cleaning the room. No particular

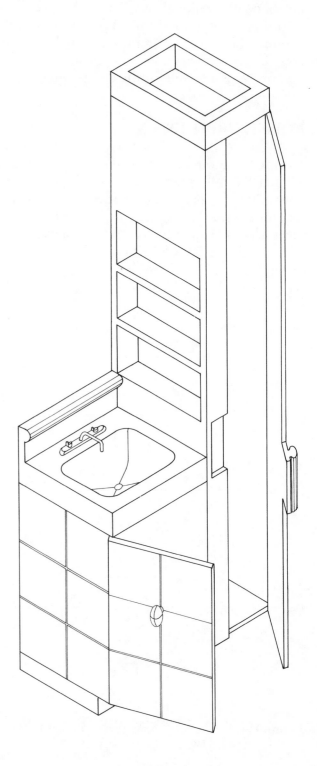

Figure 13-14. The large-scale pieces: bed, wardrobe, and sink/broom closet. *(cont.)*

Figure 13-15. The easily movable pieces: desk/table, stand, armchair, and side chair.

change from standard design is necessary for the sink itself. A cabinet with a light should be placed above the sink. The cabinet will serve some of the purposes of a medicine cabinet but should be designed without creating the overtones of a bathroom. The area beneath the sink should be enclosed for storage and for creating visual order.

An ancillary piece to the sink also is proposed. This is the old-fashioned broom closet, a vertical storage piece for brooms, mops, and buckets (see fig. 13-14). This element is placed next to the sink for convenience. Shelves are built into the exterior, on the sink side, to provide space for

toiletries, soap, and drinking glass. It also has a well on top. Once again the surfaces are partly gridded to add texture, scale, and a sense of unity with the other pieces. As with the "medicine cabinet," the "broom closet" must not look out of place in a room that serves as bedroom and living room.

In a single room the table is another essential piece of equipment. It serves as a place for working, studying, and writing; a place to have one's meals; a storage surface; and a bedside table (Fig. 13-15). With these considerations in mind, the following additions to the standard table were made to create a combination of table and desk: folding leaves at both ends to increase capacity and flexibility; a wide shelf below the desk top; an adjacent narrow shelf; and side shelving for book storage, alarm clock, or radio. The table was designed without a predetermined back or front to enhance the opportunity for rotational use and for alternative placement.

A small storage stand was posited as essential for items of personal use or value. This could be used as a stand for a TV, a plant, or a radio or as a place for a single valued object. It could also serve as a night stand. Inside are two shelves. Horizontal rods on the outside are for hanging things, just as they are on the sink and the wardrobe.

No home could be considered complete without something to sit on, other than the bed. Two chair types were proposed (Fig. 13-15). A simple side chair is suitable for use at the table/desk, for sitting, or for clothes storage over the arms and back. It is light so it can be easily moved to fulfill

a variety of functions. It has an open quality without appearing temporary or institutional. A medium-size armchair also is proposed. It uses a design vocabulary similar to the side chair but is deeper, broader, and has arms. It is based on the captain's chair, a sturdy, open, wood chair suitable for lounging, reading, or watching television. It also can be pulled up to a table and is portable and visually open.

Two additional pieces are necessary and should be included where possible. The first is a cabinet for personal storage, and the second is a variation on the chest. There is not enough space in the night stand and wardrobe to store many household items such as a dinner service, pots and pans, books, records, photos, or more clothes. All these items are common to long-term residency in single-room accommodations. The cabinet provides storage for such items on three deep shelves behind doors at the base, three open shelves in the middle, and three shelves behind glass doors at the top (Figs. 13-16 and 13-17).

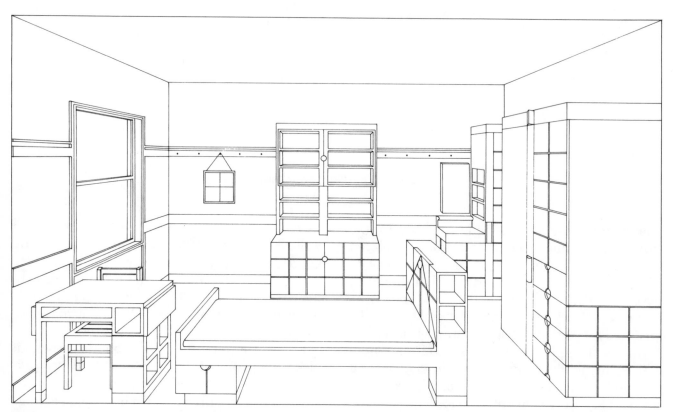

Figure 13-16. The prototype room with furniture: view across the room, showing storage cabinet in place of stand.

Chests have been forgotten in furniture design, yet they can serve many purposes in addition to storage—as a window seat, an end table, a stand, or a coffee table (Fig. 13-17). The chest is a simple and economical response to the major furniture requirements of single-room living—flexible and multiple use, provision of storage, and opportunity for alternative placement.

With the chest, probably the oldest item of furniture, we conclude this essay. In addressing the need for housing for low-income single people, we relied on historical analysis, contemporary documentation, and design and analysis conducted with a particular philosophical orientation. A single room may seem unimportant in considerations of housing problems, policies,

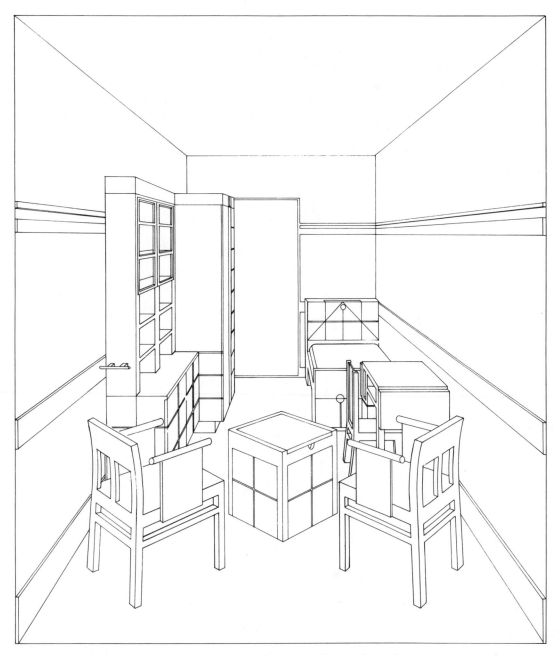

Figure 13-17. The prototype room with furniture: view from the window, showing two armchairs, storage cabinet, and chest in place of stand.

and procedures, and its design may seem super-fluous. Yet in the lives of many people, this singular space provides shelter, privacy, comfort, convenience, and a source of happiness. To make a place of a space that houses all of life's activities inside four walls challenges our comprehension of design and its limits. What better way to begin to consider architecture and housing issues than with one space and one person, one place and one life?

NOTE

1. The Parkview study was conducted in 1981–1983 by the author and students Colin Cathcart, Bob Lane, Ray Porfilio, and Peter Scaglione in the School of Architecture at Columbia University, with the Columbia University Community Services Project. The study was directed by Dr. Melvin Herman and Tony Hannigan, field supervisor.

References

Comerio, M. 1982. Inside Chinatown. Report on National Endowment for the Arts design demonstration project. San Francisco: Asian Neighborhood Design.

Ford, J. 1936. *Slums and Housing.* Cambridge, MA: Harvard University Press.

Le Corbusier, 1967. *The Radiant City.* New York: Orion Press.

Liu, J. 1980. *San Francisco Chinatown Residential Hotels.* San Francisco: Chinatown Neighborhood Improvement Resource Center.

Mostoller, M. 1985. A single room: Housing for the low-income single. In *The Unsheltered Woman,* ed. E. L. Birch, 191–216. New Brunswick, NJ: Center for Urban Policy Research.

Smith, E. L. 1985. *Furniture: A Concise History.* New York: Thames and Hudson.

Sprigg, J. 1975. *By Shaker Hands.* New York: Knopf.

Chapter 14

A Look at SRO Hotel Residents with Recommendations for Management and Design

Mary Burki

Life in a single room occupancy (SRO) hotel can be many things. It can be a time of hiding away, of blending into crowds; a time of continued or accelerated alcohol or drug abuse; or a time to begin the process of recovery from chemical dependency, a time to learn new living skills that may lead the SRO dweller away from skid row. Because it is cheap the SRO hotel may be a place to retire after many years of poorly paid labor. Whatever the case may be, an SRO hotel resident rarely selects this style of housing because it is the most desirable of the available choices, but rather he or she arrives at a hotel due to some particular set of circumstances.

The one characteristic common to all SRO residents is their income: it is either very low or nonexistent. Rent at an SRO hotel also is very low. This match between a low-income population and a low-cost form of housing brings together a special type of resident with a special type of accommodation. As with any specialized housing type, the particular characteristics and needs of SRO residents have implications for management and design.

This chapter examines these implications by first describing the SRO population and their needs and activities. Recommendations for management and design of SRO housing are then presented. Particular note is made when information is based on a review of the literature. Otherwise, this chapter is based on my own experience, which includes academic work, policy development, "hands-on" management, and development.

For my doctoral dissertation I studied SRO hotels as a form of housing for urban elderly males. I interviewed men who lived in SROs and men who had moved into renovated Section 8 apartments in the same downtown area of Portland, Oregon (Burki 1982). Several years after completing the study, I took a position managing six SRO hotels with a total of 420 units. For three years I was responsible for the total operation of each building, including staffing, budgets, policies and practices, and tenant complaints. Over that time three additional buildings were added, bringing the number of units to 670. Then I moved out of hotel management and into the acquisition and renovation of SRO hotels in this same area of Portland.

In both of these positions, my employer was a private, nonprofit organization, Central City Concern (CCC), formerly known as the Burnside Consortium. As an organization CCC works in a number of areas to help shape and carry out policies for the city of Portland. Specifically CCC acquires and renovates SRO hotels on behalf of the city, as a way to meet the city's goal of preserving the remaining stock of SRO hotels. CCC also manages SRO hotels and maintains both CCC's and other nonprofit managed hotels in the downtown area.

Portland, Oregon, is a city of 419, 810, the largest city in the state, which has a population of 2,690,000. While the state is largely dependent on forestry, agriculture, and tourism, Portland has a diversified economic structure and is reasonably sophisticated in its social and political agendas. Indeed, the city has been progressive in its policies and programs related to SRO housing. In 1979 the Portland City Council approved programs that called for funding the development of management expertise, for an ongoing emergency maintenance program, and for the acquisition and renovation of SRO units. The city also was persistent in pursuing a Demonstration Grant Award from the Department of Housing and Urban Development (HUD), which created the first allocation of Section 8 rental certificates for use with renovated SRO hotels. With support for management, maintenance, acquisition, and renovation, Portland—in conjunction with CCC —has served as a model for other communities wishing to address the problem of housing their skid-row populations.

SRO NEIGHBORHOODS

An SRO neighborhood is an urban neighborhood of residential units, businesses, and services. At a minimum an SRO neighborhood has a number of SRO buildings and businesses that cater to hotel residents. Inexpensive restaurants, small grocery stores, pawn shops, second-hand stores, and day-labor job offices are characteristic of SRO neighborhoods (Fig. 14-1). Soup kitchens, missions, medical clinics and offices of social-service agencies also are typical. Establishments that sell cheap, fortified wine are as much a part of an SRO neighborhood as are the people who drink the wine and loiter on street corners. Unfortunately crime, too, is a part of an SRO neighborhood, with drugs and stolen goods for sale on the street and predators on the lookout for unsuspecting victims. Another name for an SRO neighborhood is skid row.

Not all SRO hotels are located in SRO neighborhoods or skid-row areas. In Portland there is an area that hotel residents call "upper skid row" (Burki 1982), where a number of hotels are interspersed with apartment buildings and businesses that cater to the middle class. Gatherings on the street corner are rare in this neighborhood, and the services usually found in a skid-row area are absent. Nonetheless, the majority of SRO units in most cities are located in skid-row areas. For this reason, discussions in this chapter focus on SRO residents who live in hotels located in an SRO neighborhood.

SRO HOTEL RESIDENTS

Beyond the common bond of poverty, SRO hotel residents are a diverse population.[1] This finding is in a number of studies of elderly hotel residents (Burki 1982; Eckert 1978; Ehrlich 1976) and in studies of residents of all ages (Community Emergency Shelter Organization and Jewish Council on Urban Affairs 1985; Ille 1980; Felton et al. 1977).[2] A review of the latter three studies shows an average age of 50, suggesting that not all residents are elderly; there are younger residents as well. A considerable number of residents (about half) report never having married; an almost equal number report having been married at least once. Level of education is another example of variation in the population. With the average years of schooling reported to be about 11, the implication is that some residents did not get much beyond grade school and others completed at least some college (Ille 1980). Of the three studies only Ille (1980) reports findings on drinking behavior, but what she shows is that some residents drink excessively while others do not drink at all. A final example of diversity within the SRO population is findings on social interaction. Although the majority report at least some level of interaction, there are those who

Figure 14-1. SRO neighborhood in Portland. This is in the heart of Portland's SRO neighborhood. Within a block there are two SRO hotels—including the Estate Hotel (shown above)—a grocery store, café, tavern, social service agency, medical clinic, second-hand store, and missions. All cater to hotel residents or the homeless.

report having no contact at all with relatives or friends (Ille 1980; Felton et al. 1977).

Just as there is great variation among SRO residents, there also is variation among SRO hotels. Much of this difference is the result of management practices and the resulting self-selection by prospective tenants. Given consistent management, once a building develops a reputation or personality, it tends to be perpetuated over time. A hotel might, for example, develop a reputation for one or more of the following: having a strong sense of community among its residents, being a haven for drug users, having an intolerance for drug and alcohol abuse, being a secure place for women to reside, or having an accepting attitude toward the chronically mentally ill. Building reputations and management styles become known to residents of SRO neighborhoods, and, for the

most part, prospective tenants seek rooms in hotels they think will accept them. Management sets the tone; some establish house rules and expect compliance while others collect the rent and either ignore or attempt to profit from illegal activities that take place in the building.

The following profiles describe some of the more prevalent types of hotel tenants who reside in SRO neighborhoods. The categories are meant to be descriptive and are not mutually exclusive. They were selected because they depict life circumstances that bring individuals to residency in an SRO neighborhood. The descriptions are based partially on the literature (Eckert 1978; Levy 1968; Shapiro 1966; 1969; Siegal 1978; Winberg and Wilson 1981) but primarily on my own experience overseeing the management of nine SRO hotels and observing life in one skid-row neighborhood. It should be noted that each type of resident will not be found in each SRO hotel; some, like drug dealers, cluster together in hotels where management tolerates their behavior.

Practicing Alcoholics

The alcoholic hotel resident has a disease that makes the person's body unable to process alcohol, yet, despite the alcohol's destructive effects, the body becomes dependent on it. Often the alcoholic has a family history of alcoholism, possibly going back a number of generations. Most likely the alcoholic has a history of job losses related to drinking. It is not uncommon for alcoholics to be alienated from their families. A history of arrests and convictions resulting from actions committed while intoxicated also is common.

Practicing alcoholics are prominent in SRO neighborhoods and probably are the type of resident most associated with a skid-row area. About 60 percent of Ille's (1980) random sample of hotel residents in Portland reported heavy or excessive drinking. Some are binge drinkers who dry out periodically; some drink only during the first part of each month because that is when they have money; and some drink on a daily basis.

Practicing alcoholics can be problem tenants. Their extremely short attention spans may result in burned pots and pans in the community kitchen or overflowing sinks due to faucets left running. Their personal hygiene may deteriorate. The most serious problem presented by a drunk resident, however, is starting a fire due to carelessness with a lighted cigarette.

Despite these problems practicing alcoholics can be housed in SRO hotels. CCC's approach is to house the most recalcitrant drinkers in the agency's most indestructible building, that is, one that is constructed of steel and concrete and has painted concrete flooring. In this building surfaces are easy to clean and furnishings are minimal and sturdy. Hotel staff try to encourage alcoholic tenants to seek detoxification and ongoing treatment. Tenants who make progress are likely to be offered housing in one of CCC's "better" hotels, ones that have carpeted floors and furnishings that give a more homelike feeling.

Recovering Alcoholics

A recovering alcoholic's background and circumstances are likely to be indistinguishable from those of a practicing alcoholic. The difference is that the recovering alcoholic is making an effort to maintain sobriety. In all likelihood the recoverer has made several previous attempts to remain sober, almost always with the aid of some type of treatment program. Recovering alcoholics who have remained alcohol-free for a period of time may begin to make plans to move out of their hotels and the SRO neighborhood.

The problems associated with housing a practicing alcoholic virtually vanish when the alcoholic maintains sobriety. Efforts to assist newly recovering alcoholics to continue with their treatment program are extremely worthwhile. Most of the hotel staff that CCC hires, including managers, are recovering alcoholics who were residents of CCC's or another agency's alcohol-free housing.

Chronically Mentally Ill

There is no simple way to describe the chronically mentally ill who reside in SRO hotels. Some have a long history of institutionalization, while others have none. Some are involved in treatment programs, and others are not. Some need medication in order to control their illness, while others manage without drugs. Some have behavior problems that are a manifestation of their illness, but many do not. Some are social; others are reclusive. Some are able to maintain their personal hygiene and housekeeping, and others need assistance.

The chronically mentally ill are generally, and erroneously, considered to be poor risks in a residential setting. CCC has found that mentally ill residents housed in their buildings are acceptable tenants and mix well with other residents. However, there are exceptions, such as when residents stop taking their medication, withdraw from a treatment program, experience an escalation in their illness, or develop unhygienic habits. To reduce the likelihood of these occurrences, CCC hotel managers try to establish close working relationships with these residents and their case managers.

Physically Disabled

The physically disabled constitute a small part of the SRO resident population. Typically they include war veterans and accident victims. A few are wheelchair bound; some have severe brain damage; others have lost limbs; and a few are legally blind or deaf. Generally their condition does not present a problem that would make them unacceptable as hotel residents. However, it is not uncommon to find drug or alcohol problems in this population.

Low-Paid Workers

There are some hotel residents who appear to have no reason other than lack of financial resources for residing in an SRO hotel. They do not have a problem with alcohol or drugs and are not mentally ill. The younger ones tend to have few job skills and have probably worked only sporadically. The older, retired residents were employed as laborers in low-paid jobs, such as logging, agricultural work, and manual labor, and now receive only minimal Social Security payments. Young or old, these residents are poor, and an SRO hotel is the only type of housing they can afford. They present few problems as hotel residents.

Drug Users

Like alcoholics drug users develop a chemical dependency that drives them to seek drugs to satisfy their addiction. Steady users are not likely to be able to hold a job and develop other methods of financing their habit. Most likely this will involve victimizing others. Probable targets are residents of the user's own hotel and those who frequent the SRO neighborhood. Because of this behavior drug users make poor tenants.

Drug Dealers

Dealers come to SRO hotels to serve their clients and to conduct their business. They may live in the hotel and keep their "products" elsewhere or may use their rooms as a base of operations.

Generally drug dealers prefer to remain low key in order not to attract the attention of hotel management or police. Their goal is to protect their base of operations and to increase sales. Usually there are no limits to what dealers will do to protect their operations, so violence is nearly a foregone conclusion. This makes drug dealers unacceptable as residents.

Criminals

The criminal element in SRO neighborhoods is one that cannot be ignored. The problems of jail overcrowding and backlogged court systems exacerbate this situation, as does the release of prisoners without adequate means of support or job opportunities. Many have given up their criminal habits, becoming suitable tenants. Others continue to pursue their criminal ways with fellow hotel residents as probable victims.

Occasional SRO Residents

This group of hotel residents differs from other groups in that for the most part they are temporary residents of the SRO neighborhood. Students, artists, actors, those down on their luck, and displaced families who find themselves housed in SRO hotels generally anticipate moving to a better neighborhood eventually. They may reside in a hotel because it suits their current economic condition, but they have plans of finding a job and moving to a better neighborhood. Occasional residents constitute a very small part of Portland's SRO population but make good additions to a hotel's resident mix, provided they do not have problems such as an alcohol or a drug addiction.

THE SRO RESIDENT'S LIFE

The daily routines and activities of hotel residents tend to be as diverse as the residents themselves. A particular illness or disability, the nature of a hotel and its surrounding neighborhood, individual preferences and patterns of socializing, and levels of income all influence daily routines. For any particular resident one factor may be more influential than another in directing these routines.

There are several categories into which routines may fall: the pursuit of basic needs, medical and social services, and personal activities.

Basic Needs

Basic needs are those things essential to a resident's existence, such as sustenance or satisfying an addiction. Regarding food the hotel resident has several options. Residents with sufficient income may purchase low-cost meals at cafés and restaurants in the neighborhood. Residents with no income may wait in soup lines for a free meal, seek out some other type of meal program if it exists, or try to panhandle enough money to buy a meal. Another option is the local grocery. Nearly every SRO neighborhood has a grocery store that caters to the hotel resident's needs by including in its stock "quick, no cook" meals, such as sliced meats and cheeses, canned stew, and peanut butter. These "no cook" meals are an important source of nutrition for many hotel residents because local codes normally prohibit cooking in individual rooms due to the danger of fire.

Hotels that provide community cooking facilities for the residents' use provide a special benefit to all residents, but especially to the lowest-income residents. With access to cooking facilities, residents are eligible for food stamps and thus can purchase food and prepare their own meals. All hotels managed by CCC have either communal or individual cooking accommodations, and about 65 percent of the residents participate in the food stamp program. For many hotel residents the problem of how to get enough to eat is of paramount importance. The resolution involves some level of planning; many residents eat only one meal a day in order to stretch their limited resources.

For practicing alcoholics and drug abusers, the daily planning is likely to focus more on the pursuit of alcohol and drugs than of food. They need chemicals to relieve the pain in their bodies; food is secondary. The local grocery store or tavern is the major source of alcohol. This means drinkers

must either go out and purchase their supply or send a "runner." The alcoholic's health may determine whether he or she goes out or has someone else do so. Most alcoholics seek out their own supply, but as the disease progresses, their bodies become more and more debilitated. Because most of an alcoholic's money is spent on alcohol, meals are likely to be inexpensive groceries or those served in soup lines.

There are other basic needs including hygiene, personal services, and acquisition of clothing and household articles. All hotels provide facilities for personal bathing, but not all provide locations for washing clothes. Most hotels in Portland have laundry facilities for tenants' use. There are few laundromats in the neighborhood so in-building laundries are appreciated and well used.

Barbering is another service that may occur in-house. Because of limited resources many tenants cannot afford to pay to have their hair cut. Informally some tenants take on the function of a barber and trim fellow residents' hair; others cut their own. Those with sufficient resources use local barbershops or schools of hair design.

SRO hotel residents must be very prudent in their acquisition of clothing and household articles. Secondhand stores and service agencies that distribute free clothing and household items provide the least expensive options and usually are located in SRO neighborhoods. In Portland inexpensive retail stores are within easy walking distance of the skid-row area, so access to new goods is available to those with enough income.

Medical and Social Services

The need for medical and social services is not typically a daily occurrence; it arises intermittently. Common ailments for which SRO neighborhood residents seek medical assistance include respiratory problems; dermatological conditions; musculoskeletal pain; and general evaluations, such as blood-pressure checks and post-hospitalization visits. At least half the new cases of tuberculosis reported in Multnomah County come from the skid-row area, which comprises only 3 percent of the county's population (Reuler et al. 1986).

SRO residents in Portland have a variety of

medical services to choose from, including public and nonprofit managed clinics. Multnomah County provides in the neighborhood a free clinic that is staffed by doctors and nurses. One nonprofit group specializes in health care and has several clinics located within SRO hotels, while another operates a medical and dental clinic in conjunction with a night shelter. House calls are made to ailing SRO residents based on individual requests or referral by a hotel manager. Despite the presence of a number of clinics, some residents receive most of their medical care from emergency personnel, that is, ambulance drivers and emergency-room staff.

There also are agencies that provide a wide range of social services. In Portland SRO hotel residents can get assistance in applying for income support (such as Social Security or SSI). They can also receive free clothing, get detoxified, get treatment for alcohol or drug dependency, receive case management assistance for mental illness, get job referrals or referrals to job training programs, be assigned a payee who will manage their money, be assigned a housekeeper who will help keep their rooms clean, and other similar services. Some programs, in particular those for alcohol treatment, specialize in serving one ethnic group, such as Native Americans or Hispanics.

Personal Activities

Along with the pursuit of basic necessities and special services, hotel residents have their own set of preferred activities. If residents are not employed or otherwise engaged in regularly programmed activities, such as job training, they find other ways to pass the time.

Some hotel residents are walkers, going out each day, even several times a day, to walk about the neighborhood (Fig. 14-2). Getting out offers a welcome break from sitting in a small room. Street corners are popular places for observing the people and events of the neighborhood, and it is here that residents mix with the homeless to watch events of the day. Because SRO rooms are small, street corners serve as a combination living room, kitchen, and back yard. Over the years protocol develops as to who uses which street

Figure 14-2. This resident of the Rich Hotel takes several walks each day.

corners and groups migrate from sunny to shady corners, depending on the time of year and the day's temperature.

While hanging out on a street corner, residents will often visit with each other. They also may share a bottle of wine or panhandle, and they may be offered an opportunity to buy stolen goods or drugs. Mostly, though, they watch passersby. It is notable that there are few secrets in an SRO neighborhood, and word of mouth can be faster than the telephone.

A personal preference of many older, retired hotel residents is to spend much of the day in a local tavern sipping beer or coffee and watching whatever is on the television. These older residents are quiet drinkers and go to their favorite taverns to socialize.

Sitting in the hotel lobby is another frequent pastime (Fig. 14-3). Some people have a particular seat they prefer, and this preference may be

Figure 14-3. The Estate Hotel: lobby. The television is on during much of the day and tenants stop by to watch favorite programs or just to sit and relax.

honored by other tenants. While seated in the lobby, the resident may engage the hotel staff in conversation, watch television, play cards with another tenant, watch the street activity, or simply sit and watch comings and goings within the hotel.

There also are those residents who spend most of the day in their rooms and do not seek opportunities to socialize. This isolationist pattern reflects the resident's particular lifestyle. Even though most residents seek some level of social interaction, in general SRO tenants could not be classified as gregarious. They select certain opportunities for social interaction and avoid others. They have learned to be guarded as a means of self protection.

MANAGING SRO HOTELS

There is no single approach to the management of SRO hotels; what may be best for one situation may not be appropriate for another. The residents' needs, the nature of the particular SRO building, and the surrounding environment should all be considered in selecting the appro-

priate management approach. Whichever approach is selected it is best to prepare a management plan prior to beginning development work.

After only a short time in the SRO hotel management business, CCC found it necessary to prepare a guide for its hotel managers. The agency's management policies and practices were committed to paper in *The SRO Management Handbook* (1983). Experience has convinced me that management of SRO hotels is an evolutionary process and that any management plan requires adjustments over time.

A management plan can be simple or detailed, but at a minimum it needs to set out the parameters of how a building will be managed. Among the questions to be answered by a plan are the following: What is the underlying philosophy from which management policies and practices will evolve? Does the prospective resident population suggest the need for a particular management style? What tasks will be expected of staff? What procedures will they follow?

The question regarding prospective tenants is of particular importance because different residents often require different management approaches. Residents who have a history of acting out and causing disruptions requires a management with the capacity to respond quickly. Residents who are easily victimized require a management that provides a high degree of security.

With some understanding of the prospective resident population, further development of a management plan should consider several basic goals. One major goal is the provision of a safe environment: a management plan should suggest ways hotel staff can provide security to residents, their belongings, and the building itself. Maintaining a clean and sanitary environment is another goal: methods should be developed to assure that common areas are regularly cleaned and rooms are periodically inspected. Another goal is the provision of a supportive environment: examination of the needs and vulnerabilities of the prospective tenant group should provide clues to the types of assistance that will benefit residents.

These goals—the provision of a safe, clean, and supportive environment—are the basic objectives that any SRO hotel's management approach must consider.

Additionally there are a number of particular management issues that need consideration—such as access to the hotel, house rules, tenant selection, and staff roles. The impact of different management approaches regarding each of these issues is examined in the following sections.

Access to the Building

The way that access to a building is handled sets the tone for management. An unlocked and unmonitored front door means the management's approach is laissez-faire, while a locked and monitored front door means management intends to assert control over access. Other management approaches fall somewhere between these two types.

Issues to consider are the number of staff needed to maintain an acceptable level of control over access to the building, the personnel costs of providing the desired level of staffing, whether it is advisable to allow tenants to have keys to the front door, and whether it is advisable to have live-in staff. Around-the-clock staffing at the front desk provides the greatest control over access, but it also is the most expensive approach. If access is not monitored in some way, it is almost certain that the hotel will become a haven for illegal activity. It is essential that management take a stand regarding illegal activities in the building. A management policy forbidding illegal activities requires continual enforcement efforts, but if that policy is not set early on, it will be virtually impossible to enact it at a later time.

An alternative to 24-hour staffing is to provide tenants with a key to the front door, which is then kept locked at all times. The advantage of this approach is the greatly reduced personnel costs. The disadvantage is that it is impossible to have complete control over the keys: some will be lost and others will be stolen; some tenants will duplicate their keys, and others will fail to return the keys when they move out. The presumption of this approach is that the lock will have to be rekeyed periodically. Providing front door keys to all types of SRO hotel residents is not recommended. However, it is a viable option and, depending on the circumstances at a particular hotel, should be considered.

Twenty-four-hour supervision of the front door is needed in hotels with daily and weekly rentals, where resident turnover is high, and in large hotels with several floors, where staff has difficulty getting to know each resident personally. Around-the-clock staffing also is advisable in hotels located in high crime areas where drug dealing, prostitution, and the sale of stolen goods are commonplace.

Intercoms at the front doors of buildings that do not have 24-hour staff can be a mixed blessing. A system that allows two-way communication between each individual unit and the front door is very expensive and thus usually not a common feature of low-rent SRO hotels. A system that rings either in the hotel's office, which is often adjacent to the manager's unit, or in a single location in a central hallway is less expensive. With this type of system, the question is who answers the buzzer: only the manager or anyone who is in the hallway when it rings? The intercom facilitates access to the building by those without keys but also builds an expectation that someone is always available to answer the buzzer. This expectation can be wearing on a live-in manager, especially when the person at the front door becomes irritated because no response is forthcoming. An important feature of any intercom system is that it can be turned off by the hotel manager. This is a particularly desirable feature during the late evening and early morning hours.

An alternative to intercoms is the installation of public pay phones on each floor of the hotel with the numbers posted at the front door (Fig. 14-4). This approach reduces the burden on the hotel manager because tenants on each floor share the responsibility of answering the pay phone and notifying fellow residents of visitors.

Another issue related to monitoring access is whether to have live-in staff. Employees who live and work in the same building tend to take a more personal interest because the hotel is also their home. This provides management with extra coverage, even when a staff member is off duty. The disadvantage is that it is almost impossible for live-in staff to escape from their jobs; therein lies the danger of staff burnout. This is a

Figure 14-4. The Beaver Hotel: front door. Phone numbers for the pay phones on each floor are painted on the front door.

Figure 14-5. The Estate Hotel: front desk. Desk clerk explaining the house rules. New tenants are asked to sign a copy of the hotel rules, indicating that they understand those rules.

particularly serious problem for hotel managers. With 24-hour supervision the need for live-in staff is reduced because the on-duty staff is awake and able to monitor activity in the building around the clock. With only a locked front door, the need for live-in staff is greatly increased because staff is not awake and on duty during all hours of the day.

Residents of a hotel can be of great assistance in monitoring access to the building. This is especially true in hotels where there is no 24-hour desk coverage and tenants have keys to the front door. The more sense of community tenants feel, the more likely they are to take on some of the monitoring functions.

House Rules

As with access to the building, house rules help set the management tone. A lack of house rules implies a laissez-faire approach, while a specific set of rules implies a much more prominent role for management. Without enunciating the house rules precisely, it is virtually impossible to achieve compliance. Providing copies of the rules at the time of rental gives the staff an opportunity to discuss the rules with the new tenant (Fig. 14-5).

Concerns that house rules might well address include the following: safety, cleanliness, use of alcohol and illegal drugs, visitors, pets, reporting of maintenance problems, and the date rent is due. Rules on safety may specify no cooking in individual rooms and permit cooking only in the community kitchen, limit the use of emergency exits for emergencies only, and specify that tenants should not provide entrance to nontenants who are not their own guests. Cleanliness may be addressed by specifying that individual rooms are to be kept free of odor, garbage, and clutter and noting the location in the building where garbage may be disposed. It may be desirable to provide special alcohol-free living. In this case alcohol consumption can be prohibited on the premises provided that all residents understand and agree to such restrictions. More typically, house rules limit the consumption of alcohol to those of a legal age and then only in the tenants' rooms, never in the common areas. The use of illegal drugs should be strictly prohibited. Policies on visitors may specify hours when guests are welcome in the hotel, for example 9 A.M. until 10 P.M. on weekdays and until 12 P.M. on weekends and holidays. The prohibition of overnight guests is a common practice; small rooms, common bath facilities, and the potential for disruptive behavior all suggest that limited visiting hours will be an aid in maintaining a safe and peaceful hotel. The house rules should clearly state whether pets are allowed and, if so, what kinds. The reporting of maintenance problems should be encouraged, and it is advisable to highlight on the house rules the day of the month when rent is due.

Care should be taken in the preparation of rules to be sure that each is enforceable.

Tenant Selection

Whatever approach to tenant selection is used, the basic issues are which criteria, if any, are used to screen prospective residents, and who is responsible for tenant selections. The criteria used to screen tenants may be as simple as verifying the ability to pay rent or may involve some reference checking. The more lax the tenant selection criteria, the more likely it is that a hotel will attract problem tenants. By establishing at least some minimal criteria for tenant selection, such as a satisfactory report from a previous landlord or shelter provider, a number of prospective tenants with serious problems can be screened out prior to rental.

In buildings that are supervised around the clock, staff is awake and able to mitigate circumstances that might result in threats to safety or disruptions for other tenants. Under such management it would be difficult for a drunk resident to sneak a drinking companion and several bottles of wine up to his or her room after visiting hours without detection by hotel staff. It would be relatively easy to bring a late-night visitor into a building where there is no front desk and each tenant has a key to the front door. Minimally supervised hotels where front door keys are distributed to tenants are best saved for prospective tenants who indicate a willingness to abide by the house rules. Those who indicate an unwilling-

ness would be better housed in a hotel with more structured supervision.

Building design also can help management determine whether prospective tenants would be appropriately housed in a particular hotel. Some SRO residents in any city are frail and barely able to care for themselves. They may be unable to clean their rooms and may at times be incontinent and have a great deal of difficulty keeping themselves clean. Their alternative to living in an SRO hotel is residency in a nursing home. With assistance from visiting health-care workers and scheduled chore services, these residents can maintain themselves in an SRO hotel. It would not be advisable to house such tenants in a building with carpeted rooms and hallways; a building with easily cleanable surfaces such as tile floors would be more appropriate.

Some hotels may be used to house residents associated with a particular social-service program, such as a mental-health agency. In these cases criteria for tenant selection may include a referral by the agency and an agreement on the part of the prospective resident to continue with the agency's treatment program as a requirement for continued residency.

The criteria for screening is only one part of the selection process. The person who makes the selections also has an important role. In most cases this is the hotel manager or desk clerk; whether they live in or outside the building is likely to influence their selection decisions. Staff who live in the hotel are more likely to be familiar with the neighborhood and prospective tenants. Staff who live elsewhere are less likely to recognize a prospective tenant as the person who has repeatedly tried to enter the hotel during late-night hours via the fire escape. Thus it is generally easier for live-in staff to screen out problem tenants.

Because memories fade and staff changes, it is a good practice to keep some type of list of problem tenants. This is a common practice among housing authorities and other property managers. A list of previous tenants who have been evicted and the causes and dates of those evictions can serve as a warning to newer staff. In SRO neighborhoods such a list is best used only as a guide: the alcoholic who destroyed his room and nearly burned down the hotel while on a drinking binge may well be a model tenant as a recovering alcoholic, and access to decent housing may be a factor in facilitating his continued recovery.

Staff Duties

The traditional duties of staff who manage housing units include renting units, collecting rents, making repairs, and keeping common areas clean. Staff who manage SRO hotels are likely to be drawn into responsibilities that exceed these typical duties of housing managers in response to residents' needs. Hotel managers often become check cashers because residents have few options when it comes to cashing checks. Banks typically charge a fee to cash a check if the check casher does not have an account. Since few hotel residents have bank accounts, they are forced to pay the fee, even if it is a government check. Most banks do not solicit business from hotel residents; in fact most banks would prefer that hotel residents not enter their lobbies. The alternative to a bank often is a local grocery store, and typically they, too, charge a fee.

By having the hotel manager cash checks, the resident avoids paying a fee and the manager is able to collect the rent. This sounds ideal, and in many ways it is. It means that rent is paid before the residents have the opportunity to spend their money elsewhere; it also means residents can stash their remaining money in their rooms or on their person and thus are less vulnerable to robbery than if they had to walk back to the hotel from the bank. However, managers who cash checks may become vulnerable because they will need to hold enough cash to continue cashing checks. The best guide is to determine the norm for the neighborhood: Do managers of other SROs cash checks? If so, how much money do they keep? And is there a history in the neighborhood of hotel managers being robbed? Safety for the hotel staff must be the top priority.

Dispensing medication is another role into which hotel staff may be drawn. Many older and chronically mentally ill residents are forgetful about taking medication, and staff can help regulate this activity. The advantage of dispensing medicine is that many of the drugs help mitigate behavioral problems. By dispensing drugs the hotel staff reduces the likelihood of having to deal with a medical or behavioral crisis. However, hotel staff are likely to be untrained, and the potential to dispense the wrong medication is always present. Even though it would seem possible to design a safe system for dispensing medication, it is an activity best left to qualified personnel. In many SRO neighborhoods there are service agencies with personnel trained to do this job. If there are no such agencies, it may be best to help start one.

It is important that the management agent for an SRO hotel define the staff's role. Is it a traditional approach to property management or does it include more activities? If it includes more activities, what are those activities? A decision to move beyond the traditional role should consider the skills of the hotel staff, the residents' needs, and any alternative solutions. Often there are agencies in the community that can provide a particular service and thus eliminate the need for the hotel staff to take on additional duties.

Thoughtful consideration of these issues—access, house rules, tenant selection, and staff duties—will aid in the development of an appropriate management approach. It also is important to establish criteria for selecting hotel personnel, procedures for record keeping and accounting, standards and practices for maintenance and upkeep as well as policies for addressing tenant-landlord problems. Management is the key to providing decent, safe, sanitary, and supportive housing in an SRO hotel, and a concerned and caring hotel manager is essential to successful management.

DESIGNING SRO HOTELS

A basic premise of design is to know the target group for whom the design is intended. This is particularly true in the design of SRO hotels. Without having a sense of the residents and their daily routines, it is difficult to respond to their special needs for such features as cooking facilities or security.

The first step, then, is to determine who is most likely to live in the hotel. Whatever the reasons behind the development of an SRO hotel, there is some expectation of who will reside in the building. By identifying the prospective residents, particular design features that will foster successful residency or management can be included.

There is no set approach to hotel design, but one technique is simply careful consideration of how residents and management will use the building. If a hotel is to house only recovering alcoholics who are participating in a treatment program that has a goal of fostering social interaction, then inclusion of community rooms will help residents achieve this goal. If tenants of a building suffer from serious mental confusion, as can be the case with some elderly or mentally ill and most practicing alcoholics, then it will be helpful to have individual room sinks fitted with faucets that shut off automatically. If women and children are to be housed as a family unit, rooms that are too small to accommodate a mother and her children would create undue stress and be a hindrance to residency. If practicing alcoholics are to be housed, then cooking units in individual rooms should be avoided since the danger of fire is greater with cooking facilities in each room.

After assessing the user group, the next step is to hold discussions with those who have, or have had, responsibility for managing or maintaining SRO hotels. These people can provide insights into hotel design in general and, if they have personal knowledge of a building, can provide invaluable details on the assets and liabilities of that building. A hotel manager can detail the weaknesses in a building's security; someone unfamiliar with the building might fail to realize that a primary source of illegal entry is the exterior fire-escape ladder. Hotel managers and maintenance staff also are likely to know which locks work best under particular conditions.

The final step before designing is personal observation. The designer should observe a number of hotels in operation and pay particular attention to patterns of use. Three excellent books that discuss techniques for observation are *Curious Naturalists* (Tinbergen 1958), *Unobtrusive Measures* (Webb, Campbell, Schwartz, and Sechrest 1966), and *Inquiry by Design* (Zeisel 1981). The following list of questions can serve as a guide for the observing designer. Their purpose is to stimulate thought and to encourage the observer to consider the advantages and disadvantages of various design alternatives.

1. Lobby

   - Is there a lobby? How is it used? By whom? Are some areas used more than others? If there are windows facing the street, how is the space near the window used?
   - What furniture is there? How is the furniture arranged in the space?
   - Is there a television? Is it a dominant feature? Where is it located?
   - Does the layout and furnishing enhance or hinder social interaction? How?

2. Front Desk or Manager's Office

   - Where is the front desk or manager's office located? What is the size of this space?
   - What furnishing and equipment are located there?
   - What can be seen from the desk or office?
   - How often is the desk clerk or manager there?
   - Does the desk clerk or manager interact with people as they come and go from the building?

3. Community Kitchens

   - How many are there? Are they used? By whom? Are some used more often than others?
   - How well is the kitchen(s) maintained?
   - What types of appliances and utensils are there? What appliances are most used? Is there any other furniture there?
   - What areas are used most often?
   - How many people are in a kitchen at the same time? What is the peak number?
   - Do conflicts arise in using the kitchen? Have residents or staff created schedules for kitchen use? What happens at major meal times?
   - Where do people eat: in the kitchen, in their rooms, or elsewhere? How long do individuals typically stay in the kitchen? Do people stand around and talk while they are cooking? Do they use the kitchen to socialize even when they do not have to prepare meals?
   - Could a change in layout improve usage?

4. Bathroom

   - How many bathrooms are there? How many toilets and fixtures are in each?
   - Are some bathrooms used more often than others? Is it because they offer more privacy, have a shower rather than just a tub, have a shower head that people prefer, or is the

shower less likely to have fluctuations in water temperature?
- How clean are the bathrooms? How often are they cleaned? By whom?

5. Laundry Room

- Is there a laundry room? Where is it located in the building?
- How many machines are located there?
- Is it designed to provide tenants with a sense of security?
- Do people stay while doing laundry?
- Is there a place to sit while doing laundry? Do people use the seating?

6. Garbage

- How is the garbage handled? Are there garbage rooms in the hotel for tenants' use or must they take their garbage to a dumpster located outside the building?
- Is garbage build-up a problem?
- Is there a rodent or pest problem due to the way garbage is handled?

7. Hallways

- Is there sufficient lighting in the hallways? Are there any dark corners? Where?
- Do tenants tend to keep their doors open when they are in their rooms? If they do, why (for example, ventilation, because the room is too small, lighting, to see others pass by)?
- If the hallways are noisy, where is the source of the noise (for example, is it from inside or outside the building)?
- How well are the hallways maintained?

8. Rooms

- What size is the room? How many people stay in the room?
- What type of furnishings are there? How are they arranged?
- What do tenants do in their rooms? How much time do they spend in their rooms?
- How much socializing takes place in the rooms? How many visitors are typically there at one time and for how long?
- Where do they sit when they come to the room?
- How many personal belongings have to be stored? Where are personal belongings stored (for example, in drawers, hung on walls)?
- Have tenants personalized their rooms? How?
- If it is cold outside but windows are open, why is that?

- Is there enough light?
- Is there enough ventilation? Where does it come from?
- How many electrical outlets are there? How many are used? What type of electrical appliances and lights do residents have?

9. Outside the Building

- What happens on the sidewalks outside the building?
- Have storefronts been covered over to form blank walls?
- Are there abandoned entryways that now serve as gathering places for illegal activities?

Design Goals

While preparing an SRO hotel design, there are three basic goals to keep in mind: the first is safety; the second is durability and maintenance; and the third is livability. This chapter presumes that most SRO development will occur through renovation of existing structures, the main reason being cost. For the most part rehabilitation is still less costly than new construction.

Overstating the importance of safety considerations in the design of SRO hotels is almost impossible. As has been noted hotels tend to be located in areas of high crime. It is important to design a building to provide maximum protection for the residents. Because a hotel is likely to get hard use from its residents, durability and ease of maintenance are important design factors. Durable products may be more costly than their less durable counterparts, but expensive maintenance repairs can create large deficits in an operating budget. The design of a livable environment is no less important than issues of safety and durability. An SRO hotel should have an environment that invites social interaction yet protects the individual's right to privacy.

Careful consideration of safety, durability, and livability issues should lead to preparation of a sensitive SRO hotel design that addresses the needs of both the resident group to be housed and the managing agent. How close a project will resemble this ideal depends on the level of funding available to carry out the renovation. In all likelihood some elements of the design will need to be eliminated. An awareness of the basic goals of SRO design will provide a guide as to which features should not be eliminated, which can be modified but should not be eliminated, and which can be dropped from further consideration without compromising the renovation.

The nine SRO hotels that I supervised ranged in size from 37 to 156 units and housed almost every type of resident. The following design recommendations represent an accumulation of knowledge gained from this experience. Each of the hotels had been renovated to some degree, some more extensively than others. Some were renovated prior to my coming to work for the agency, and some were renovated during my tenure. As a result I was forced to live with both my own and others' design mistakes. In addition to my own observations, hotel managers, their staff, and tenants told me what they like and dislike about their buildings. The maintenance staff has told me what works and does not work, what is easy to repair, and what cannot be repaired. Service repair people educated me about boilers, steam-heat systems, hot-water heaters, and the like.

Enhancing Safety

A front door that is locked 24 hours a day is a big help in keeping undesirable nonresidents out of the building.

A front desk located near the hotel's entrance will allow for better monitoring of hotel tenants and guests than one located some distance from the front door.

A live-in manager's unit is best located with an orientation to the street or to the major corridor. Location in a secluded corner of the building is quieter but reduces the manager's ability to supervise.

Front doors with windows provide greater security for tenants entering and leaving the building (Fig. 14-6). The general rule is that the larger the pane of glass, the more likely it will be broken, but the smaller the window, the less security it provides. A window in the upper half of the door seems to be a good compromise.

The hotel's office is best placed in a highly visible location both because this allows for super-

Figure 14-6. The Butte Hotel: front door. The entryway has both a side window and a glass door panel. This arrangement provides good security by eliminating blind spots and allowing exiting tenants a full view of the sidewalk.

vision and because it fosters interaction between hotel staff and residents.

Exterior fire escapes allow for entry into the building from the street. Under some circumstances internal stairwells can be substituted. In all likelihood construction of an internal stairway will mean the loss of some rooms but will provide greater security.

Installing alarms on fire exit doors so that an open door will set off an alarm helps reduce use of fire doors for nonemergency use. A choice management must make is where the alarm should sound. It is good to have it sound at the site of the opened door because this encourages residents within earshot to help monitor exit door traffic. In large buildings it may be desirable to have some type of notification at the front desk or manager's office when an exit alarm has sounded. This presumes that most exit doors are not in earshot of front desks or managers' offices.

Locks on the doors of tenants' rooms should be sturdy and difficult to pick. Dead bolts provide good security.

Sprinkler systems are costly to install but are worth every penny. Not only do they save lives but also they save property. Buildings with sprinklers may also cost less to insure. Local codes will specify when a sprinkler system is required; even if not required, one should be installed.

Smoke detectors are an invaluable aid to fire prevention. The more tamperproof, the better the system. Battery-operated detectors may be deactivated by a resident and the battery used in a radio or sold. A hardwired system is best, and local fire regulations will determine if an independent monitoring service is required. Placement of a detector on the wall (if regulations allow) rather than on the ceiling also helps mitigate activation from cigarette smoke.

Doors that separate corridors from stairways and do not contain transparent glass often are propped open, thus defeating their purpose: preventing the spread of fire. Installation of glass panels in the upper portion of the door allows for visual access in either direction, and as a result, reduces the need to prop open the doors.

Enhancing Durability and Maintenance

Upgrading the plumbing system in a building can be costly but is probably well worth the expenditure. An engineer should examine the system and make recommendations. Particular attention should be paid to the condition of the waste pipes, water pressure, and flow. The amount of damage leaking or broken fixtures and pipes can cause is considerable. Piecemeal repairs are time consuming, and walls or floors may have to be torn up to provide access to the problem. The resulting patchwork will probably look like patchwork, and the disruption to tenants is likely to be substantial.

The electrical system also should be upgraded. A fire as the result of overloaded circuits or frayed wiring would threaten lives and is likely to cause damage to the building.

Careful consideration should be given to the installation of safety devices, such as an automatic water feed on an old but adequate steam-heat system. Replacing the old system with a newer, more energy efficient model is often desirable but may not be cost effective.

New elevators require few if any repairs but are costly to install. On the other hand old elevators tend to need ongoing adjustments and repairs by qualified mechanics. The cost of this service, which is apt to include specially manufactured parts, can be considerable. It is best to get an opinion from an expert as to whether to replace or repair elevators.

Valves and vents on steam radiators are likely to be old and in need of replacement. A rule of thumb to follow when selecting replacements is to choose sturdy, unobtrusive valves and vents. Large or protruding parts may attract attention and thus invite tampering.

Some renovated SRO hotels provide cooking facilities in each tenant's room rather than in community kitchens. Pullman, or one-piece, kitchen units often are used as they include a sink, several burners, and a small refrigerator. These units are easy to install and often less expensive than purchasing component parts (Fig. 14-7). However, they can be costly to repair, especially when the compressor is damaged. Moving a pullman unit for easier access means disconnecting the sink's plumbing. An alternative is to build in the component parts, small sink, countertop with cupboard space, hot plate, and a space for a small refrigerator. This allows for repair and replacement of the individual components as needed (Fig. 14-8).

Floor coverings in rooms and hallways of SRO hotels are subjected to heavy use and, in some cases, abuse. As many hotel residents smoke, cigarette burns are a common form of damage. Carpet is attractive and muffles sound but can be difficult to keep clean, shows wear, and is hard to repair once damaged. Linoleum tile is easy to clean and individual tiles can be replaced if damaged; however, it has no sound-muffling qualities and can give the impression of an institution. Before making decisions regarding floor coverings for rooms and hallways, it is best to reflect on who will be living in the hotel. If residents will include practicing alcoholics or those who are

Figure 14-7. The Butte Hotel: pullman kitchen unit. The unit has two burners, countertop space, a sink, a refrigerator, and a storage area. The above-counter cupboards can be purchased separately. The side splash guards were custom designed.

incontinent, tile flooring is recommended. Area rugs or hallways runners can always be added at a later time. For most other types of SRO residents, the kind of floor covering selected need only be a matter of the developer's and managing agent's preference.

Stair treads are best covered with some type of rubberized product. Carpeted stairs may be attractive, but carpet wears quickly on stairs and frayed carpet can be dangerous. The rubberized treads are very durable and provide a firmer base for those who are unsure of their footing.

Ceramic tile and floor drains in community bathrooms are mandatory because it is virtually assured that the toilet, shower, and basins will overflow at some point. When an overflow occurs the water will seek a lower level and, without a properly located floor drain, that lower level will be the floors below. Overflowing toilet water is particularly unpleasant, especially when it leaks into a resident's room or a commercial space.

Surface finishes should be selected with attractiveness and ease of cleaning in mind. A gloss-finish paint is much easier to clean than a flat-base-finish paint and, as a result, looks better for a longer period of time.

Hallway wainscoting is best if it has no ledge on the upper side. This is because a ledge provides an all-too-convenient depository for cigarette butts. One solution is to invert the wainscoting, turning the bottom side, and most likely the narrower side, upward. In that way the old wainscoting can be used in the renovation, only upside down.

Wall-mounted ashtrays are recommended for hallways, and near public telephones and entry doors. Their presence makes the disposal of cigarette butts and other small bits of trash an easy task.

To facilitate cleaning sidewalks outside the building, an exterior faucet is recommended.

Enhancing Livability

Community spaces should be carefully designed to foster maximum use and interaction among residents.

Community kitchens should be designed to provide space for food preparation, cooking, and cleaning up. Appliances to include are range tops, ovens, instant hot-water taps, and possibly a microwave oven. Garbage disposals should be avoided; they can be maintenance headaches. Self-cleaning ovens are more expensive but well worth the cost. CCC is currently testing solid-top ranges in the hope that they will be more durable and easier to keep clean than stoves with typical ring-type burners. Community refrigerators can be a problem, so it is recommended that each unit have its own.

It is best to provide comfortable eating spaces in the community kitchens. This may be as simple as adding a table and four chairs to an existing kitchen. By doing so, the number of rug burns in the hallways, which result from hot pans being placed on the carpet while tenants search for

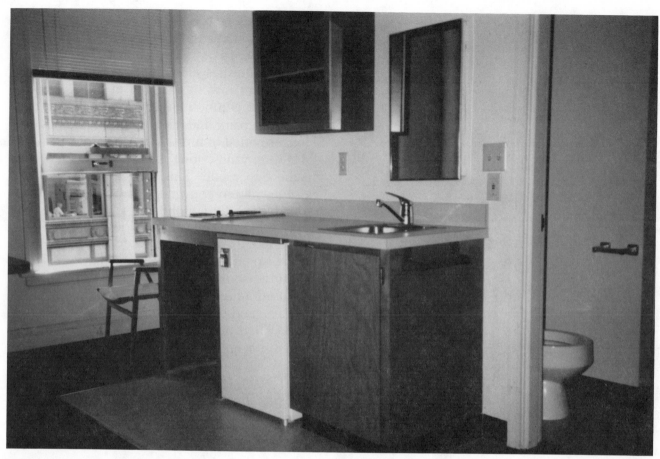

Figure 14-8. The Morrison Hotel, Seattle: alternative to pullman kitchen units. Individual cooking facilities are made of component parts: a two-burner hot plate mounted in the countertop, a refrigerator that slides under the counter, a stainless-steel sink, and cupboard space above and below the counter.

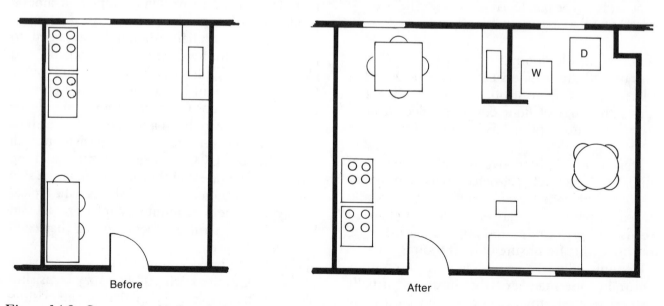

Figure 14-9. Community kitchen: before and after expansion. The enlarged kitchen with its new layout has been well received by hotel tenants. Residents now sit at the square table near the window; before they tended to sit *on* the table behind the door.

their room keys, will be reduced.

Minor changes can make a substantial difference in use patterns. Figure 14-9 shows the layout of a community kitchen before and after remodeling. Before remodeling, the kitchen was crowded and the stoves blocked much of the window. In remodeling, the stoves were moved to provide seating near the window, a wall was removed to provide additional seating, and a washer and dryer were installed. Almost immediately after the remodeling, more tenants began using the kitchen, and ate their meals there instead of taking them back to their rooms.

There is no rule of thumb on the number of residents who can comfortably share a single community kitchen (Fig. 14-10). In several hotels managed by CCC, up to 40 residents share a single kitchen equipped with two four-burner stoves with ovens and a single two-sided sink. Although

this may not be ideal, tenants work their schedules around each other and managers do not receive complaints. For planning purposes the guide might be one kitchen per floor or one for every 30 units.

Every effort should be made to provide common space, in addition to a community kitchen, where residents can gather. This might include a lobby with a view of the street, a lounge area with no exterior windows, or both if space and finances permit. Recognizing that televisions are almost synonymous with SRO hotel lobbies, it is best to keep them away from the front windows since when turned on they tend to be a major barrier to social interaction. If the window area of a lobby is television-free and space for sitting is provided, conversations are almost sure to take place (Fig. 14-11).

Providing space for reading and playing cards

Figure 14-10. The Rich Hotel: community kitchen. This kitchen is in almost constant use. In addition to serving as a place for meal preparation, it is used as a gathering place where residents talk and play cards.

Figure 14-11. The Foster Hotel: front lobby without TV. With the television removed from the front lobby, tenants now use the area for visiting, reading, and sitting.

or other games, in addition to a space for sitting and watching television, is a good idea. These activities might be encouraged in a lounge area that does not have a view of the street. Locating lounges along major building corridors is recommended to facilitate social interaction between lounge users and those who pass by.

Like community kitchens, laundry facilities are not essential elements of SRO hotels, but they add considerably to the livability of a building. Located near a lobby or a lounge or on individual floors of the hotel, their goal should be to provide a safe location where the noise from the machines will not disrupt adjacent activities. It is best to avoid putting laundry facilities in unsupervised areas, such as basements.

Pay phones on each floor of a hotel provide an added convenience for tenants. Most tenants cannot afford their own phone, and most operators of SRO hotels cannot afford to install telephones in each room. As noted earlier pay phones on individual floors become a shared resource, with tenants answering incoming as well as making outgoing calls.

Individual, locking mail boxes provide maximum privacy for residents, but space requirements and the cost of purchasing such boxes is considerable. Also the control of mail-box keys can be a problem. Another option is the delivery of mail by the postal carrier directly to the on-duty staff. In this situation, staff would then distribute the mail either to individual tenants' rooms or sort the mail and place it in individual mail slots, if available, for later pickup by tenants. Most older hotels already have mail slots so this method involves almost no cost. A variation on this approach is to have a single large and secure mail box just inside the entrance doorway. This option works well for hotels that do not have round-the-clock staffing because mail can be safely delivered to a building even when staff is not present. Once staff return the mail can be distributed either to rooms or to mail slots.

There are two basic types of restroom facilities in SRO hotels: those that are designed for use by one person and those that are designed for use by several people. The single-person model may be a room that contains a toilet, a sink, and a tub or a shower—in which case all the facilities are tied up by a single person—or separate rooms for a toilet and a tub or shower. In either situation the single-person model provides maximum privacy for users. The multiple-person design may contain several toilets, sinks, and tubs or showers. If space or cost does not permit single-person facilities, every effort should be made to design maximum privacy into a multiple-person restroom. This would include partitions with locking doors for tub and shower areas as well as for toilets. Also sufficient area for dressing should be provided within each tub or shower area.

Factors that help to determine the number of restrooms needed are the sex of the residents and whether single- or multiperson facilities are possible. Single-person facilities can be unisex; multiperson facilities should be single-sex. Based on experience in Portland, one toilet for up to 8 to 12 persons on a floor seems to work, with about the same number of persons able to share a shower. Tubs are used infrequently but should be available nonetheless. This may seem like an insufficient number of facilities, but it should be remembered that most SRO residents are not wedded to fixed schedules during the day; many have the flexibility to adjust their daily routines. The 8-to-12-person figure should be considered a maximum number for sharing restroom facilities and efforts to reduce that ratio are encouraged.

SRO hotel rooms vary in size, but furnishings tend to be quite standard: bed, dresser, chair, sink, and mirror (Fig. 14-12). Storage areas, such as a wall-mounted cabinet or a regular closet, are very useful because dressers provide only minimum storage. If space permits the addition of a table is recommended.

CCC has found that miniblinds are both durable and attractive window coverings that present few maintenance problems. Window screens can be torn, bent, thrown into the light well, lost, or otherwise abused. This does not mean screens should not be provided, but the operating budget needs to include funds for repair and replace-

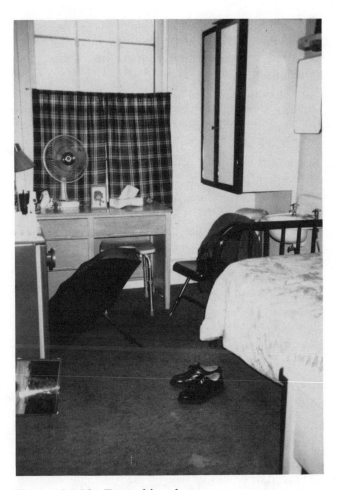

Figure 14-12. Typical hotel room.

ment, or a deposit can be required. In order to maintain maximum ventilation of small SRO rooms, it is best to avoid sealing the upper sash when storm windows are installed. Any ventilation is better than none.

One final way to enhance livability is to provide space for various services within the hotel. Providing a location for local social-service agencies allows their case managers, clinic staff, or other service providers to meet with tenants, thus enabling agencies to spend more time with the hotel's residents. This can help relieve hotel staff of the responsibility of providing social services as well as managing the hotel.

The design and management of SRO hotels require a great deal of forethought and planning.[3] To do a good job at either necessitates a sensitivity to and respect for the residents and their particular needs. Common sense and a willingness to make the trade-offs that will inevitably arise between livability, security, cost, durability, and management style are essential. Haste in design decisions should be avoided. Openness to modifying management approaches should be maintained.

SRO hotels are an essential part of our nation's housing stock. Most likely their residents are individuals whom landlords or care facilities do not want to house. They also are part of the population who many city officials and business people wish would simply disappear. But without SRO hotels to house these low-income people, most would be added to the ranks of the homeless. With care, SRO hotels can become dignified environments for housing some of our poorest citizens.

NOTES

1. Findings from Ille's (1980) study of 100 randomly selected residents show Portland's SRO population to be primarily male (only 7 percent are female); primarily older (68 percent are 45 years of age or older) but also having a substantial number of younger residents (18 percent between the ages of 25 and 34), with an average age of 50. About one-half the residents (43 percent) report being divorced or separated while a slightly higher number (46 percent) report having never married. The vast majority (92 percent) live alone. Just over one-half (52 percent) completed high school, and 13 percent had less than seven years of schooling. Of the 39 percent who report being employed, the most common positions were service worker (44 percent), laborer (21 percent), farm laborer (13 percent) and clerical (13 percent). About one-third (36 percent) reported that they consumed an excessive amount of alcohol, that is, an equivalent of eight ounces of hard liquor or more per drinking occasion, while just under one-quarter (24 percent) reported consuming either light amounts (one ounce or less) or no alcohol at all.

By comparison findings from Chicago (CESO 1985) and New York (Felton et al. 1977) show that SRO populations in those cities differ in some ways but also show many similarities to the SRO population in Portland. Both New York and Chicago have a larger number of female SRO residents, about 47 percent and 20 percent, respectively. Agewise, however, the three cities are quite similar with average ages of 46 (Chicago) and 52 (New York). The percentage of residents who never married is almost identical—49 percent in the Chicago study and 48 percent in the New York sample. Like Portland's population, most of Chicago's SRO residents live alone (82 percent). (No information on this was reported in the New York study.) Level of education appears to be comparable between Portland and New York, where the average grade completed is just over 11. (Reporting differences prevent comparison with the Chicago sample.) As far as employment, the Chicago study reports 42 percent employed, the majority of whom are service or operatives/laborers (68 percent). (No similar figures were available in the New York study.) Information on alcohol consumption was presented only in the Portland study. Even though measures of social interaction were used in all three studies, comparison is difficult. However, each reported levels of social interaction among the majority of residents.

2. Felton et al.'s (1977) study divided a sample of SRO residents into categories of young and old for the purpose of examining differences between the two groups. Figures from that study, which are reported in this chapter, represent a compilation of the two groups.

3. Further assistance on designing SRO hotels can be found in two publications: *Single Room Occupancy Development Handbook* (Church et al. 1985) published by the Portland Development Commission and *SRO Rehabilitation Technical Guide* (1986), prepared by the Asian Neighborhood Design.

References

Asian Neighborhood Design. 1986 (1st draft). *SRO Rehabilitation Technical Guide*. Typescript. San Francisco: Asian Neighborhood Design.

Burki, M. A. 1982. *Housing the Low Income Urban Elderly: A Role for the Single Room Occupancy Hotel*. Ph.D. dissertation. Portland, OR: School of Urban and Public Affairs, Portland State University.

Central City Concern. 1983. *SRO Housing Management Handbook*. Portland, OR: Central City Concern.

Church, W., S. Galbreath, and A. Raubeson. 1985. *Single Room Occupancy Development Handbook*. Portland, OR: Portland Development Commission.

Community Emergency Shelter Organization and Jewish Council on Urban Affairs. 1985. *SROs: An Endangered Species*. Chicago: Community Emergency Shelter Organization.

Eckert, J. K. 1978. *Older Persons Living in Single Room Occupancy Hotels: A Study in Medical Anthropology.* Ph.D. dissertation. Evanston, IL: Northwestern University.

Ehrlich, P. 1976. *Study of the St. Louis "Invisible" Elderly: Needs and Characteristics of Aged "Single Room Occupancy" Downtown Hotel Residents.* Typescript. Department of Community Development, Southern Illinois University.

Felton, B., S. Lehman, A. Adler, and M. Burgo. 1977. Social supports and life satisfactions among old and young SRO hotel tenants. Paper read at Annual Gerontological Society Meeting, San Francisco.

Ille, M. M. 1980. *Burnside: A Study of Hotel Residents in Portland's Skid Row.* Typescript. Portland, OR: Central City Concern.

Levy, H. 1968. Needed: A new kind of single room occupancy housing. *Journal of Housing* 25:572–580.

Reuler, J. B., M. J. Bax, and J. H. Sampson. 1986. Physician house call services for medically needy inner-city residents. *American Journal of Public Health* 76:1131–1134.

Shapiro, J. H. 1966. Single room occupancy: Community of the alone. *Social Work* 2:24–33.

———. 1969. Dominant leaders among slum hotel residents. *American Journal of Orthopsychiatry* 39:644–650.

Siegal, H. A. 1978. *Outposts of the Forgotten.* New Brunswick, NJ: Transaction Books.

Tinbergen, N. 1958. *Curious Naturalists.* Garden City, NY: Anchor Books.

Webb, E. J., D. T. Campbell, R. D. Schwartz, and L. Sechrest. 1966. *Unobtrusive Measures.* Chicago: Rand McNally.

Winberg, E., and T. Wilson. 1981. *Single Rooms: Stories of an Urban Subculture.* Cambridge, MA: Schenkman.

Zeisel, J. 1981. *Inquiry by Design.* New York: Cambridge University Press.

Chapter 15

The Single Room Occupancy Hotel

A Rediscovered Housing Type for Single People

Karen A. Franck

The proportion of one-person households in the United States is relatively high: 24 percent of all households in 1985 compared to 30 percent married couples without children and 36 percent family households with children (U.S. Bureau of the Census 1985). This proportion would be even higher if the census included those people who live in single room occupancy (SRO) hotels and if more single people could afford to live alone. However, housing options designed to meet the needs of single people have decreased dramatically due to urban renewal and gentrification, with the loss of rooming houses, residences for single men and single women, and SRO hotels. Until recently policy makers, planners, and others involved in urban redevelopment saw no advantages in SRO housing; in fact most saw it only as a problem to be resolved through the destruction or conversion of SRO hotels to other uses. Moreover, they neglected to consider where the displaced residents would live and failed to consider them in the development of subsidized low-income housing, which was primarily for families with children.

Single people today are expected to live alone in conventional apartments or houses or to share these with other people. Yet many cannot, by themselves, afford the rents of apartments, much less houses. Sharing with relatives or friends can become very cramped; and many, with or without opportunities for sharing, find themselves homeless. Others may prefer not to share apartments, particularly since they are only rarely designed for sharing by unrelated adults. Others, who may qualify for subsidized housing consisting of complete apartments or who can afford conventional apartments outside the downtown area without subsidies, may prefer SRO hotels for their services, their downtown locations, or the lifestyles they support. The latter group includes students, young or middle-aged working people, and older people who have grown accustomed to living in SRO hotels or who do not wish to leave neighborhoods to which they have cultural or other attachments. Younger and older people with various problems—including alcoholism, frailty, physical handicaps, or mental disturbances—may need services that SRO housing can provide on-site or nearby. Similarly SRO housing with services can serve homeless people who need both housing and services such as health care, counseling, and advocacy in applying for benefits. This chapter describes the potential of the SRO housing type to meet the needs of this wide variety of people. Although the chapter focuses on single people because they constitute the majority of SRO residents, couples also are SRO residents and should not be excluded from considerations in the planning and designing of SRO housing.

The chapter is based on research I conducted when I visited a total of 21 renovated SRO hotels during 1984 and 1985 in Portland, Oregon; Denver; Seattle; San Francisco; and Boston.[1] These visits included tours of the buildings and interviews with the managers or with members of the organizations in charge of management. Design, management, and population characteristics varied widely, as did the degree of renovation. Almost all the buildings, however, had retained their SRO building form of single furnished rooms and shared bath, kitchen, and other facilities; only two had been converted to apartment buildings.

The chapter begins with a discussion of the social advantages of SRO housing. This is followed by a description of three types of renovated residential hotels I visited: those housing heterogeneous populations, including vulnerable residents; those targeted for the elderly; and those housing predominantly younger people. In this discussion nine of the SRO hotels visited are described in detail to illustrate the salient characteristics of SRO housing for different populations and to reveal important design, management, and policy issues. These issues are discussed in the last three sections of the chapter.

SOCIAL ADVANTAGES

Central to the social advantages of renovating or developing SRO hotels are their convenient downtown locations, the services they usually provide, and the additional services they can offer to aid vulnerable residents. Additional advantages pertain to the social environments SROs can promote. Research in several cities indicates that residents in SROs are not the socially isolated loners they were once presumed to be. In her study of nine SROs in New York, Shapiro (1971) found that residents had friends in the building and that some residents served as protectors and spokespeople for other residents and helped with chores, such as cooking. She notes that "we found a profoundly social community . . ." (Shapiro 1971, 23). In a survey of residents in 12 skid-row hotels in San Diego, Erickson and Eckert (1977) found that 87 percent of the residents reported that they knew other

residents in the building and over half of them said other residents helped them out from time to time. In Chicago researchers found extensive networks of helpful and social relationships among SRO residents and discovered that 84 percent of those eligible to vote were registered and that 40 percent attended church (Community Emergency Shelter Organization 1985). Thirty-one percent of the respondents reported social reasons for choosing their place of residence (that is, living near friends or relatives or referred by a friend).

The location of SRO housing often allows residents to maintain social networks that moving to conventional housing in other locations might sever. This is particularly true among minority elderly groups, such as the Chinese in San Francisco. In 1980 SROs in San Francisco's Chinatown accommodated 5,000 elderly or half of all elderly in Chinatown (Liu 1980). Liu reports that living in residential hotels in Chinatown for these people is a matter of choice, not necessity: many residents choose to live near their friends rather than to move away to live with sons and daughters who have moved to suburban homes. For these elderly "life in suburban America would be a form of living death" (Liu 1980, 5), where they would have little chance to be with people who share their language, traditions, and habits or to purchase the goods and services they are accustomed to in Chinatown.

Because many SRO residents are not transient, they are able to develop networks of friendship or acquaintance within the hotels and extending into the surrounding neighborhood. In the Chicago survey half of the residents interviewed had lived in their present unit for two years or more; 29 percent for four or more years. Research cited by Werner and Bryson (1982) indicates that 34 percent of SRO residents in San Francisco had lived in the same building for three years. Residents also may move from one SRO to another but remain in the same neighborhood.

Significantly SROs also allow people to be removed from social interaction if they so choose because the joint use of kitchens, lobbies, or other spaces does not depend on social interaction or exchange. What seems to be important to SRO residents is independence. Burki (1982) interviewed SRO residents who were eligible for

Section 8 elderly housing but had chosen not to move. One of the aspects of their housing they describe as positive was that it allowed independence. Similarly the Chicago researchers suggest that "independence, not isolation, characterizes SRO life" (Community Emergency Shelter Organization 1985, 16). Some SRO residents, however, take self-reliance and independence to an extreme. Erickson and Eckert (1977) report that most SRO residents in their study in San Diego reported that in times of need they would turn to "no one." Some managers of the hotels described later noted that residents could be extremely reserved, having no close relationships and very little contact with other people. There is little reason, however, to view this as a social problem; it is more appropriately viewed as a lifestyle or as a response to individual life circumstances.

Indeed, SROs allow for a diversity of lifestyles and tolerate a diversity of everyday habits and demeanors that show a high degree of independence and that would often not be allowed in conventional housing, particularly housing for the elderly. In the latter, residents may be expected to be neatly dressed; to participate in group activities; to eat at prescribed times or to do their own cooking; and to refrain from certain activities, such as drinking or consorting with people the management considers undesirable. Male residents may be expected to shave. The lack of such requirements or expectations in many SROs is an additional advantage as long as residents' behavior does not disturb the lives of other residents and as long as management is able to maintain a safe and secure environment. Depending on the lifestyles and habits of the residents, this may require a very vigilant staff and clearly stated and enforced rules.

Until recently the law defined SROs as substandard housing partly because they lack private kitchens; but many residents may not see this lack as a great drawback. In Burki's research (1982) only 18 percent of the SRO residents who had moved to Section 8 elderly housing mentioned having a kitchen as a major advantage of their new housing and 35 percent prepared no more than half their meals in their apartments. For this group having one's own kitchen and bath were not the most important differences between the SRO and Section 8 housing; the other ten-

ants and the quality of the building and its management were more important. In the Chicago research the items respondents most frequently reported as positive were the following: the rent rates in their hotels (18 percent), the location of the hotel (18 percent), relationships with other tenants (14 percent), the privacy (14 percent), and the security (10 percent). Dislikes centered on vermin (9 percent), poor building services (8 percent), and the small room sizes (5 percent). Shared bathrooms and the lack of kitchens were less frequently mentioned (2 percent). Significantly many of the qualities that residents disliked can be improved without changing the fundamental characteristics of the SRO hotel and some of those that they liked can be supported and strengthened.

An additional social advantage of SROs is the diversity of population they house. While the racial diversity of the hotels visited in the present research was not substantial, the diversity in terms of age, sex, background, and lifestyle was impressive. This diversity can contribute to the presence and strength of mutual-aid networks. The first type of hotel to be discussed manifests the greatest diversity, but even those targeted for the elderly or for younger people possessed a heterogeneity that was noticeable and that seems to distinguish the SRO housing type from other types.

HOTELS WITH HETEROGENEOUS POPULATIONS

Most of the buildings I visited in this research (15 of 21) house a mixture of residents, many of whom are vulnerable because of alcoholism, mental disturbances, frailty, or other problems. Several of the hotels housing heterogeneous populations were formerly large and fairly grand hotels or residences for single women, and they continue the earlier purpose and functioning of residential hotels by providing linen and housekeeping services, a spacious ground-floor lobby, and a 24-hour desk clerk.

One of these is the Civic Center Residence (CCR) in the Tenderloin district of San Francisco (Fig. 15-1). A large and imposing building of 224 rooms on eight floors, the CCR was for-

Figure 15-1. Civic Center Residence, San Francisco.

Figure 15-2. Civic Center Residence: front desk and lobby.

merly a residence for single working women that was owned and managed by the Salvation Army until 1981, when the Salvation Army proclaimed that this kind of residence was no longer needed and attempted to sell it to a developer. Long-term residents protested and were able to persuade the Tenderloin Neighborhood Corporation (TNDC), a nonprofit development corporation, to purchase and manage the building. There are three lounges on the first floor, including a large and gracious lobby with a front desk and a desk clerk (Fig. 15-2). A laundry room, a music room, and a canteen are in the basement. There also are a children's play room and a roof deck. While there are no kitchens for residents to use, the CCR serves two meals a day seven days a week in the dining room located on the first floor. Linen and maid service are also provided.

Residents of the CCR vary in many ways, although most of them are women. There are young and middle-aged working men and women, a number of whom moved in during the Salvation Army's ownership; some elderly men and women, some of the latter having moved in when they were younger, working women; several displaced homemakers; several single parents with small children; several Vietnam veterans with emotional problems; several mentally disturbed persons; and a number of foreign students.

There is a live-in manager who, along with other staff members, does a considerable amount of counseling with residents. All together there are 17 staff members, including desk clerks and kitchen staff; 14 of them live in the building. In 1984 the manager's goal was to create "an extended family environment," and it appeared that she succeeded with those residents who were interested in participating. Holidays, birthdays, and other special occasions were celebrated with enthusiasm. The CCR, housing one of the most heterogeneous groups of residents of any of the hotels visited, has a warm and congenial atmosphere. Given the mixture of residents and the problems some of them have, the strong community spirit that exists depends considerably on the skills and dedication of the staff.

In 1984 rents at the CCR ranged from $366 to $386 a month, which included meals and maid service. Many residents and potential residents could not afford these rates, resulting in a high vacancy rate. TNDC then developed a new payment plan: $215 to $250 a month with the option of an additional $195 a month for meals and maid service. Following a marketing campaign in 1988, there is no longer a vacancy problem. TNDC also has contracted with service providers to lease rooms for their clients. One such program is for homeless veterans who have drug- or alcohol-dependency problems; another is a rehabilitation program for homeless people that gives them temporary housing and referrals for employment.

The Bush Hotel, in the Chinatown section of Seattle, was built in 1915 and operated for many years as a first-class businessmen's hotel of 195 rooms, conveniently located near the train station. It was purchased by the Seattle Chinatown International Preservation and Development Authority, and renovations were completed in 1981. It is now a combination SRO hotel and community center with retail spaces (Fig. 15-3). There are 88 SRO rooms for transient and long-term residents; 16 Section 8 apartments with small kitchens and baths; and 6 apartments and a community room for persons leaving mental institutions, which are administered by a special program. Some of the SRO rooms have private bathrooms. There are no kitchen facilities for the SRO rooms, but hot plates are permitted. The original lobby and front desk have been retained along with 24-hour desk service (Fig. 15-4).

As a community center the Bush contains a wide variety of spaces for social-service programs and for offices of social-service agencies. The offices of the Development Authority are in the building along with services for the Chinatown neighborhood that include counseling, a health clinic, a meal program for the elderly, an assembly hall, and the offices of a Chinese neighborhood newspaper. These spaces are reached through the back or the side entrances to the building, while the SRO rooms are best reached through the front entrance and the lobby. At the street level, off an interior walkway extending from the side entrance, are retail spaces—including a Korean restaurant, two antique stores, and a jewelry store. Other storefronts, including a grocery store (Fig. 15-5), are accessible from the street in front of the building. A greenhouse graces the roof, and the city has built a park in the back of the building.

Figure 15-3. The Bush Hotel, Seattle.

The SRO residents at the Bush are almost all men; many are elderly who lived at the Bush while they were employed but are now retired. Others are still employed. Most of the residents are from minority groups, including native Alaskan, Native American, Filipino, Chinese, Southeast Asian, and black. About one-half to three-quarters are alcoholics. A core group of 40 to 50 people have lived at the Bush six months or more, and within that group are some who have lived there 20 to 40 years. Among these are migrant workers and cannery workers who send money to their families in Alaska or the Philippines, families they may not have seen for 20 years or more. Some residents can afford to live in conventional apartments or are eligible for the Section 8 apartments in the building, yet they prefer not to move. The manager reports that one resident did not want his room painted. "They are entrenched in their own rooms. . . . They put their feelings for family or other things they're missing into their room, their space."

The hotel is known on the street as an old men's hotel, but some young men do move in to prey on older residents. Problems relating to drugs and fist fights do occur, and those tenants are evicted. Other younger men do not cause problems and seem to be following the pattern of the older residents of keeping largely to themselves. According to the manager many of the residents are life-long loners who prefer to go their own ways. In fact, when some residents die, the manager is unable to locate their relatives, which is not uncommon in SRO hotels with res-

THE BUSH HOTEL

Located in downtown Seattle, just out of the heavy traffic district, offers the finest accommodations for the traveler at truly "sensible rates," with service equalled only by much higher priced hotels.

You will like this hotel for its friendly atmosphere The Bush is keeping pace with low cost travel comfort by introducing its **"one price policy"** for all.

5 Minutes to
27 hole Municipal
Golf Course

5 Minutes to
Finest Salmon
Fishing

5 Minutes to
Boeing Airport

5 Minutes to
Shows, Shops and
Parks

A TYPICAL $1.00 ROOM

NEW LOWER RATES . . . ONE PRICE POLICY

One Person $1.50   Two Persons $2.00
With Private Bath and Free Garage

One Person 75c and $1.00   Two Persons $1.25 and $1.50
With Detached Bath—Garage Storage 25c

All Rooms Have Outside Exposure and Modern in Every Detail
Special Weekly and Monthly Rates

PRINTED IN U.S.A.

Figure 15-4. Early brochure of the Bush Hotel. Lobby and rooms look very similar today.

Figure 15-5. The Bush Hotel: grocery store next to hotel entrance.

idents like those at the Bush. The manager reports, "Some men have become totally isolated from their families. SROs provide a place for these people to gather and chitchat and have some involvement without commitment."

Rents are $155 to $200 a month for the SRO units and $20 for an additional person. Residents must have a steady source of income when they move in. The staff includes a manager who does not live in the building, five desk clerks, three housekeepers, three janitors, and one maintenance man.

The Bush is an unusual example of a renovated SRO hotel because it incorporates a wide variety of social and commercial uses. The various social services and facilities at the Bush are geared more toward the residents of the surrounding neighborhood or toward visitors to Chinatown. The SRO residents tend not to use any of the services in the building. Nonetheless, the different commercial spaces help finance the SRO housing, and the proximity of all the differ-

Figure 15-6. The Butte Hotel, Portland: The Butte is on the right.

ent social and commercial services makes the Bush Hotel a pleasant and lively setting. This is quite the opposite of a dreary and deteriorated SRO shunned by all but its own residents. On a tour of the Bush Hotel in 1982, the staff director of the U.S. House Committee's Task Force on Rental Housing was so impressed by its sense of community and its success that he was relieved of "all his previous misgivings about whether federal assistance should be provided to the SRO-type living style" (Werner and Bryson 1982, 1002).

The Butte was one of the four hotels in Portland selected to participate in the SRO/Section 8 demonstration program in 1983. The Portland Development Commission provided low-interest financing for the rehabilitation and local lenders provided additional financing. Residents who qualify receive rent subsidies from the Public Housing Authority of Portland.

Once a hotel for loggers, dock workers, and mine workers and then reportedly a brothel in the 1940s, the Butte was purchased and renovated by the Central City Concern (CCC, formerly the Burnside Consortium) and reopened in 1984 (Fig. 15-6). It has a total of 37 rooms on two floors above ground-floor commercial spaces, with no hotel spaces on the ground floor other than the small entrance vestibule. Each room has a pullman kitchen. There is no lobby or common social space, but in the basement there is a senior center sponsored by another agency, which older residents may use. An elevator and four rooms for the handicapped allow elderly or disabled residents to live in the bulding. Many of the rooms are 100 to 130 square feet and are long and rectangular, allowing for a separation of functions (see figure 15-18). Residents have their own keys to the front door, which is always locked. There is no buzzer, intercom, or desk clerk so the building is difficult to enter. Storefront spaces include a health clinic, a printing shop, a nonprofit restaurant, and a dry cleaner.

Most of the residents are male; they range in age from 20 to 90; most are low-income recovering or practicing alcoholics who are in control of their drinking. A dozen have jobs; others do part-time or casual labor. Several of the seven women residents were referred from a nearby shelter for battered women. Residents pay 30 percent of their gross income for rent, which is $229 a month, and some receive full subsidies because they have no income. All rentals are one-year leases.

Both the manager and the assistant manager live in the building. They screen applicants carefully, interviewing them two or three times, and require that residents be quiet tenants, allowing "no sloppy drunks." The building is very well maintained and the manager is extremely diligent, treating residents with respect and understanding but also with firmness. He does some counseling with residents and refers many to the appropriate agencies and services. According to him, the Butte provides occupants with "the nicest living conditions they've had in years, or ever. Many of the people thank me when they pay the rent." As in all the rehabilitated SROs in Portland, the halls and rooms are newly painted and carpeted, with new plumbing and new lighting throughout the building. Several residents have done additional decorating of their rooms, including planting flower boxes on their windowsills.

The Estate, also in Portland, is one of the first SRO hotels to be renovated and managed by CCC (see figure 14-1). Formerly occupied by loggers and other laborers, it now contains 156 rooms—many of the rooms are as small as 80 square feet (Fig. 15-7)—and houses a large number of practicing alcoholics. The lobby is on the ground floor facing the street, and the front door is controlled from the front desk where there is a desk clerk 24 hours a day (see figure 14-3). Storefronts include a grocery store; a luncheonette; and an outreach program for residents of the Estate and others from the neighborhood, which offers used clothing and cooking equipment and assistance with housekeeping and personal hygiene. There is a community kitchen on each of the three residential floors, and a laundry is located in the basement. The fourth floor is an alcohol-free community. As the manager pointed out, the concrete floors are good design features for the Estate: there is no carpet to wear down and the floors can easily be mopped.

The residents are almost all male, from different racial backgrounds and of different ages. One-third of them are daily drinkers. Rents are $8 a night, $32 a week, and $110 a month. Linens

Figure 15-7. The Estate Hotel, Portland: resident's room.

are provided, and rooms are checked each week. There are a live-in manager, a janitor, and a housekeeper, as well as five desk clerks. Rules on noise and guests are strictly enforced. People who are known to be drug pushers, prostitutes, or violent alcoholics are turned away. A hard-nosed but sensitive resident manager contributes to the livability of the Estate. The manager reported that residents have become involved in the upkeep of the building and that a sense of community has developed. He advises: "You have to take time, and you have to understand them. . . . In order to do what I wanted to and make it an involved hotel, you have to listen. A lot of it is true caring." By virtue of its design and its management, the Estate is able to fulfill an essential but often forgotten function: providing safe and sanitary low-cost housing for various people, including practicing and recovering alcoholics.

HOTELS TARGETED FOR THE ELDERLY

Many of the hotels previously described have elderly residents who live with a wide variety of other tenants. But several other hotels that were visited house 50 percent or more elderly residents. Two in San Francisco are owned and managed by the Chinese Community Housing Corporation (CCHC): the Clayton and the Tower.

The Clayton, located in Chinatown, once housed seamen and other working men (Fig. 15-8). It now contains 82 rooms on three floors above the ground-floor commercial spaces. The commercial spaces include two small restaurants, a printing shop, and an accounting office. A senior center in the basement provides medical attention, counseling, and meals to elderly people in the neighborhood. On each residential floor there is a kitchen with a small dining room next to it. The floors are segregated by sex: the first for women, the upper two for men (Fig. 15-9). All the residents are over 60; many of them are Chinese and Filipino; some of the men have lived there 30 years or longer. Although some of the residents are employed, most receive their income from Social Security. The average rent is $125 a month.

There is a resident manager and janitor. Tenants are supplied with sheets. While the men tend to be loners, the women are friendlier with each other. Although they rarely share cooking, they often chat as they eat, each in her own room with the door open, conversing across the narrow hallway. The atmosphere at the Clayton seems quiet and sedate.

The Tower (Fig. 15-10), in the North Beach district on the edge of Chinatown, was originally home to poets and Italian fishermen (Jack Kerouac reportedly lived there). In the 1960s residents were hippies; in the 1970s and 1980s the Tower became a shelter of last resort. At that time the landlord, in an attempt to vacate the

Figure 15-8. The Clayton, San Francisco.

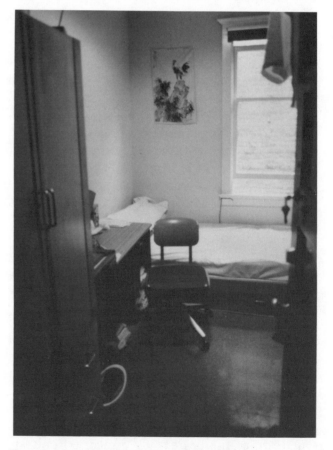

Figure 15-9. The Clayton: resident's room.

building, hired ex-convicts to manage the hotel and to harass tenants. When CCHC and the Economic Development Potential purchased the building in 1983, 17 residents were living there and drug dealing was rampant. This problem continued and required the eviction of several residents to be resolved.

The elderly residents at both the Clayton and the Tower are the type of people described by Liu (1980): elderly Asians who enjoy living in or near the Chinatown neighborhood and who benefit from its commercial and social services. Some, or even many, would rather live in SRO accommodations and be in Chinatown than live in larger or more complete dwellings elsewhere. By improving the safety, cleanliness, and livability of SRO housing in the Chinatown area, CCHC is helping these residents maintain their ties to the neighborhood.

HOTELS FOR YOUNGER PEOPLE

These buildings house primarily young or middle-aged independent people who for the most part have no particular vulnerabilities. They are the Stewart House in Seattle, the Aarti in San Francisco, and the Apex Belltown Co-op in Seattle. Each is an SRO building without the vigilant management that is characteristic of the renovated hotels for more heterogeneous populations.

The Stewart House, in the Pike Place Market area of Seattle, is remarkable in several ways. The original building, built in 1902, was one of the early wood-frame workingmen's hotels in the area (Fig. 15-11). The building was operated as a hotel until 1977, when it was closed for noncompliance with codes. As part of the preservation and renewal plan for the Pike Place Market, which gives preference to restoration and rehabilitation over new construction, the Pike Place Market Preservation and Development Authority decided to maintain the building's traditional use as an SRO and to restore it to its original appearance, with historic accuracy to qualify for tax deferments. Accordingly the asphalt siding was removed and a second layer of wood siding was applied; existing skylights were reglazed and brought up to code. In addition to restoring the

Figure 15-10. The Tower, San Francisco.

Figure 15-11. The Stewart House, Seattle. Original 1902 building is on the right.

original building, now consisting of 39 SRO units, a second connecting building was built to house 48 Section 8 apartments. The SRO units, ranging from 100 to 150 square feet, have small sinks, refrigerators, and stoves. As in many of the hotels, the original furniture in the rooms—bed, table, chair, and chest of drawers—was retained (Fig. 15-12). All the woodwork, including wood floors, has been refinished, creating a very spare but warm and airy feeling. In a small lounge, which was the original lobby, are the hotel's original captain's chairs. The new lobby and front desk are shared with the Section 8 apartments, as is the courtyard.

Each of the 34 rooms on the two floors is 100 square feet or smaller. Some tenants have added lofts, with the permission of management. There is a kitchen on each floor but without a refrigerator; tenants can have refrigerators in their rooms. There is one community lounge on the second floor. The residents, young white men and women who are working and elderly Chinese men and women, live on integrated floors. The management plans to maintain this population

mix of 50 percent young people and 50 percent elderly Asians. In screening applicants the manager tries to evaluate a person's ability to live in this mixed population. The average rent is $140 a month. There is a live-in manager.

Twelve hundred square feet of commercial space below the Stewart House, which is on a slope, includes a barber shop, a low-cost cafeteria, and various stores and cafés popular in the Pike Place Market area.

The SRO tenants at the Stewart House are young working people whose average age is 30. There are 32 men and 8 women. Seven are seamen who like to keep a pied-à-terre to come home to. In keeping with the tradition of the building, preference is given to seamen. Rents range from $168 to $203 a month, depending on the size and the location of the room. There is a live-in manager, a part-time assistant manager, and a desk clerk who is on duty in the mornings. The SRO units are popular, with a waiting list of 150. The manager reports that "seamen make a good community, like men on a ship."

The Aarti in San Francisco was supposedly

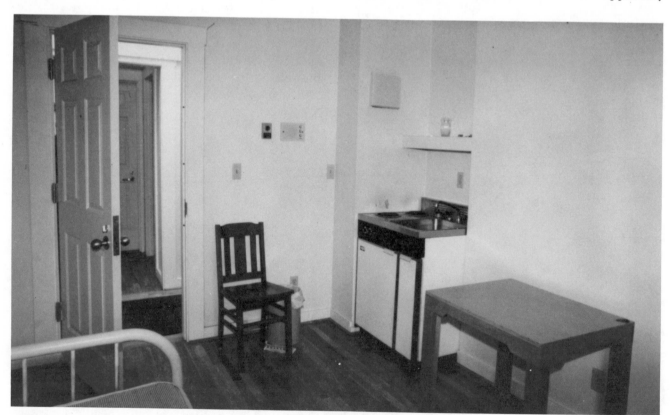

Figure 15-12. The Stewart House: two views of an unoccupied room.

built as a brothel right after the 1906 San Francisco earthquake to serve the many workers rebuilding the city (Fig. 15-13). Over the years it was a flophouse and then a "shooting gallery" for addicts; it was finally closed down by the police. The building was eventually purchased by the Tenderloin Neighborhood Development Corporation (TNDC), which also owns the Civic Center Residence. The renovated Aarti consists of 40 small rooms, many of which are only 60 square feet. Each of the three floors of rooms, over the ground-floor commercial spaces, has a large and airy common kitchen and adjoining dining/living space. The kitchens are equipped with large commercial stoves and refrigerators. The living/dining spaces are furnished with comfortable couches and armchairs (Fig. 15-14). The atmosphere in these spaces, as in the building generally, is warm, friendly, and lived-in.

TNDC worked with the Asian Neighborhood Design (AND), neighborhood residents, and future tenants in redesigning the building (Comerio 1982). AND helped develop built-in furniture for the rooms. In one room a storage

platform was designed to be built over the door, supported by drawers and a closet on each side. Much of the construction was done by the tenants, and each was allotted $100 to furnish his or her room. Comerio reports: "We saw each of them become aware of and make choices about their living environment. They transformed a hotel into a home" (Comerio 1982, np). Residents also have stripped and refinished all the doors and paneling in the hallways and some have planted a flourishing roof garden.

All the residents at the Aarti are young or middle-aged. Many are single black men. There are a number of single white men and women, a few Asian men and women, and even a few single parents who share their small rooms with children. Some of the residents receive public assistance; some work and some are students. The highest rent is $198 a month, with double occupancy costing $227. There is a live-in manager who works part-time and two part-time maintenance men. The door is always locked; there is a buzzer system. Unlike in many renovated SROs guests are allowed to stay the night at no extra

Figure 15-12. *(cont.)*

Figure 15-13. The Aarti, San Francisco.

Figure 15-14. The Aarti: common kitchen and part of common living room.

charge. Residents are responsible for the housekeeping of their rooms and several voluntarily clean other areas as well.

Some residents share cooking and take turns babysitting the small children who live there. Several are interested in establishing a cooperative ownership structure and hold monthly meetings on the subject. Those who are eager to form

a cooperative complain that too many of the residents are uninterested in it and live there "only because the rent is cheap." In 1986 residents of the Aarti signed a renters' cooperative agreement with TNDC, which is the next phase in forming a cooperative. Residents now have more control over discretionary funds, and the manager is hired and supervised by the Aarti board of directors composed of Aarti residents. The spirit of the Aarti is remarkable; rather like a very homey college dormitory but with a more heterogeneous population.

The Apex Belltown Co-op in Seattle is what many Aarti residents hope the Aarti will become: a cooperative. The Apex, formerly a 58-room SRO, reopened in 1984 as a limited-equity SRO cooperative, the only one in the country (Fig. 15-15). The history of its transformation is complicated (Collins 1985) and involves the care and commitment of a number of organizations and individuals, including a local architect, Ann Hirschi. Hirschi and others were determined to protect low-cost housing in downtown Seattle, where land prices and rents are being driven up by the prospect of high-density, high-profit development. They also were intent on maintaining the SRO building type and lifestyle, meaning that living rooms, kitchens, and bathrooms are shared and the individual bedrooms are small (130, 280, and 440 square feet).

A long struggle to realize these intentions led to an intricate ownership arrangement for the Apex. A condominium structure was created so that the earlier owner of the building owns the ground-floor furniture store and the 21-share cooperative owns the upper two floors. Each resident makes a down payment of $1,155 and then pays $161, $246, or $331 a month in carrying costs.

There are 21 single rooms on two residential floors. The corner of the building with the best views of the bay was reserved for one of the shared dining/living/kitchen areas on each floor (Figs. 15-16 and 15-17). Each floor also has another shared kitchen and another shared living room. Five residents share each kitchen and have their own individual refrigerators in the kitchens. The shared areas have been decorated and furnished by residents and are warm and inviting spaces. Residents also have done colorful tile and mosaic work in the bathrooms and kitchens. Decks on the second floor and the roof provide outdoor space.

To live at the Apex one has to be an artist, which is defined as earning substantial income from or devoting substantial time to the fine arts, dramatic arts, photography, dance, or writing. Eighty percent of the residents must earn incomes below $18,000. Two-thirds of the residents are women. Ages range from 20 through 50. Many have jobs that are not related to their artistic interest; some are studying art. There is no live-in manager, and tenants do all the maintenance chores themselves. Some help is given by a management firm. Residents at the Apex work hard to assign and do the chores of maintaining the building. They also are grappling with the problems of sharing kitchens; these seem to center on different perceptions of what are acceptable levels of tidiness and cleanliness.

Like the Aarti, but unlike many SROs that have more extensive management and housekeeping services, residents of the Apex have to coordinate tasks and exchange information in order to manage the building themselves. These two buildings depend on interaction and cooperation among residents. This alters the model of SRO housing as a hotel where management relieves tenants of responsibility and they can remain quite isolated if they so choose, as at the Bush Hotel. The cooperative ownership structure at the Apex also provides a level of legal and emotional commitment that is absent from other types of renovated SROs and that is not originally part of the SRO model. The Apex and the Aarti illustrate how the SRO building type can be adapted to a type of collective housing for people interested in cooperative living arrangements.

Figure 15-15. Apex Belltown Co-op, Seattle.

Figure 15-16. Apex Belltown Co-op: common living area.

Figure 15-17. Apex Belltown Co-op: common kitchen.

DESIGN ISSUES

Perhaps the most fundamental design question regarding SROs is whether they should be converted to apartments with private kitchens and baths or be renovated to maintain the SRO style of shared facilities. In this research some of the most costly renovations involved conversions of SROs to apartments. In Denver the Ecumenical Housing Corporation purchased and converted the Olin from 150 hotel rooms to 107 Section 8 apartments. In Boston Rogerson House, a non-profit organization working with the elderly, purchased and then converted the Beacon from 373 hotel rooms to 132 Section 8 apartments. Such conversions reduce the number of low-cost housing units available. A strong argument has been made for the cost effectiveness of maintaining the SRO format; experts have estimated that for the cost of converting SRO units to one Section 8 apartment and subsidizing it, the government could renovate and subsidize four SRO units (National Trust for Historic Preservation 1981; Werner and Bryson 1981). Other arguments in favor of shared facilities are that they generate more social interaction between residents and allow for more support and opportunity for assistance, when needed, from staff.

The SRO housing model, whereby residents live in private furnished rooms and share essential facilities, requires very careful design of the private rooms as well as of the shared spaces. Subtle aspects of the design of these spaces become more important than the design characteristics of bedrooms, living rooms, kitchens, or bathrooms in conventional apartments. The private room must fulfill many more functions than a bedroom, and the shared spaces must supplement the private spaces extensively and must serve a large number of unrelated individuals without appearing institutional.

Not only should an SRO unit accommodate a great variety of functions, but also it should promote feelings of privacy, security, and personal identity. The functions of an SRO room and how room and furniture design can support these functions are aptly described by Mostoller in chapter 13. The hotels visited in this research reinforce the value of many of the guidelines Mostoller has developed. First is the need to de-

sign a room and furniture that will support a wide variety of activities and the storage space to support those activities. These include sleeping, eating, reading and writing, relaxing, entertaining, personal hygiene, grooming, and housekeeping. Mostoller omits meal preparation because he assumes the existence of a shared kitchen rather than cooking facilities in each room. However, if kitchen facilities are included in the rooms, this adds an additional set of functions.

Regarding room size and shape, Mostoller recommends a "long room," the optimum dimensions being 16 feet long and 8 feet wide. The long dimension allows a division of the room into subspaces differentiated by function. Several rooms I visited had this feature. At the Butte two residents had divided their rooms into a sleeping area (bed and side table) and a sitting/eating area (table and chairs or lounge chair) (Fig. 15-18). However, the square footage Mostoller recommends (128 square feet) is larger than many existing SRO rooms and larger than the minimum established by the city of Portland. What does seem important, however, is the long dimension so that given a choice, as in new construction, an oblong room (such as an 8-foot by 12-foot room of 96 square feet) is preferable to a square room (such as a 10-foot by 10-foot room of 100 square feet). L-shaped rooms also allow a separation of zones (see Leavitt's description of the congregate house in chapter 8.) There is nothing, however, except maybe the cost of construction, to justify a complete standardization of rooms within a SRO building. Many of the hotels visited had rooms that varied in size and shape and were sometimes rented at different rates. This variety is likely to give residents a greater sense of individuality. Variations in both size and shape should be considered.

Ceilings higher than the current norm of 8 feet are very important. They give a greater feeling of spaciousness and offer a greater opportunity to build lofts, as some residents have done at the Aarti and the Tower. Other considerations in room design include good ventilation, some system of shades or blinds for windows, and enough electrical outlets. In hotels I visited several residents had TVs as well as stereos and electric musical instruments.

All the hotels visited, except the Tower, pro-

Figure 15-18. The Butte Hotel: separate sitting and sleeping spaces in one resident's room.

vided furniture in the rooms. This often was furniture that was in the hotel prior to its renovation and usually included a sink, a bed, and a chest of drawers and sometimes a chair and a table or a desk. Some hotel rooms had a built-in closet or a wardrobe, but some did not. At the Clayton a nonprofit design firm designed captain's beds with drawers, desks, and dressers to make maximum use of space in the small rooms.

In general the rooms visited support the importance of the furniture design characteristics outlined by Mostoller: that items of furniture fulfill multiple functions, that the furniture not be bulky, and that items be designed to incorporate storage space. The need for storage space is acute, including storage space for cooking utensils and cans or packages of food. Being able to put things away, either on display or hidden, gives residents a chance to make their rooms more orderly and more comfortable for entertaining. And being able to choose which items will be on display and which will be hidden from view gives them more control over their rooms. Making pieces light enough to move allows residents to rearrange the furniture, which is another way for them to exert control and arrange things in an order that they have selected. However, when the rooms are very small, built-in pieces free floor space for movement, as at the Aarti (Comerio 1982).

Some residents also like to decorate their rooms (Fig. 15-19 and 15-20). Having an opportunity to do this gives residents the chance to establish a sense of familiarity and self-identity, to make themselves "at home."

The kitchen, lobby, and other indoor and outdoor seating spaces offer residents a respite from their own rooms while still being in their own building. Such spaces offer an opportunity to observe activities and people and to interact with others or not, depending on one's inclination. A range of social spaces that vary in size and purpose also is valuable. A choice of spaces insures a greater probability that a resident will find a space to be alone, or with very few other people, or where the other occupants are congenial. Outdoor spaces in a back yard, courtyard, or on a roof deck also are desirable. The Aarti, the CCR,

Figure 15-19. The Biltmore Hotel, Portland: resident's room.

and the Apex all have roofdecks, and the Stewart House has a courtyard.

Only one hotel visited—the Butte—has no social spaces whatsoever, and one—the CCR—has an amazing range of them. The Aarti and the Apex have living/dining spaces on each floor. Similarly the Heights in New York City has a small lounge on each floor, a dining room on the ground floor, and a basement recreation room that opens onto a back yard (Fig. 15-21).

Shared bathrooms and kitchens must supplement the private rooms by providing necessary facilities; they must accommodate heavy use and use by different individuals at the same time. Yet these facilities should not appear so durable or efficient that they assume an overly institutional character. One recommendation for bathrooms is to separate the watercloset from the bath or shower to allow each to be used simultaneously by different people.

The advantages of shared kitchens over a kitchen unit in each room are lower cost, the opportunity for social interaction, and the chance for staff to oversee cooking conditions, a particularly important issue in buildings where residents are forgetful about leaving the stove on or letting garbage accumulate. If community kitchens are chosen, private refrigerators in each room are essential because of theft from shared refrigerators. The Apex provides an individual refrigerator in the common kitchen for each of the residents who share that kitchen. Presumably that works because so few residents use each kitchen and because the building is a cooperative. The kitchens should include space for a table and chairs where residents may eat or sit while their food is cooking. A dining/living space that extends out from the kitchen is another possibility, as at the Apex and the Aarti.

The SRO hotel, unlike many conventional apartment buildings, often includes storefronts and additional interior spaces that can be leased out for commercial purposes or for social-service programs. These spaces can generate revenue that helps support the operation of the hotel. Most of the hotels visited have several store fronts. In Portland, with the gentrification of the Burnside neighborhood where many hotels are located, the rental of storefront spaces brings in revenue and creates a lively street life that many residents enjoy watching. Some uses, however, such as a jazz club, generate noise that keeps residents awake. The choice of commercial tenants should be compatible with residential life and, when possible, provide services for tenants, such as low-cost restaurants and grocery stores.

Storefront spaces also can be leased to social agencies and programs that benefit the SRO residents living above. The Butte and the Clayton lease space to senior citizen centers that residents may use. The Bush Hotel is particularly unusual in containing a wide variety of commercial spaces *and* social-service programs. It is essential, however, that access to the commercial spaces and to the social-service spaces be independent of the interior of the hotel. In the Bush Hotel all the commercial spaces are reached through entrances that are separate from the hotel entrance. An SRO hotel, because it is housing for long-term occupancy and serves the function of home

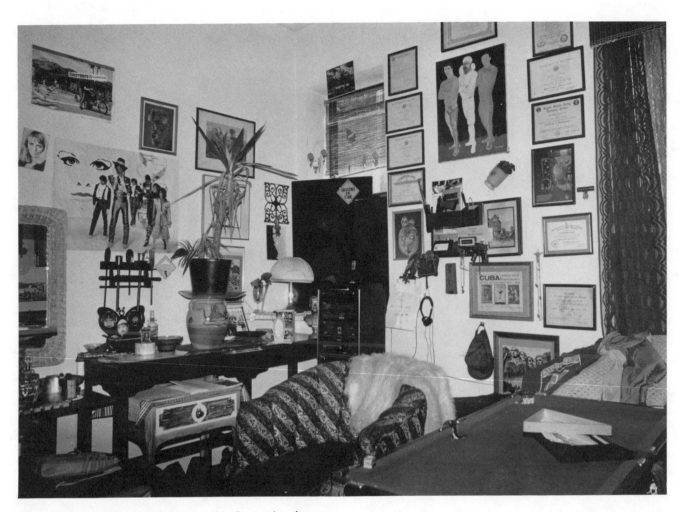

Figure 15-20. The Heights, New York: resident's room.

for its residents, should not be public as a hotel for transients is, where the lobby may contain stores, restaurants, and cafés, all easily accessible to the public as they pass through the hotel entrance and lobby. Even social-service spaces that serve hotel residents but also bring in clients from outside the hotel should have entrances independent of the hotel's circulation space.

Storage space outside the individual rooms is another design concern. At a few hotels visited but not described here (the Barth and the Olin in Denver), such storage space is provided and is rented by residents. Rather than assuming that potential residents will have no belongings and will accumulate none, it makes more sense to view them as people with a past and a future, either of which may contain valued material items. Having storage space available in their own rooms and elsewhere should enable residents to pursue richer and more orderly lives.

That, indeed, may be the ultimate goal of renovating SROs—to enhance both of these aspects of life.

The difficulty of meeting the paired goals of richness and order is particularly great when choosing and maintaining materials and finishes. Durability in the face of hard use and possible abuse and ease of cleaning and maintenance suggest neutral, hard surfaces while the need for warmth and texture suggest softer, richer surfaces (including carpeting). As Burki describes in chapter 14, many SRO design decisions should be based on a careful consideration of the needs and habits of the particular types of residents to be housed. This is particularly true in the choice of materials. Durability and ease of maintenance are extremely important in hotels where many residents have problems with personal and environmental cleanliness. This is the case at the Estate, where the concrete floors, despite their

Figure 15-21. The Heights: back yard.

institutional quality, are appropriate. In this example the need to maintain order, in the form of cleanliness, outweighs the need to have a rich and textured environment. It is essential, however, to have other hotels, with warmer, less institutional interiors, to which residents may move when they gain control over their behavior. The Butte meets this need by providing a greater balance between richness and order.

MANAGEMENT ISSUES

The hotels visited in this research house a significant variety of residents. This illustrates both the variety of people who can be accommodated in an SRO building, such as the Civic Center Residence, and the range of uses for which the SRO model can be adapted—from the Bush Hotel (which is closest in design and management to a hotel for transients) to the Apex (which is financially and socially a cooperative). Some of the

hotels I visited serve a high proportion of residents with special needs, such as the Estate and the Butte. Neither of these, however, is exclusively for such residents. Other buildings, also based on the SRO model, provide housing exclusively for people who have similar special needs. In New York City the three SRO residences sponsored by St. Francis Friends of the Poor house chronically mentally ill people, and the West Side Cluster houses mentally handicapped women (Greer 1986). Some hotels are intended exclusively for recovering alcoholics, such as the Leo Hotel in Los Angeles, owned and operated by the SRO Housing Corporation, and the Arlington in San Francisco, operated by the St. Vincent de Paul Society. The model of single furnished rooms, shared kitchens and baths, and support services also is being adopted for housing homeless people with AIDS.

This adaptability, and usefulness, of the SRO model should not, however, obscure its potential for providing low-cost housing for people without special needs and for integrating people of different ages, backgrounds, and daily pursuits, including working people of all ages.

The population being housed in a particular building should help determine what management approach is used. Hotels that house some residents with special needs—such as the Civic Center Residence, the Butte, and the Estate—have managers and other staff who are vigilant and involved, providing counseling and referrals to other services. Hotels such as the Bush and the Tower are well maintained and managed, with particular attention to maintaining security, but residents are not as closely monitored for other needs. And at the Aarti, the Stewart House, and the Apex, residents are almost completely on their own. As outlined by Burki these approaches are appropriate responses to the needs of the particular types of residents being housed.

My research indicates that in buildings where many of the residents are vulnerable, a live-in manager is necessary; his or her job is to manage the property and to serve as counselor, advisor, advocate, and disciplinarian. Thus the manager takes on standard property management and social-service responsibilities. This can be quite a burden. The qualities of firmness and sensitivity, care, and experience exhibited by resident managers in carrying out these responsibilities contribute significantly to the success of many of the hotels visited. In many cases resident managers have had, in their lifetimes, experiences and problems similar to those of the residents; this gives them insights and a firmness that are invaluable.

A different management approach is presented by The Heights in New York City. First, property management and social-service functions are separated and assigned to different on-site staff members (Baxter 1986). Second, although the residents in that SRO are a heterogeneous population and include several with mental or physical handicaps, there is no live-in manager and there is no management or service staff on duty at night or on weekends. Instead, several residents have been trained to be desk clerks and are responsible for dealing with emergencies during these periods. These desk clerks are able to handle emergency situations and have learned useful

skills. The residents, as individuals and as a group, have developed a sense of independence and empowerment. "Independence (some tenants refer to it as emancipation) is highly regarded by most tenants. Those tenants who are more dependent and needy and would otherwise be unable to exercise their desire for independence, are backed up by the more able tenants" (Baxter 1986, 29). Also there is less of a problem of staff burnout than with a resident manager. The Heights, however, also has a full-time director (a management position) and several social-service staff, all of whom work intensively with tenants during the week to deal with the problems that arise and to support tenants' involvement in management. This model gives significant responsibility and independence to residents, but a vigilant, involved, and committed staff still is required to support that process.

Another characteristic of the more vigilant management approach is a clearly stated and enforced set of rules concerning the hours when visitors are allowed, quiet hours, the disallowance of drinking in public spaces, and the disallowance of disorderly or destructive behavior. Some hotels in Portland have the strictest guest policy: no overnight guests at all. Most of the hotels visited, however, require that residents inform the manager when they have a guest and pay a nightly fee; some have limits on how long a guest can stay. The arguments in favor of allowing no overnight guests are that guests create an added burden on facilities and can cause problems of crime, other destructive or illegal behavior, and noise. Allowing no overnight guests at all, however, undermines one of the benefits of SRO housing: providing private accommodations that allow residents to maintain, or to re-establish, personal and social relationships. Being able to have an overnight guest, when this does not cause problems for other residents, is essential to this goal.

Both security and high-quality maintenance are essential in SRO housing. (Burki presents many recommendations for meeting both of these requirements.) The physical condition and cleanliness of the building affect residents' own attitudes. At one of the cleanest hotels visited, the manager feels that his efforts encourage residents to clean up after themselves (which shows up partly in improved personal hygiene). Providing a stable, clean, and orderly environment is his goal. He feels that a resident "living here and working can do a better job than if he's living in the Mission or an unstable environment." His experience, and that of other managers, demonstrates the kind of profound effect good SRO housing can have on residents who have previously been homeless or virtually homeless. Having a safe, clean, and supportive place to live, however simple, is empowering.

SRO housing can be empowering in other ways as well. Residents at the Aarti seem to have been empowered by their involvement in its renovation and its development as a cooperative. Similarly, The Heights, by following a model of significant tenant involvement in management, and in the planning and design of the building, is following an explicit goal of empowering residents, despite their heterogeneity and their various vulnerabilities. While the latter may make the process more difficult, it seems not to have lessened the success of the endeavor. The heterogeneity of the population increases the probability of finding tenants with skills and interests in tenant mangement and allows the more self-sufficient tenants to support the more needy ones.

POLICY ISSUES

When I began this research in 1984, my inclination and that of others was to compare renovated SRO hotels to apartments with private kitchens and baths. Since then both the loss of low-cost rental housing and the problem of homelessness have become even more severe. Therefore it seems only appropriate to see SRO housing as one solution to housing homeless singles and couples and, accordingly, to compare SRO housing with the more problematic alternatives of living on the streets or in shelters. This poses a dilemma, however: Do we no longer work toward increasing the stock of low-cost rental apartments? No, but it does mean that we recognize the social, psychological, and health advantages of the SRO housing type over no place to live at all. These advantages are profound.

Without permanent housing, constant and endless effort is required simply to fulfill basic needs: keeping warm and dry, keeping clean and dressed, getting enough restful sleep, and staying safe. None of the routines of daily life can be taken for granted; each has to be figured out and resolved anew each day (Rivlin 1986). And very few, if any, of the objects or materials of daily life can be accumulated and used. There is no opportunity to assume a spatial, temporal, or social order to everyday living (Dovey 1986). All is unpredictable.

Permanent housing, particularly when it is safe and clean, allows a person to re-establish daily routines, to have at least some of the objects and materials that support those routines, to take many of the basic activities and conditions of living for granted, and to establish a spatial and temporal order in one's life. Although getting enough to eat and acquiring necessary clothing and other items can continue to be difficult, having a permanent place to live and additional support services can enable residents to apply for benefits or to receive job training or job referrals.

Beyond fulfilling the basic requirements, having a place of one's own means having a place to be and to be oneself, alone or with others one has invited in, perhaps with possessions, at least with control over the space. All this supports the strengthening of self-identity and offers opportunities for growth.

Having a permanent place to live also allows a person to form and maintain relationships with others (Leavitt 1988). Without housing it is very difficult to keep clean or properly dressed, both of which significantly affect relationships with other people. It is very difficult to hold a job, to have friends, to see relatives, or to pursue an intimate relationship. Living in an SRO hotel, particularly when it is clean, safe, and supportive, allows these simple contacts to occur. Baxter (1986) describes such contacts at The Heights. Tenants are contacting friends and relatives they have not seen for years and, given the privacy of their rooms, are able to explore their own sexual identities. They can now receive mail, phone calls, and guests. Friends, relatives, and others know where they are and can reach them. Some residents have invited their children residing in foster care to stay with them for weekends or holidays.

One way to encourage and to simplify SRO

development is to amend building codes and other building regulations to make SROs standard, regulated housing. One of the biggest barriers to the renovation and new construction of SROs has been their legal standing as substandard housing because of the lack of private bathrooms and kitchens and the small size of the rooms (Werner and Bryson 1981). Without an ordinance that directly addresses SRO-type accommodations and that does not contradict other ordinances that also apply to such buildings, it is difficult, costly, and time consuming to develop SRO housing. Hamberg (1984) analyzes the various complicated codes and regulations that affect renovation and development of SRO-type accommodations in New York City. Baxter (1984) recounts the resulting problems encountered in converting a tenement apartment building to SRO housing. Codes and regulations are needed to support the essential SRO characteristics of small units and shared facilities, but also to make them safe, sanitary, and livable, just as regulations for other types of housing do.

In order to adopt the SRO Demonstration Program in Portland, the city's building code was amended to incorporate an SRO ordinance. This ordinance requires that each SRO unit be at least 100 square feet, that cooking and sanitary facilities be provided in the individual units or in a shared space, and that there be a minimum of one bathroom for each 12 units. Other cities have different ratios of bathrooms to units: 1 to 10 in Los Angeles and San Francisco and 1 to 6 in the New York Housing Maintenance Code in New York. Those involved in the renovation of particular buildings often adopt lower ratios: The SRO Housing Corporation in Los Angeles provides a bathroom for every 5 units and the Department of Housing Preservation and Development in New York required The Heights to provide one for every four units.

Suggestions for amendments to the New York City building code for the creation and regulation of "mini-dwelling units" list a minimum of one washbasin and one watercloset for every four persons and one bath or one shower for every six persons (Settlement Housing Fund 1983). These suggestions recommend the equivalent of a pullman kitchen in every room, a minimum floor space of 120 square feet for one person, a laundry room for buildings with more than 50 units, a 24-hour desk clerk for such buildings, and an intercom system for smaller buildings.

One final policy and design issue concerns the concentration of SRO units in a single building composed only of such units. While that is now the standard in SRO housing, it was not always so. Earlier in this century single rooms with private or shared baths were incorporated into buildings with many other unit plans, such as in the Ansonia in New York (see chapter 2) or the Shelton, which was a residence for professional men. Although none of the suites at the Shelton had a full kitchen, some suites had a living room, a bedroom, a pantry and a bath while others simply consisted of a room and bath. While these buildings may have been more commodious than current SRO hotels, the principle of a greater mixture of unit types is a valuable one. While the benefits of concentrating SRO units in a single building are considerable, particularly when residents have need of additional services, the integration of SRO units into apartment buildings may be beneficial in other instances. One possibility is to design suites of single rooms with shared kitchens and social spaces and either private or shared bathrooms. Such suites could be adaptations of the GoHome or the quad units (see chapter 1). These could be incorporated into buildings composed of other apartment types. Although these would no longer be SRO hotels, they would provide low-cost housing for single people on the model of single furnished rooms and shared facilities.

There also are serious risks in making SRO housing standard, regulated housing without taking additional precautions to make it affordable for those who need it most. Some SRO buildings in New York City are attracting young professional people as tenants. They may become more attractive tenants to landlords than the older residents on fixed incomes and they may be quite willing to pay higher rents (Basler 1986). Developers in San Diego are building SRO housing in the private market and may be able to attract residents able to pay relatively high rents. Controlling rents through different forms of government subsidy, both in for-profit and nonprofit SRO housing or through the purchase and operation of SRO hotels by semipublic and nonprofit organizations, may provide a solution (see chapter 12). Other precautions should also be explored, however, to ensure that SRO housing does not simply become another form of urban housing that the poor cannot afford.

It is most important at this point to recognize the value of the SRO hotel, in all its variations, and to exploit its potential as low-cost housing for single people. As more and more public attention is being focused on homeless families, it is imperative that we not forget homeless singles, that we not pursue housing programs that put such high priority on families that single people are, again, neglected.

NOTE

1. The research described in this chapter was supported by a grant from the National Science Foundation (Grant CEE-830721-13) for a study of "Social and Spatial Innovations in American Housing." The 21 hotels were selected for visits because (1) they were located in cities where other types of housing innovations were also located and were visited as part of the same research endeavor and (2) they had recently undergone some degree of renovation. Thus they do not constitute a representative sample of SRO hotels, but they do illustrate the possible variations in renovated SRO hotels. Much of the information on the nine cases described in this chapter was gathered in 1984 and 1985. The rents reported are those in effect in 1988. I am grateful to my research assistants Maria D'Isasi, Christine Balint, and Stephanie Kidd, who have helped me on this study. I would like to thank Tony Holmes for his work on the photographs in this chapter.

References

Basler, B. 1986. Young professionals join the needy as SRO tenants. *New York Times* (Jan. 22):B1, B4.

Baxter, E. 1984. *Interim progress report: The development of a community based housing model for homeless single adults*. Report to the Ittleson Foundation, New York.

————. 1986. *The Heights: A Community Housing Strategy*. New York: Community Service Society of New York.

Burki, M. 1982. *Housing the Low-Income, Urban Elderly: A Role for the Single Room Occupancy Hotel*. Ph.D. dissertation. Portland, OR: School of Urban and Public Affairs, Portland State University.

Collins, A. 1985. Artist's Co-op. *Arts and Architecture*. (Winter):56–59.

Comerio, M. 1982. Inside Chinatown, Unpublished report on National Endowment for the Arts design demonstration project. San Francisco: Asian Neighborhood Design.

Community Emergency Shelter Organization and Jewish Council on Urban Affairs. 1985. *SROs: An Endangered Species, Chicago's Single Room Occupancy Hotels*. Chicago: Community Emergency Shelter Organization.

Dovey, K. 1986. Home and homelessness. In *Home Environments*, ed. I. Altman and C. M. Werner, 33–64. New York: Plenum.

Erickson, R., and K. Eckert. 1977. The elderly poor in downtown San Diego hotels. *The Gerontologist*. 17:440–446.

Fulton, W. 1985. A room of one's own. *Planning* (Sept.):18–20.

Greer, N. 1986. *The Search for Shelter*. Washington, D.C.: The American Institute of Architects.

Hamberg, J. 1984. *Building and Zoning Regulations: A Guide for Sponsors of shelters and Housing for the Homeless in New York City*. New York: Community Service Society.

Leavitt, J. 1988. The House of Ruth. *Nation* (Apr. 2):473–474.

Liu, J. K. C. 1980. *San Francisco Chinatown Residential Hotels*. San Francisco: Chinatown Neighborhood Improvement Resource Center.

National Trust for Historic Preservation. 1981. *Rehabilitating Residential Hotels*. Washington, D.C.: National Trust for Historic Preservation.

Rivlin, L. C. 1986. A new look at the homeless. *Social Policy* (Spring):3–10.

Settlement Housing Fund. 1983. *Proposal to Amend State and City Codes for Single Room Occupancy Housing*. New York: Settlement Housing Fund.

Shapiro, J. H. 1971. *Communities of the Alone*. New York: Association Press.

U.S. Bureau of the Census. 1985. Current Population Reports, series P-20, #402 Households, Families, Marital Status and Living Arrangements. Washington, D.C.: U.S. Government Printing Office.

Werner, F., and D. D. Bryson. 1982. A guide to the preservation and maintenance of single room (SRO) housing. *Clearing House Review* (Apr.):999–1009.

Contributors

Sherry Ahrentzen is an associate professor in the Department of Architecture at the University of Wisconsin–Milwaukee. She is currently engaged in research on the housing and neighborhood design implications of home-based work, a project funded by the National Endowment for the Arts. Her previous research, funded by the U.S. Department of Housing and Urban Development, focused on the housing preferences and mobility of female-headed households. She has a Ph.D. in Social Ecology from the University of California, Irvine.

Mary Burki is a housing developer with Common Ground, a nonprofit organization in Seattle, Washington, which helps clients develop low-income housing. She was previously the director of Property Development and Management for Central City Concern in Portland, Oregon, where she was responsible for the development, management, and operation of single room occupancy hotels. Her doctoral dissertation entailed a survey of occupants of such hotels. She has an M.A. in Urban Studies and a Ph.D. in Sociology from Portland State University.

Christine C. Cook is an assistant professor in the School of Urban and Regional Studies at the University of New Orleans. She has extensive research and community service experience with transitional housing for single-parent families. She is a past president of the Minnesota Association of Women and Housing and has served on several task forces and boards of directors for

state and local agencies and nonprofit organizations. She is a co-author of *Expanding Opportunities for Single Parent Families through Housing*. She has a Ph.D. in Housing and Urban Sociology from Ohio State University.

Elizabeth Cromley is an associate professor of architectural history in the Department of Architecture, State University of New York, Buffalo. She is the author of *Alone Together: New York's Early Apartment Houses*. She has spent the last several years researching the development of American apartment houses during the nineteenth and early twentieth centuries, focuing on architectural responses to the issues of publicity, privacy, and household technology. She is now conducting research on the history of the bedroom. She has a Ph.D. in Art History from the City University of New York.

Charles R. Durrett is a partner in McCamant & Durrett, a consulting firm specializing in cohousing and community design. He is also employed by the San Francisco Mayor's Office of Community Development, where he designs and supervises the construction of child-care facilities. He has a B. Arch. from California Polytechnic State University.

Karen A. Franck is an associate professor in the School of Architecture at the New Jersey Institute of Technology. She has recently completed research, funded by the National Science Foundation, on recent innovations in housing in the

331

United States, particularly housing designed for low-income single persons, single-parent families, intergenerational households, unrelated persons sharing a dwelling, and people working out of their homes. Her current research, funded by the National Endowment for the Arts, focuses on the history of the design of public housing. She was formerly the director of Research for the Institute of Community Design Analysis in New York. She has a Ph.D. in Environmental Psychology from the City University of New York.

Jacqueline Leavitt is an acting associate professor in the School of Architecture and Urban Planning at the University of California, Los Angeles. For several years she has been engaged in research and design activities concerning housing for single-parent families and homeless persons. She has served as a planning consultant to several agencies in Sweden and the United States. With Troy West, she was the first prize winner for the New American Home Competition. She is a co-author of *Housing Abandonment in Harlem: The Making of Community Households.* She has a Masters degree and a Ph.D. in Urban Planning from Columbia University.

Kathryn M. McCamant, a partner in McCamant & Durrett, has co-authored a book with Charles Durrett on cohousing communities in Denmark, *CoHousing: A Contemporary Approach to Housing Ourselves.* She is an author, lecturer, and consultant on housing. Her previous work with nonprofit housing development involved community organizing and working with resident groups on several design and construction projects. She has a B.S. in Architecture from the University of California, Berkeley.

Michael Mostoller is a professor in the School of Architecture at the New Jersey Institute of Technology and a partner in the firm Mostoller Travisano Architects. He has been engaged for several years in the study and design of single room occupancy hotels. His design prototypes for rooms and furniture for single room occupancy hotels won an award from the New York Chapter of the American Institute of Architects. He has also served as an advisor to community groups on housing and site design for low-income and homeless persons. He has an M. Arch. degree from Harvard University.

Sylvia Novac is currently a doctoral candidate in sociology at Ontario Institute for Studies in Education. She has written a number of papers and reports for various government and nonprofit agencies on women's housing issues in urban and rural settings. She has an M.A. in Environmental Studies from York University, Ontario, Canada.

Norbert Schoenauer is a professor emeritus in the School of Architecture at McGill University in Montreal, Canada. He has been engaged for many years in the planning and design of housing; several of his projects have won awards. He has written a number of books on housing, including the three-volume work, *6,000 Years of Housing,* which has been translated into several languages. He has a Certificate in Architecture from the Royal Academy of Fine Arts in Copenhagen and an M. Arch. degree from McGill University.

Joan Forrester Sprague is a consulting architect and planner who works on innovative projects that address the development needs of economically disadvantaged women and children. She was formerly executive director and president of the Women's Institute of Housing and Economic Development, which she co-founded. She is the author of the first editions of *A Development Primer: A Manual on Transitional Housing* and *Taking Action: A Comprehensive Approach to Housing Women and Children in Massachusetts.* She has a B. Arch. degree from Cornell University and an M.A. in Education from Harvard University.

Jill Stoner is an assistant professor in the College of Environmental Design, University of California, Berkeley, and a partner in Stoner Duncan Architects. Through design competitions, she has pursued her interest in the design and construction of alternative housing. She was the second-place winner in the New American Home Competition and a finalist in the Inner City Infill Housing Competition for Harlem. She has an M. Arch. degree from the University of Pennsylvania.

Gerda R. Wekerle is an associate professor in the Faculty of Environmental Studies at York University in Ontario, Canada. She has been engaged for many years in research, writing, and lecturing on women's needs in urban environments. She is co-editor of *New Space for Women* and cofounder of the journal *Women and Environments*. She has served as a consultant to many Canadian agencies. With Joan Simon, she conducted post-occupancy evaluations of housing developments for single-parent families in Canada. She has a M.A. and a Ph.D. in Sociology from Northwestern University.

Alison Woodward teaches in the Department of Social and Political Science at the University of Antwerp in Belgium. For the last ten years, she has been conducting research on various aspects of community and housing in Sweden and has recently completed a comparative survey study of several communal housing projects in Sweden. Her dissertation addresses the relationship between ideology and planning in Swedish and American new communities. She has a Ph.D. in Sociology from the University of California, Berkeley.

Index

Aarti (San Francisco), 318–320, 324, 328
Abigail West Shelter (Boston), 188–195, 204, 206
  design and planning issues, 189–195
  plans for, 192, 194
Abused women/families. *See* Family abuse
Accessory apartments, xiii, 166
Adam, Katrin, 150
Affordability. *See* Housing costs
Aitcheson, Susan, 150
Alcoholic residents
  special SRO housing for, 326
  in SRO housing, 254, 286, 288–289, 314–315
Amerikanerhaus (Zurich), 56–58
Ansonia (New York), 41–42, 329
Apartment hotels. *See also* Apartment houses (nineteenth-century); Catering flats
  housekeeping arrangements, 22, 41
  nineteenth-century New York, 22, 41
Apartment houses (nineteenth-century)
  assumptions underlying, 20–21, 43–45
  building services in, 34–35
  design issues, 22–31
  dining rooms in, 32–33
  housekeeping and cooking in, 32–35
  plans, 24, 26, 37, 39, 42
  present-day parallels, 43–44
  privacy and sharing in, 20–22, 25–31
  public spaces in, 23–28

social homogeneity in, 42–43
  staff in, 34–35
Apartment houses, collective. *See* Cooperatives; *Einküchenhaus*; *Kollektivhus*
Apex Belltown Cooperative (Seattle), 317, 320–321, 324
Artists, housing for, 132, 138, 172. *See also* Apex Belltown Coop; GoHomes
Asian Neighborhood Design (AND), 319–320
Austin, Alice Constance, 4

Bachelor flats, 38, 41
Backström and Reinius, 65
Balfour, E. J. A., 49–50
Barbizon, The (New York), 249, 250
Barshit, M., 60
Bathroom design
  in housing for single-parent households, 165
  in SRO housing, 297–298, 305, 324
Battered families/women. *See* Family abuse
Baxter, Ellen, 257
Beguinage, The (Toronto)
  demographic profile, 235–236
  description and plans, 226–227, 228–229, 230, 232–233
  planning process, 228–229
  unit costs and subsidy program, 234–235
Behrendt, W. C., 55
Bergen County (New Jersey), 161
  plans for congregate housing, 164–170

Berlin, collective apartment buildings in, 55–56
Blenda (Uppsala, Sweden), 81–85, 86, 87, 88
Boarding houses, 21, 246–247, 263–264. *See also* Single room occupancy housing
Boi i Gemenskap (BIG)/Live Together in Community group, 72, 76
Bondebjerget (Denmark), 98, 99, 120
Bone, Sylvester, 147, 148
Boston
  housing for single-parent households. (*See* Abigail West Shelter; Tree of Life)
  shared housing in, 11
  urban planning and policy in, 188–189, 195, 207
Boston Redevelopment Authority (BRA), 195–196, 199
Braun, Lily, 55
Building codes, for SRO housing, 329
  as barrier to housing innovations, 134
  and party wall, 134–135, 139–140
  in SRO housing, 328–329
Building services
  in nineteenth-century apartment buildings, 34–35
  in party wall, 130–131, 132, 134, 136–137
  in SRO hotels, 299–301
Burnside Consortium. *See* Central City Concern
Bush Hotel (Seattle), 249, 312–314, 324

335

Butte Hotel (Portland, Oregon), 314–315, 324

Campbell, Helen, 33–34
Campden House Chambers (London), 49–50
Campus Court (Eugene, Oregon), 8–9
Canada Mortgage and Housing Corporation (CMHC), 224–225, 228, 230
Canadian Non-profit Housing Program, 222, 224–225, 227, 229, 234
Catering flats (London), 48–50. *See also* Apartment hotels
Central City Concern (CCC), 253
    and alcoholic tenants, 288
    SRO hotel renovations, 286, 314, 315
Central Park Apartments (New York)
    description, 23, 24–25, 26
    facade design, 29–30
    services and building maintenance in, 34
Century, The (New York), 38–39, 41
Child care, xiii, 6
    in Danish cohousing, 97, 106–107, 123
    in housing for single-parent households, xiii, 171, 182–183, 198–199, 206, 213, 218–219
    in nineteenth-century apartment buildings, 22, 34
    and single-parent families, 145–146, 218
    in Swedish collective housing, 64, 68, 92
    in women's co-ops, 230, 234
Children. *See also* Child care; Single-parent households
    in collective housing, 6
    in Danish cohousing, 94, 100, 115, 117–118, 121
    in housing for single-parent households, 220–221
    mobility problems with, 162–164
    in nineteenth-century apartment buildings, 22
    rental housing restrictions on, 145

in shared housing, 132, 138, 139
in Swedish collective housing, 67, 73, 86, 88, 89, 92
Childs, Bertman, Tseckares, and Casendino, 205
Chinese Community Housing Corporation (CCHC), 316, 318
Church, Bill, 16–17
Civic Center Residence (San Francisco), 249, 310–312, 324
Clayton (San Francisco), 316–317, 322, 324
Cohousing (Denmark), xiv, 95–125
    characteristics, 95, 98, 100–101
    common house plans, 108, 118, 119
    demographic profile, 102, 104
    design issues, 111–121
    evolution, 96, 101–104
    list of developments, 97
    ownership and financing, 97, 98, 102, 107
    participatory development process, 109–111
    private house plans, 108, 114, 120
    site plans, 99, 103, 105, 108, 122
Cohousing (issues in U.S.), 121–125
Collective housing. *See also* Apartment houses (nineteenth-century); Cohousing (Denmark); Congregate housing; *Dom-kommuna*; *Einküchenhaus*; GoHomes; Group housing; *Kollektivhus* (Denmark); *Kollektivhus* (Sweden)
    advantages, 6–7
    American examples, 13–17
    architectural expression in, 44
    characteristics, 17
    definition and characteristics, 3
    historical discussion, xii–xiii, 3–4
    opposition to, in Germany, 55–56
    overview, 3–19
    privacy issues in, 6–7
    size and viability, 69
    for single men (historical, U.S.), 38

for single women (historical, U.S.), 4, 35–38
for special groups, 4–5
Comerio, Mary, 263, 320
Common house (Danish cohousing), 100, 104–107, 116–120
Common house (U.S.), 17
Communal housing (Sweden). *See Kollektivhus* (Sweden)
Communal Housing Now, 73, 76
Community-Household Model, 163
Comunitas, 193
Congregate housing. *See also* Collective housing
    characteristics, 4–5, 164
    for elderly, 124, 163
    intergenerational, 164–170
    for single-parent households, 164–170, 202–203
Constance Hamilton Cooperative (Toronto)
    demographic profile, 235–236
    description and plans, 225–226, 231
    planning process, 228–230
    unit costs and subsidy program, 234–235
    management board, 230
Cooking. *See* Meal preparation and dining
Cooperative housing. *See also* Collective housing
    Canadian programs for, 224–225
    communal activities in, 237–238, 241
    demography of women's co-ops, 235–236
    design issues, 229–230, 234, 239–241
    GoHomes as, 9–11
    in Great Britain, 50–53
    participatory planning of, 236–237
    planning process, 227–228
    plans for, 228–229, 231–233
    for single-parent households, 150
    social benefits, 236–238
    in SRO hotels, 320–321
    subsidy pool in, 234–235
    in Sweden, 74

unit costs in, 234–235
women's, 4, 223–241
Coordinator Architects, 82, 83
Copenhagen, collective housing
in, 53–55

Dakota, The (New York), 27, 28–29
facade design, 28–29
Dayton Court (Minneapolis–St. Paul). *See also* New American House Competition
cost concerns, 175–176, 182–183
description and plans, 176–182
planning and approval process, 174–175, 176, 183–184
Dayton-Hudson Foundation, 170, 183
Demographics
change in U.S. households, ix
household income, xi–xii
household types, xi
of residents of Swedish collective housing, 67–68, 84–85
of single-parent households, 143, 201
of SRO hotel tenants, 286, 312
of women's co-ops, 235–236
working mothers, xi
Denmark, collective housing in, 53–55, 69. *See also* Cohousing (Denmark)
Design issues. *See also* Participatory design and planning
in cooperative housing, 229–230, 234, 239–241
in Danish cohousing, 111–121
in housing for single-parent households, 162–167, 170, 198–199, 212–213, 220–221
in intergenerational housing, 166
and mobility, 162–164
in nineteenth-century apartment buildings, 22–31
and the party wall, 127–135
in SRO housing, 271–272, 296–306, 322–326
in Swedish *kollektivhus*, 89–92
Dining area design
in Danish cohousing, 117–118, 180

in mingle units, 7
in SRO housing, 301
in Swedish collective housing, 86, 87, 90–91
Disabled residents
integrated housing for (Sweden), 76, 80, 91
in SRO housing, 289
Dom-kommuna (Soviet Union), 59–62
Double House, 151
Double master bedroom plans. *See* Mingles/mingle unit
Drew Economic Development Corporation, 151, 167
Dubnoff, Ena, 150, 152–153, 167

Echo houses, definition, xiii
Einküchenhaus (Germany/Austria/ Switzerland), 55–59
Elderly residents
analogy with single-parent households, 161–164
characteristics, 162
in Danish cohousing, 102, 123
housing types for, 4–5, 163
in intergenerational housing, 11, 15, 132, 135, 164–165, 170
in SRO housing, 286, 309–310, 316–317
in Swedish service-integrated housing, 75–76, 79–81, 84–85, 86
Electrical services. *See* Building services
Elfvinggården (Stockholm), 65–66
Engkvist, Olle, 65, 66
Estate Hotel (Portland, Oregon), 292, 315, 325–326

Family abuse, 146, 187
Family composition. *See also* Demographics; Household Composition
Family hotels. *See* Apartment hotels
Female-headed families. *See* Single-parent households
Fick, Otto, 53–54, 55
Fifth Avenue Plaza (New York), 33
Fiona House (London), 147–149
Flagg, Ernest, 33, 247

Flexibility in use of space
in Danish cohousing, 119–120
in housing for single-parent households, 167
in intergenerational housing, 170, 171
Flexibility of dwelling units
in Danish cohousing, 121
in GoHomes, 10
in nineteenth-century apartment buildings, 41
Florence, The (New York), 33
Florence Hotel (Los Angeles), 254, 255, 256
Flynn, Raymond L., 186, 188, 195
Fourier, C.-F.-M., 47–48
France, collective housing in, 47–48
Fristad (Stockholm), 79–81, 85, 86, 87–89, 91
F-type unit *(dom kommuna)*, 60–62
Furniture, in housing for single-parent households, 167
Furniture, in SRO housing, 263–284, 305, 322–323
design issues, 279–284
essential pieces, 272
historical types, 263–267
prototype pieces, 279–283

Gårdesgården (Stockholm), 65–66
Gessner, Albert, 55
Gilman, Charlotte Perkins, 33–34
Ginsberg, Moses, 60, 61, 62
Godin, Jean-Baptiste André, 48
GoHomes, 9–11, 17, 329
Goldsmith, Phil, 225, 226–227, 230
Government. *See* Housing policies
Granny flats. *See* Accessory apartments
Group houses, 5, 11–13, 17. *See also* Innovative housing; Shared housing; Shared living house
Gudmand-Høyer, Jan, 101, 115
Guessens Court (Great Britain), 51
Guest rooms, 15, 17, 97, 104, 107, 118

Haight House (New York), 33, 34
Halls. *See* Public areas

Handicaps. *See* Disabled residents

Hardenburgh, Henry, 27, 28, 30

Hardy, Rodney D., 170, 174, 182

Hässelby Family Hotel (Sweden), 73

Hayden, Dolores, xii, 47, 73, 167, 221, 223, 224

Heights, The (New York), 254–255, 257, 258, 324, 329
  management and social services, 327, 328

Heimhof (Vienna), 58–59

Hellwig, Otto, 58

Hemgården apartment building (Stockholm), 62–63

Herrick, Christine, 27, 35

Hirschen, Sandy, 150

Hirschi, Ann, 320

Ho, Mui, 150

Homelessness, 250–251, 328

Home maintenance. *See also* Meal preparation and dining; Service-integration model; Tenant management model; Women
  collective aspects, 34–35
  in Danish *kollektivhus*, 54–55
  household appliances and, 44
  in housing for single-parent households, 146
  in nineteenth-century apartment houses, 22, 32–35
  in Swedish collective housing, 63–64
  theories of, 47–48

Homesgarth (Great Britain), 50–52

HOMES proposal, 224

Household composition. *See also* Demographics; Single-parent households
  postwar changes in, ix
  in SRO housing, 308–309
  in Swedish collective housing, 67
  in Toronto co-ops, 235–236

Housekeeping services staff
  in British cooperative quadrangles, 50–51
  in Danish *kollektivhus*, 54
  in *Einküchenhaus*, 55, 59
  in family hotels, 22
  in nineteenth-century apartment houses, 22, 33–35

in Swedish *kollektivhus*, 63–64, 66, 68

Housework. *See* Home maintenance

Housing and Urban Development (HUD), 175
  demonstration grants for SRO housing, 253, 257, 286, 314, 329
  estimates, homeless rate, 251
  SRO housing policy, 253

Housing costs
  in Danish cohousing, 102
  and New American House designs, 175–176, 182–184
  rising of, x
  in shared housing, 5, 7, 9–10, 11
  and single-parent households, 144–145
  for SRO housing, 311–312, 313, 320, 321, 329–330
  in Swedish collective housing, 89
  and women's co-ops, 234–235

Housing policies
  alternative policy development, xiii
  assumptions behind, x
  for nontraditional families, 143–144
  origins, ix–x

Howard, Ebenezer, 50–53

Hubert, Pirsson, and Hoddick, 25, 26

Hudson View Gardens (New York), 4

Hungle, Penny, 189

Hunt, Richard Morris, 23, 25

Huvertusvereniging (Mother's Home, Amsterdam), 146–148

Inner City Infill Housing Competition, 137–140

Innovative Housing, 11–13, 124

Integration of household types, xiii
  in Danish cohousing, 96, 105, 123
  in housing for single-parent households, 151, 165–166, 198, 199, 202, 206
  in intergenerational housing, 11, 15, 165–166

lack of in nineteenth-century apartment houses, 42–43, 54

and New American House, competition and designs, 170, 171–173

in shared housing, 11, 12

in SRO housing, 257, 287, 308, 310–315, 328, 329

in Swedish collective housing, 67, 84–85, 86, 88, 92

in women's co-ops, 235–236, 239

Israels, Charles, 30, 31, 35, 43

Jackson and Associates, 257–258

Jane Club (Chicago), 4

Jernstøbereit (Denmark), 98, 116, 121, 122

Jystrup Savværket (Denmark), 106–108, 112

Katthuvudet (Sweden), 78–79, 90

Kellum, John, 36

Kilham, Walter, 27

Kinköping project, 74, 76, 77

Kitchen design
  in Danish cohousing, 112, 116, 117
  in shared housing, 9, 10, 11
  in SRO housing, 297, 300–303, 323–324
  in Swedish collective housing, 81, 89–91
  in transitional housing, 221

Kofoed, L. Christian, 54

Kollektivhus (Denmark) 53–55, 95

Kollektivhus (Sweden), 62–69, 71–93, 95
  definition, 71, 72
  demand for, 72–73
  demographics, 67–68, 84–85
  design issues, 89–92
  historical discussion, 62–67, 72–73
  list of projects, 75
  management models, 74–79
  meal service in, 86–88
  problems encountered in, 86, 92
  social and material advantages, 73–74, 88–89
  tenant surveys, 67–68, 85–89

Kopp, Anatole, 59–60

Kropotkin, Peter Alekseevich, 48

Lander, A. Clapham, 50, 52
Las Flores (California), 8
Latimer, George, 174, 182
Laundry facilities
   in nineteenth-century
      apartment houses, 27, 32, 34
   in SRO hotels, 290, 298, 304
Lawton, Powell, 164
Le Corbusier, 271
League of Women Voters (Bergen
   County, New Jersey), 161,
   164–170
Lerup, Lars, 44, 151
Levenson, Conrad, 151, 154–155
Lewis Homes (California), 8
Life-care communities, 4–5
Lind, Svend Ivar, 67
Lissitzky, El, 60, 62
Littell, E. T., 27, 32, 38–39
Llan del Rio (California), 4
Lobbies. *See* Public areas; Single
   room occupancy housing
Lodging house, 246. *See also*
   Boarding houses; Single room
   occupancy housing
London
   catering flats in, 48–50
   cooperative housing in, 48, 50–
      53
   housing for single-parent
      households, 147
Longacre, The (New York), 250
Lui, John, 263
Lundagården (Stockholm), 66–67

Management issues (discussion of)
   in Danish cohousing, 101
   in housing for single-parent
      households, 170, 199, 217–
      218, 225
   in SRO housing, 292–296, 321,
      326–328
   in Swedish collective housing,
      74–79
   in women's co-ops, 225, 236–
      237, 238, 241
Marieberg (Stockholm), 66–67
Markelius, Sven, 63–64
Markell Evangeline Residence
   (New York), 247
Marlborough Chambers
   (London), 49
Massachusetts, subsidies to
   housing in, 191, 193

Meadow Way Green (Great
   Britain), 51
Meal preparation and dining
   in collective housing (U.S.), 15,
      16
   in Danish cohousing, xiv, 100,
      106
   in Danish *kollektivhus*, 54–55
   in German *Einküchenhaus*, 55
   in nineteenth-century
      apartment houses, 32–33
   in shared housing, 10, 11, 13
   in SRO hotels, 290
   in Swedish *kollektivhus*, 86–88
Medical care, in SRO housing,
   290–291, 296
Meltzer, Marvin, 151, 154–155
Men. *See also* Bachelor flats;
      Catering flats
   single room occupancy housing
      for, 247
   in women's co-op housing, 239
Mentally ill, in SRO housing, 249,
   257, 288, 311, 326
Michelson, Val, and Associates,
   211
Milinis, I., 61, 62
Mills Hotel (New York), 247
Mingles/mingle unit, 7–8. *See also*
      Shared housing
Minneapolis–St. Paul
   community consciousness, 183–
      184
   housing for single-parent
      households. (*See* Dayton
      Court; Passage Community)
Minnesota Association of Women
   in Housing, 183, 210
Mobility
   designing for, 162–164
   restricted, for single parents,
      161–162
Modular construction, 193, 195
Morphew, Reginald, 49
Mother's Home (Amsterdam). *See*
   Huvertusvereniging
Mumford, Lewis, x, 166
Muthesius, Hermann, 55
Myrdal, Alva and Gunnar, 63

Narkomfin (Moscow), 60–62
National Shared Housing
   Resource Center, 11

Neighborhoods
   integrating cohousing into, 113–
      114
   integrating housing for single-
      parent households in, 167,
      171
   opposition to cohousing, 101
   opposition to transitional
      housing for single-parent
      households, 196–198, 206
New American House Competition, xiii. *See also* Dayton
      Court
   conclusions from, 182–185
   design requirements, 170, 175–
      176
   designs for, 135–137, 172–173
New York City
   loss of SRO housing, 250
   nineteenth-century housing
      trends, 21–22
   programs for homeless in, 253
   SRO rehabilitation in, 253
NOARK Architects, 78, 83
Nontraditional households. *See
   also* Demographics; House-
      hold composition
   growth in numbers, xi
   historical discussion, xii
Notter, Finegold, and Alexander,
   203–204

Orion (Stockholm), 79
Ostberg, Ragnar, 65

Parisian Buildings (New York), 28
Park Avenue Hotel (New York),
   36–37
Parkview Hotel (New York), 268–
   270, 276
Participation by residents in
      management, maintenance
      of, xiv. *See also* Tenant
      management model
   in Danish cohousing, 100, 106
   in housing for single-parent
      households, 170
   in shared housing, 11, 13
   in SRO housing, 257, 321, 327,
      328
   in Swedish collective housing,
      86–87, 88
   in women's co-ops, 237, 238

Participatory design and planning,
    xiv
    in collective housing (U.S.), 17
    in Danish cohousing, 100–101,
        109–111
    in housing for single-parent
        households, 196–198
    in intergenerational housing,
        166
    in shared housing, 13
    in Swedish collective housing,
        90
    in SRO housing, 319–320, 321
    in women's co-ops, 227–229,
        236–237
Party wall, 127–142
    as design element, 130–135
    in multi-household suite, 138
    social functions, 126–132
    structural functions, 132–134
    transformation strategies for,
        130–135
Passage Community (Minne-
    apolis), 209–222
    description and plans, 208–209,
        214–216
    design issues, 212–213, 217,
        220–221
    financial problems, 218–219
    financing, planning and
        development process, 209–
        213, 217
    social services and
        management, 217–218
Pasternak, A., 60
Pavilion Limited Partnership, 203–
    205
Pedestrian streets (Danish
    cohousing), 104, 106–107
Phalanges, 47–48
Physically handicapped. *See*
    Disabled residents
Portland (Oregon)
    housing policies, 286
    Redevelopment Commission,
        252, 253, 314
    SRO housing in, 253, 314–315,
        329
Prästgårdsmarken (Sweden), 78–
    79, 81–85, 86, 87, 88
Price, Bruce, 23, 24, 26
Privacy
    in collective housing, 6
    in Danish cohousing, 95, 100, 107

    in housing for single-parent
        households, 164, 166–167
    in intergenerational housing,
        166
    in shared housing, 6, 7, 8–9, 10
    of single-family detached house,
        x, 4, 121, 127, 129
    in SRO housing, 309–310, 322
    in Victorian family life, 21
Privacy, balance with sharing, xiv,
    44
    in collective housing, 17
    diagrams of private and shared
        spaces, 190
    in housing for single-parent
        households, 212, 213
    in nineteenth-century
        apartment houses, 20–22, 25–
        31
    in suites, 130, 132, 135
    in Swedish collective housing,
        68
Privacy, transitions to shared
    areas
    in Danish cohousing, 111–112
Prokhorov, S., 61, 62
Public areas
    in Danish cohousing, 111–114
    design criteria for SRO housing,
        297–298, 301, 303
    in housing for single-parent
        households, 220–221
    lobbies and lounges in SRO
        housing, 291–292, 297, 303–
        304, 323–324
    in nineteenth-century
        apartment houses, 23–28
    in Swedish collective housing,
        74, 90–92
Putnam, John Pickering, 25–26

Quadrangle Architects, 225, 227
Quads, 8–9, 329. *See also* Collec-
    tive housing
    as SRO housing, 329
Queen Anne's Mansions
    (London), 49

Ralåmbhus (Stockholm), 65
Raubeson, Andy, 253
Residential clubs and hotels, 247,
    264. *See also* Apartment
    hotels; Single room
    occupancy housing

Resident management. *See* Man-
    agement issues; Partici-
    pation of residents in manage-
    ment, maintenance of;
    Tenant-management model
Resident selection
    in nineteeth-century apartment
        houses, 42–43
    in SRO housing, 295–296
    in Swedish collective housing,
        84
Retail stores, in SRO housing,
    312, 313, 324
Retirement communities, 4–5
Rio (Stockholm), 79–81, 84, 85,
    86, 88, 89
Riverside Apartments (Brooklyn),
    27–28
Robson, E. R., 49
Rono, Gwen, 13–14
Rooming houses. *See* Single room
    occupancy housing
Rubin, Jenny, 67–68

Saegert, Susan, 5, 163
St. Paul Heritage Preservation
    Commission, 171, 175
San Francisco, SRO housing in,
    250, 310–312, 317–318
Savværket. *See* Jystrup Savværket
    (Denmark)
Schorr, Alvin, 162–163
Schultze-Naumberg, Paul, 55–56
Schwank, Otto, 56–59
Schwimmer, Rosika, 55
Seattle, SRO housing in, 312–314,
    317–320
Second-stage housing. *See* Single-
    parent households, housing
    for; Transitional housing, for
    single-parent households
Service-integration model
    (Sweden), 74, 76, 79–81
    meal service problems, 86–87
78 Irving Place (New York), 30
Shaker furniture, 265–267
Shared housing. *See also*
    GoHomes; Group houses;
    Mingles/Mingle unit; Party
    Wall; Quads
    advantages of, 5–6
    definition, 3, 17
    history of, in U.S., 3–5

suites for, 138–140
survey (U.S.), 5
U.S. programs for, xiii
Shared housing programs. *See* Innovative housing; Shared housing; Shared Housing Resource Center; Shared Living House
Shared Living House (Boston), 11
Sharing, social interaction. *See also* Privacy, balance with sharing; Privacy, transitions to shared areas
  in Danish cohousing, 95, 100, 101, 111–112, 113, 116
  in housing for single-parent households, 164, 167–168
  in nineteenth-century apartment houses, 44–45
  in shared housing, 7–8, 9, 10, 11, 13, 15
  in SRO housing, 286, 309–310, 328
  in suites, 129, 130, 135
  in Swedish collective housing, 73, 85, 86, 88
  types of, xiv, 6–7, 237
  in women's co-ops, 234, 237–238
Shelton Club (New York), 247
Sherman, Harvey, 170, 174–176, 182
Sherwood House (New York), 33
Shockley, Brenda, 167
Simon Architects, 225, 226
Simon, Joan, 225, 230
Single-family detached house characteristics, xii, 4, 129
  dominance after World War II, xii, 4, 248
  problems of, xii–xiii, 7, 95, 101, 121, 122
Single-parent households
  analogy with elderly, 161–164
  characteristics, 143–145, 162, 220
  in Danish cohousing, 102
  definition, 143
  demographics, xi, 143, 201
  housing costs and, 182–185
  inadequate housing for, 145
  in shared housing, 7, 12, 13, 132, 138
  social and economic problems, 162–164

social services for, 146
  in Swedish collective housing, 67
  in women's co-op housing, 234–236
Single-parent households, housing for, 44, 143–144. *See also* Single-parent households
  congregate, 164–170
  construction cost problems, 175–178, 182, 206, 226, 234–235
  costs of renting/purchasing, 183, 234–236, 240
  definition and characteristics, 144–146
  design issues, 162–167, 170, 189–191, 198, 202–204, 220–221, 229–230, 234, 239
  early developments (Europe), 146–149
  list of developments (U.S.), 156–158
  management issues, 170, 199, 217–218, 238–239
  need for, 144–146, 195, 201, 202
  neighborhood characteristics, 145, 184, 221, 239
  opposition to, 196–198, 206
  overview, 143–160
  policies and programs for, 183, 191–193, 199–200, 202, 211, 224–225
  security, 146, 191, 203, 220–221
  size problems, 206–207
  social services in, 146, 147, 198–199, 217–218
  transitional, 144, 147, 187–222
Single-person households
  housing for, 138, 139. (*See also* Apartment hotels; Bachelor flats; Catering flats; Cohousing (Denmark); *Kollektivhus* (Sweden); Men, Shared housing; Single room occupancy housing; Women)
  increase in, ix, xi, 308
Single room occupancy hotels. *See* Single room occupancy housing
Single room occupancy housing, 245–330
  advantages, 245, 252, 309–310, 328–330

definition, 245
  demonstration grants for, 253, 257, 286, 314
  design issues, 271–272, 296–306, 322–326
  deterioration and destruction, 248–249, 250
  furniture for. (*See* Furniture, in SRO housing)
  historical discussion, 246–250, 263–264
  house rules in, 294–295, 327
  independence in, 309–310, 327, 329
  interaction in, 309–310
  management issues, 292
  manager's office/front desk in, 293–294, 297, 299
  medical and social services, 290–291, 296
  neighborhood characteristics, 286
  overview, 245–262
  plans for, 256, 258
  policies and programs for, 252–257, 286, 314, 328–330
  prototype room, 263, 322
  rehabilitation of, 253
  renovation costs, 252, 254–255
  rental costs, 252, 254, 329
  resident characteristics, 286–287, 314–315
  residents' activities in, 268–269, 289–292
  room design criteria, 271–279, 298, 322
  security and access, 292–294, 296, 298–300
  services in, 245, 252
  social services in, 254, 257, 312, 327
  staff levels and duties, 293–294, 296, 327
  tenant selection, 295–296
  use of zoning in, 268–270, 273, 276
6 John Ericssongatan (Stockholm), 63–65
Skråplanet (Denmark), 101, 102, 103
Smaragden (Stockholm), 65–66
Smith, Ted, 9–11
Social Democratic Union of Swedish Women, 63, 72

Social services in housing, xiii–xiv. *See also* Service-integration model (Sweden); Single-parent households; housing for; Single room occupancy housing
Sol & Vind (Denmark), 110, 113, 117, 118
Sollentuna (Stockholm), 69, 72
Sollershott Hall. *See* Homesgarth
Solomon, Dan, 11–13, 124
Soviet Union, collective housing in, 59–62
Sparksway Common (California), 150
SRO Housing Corporation (Los Angeles), 253, 254, 329
SRO housing. *See* Single room occupancy housing
Stacken (Sweden), 76, 77–78
Stark, Albin, 65, 67
Stewart, A. T., 36
Stewart House (Seattle), 318, 324
Stewart's Hotel (New York), 36–37
Stockholm
    collective apartment houses in, 62–67
    pressure for collective housing, 76
    role in communal housing projects, 79
Stolplyckan (Sweden), 74, 76–77
Storage
    and party wall, 134, 136
    in SRO housing, 281–283, 325
Strindberg, Johan August, 48, 63
Stuckert, Mary Coleman, 4
Stuyvesant Apartments (New York), 23, 25, 32
Subsidies
    Chapter 707 (Massachusetts), 191, 193
    for cooperative housing (Canada), 224, 234–235, 240
    federal proposals, xiii
    for housing for single-parent households, 183
    Section 8, 150, 193, 208–209, 218, 252, 253, 257, 285, 286
    for SRO housing, 252–253, 257, 286, 329
    Title XX, Special Needs Subsidies, 219
Substandard housing
    definition, 159

and single-parent households, 145
    SRO housing defined as, 248–249, 310, 329
Suite. *See also* GoHomes; Quads
    in city infill housing, 137–140
    definition and characteristics, 131, 134–135
Sullivan, Gail, 191
Sum-Shchik, G., 60
Sunlight (Portland, Oregon), 16–17
Svedberg, Hillevi, 65
Svenska, Bostäder Architects, 80
Sweden, collective housing in. *See* *Kollektivhus* (Sweden)

Tenant-management model (Sweden)
    characteristics, 76–79
    definition, 74
    examples, 81–84
    meal service in, 87–88
Tenderloin Neighborhood Development Corporation (TNDC), 310, 319, 320
Terra Vista (California), 7–8
338 Harvard Street (Boston), 13–16
Tinggården (Denmark), 102
Toronto
    cooperative housing. (*See* Beguinage; Constance Hamilton Cooperative)
    urban planning in, 163
Tower (San Francisco), 316–317
Traditional family
    demographic shift in, xi
    dominant image of, 161, 248
Transitional housing, for single-parent households. *See also* Abigail West Shelter; Passage Community; Single-parent households, housing for; Tree of Life
    definition, 144, 187
Tree of Life (Boston), 195–204
    compared to West Shelter, 204, 206–207
    design issues, 198–199
    opposition to, 196–198, 206
    plans, 197, 200, 203–205
    program goals, 198
Trudeslund (Denmark), 104–106, 112, 113, 116

Turner, Thackeray, 49–51
21 East 21st St. (New York), 23, 24, 26

University Gardens (San Diego), 254, 257, 259–260
Urban Innovations Group, 256
Urban Renaissance, 203–204
Urban renewal, ix
    effect on single-parent households, 162–163
    effect on SRO housing, 250

Vacant Lots project, 151, 154–155
Vaerbro Park (Copenhagen), 69
van der Velde, Henry, 55
Vandkunsten, Tegnestuen, 104, 107
van Eyck, Aldo, 146–147
Vanport City (Oregon), xii
Vaux, Calvert, 28, 29
Vera Institute of Justice, 263, 276
Vest Pocket Community (Fairfax, California), 11–12, 124
Vienna, collective apartment housing in, 58–59
Vladimirov, V., 60
Vogel-Heffernan, Mary, 212, 217

Waagensen, Bent, 67–68
Warren Village (Denver), 149–150, 195, 207, 209, 218
Welwyn Garden City (Great Britain), 51
West, Nina, 147, 165
West Shelter. *See* Abigail West Shelter
West, Sheree, 5–6
West, Troy, 158, 165, 167
    and Dayton Court, 174, 176
White, A. T., 27–28
Whittier Alliance, 211, 212
Wight, P. B., 34–35, 42
Willowbrook Green, 150–153, 167
Windsor Hotel (New York), 22
Women
    abused. (*See* Family abuse)
    collective housing for working singles, 4, 35–38
    domestic role in Sweden, 66–67, 71
    efforts to reduce household tasks of, 33–34, 48, 50–51, 60–63, 66, 71, 73, 77

housing costs and, 234–235
housing issues, 223–224
increase in working, xi
in nineteenth-century
   apartment houses, 43
single room occupancy housing
   for, 247, 250
social advantages in collective
   housing, 71–72, 88–89
Swedish collective housing for, 65
Women's Community Housing
   (WCH), 209–212, 219
Women's Development
   Corporation (WDC), 150–151
Women's Institute for Housing
   and Economic Development,
   186–187, 196

and Tree of Life, 196, 198
and West Shelter, 186–189, 193,
   195, 204, 206
Workers' Cooperative Colony
   (New York), 4
Working Women's Home (New
   York), 35–37
Workplace in the home
   in Danish cohousing, 123
   in GoHomes, 10, 11
   in housing for single-parent
      households, 234
   and New American House
      Competition, 170
   in New American House
      Designs, 136, 171–173, 189
   in suites, 131–132, 137, 138–139

Yerba Buena project (San
   Francisco), 250
Yrkeskvinnornas Hus
   (Stockholm), 65–66
YWCA (St. Paul), 209, 210, 219

Zilliakus, Jutta, 69
Zoning
   barrier to alternative housing,
      143
   and New American House
      designs, 175
   and party wall, 134, 139–140
   and Tree of Life, 191
Zurich, collective apartment
   building in, 56–58